STP NATIONAL CURRICULUM MATHEMATICS 10A

D0626711

L. BOSTOCK, B.Sc.

S. CHANDLER, B.Sc.

A. SHEPHERD, B.Sc.

E. SMITH, M.Sc.

STANLEY THORNES (PUBLISHERS) LTD

First published in 1998 by
Stanley Thornes (Publishers) Ltd,
Ellenborough House,
Wellington Street,
CHELTENHAM GL50 1YW

98 99 00 01 02/ 10 9 8 7 6 5 4 3 2 1

A catalogue record of this book is

ISBN 0-7487-3190-3

Artwork by Mike Ing, Linda Jeffre

Front cover image produced using
makers of The Happy Cube © Laureyssens/ Creative City Ltd 1986/ 91.
Distributed in UK by: RIGHTRAC, 119 Sandycombe Road, Richmond Surrey TW9 2ER
Tel: 0181 940 3322

The publishers are grateful to the following for granting permission to
reproduce photographs or other copyright material:
Richard Rogers Partnership/ The New Millennium Experience Company Limited – p. 346
Magnet – p. 349
Argos – p. 349

The authors and publishers are grateful to the following examination boards for permission to reproduce questions from their past examination papers. (Any answers included have not been provided by the examining boards, they are the responsibility of the authors and may not necessarily constitute the only possible solutions.)

London Examinations, A division of Edexcel Foundation (London)
Northern Examinations and Assessment Board (NEAB)
University of Cambridge Local Examinations Syndicate (MEG)
The Associated Examining Board (SEG)
Welsh Joint Education Committee (WJEC)

Typeset by Tech-Set, Gateshead, Tyne & Wear.
Printed and bound in China

SUMMARY 1

**TYPES OF
NUMBER**

A **factor** of a number will divide into that number exactly.

A **multiple** of a number has that number as a factor,

e.g.   12 is a multiple of 3.

A **prime number** has only 1 and itself as factors, e.g. 7.
Remember that 1 is not a prime number.

Square numbers can be drawn
as a square grid of dots, e.g. 9:

Rectangular numbers can be
drawn as a rectangular grid of dots, e.g. 6:

Triangular numbers can be drawn
as a triangular grid of dots, e.g. 6:

The **reciprocal** of a number is 1 divided by that number,

e.g.   the reciprocal of 4 is $\frac{1}{4} = 0.25$

and   the reciprocal of 0.8 is $1 \div 0.8 = 1.25$

Positive and negative numbers are collectively known as **directed
numbers**.

The *rules for multiplying and dividing directed numbers* are

> when the signs are the same, the result is positive.
> when the signs are different, the result is negative.

The same rules apply to adding and subtracting directed numbers,

i.e. $+(-2)$ is the same as $+1(-2) = (+1) \times (-2)$

so $3 + (+2) = 3 + 2 = 5$ and $3 - (-2) = 3 + 2 = 5$
    $3 + (-2) = 3 - 2 = 1$ and $3 - (+2) = 3 - 2 = 1$

A **square root** of a number is another number which, when multiplied
by itself, gives the first number.

A number has two square roots, one positive and one negative,

e.g.   if $x^2 = 4$, then $x = \pm\sqrt{4} = \pm 2$.

Note that $\sqrt{4}$ means the positive square root of 4.

A number written in **standard form** is a number between 1 and 10
multiplied by a power of ten,

e.g. 1.2×10^5

1

OPERATIONS OF
×, ÷, +, −

The sign in front of a number refers to that number only.

When a calculation involves a *mixture of operations*, start by calculating anything inside brackets, then follow the rule 'do the multiplication and division first.'

FRACTIONS

Fractions are *added* or *subtracted* by first changing them into equivalent fractions with the same denominators, then adding or subtracting the numerators.

To *multiply one fraction by another fraction*, we multiply their numerators and multiply their denominators,

e.g. $\quad \frac{1}{2} \times \frac{5}{3} = \frac{1\times5}{2\times3} = \frac{5}{6}$

To *divide by a fraction*, we multiply by the reciprocal of the fraction,

e.g. $\quad \frac{1}{2} \div \frac{5}{3} = \frac{1}{2} \times \frac{3}{5} = \frac{3}{10}$

To multiply or divide with *mixed numbers*, e.g. $1\frac{3}{4}$, first change the mixed numbers to improper fractions.

A *fraction can be changed to a decimal* by dividing the denominator into the numerator,

e.g. $\quad \frac{3}{8} = 3 \div 8 = 0.375$

A *fraction can be expressed as a percentage* by multiplying the fraction by 100,

e.g. $\quad \frac{2}{5} = \frac{2}{5} \times 100\% = \frac{2}{5} \times \frac{100}{1}\% = 40\%$

To find *a fraction of a quantity*, we multiply that fraction by the quantity,

e.g. $\quad \frac{1}{2}$ of $\frac{3}{4}$ lb means $\frac{1}{2} \times \frac{3}{4}$ lb, and $\frac{3}{8}$ of £24 = £$\left(\frac{3}{8} \times 24\right)$

To express *one quantity as a fraction of another*, first express both quantities in the same unit, then place the first quantity over the second,

e.g. $\quad$ 24 p as a fraction of £2 is $\frac{24}{200}\left(=\frac{3}{25}\right)$

DECIMALS

To *multiply decimals* without using a calculator, first ignore the decimal point and multiply the numbers. Then add the decimal places in each of the decimals being multiplied together; this gives the number of decimal places in the answer,

e.g. $\quad$ 7.5 × 0.5 = 3.75 $\qquad\qquad\qquad\qquad$ (75 × 5 = 375)

$\qquad\quad$ [(1) + (1) = (2)]

To divide by a decimal, move the point in *both* numbers to the right until the number we are dividing by is a whole number,

e.g. $\quad$ 2.56 ÷ 0.4 = 25.6 ÷ 4 = 6.4

A decimal can be expressed as a percentage by multiplying the decimal by 100,

e.g. $0.325 = 32.5\%$

Recurring decimals arise when some fractions are changed to decimals and the result is a recurring pattern of numbers that repeats indefinitely,

e.g. $\frac{1}{11} = 1 \div 11 = 0.090909\ldots = 0.\dot{0}\dot{9}$

**ROUNDING
NUMBERS**

To round (i.e. to correct) a number to a specified place value or number of significant figures, look at the figure in the next place: if it is 5 or more, add 1 to the specified figure, otherwise leave the specified figure as it is. When a number has been rounded, its true value lies within a range that can be shown on a number line. For example, if a nail is **23.5** mm long correct to 1 decimal place, then the length is from **23.45** mm up to, but not including **23.55** mm as shown on this number line.

If x cm is the length of the nail then,

$$23.45 \leqslant x < 23.55$$

23.45 is the **lower bound** and **23.55** is the **upper bound** of x.

PERCENTAGES

A *percentage can be expressed as a fraction* by placing the percentage over 100,

e.g. $33\% = \frac{33}{100}$,

and *a percentage can be expressed as a decimal* by dividing the percentage by 100, that is, by moving the decimal point two places to the left,

e.g. $33\% = 0.33$

To find *one quantity as a percentage of another quantity*, we place the first quantity over the second quantity and multiply this fraction by 100,

e.g.   24 p as a percentage of £2 is $\frac{24}{200} \times \frac{100}{1}\% = 12\%$

To find *a percentage of a quantity*, change the percentage to a decimal and multiply it by the quantity,

e.g.   32% of £18 $= 0.32 \times £18 \; (= £5.76)$

Percentage change
Changes are expressed in percentage terms as a percentage of the quantity *before* any changes are made.
For example, if a shirt is sold for £25 at a discount of 10%, the discount is 10% of the price before it is reduced,

i.e.   £25 = original price − 10% of original price
              $= 90\% \times$ original price

To *increase* a quantity by 15%,
we find *the increase* by finding 15% of the quantity;
we find *the new quantity* directly by finding 100% + 15%,
i.e. 115%, of the original quantity; so we multiply it by 1.15.

To *decrease* a quantity by 15%,
we find *the decrease* by finding 15% of the quantity,
we find *the new quantity* directly by finding 100% − 15%,
i.e. 85%, of the original quantity; so we multiply it by 0.85.

Compound percentage change is a percentage change that
accumulates. If, for example, the value of a house increases by 5% of its
value at the start of each year;
its value after one year, is 105% of its initial value,
after another year, its value is 105% of its value at the start of that year,
i.e. 105% of its increased value, and so on.

Interest
When a sum of money is borrowed or lent, interest is usually charged on
a yearly basis and is given as a percentage of the sum borrowed,
e.g.   3% p.a.

RATIO

Ratios are used to compare the relative sizes of quantities.
For example, if a car is 400 cm long and a model of it is 20 cm long, we
say that their lengths are in the ratio 400 : 20.

Ratios can be simplified by dividing the parts of the ratio by the same
number,

e.g.   400 : 20 = 20 : 1   (dividing 400 and 20 by 20).

A *map ratio* is the ratio of a length on the map to the length it represents
on the ground. When expressed as a fraction (or sometimes as a ratio),
it is called the **Representative Fraction**.

Division in a given ratio
To divide £200 into three amounts of money in the ratio 2 : 5 : 3,
means that £200 has to be divided into 2 + 5 + 3 = 10 equal parts;
so the first amount is 2 of these parts, that is, $\frac{2}{10}$ of £200,

the second amount is $\frac{5}{10}$ of £200 and the third amount is $\frac{3}{10}$ of £200.

**DIRECT
PROPORTION**

When two quantities are related so that when one of them trebles, say,
the other also trebles, the quantities are directly proportional (that is,
they are always in the same ratio).

INVERSE PROPORTION

When two quantities are related so that when one of them trebles, say, the other becomes a third of its original size, the quantities are inversely proportional and their product is constant.

INDICES

When a number is written in the form 3^4, 3 is called the *base* and 4 is called the *index* or *power* and 3^4 means $3 \times 3 \times 3 \times 3$.

3^{-4} means $\dfrac{1}{3^4}$, $3^0 = 1$, in fact $a^0 = 1$ for all values of a (except $a = 0$).

Rules of indices

We can multiply different powers of the same base by adding the indices,

e.g. $3^4 \times 3^2 = 3^{4+2} = 3^6$

We can divide different powers of the same base by subtracting the indices,

e.g. $3^4 \div 3^2 = 3^{4-2} = 3^2$

UNITS

Metric units of length:

$1\,\text{km} = 1000\,\text{m}, \quad 1\,\text{m} = 100\,\text{cm}, \quad 1\,\text{cm} = 10\,\text{mm}$

Metric units of mass:

$1\,\text{tonne} = 1000\,\text{kg}, \quad 1\,\text{kg} = 1000\,\text{g}, \quad 1\,\text{g} = 1000\,\text{mg}$

Metric units of capacity:

$1\,\text{litre} = 1000\,\text{ml} = 1000\,\text{cm}^3 \quad$ so $\quad 1\,\text{ml} = 1\,\text{cm}^3$

Imperial units of length:

$1\,\text{mile} = 1760\,\text{yards}, \quad 1\,\text{yard} = 3\,\text{feet}, \quad 1\,\text{foot} = 12\,\text{inches}$

Imperial units of mass:

$1\,\text{ton} = 2240\,\text{pound (lb)}, \quad 1\,\text{stone} = 14\,\text{lb},$

$1\,\text{lb} = 16\,\text{ounces (oz)}$

Imperial units of capacity:

$1\,\text{gallon} = 8\,\text{pints}$

For an *approximate conversion between metric and Imperial units*, use

$5\,\text{miles} \simeq 8\,\text{km}, \quad 1\,\text{inch} \simeq 2.5\,\text{cm}, \quad 1\,\text{m} \simeq 39\,\text{inches}$

$1\,\text{kg} \simeq 2.2\,\text{lb}, \quad 1\,\text{tonne} \simeq 1\,\text{ton},$

$1\,\text{litre} \simeq 1.75\,\text{pints}, \quad 1\,\text{gallon} \simeq 4.5\,\text{litres}$

Area is measured by standard–sized squares.

$$1\,cm^2 = 10 \times 10\,mm^2 = 100\,mm^2 \qquad 1\,m^2 = 10\,000\,cm^2$$

$$1\,km^2 = 1\,000\,000\,m^2$$

$$1\,hectare = 10\,000\,m^2, \qquad 1\,acre = 4840\,square\,yards,$$

$$1\,hectare \approx 2.5\,acres$$

Volume is measured by standard–sized cubes.

$$1\,cm^3 = 10 \times 10 \times 10\,mm^3 = 1000\,mm^3$$

$$1\,m^3 \; = 100 \times 100 \times 100\,cm^3 = 1\,000\,000\,cm^3$$

AREA

The **area of a square** $= ($ length of a side $)^2$.
The **area of a rectangle** $=$ length $\times$ breadth.

The **area of a parallelogram** is given by
$A =$ length $\times$ height.

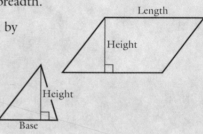

The **area of a triangle** is given by
$A = \frac{1}{2}$ base $\times$ height

The **area of a trapezium** is equal to
$\frac{1}{2}($ sum of the parallel sides $) \times ($ distance between them $)$
$= \frac{1}{2}(a+b) \times h$

The height of a triangle or parallelogram
means the perpendicular height.

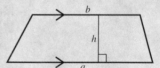

CIRCLES

The **circumference** is given by $C = 2\pi r$,
where r units is the radius of the circle
and $\pi = 3.1415\ldots$
The **area of a circle** is given by $A = \pi r^2$

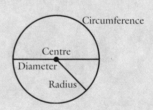

Part of the circumference of a circle
is called an *arc*.

Length of the arc AB $= \dfrac{A\widehat{O}B}{360^\circ} \times 2\pi r$

The slice of the circle enclosed by the arc
and the radii is called a *sector*.

The **area of the sector** AOB $= \dfrac{A\widehat{O}B}{360^\circ} \times \pi r^2$

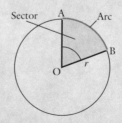

VOLUME

The **volume of a cuboid** = length × breadth × height

A solid with a constant cross-section is called
a **prism**.
The **volume of a prism** is given by

area of cross-section × length

The **volume of a cylinder** is given by $V = \pi r^2 h$

DENSITY

The *density* of a material is the mass of one unit of volume of the
material, for example the density of silver is $10.5\,\text{g/cm}^3$,
i.e. $1\,\text{cm}^3$ of silver weighs $10.5\,\text{g}$.

**DISTANCE,
SPEED AND TIME**

The relationship between distance, constant speed and time is given by

Distance = Speed × Time

Average speed for a journey $= \dfrac{\text{Total distance covered}}{\text{Total time taken}}$

**ALGEBRAIC
EXPRESSIONS**

Terms such as $5n$ mean $5 \times n$, i.e. $n + n + n + n + n$.
Similarly ab means $a \times b$.
Like terms such as $2x + 5x$ can be simplified to $7x$.

The **coefficient** of a letter means the number, including the sign, it is
multiplied by. In the expression $3x - 4y$, for example, the coefficient
of x is 3 and the coefficient of y is -4.

The same rules apply to fractions with letter terms as to fractions with
numbers only,

i.e.   *fractions can be simplified* by cancelling common factors of the
        numerator and denominator,

e.g. $\dfrac{x^2}{2xy - x^2} = \dfrac{\cancel{x^2}}{\cancel{x}(2y - x)} = \dfrac{x}{(2y - x)}$

To *add or subtract fractions*, first change them into equivalent fractions
with a common denominator, then add or subtract the numerators,

e.g. $\dfrac{3}{2x} + \dfrac{5}{4y} = \dfrac{6y}{4xy} + \dfrac{5x}{4xy} = \dfrac{6y + 5x}{4xy}$

To *multiply fractions*, multiply the numerators and multiply the denominators,

e.g. $\dfrac{2x^1}{3y_1} \times \dfrac{5y^{2y}}{7x_1} = \dfrac{2 \times 5y}{3 \times 7} = \dfrac{10y}{21}$

and to *divide by a fraction*, turn it upside down and multiply,

e.g. $\dfrac{x}{x-2} \div \dfrac{2x^2}{3x-1} = \dfrac{x}{x-2} \times \dfrac{3x-1}{2x^2}$

Expansion of brackets

$x(2x-3)$ means $x \times 2x + (x) \times (-3)$.
Therefore $x(2x-3) = 2x^2 - 3x$

$(a+b)(c+d)$ means $a \times (c+d) + b \times (c+d)$
$$= ac + ad + bc + bd$$

i.e. each term in the second bracket is multiplied by each term in the first bracket. The order in which the terms are multiplied does not matter, but it is sensible to stick to the same order each time,

e.g.

$(2x-3)(4x+5) = (2x)(4x) + (2x)(5) + (-3)(4x) + (-3)(5)$
$$= 8x^2 + 10x - 12x - 15$$
$$= 8x^2 - 2x - 15$$

In particular, $(x+a)^2 = (x+a)(x+a) = x^2 + 2ax + a^2$
$$(x-a)^2 = (x-a)(x-a) = x^2 - 2ax + a^2$$
$$(x+a)(x-a) = x^2 - a^2$$

$x^2 - a^2$ is called the **difference between two squares**.

Factorising

Factorising is the reverse of the process of expanding (multiplying out) an algebraic expression.

A *common factor* of two or more terms can be seen by inspection and 'taken outside a bracket',

e.g. $2ab + 4bc = 2b(a + 2c)$

(This can be checked by expanding the result.)

To factorise an expression such as $x^2 + 3x - 10$, we look for two brackets whose product is equal to the original expression.
We start by writing $x^2 + 3x - 10 = (x+ \ )(x- \ )$.
We then look for two numbers whose product is 10 and whose difference is 3; this gives $x^2 + 3x - 10 = (x+5)(x-2)$
Not all quadratic expressions factorise.

FORMULAS

A formula is a general rule for finding one quantity in terms of other quantities, for example, the formula for finding the area, A cm^2, of a rectangle measuring l cm by b cm, is given by $A = l \times b$

A is called the **subject of the formula**.

When the formula is rearranged to give $l = \dfrac{A}{b}$, l is the subject.

The process of rearranging $A = l \times b$ to $l = \dfrac{A}{b}$ is called *changing the subject of the formula*. It is achieved by thinking of $A = l \times b$ as an equation which has to be 'solved' to find l.

The nth term of a sequence is sometimes expressed in terms of n, the position number of the term. Any term of the sequence can then be found by giving n a numerical value.

For example, when the nth term is $3n - 2$,

the 10th term is given by substituting 10 for n, i.e. by $3(10) - 2 = 28$

SOLVING EQUATIONS

An equation is a relationship between an unknown number, represented by a letter, and other numbers, for example $2x - 3 = 5$

Solving the equation means finding the unknown number.

Provided that we do the same thing to both sides of an equation, we keep the equality; this can be used to solve the equation.

When an equation contains brackets, first multiply out the brackets,

When an equation contains fractions, multiply each term in the equation by the lowest number that every denominator divides into exactly. This will eliminate all fractions from the equation.

Simultaneous equations

A pair of simultaneous equations in two unknowns can be solved algebraically by eliminating one of the letters. It may be necessary to multiply one or both equations by numbers to make the coefficients of one of the letters the same in both equations.

For example, to solve $2y - x = 7$ [1]

and $3y + 4x = 5$ [2]

[1] $\times 4$ gives $8y - 4x = 28$ [3]

then [2] + [3] eliminates x to give $11y = 33$

so $y = 3$ and, from [1], $x = -1$

It may also be necessary to rearrange one or both equations so that the letter terms are in the same place in both equations.

Quadratic equations
A quadratic equation can be solved algebraically if the left-hand side can be factorised,

e.g. $x^2 - 3x + 2 = 0$ becomes $(x - 2)(x - 1) = 0$

Now we use the fact that if the product of two numbers is zero then one or both of the numbers must be zero.

Therefore as $(x - 2)(x - 1) = 0$

then either $x - 2 = 0$ in which case $x = 2$

or $x - 1 = 0$ in which case $x = 1$

Hence the equation $x^2 - 3x + 2 = 0$ has two solutions;
$x = 2$ and $x = 1$.

A quadratic equation should be rearranged in the order
$ax^2 + bx + c = 0$ before factorisation is attempted.

Polynomial equations contain terms involving powers of one unknown, x say,

e.g. $x^3 - 2x = 4$ and $2x^2 = 5$ are polynomial equations.

Equations containing an x^2 term and a number only, may be solved by finding square roots.

More complex equations can be solved by **trial and improvement**, that is by trying possible values for x until we find a value that 'fits' the equation.

Equations can also be solved by drawing a suitable graph.

Inequalities
An inequality remains true when the same number is added to, or subtracted from, both sides,

e.g.   if $x > 5$ then $x + 2 > 5 + 2$

              and $x - 2 > 5 - 2$

An inequality also remains true when both sides are multiplied, or divided, by the same *positive* number,

e.g.   if $x > 5$ then $2x > 10$

              and $\dfrac{x}{2} > \dfrac{5}{2}$

However multiplication or division by a negative number must be avoided because this destroys the inequality.

Inequalities in two unknowns

An inequality in two unknowns can be represented by a region of the x–y plane. For example, the *unshaded* area in the diagram represents the inequality

$y \leqslant -1.5x + 6$

The boundary line is

$y = -1.5x + 6$ and is

included in the region; this is indicated in the diagram by a solid line.

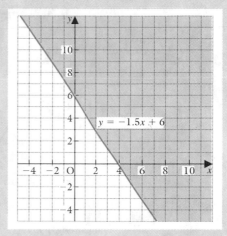

To represent the inequality $y < -1.5x + 6$, we use a broken line to represent the boundary line $y = -1.5x + 6$ as it is not included in the region.

GRAPHS

The equation of a line or curve gives the y-coordinate of a point in terms of its x-coordinate. This relationship between the coordinates is true only for points on the line or curve.

Gradient gives the rate at which the quantity on the vertical axis is changing as the quantity on the horizontal axis increases.

The *gradient* of a straight line can be found from any two points, P and Q, on the line, by calculating

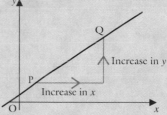

$$\frac{\text{increase in } y \text{ in moving from P to Q}}{\text{increase in } x \text{ in moving from P to Q}}$$

When the gradient is positive, the line slopes uphill when moving from left to right.
When the gradient is negative, the line slopes downhill when moving from left to right.
The gradient, or slope, of a curve changes from point to point.

Straight lines and parabolas

An equation of the form $y = mx + c$ gives a straight line where m is the gradient of the line and c is the intercept on the y-axis.

An equation of the form $y = ax^2 + bx + c$ gives a curve whose shape is called a parabola and looks like this:
When the x^2 term is negative, the curve is 'upside down'.

Cubic curves

When the equation of a curve contains x^3 (and maybe terms involving x^2, x and a number), the curve is called a *cubic* curve.

These equations give cubic curves:

$$y = x^3, \quad y = 2x^3 - x + 5, \quad y = x^3 - 2x^2 + 6$$

A cubic curve looks like 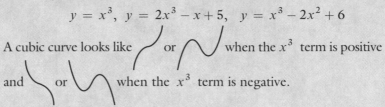 or ⌒⌄ when the x^3 term is positive

and ⌄⌒ or ⌣⌄ when the x^3 term is negative.

Reciprocal graphs

The equation $y = \dfrac{a}{x}$ where a is a number,

is called a *reciprocal equation*.

An equation of the form $y = \dfrac{a}{x}$, where

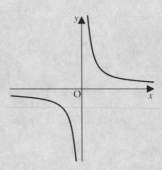

a is a constant (that is, a number), gives a
two-part curve called a *reciprocal curve* or
a *hyperbola*. The diagram shows the curve
when $a > 0$.

Any two quantities, x and y, that are **inversely proportional**, are related

by the equation $y = \dfrac{k}{x}$ and the graph representing them is a hyperbola.

PARALLEL LINES

When two parallel lines are cut by a transversal

the **corresponding angles** are equal,

the **alternate angles** are equal,

the **interior angles** add up to 180°.

ANGLES OF ELEVATION AND DEPRESSION

If you start by looking straight ahead,
the angle that you turn your eyes
through to look *up* at an object
is called the angle of elevation,
the angle you turn your eyes
through to look *down* at an object
is called the angle of depression.

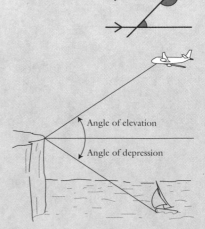

Angle of elevation

Angle of depression

THREE-FIGURE BEARINGS

The three-figure bearing of a point A from a point B gives the direction of A from B as a clockwise angle measured from the north.

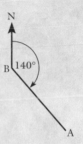

In this diagram, the bearing of A from B is 140°.

TRIANGLES

The three angles in a triangle add up to 180°.

An *equilateral triangle* has all three sides equal and each angle is 60°.

An *isosceles triangle* has two equal sides and the angles at the base of these sides are equal.

QUADRILATERALS

A quadrilateral has four sides.
The four angles in a quadrilateral add up to 360°.

Special quadrilaterals
In a square
- all four sides are the same length
- both pairs of opposite sides are parallel
- all four angles are right angles.

In a rectangle
- both pairs of opposite sides are the same length
- both pairs of opposite sides are parallel
- all four angles are right angles.

In a rhombus
- all four sides are the same length
- both pairs of opposite sides are parallel
- the opposite angles are equal.

In a parallelogram
- the opposite sides are the same length
- the opposite sides are parallel
- the opposite angles are equal.

In a trapezium
- just one pair of opposite sides are parallel.

POLYGONS

A polygon is a plane figure bounded by straight lines, e.g.

A **regular polygon** has all angles equal and all sides the same length.

The **sum of the exterior angles** of any polygon is 360°.

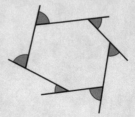

The **sum of the interior angles** of any polygon depends on the number of sides. For a polygon with n sides, this sum is $(180n - 360)°$ or $(2n - 4)$ right angles.

PYTHAGORAS'
THEOREM

Pythagoras' theorem states that in any right-angled triangle ABC with $\widehat{C} = 90°$, $AB^2 = AC^2 + BC^2$

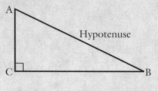

Conversely, if in a triangle PQR $PR^2 = PQ^2 + QR^2$, then $\widehat{Q} = 90°$ and if $PR^2 \neq PQ^2 + QR^2$ then $\widehat{Q} \neq 90°$

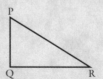

CONGRUENCE

Two figures are congruent when they are exactly the same shape and size. (One figure may be turned over or round with respect to the other.)

SIMILAR
FIGURES

Two figures are similar if they are the same shape but different in size, that is, one figure is an enlargement of the other. (One figure may be turned over or round with respect to the other.) It follows that the lengths of corresponding sides are all in the same ratio.

Similar triangles
Two triangles can be proved to be similar if it can be shown that either the three angles of one triangle are equal to the three angles of the other or the three pairs of corresponding sides are in the same ratio.

**ANGLES IN
CIRCLES**

Angles standing on the same arc of a circle and in the same segment are equal.

The angle subtended at the centre of a circle by an arc is twice the angle subtended at the circumference by the same arc.

The angle in a semicircle is a right angle.

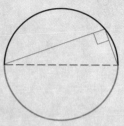

LOCI

A *locus* is the shape given by the *positions* of all the points that satisfy a given rule.

The locus of a point that moves so that it is at a fixed distance from a given point is the circumference of a circle.

The locus of a point that moves at a constant distance from a fixed straight line is a pair of parallel lines. In the case of a line of finite length, semicircular ends join the lines.

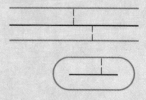

The locus of a point that moves so that it is equidistant from two fixed points, A and B, is the perpendicular bisector of the line joining A and B.

The locus of a point that moves so that it is equidistant from two intersecting straight lines is the pair of bisectors of the angles between the lines.

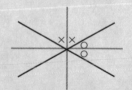

TRIGONOMETRY   In a right-angled triangle

the **tangent of an angle** $= \dfrac{\text{side opposite the angle}}{\text{side adjacent to the angle}}$

the **sine of an angle** $= \dfrac{\text{side opposite the angle}}{\text{the hypotenuse}}$

the **cosine of an angle** $= \dfrac{\text{side adjacent to the angle}}{\text{the hypotenuse}}$

or more briefly,

$$\tan \widehat{A} = \frac{\text{opp}}{\text{adj}} = \frac{\text{BC}}{\text{AB}}, \quad \sin \widehat{A} = \frac{\text{opp}}{\text{hyp}} = \frac{\text{BC}}{\text{AC}}, \quad \cos \widehat{A} = \frac{\text{adj}}{\text{hyp}} = \frac{\text{AB}}{\text{AC}}$$

VECTORS   A *vector* is any quantity that needs to be described by giving both its size (magnitude) and its direction.

A quantity that needs only size to describe it is called a *scalar*, e.g. time.

A vector can be represented by a straight line with an arrow to show direction, e.g.

When vectors are drawn on squared paper they can be described in terms of the number of squares needed to go across to the right and the number of squares needed to go up.

They are written in the form $\begin{pmatrix} a \\ b \end{pmatrix}$ where a is the number of squares across and b is the number of squares up.

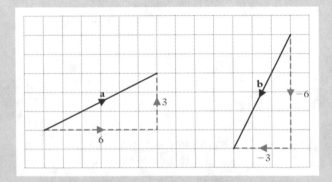

In the diagram, $\mathbf{a} = \begin{pmatrix} 6 \\ 3 \end{pmatrix}$ and $\mathbf{b} = \begin{pmatrix} -3 \\ -6 \end{pmatrix}$

TRANSFORMATIONS

Reflection in a mirror line

When an object is reflected in a mirror line, the object and its image form a symmetrical shape with the mirror line as the axis of symmetry.

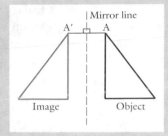

When an object has been reflected, corresponding points on the object and the image are the same distance from the mirror line. Therefore the mirror line can be found by joining a pair of corresponding points on the object and the image, AA′ say, and then finding the line that goes through the midpoint of AA′ and is perpendicular to it.

Translation

An object is translated when it moves without being turned or reflected to form an image.

A *translation* can be described by the vector which gives the movement from a point on the object to the corresponding point on the image.

In the diagram, the movement of the point A to the point A′ is 9 units to the left and 3 units up, so the translation is described by the vector $\begin{pmatrix} -9 \\ 3 \end{pmatrix}$.

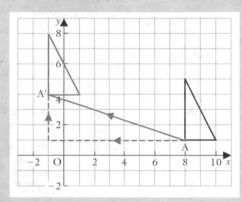

Rotation

When an object is rotated about a point to form an image, the point about which it is rotated is called the *centre of rotation* and the angle it is turned through is called the *angle of rotation*.

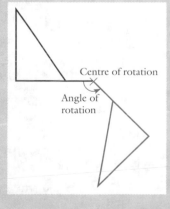

Enlargement

When an object is enlarged by a scale factor 2, each line on the image is twice the length of the corresponding line on the object. The diagram shows an enlargement of a triangle, with centre of enlargement X and scale factor 2. The dashed lines are guide-lines.

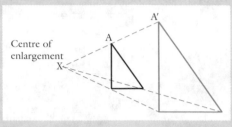

$$XA' = 2XA$$

When the scale factor is less than one, the image is smaller than the object.

When the scale factor is negative, the guidelines are drawn *backwards* through the centre of enlargement, O, so that, if the scale factor is -2,

$$OA' = 2OA.$$

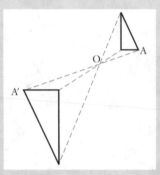

This produces an image each of whose lines is twice as long as the corresponding line on the object. The image is also rotated by $180°$ with respect to the object.

Compound transformation

A compound transformation is the result of one transformation followed by another, for example, the result of reflecting an object in the y-axis and then rotating the image obtained through $30°$ about the origin.

STATISTICS

A **hypothesis** is a statement that is not known to be true or untrue.

Discrete values are exact and distinct, for example, the number of people in a queue.

Continuous values can only be given in a range on a continuous scale, e.g. the length of a piece of wood.

For an ungrouped set of values,

- the **range** is the difference between the largest value and the smallest value
- the **mean** is the sum of all the values divided by the number of values. For a frequency distribution, the mean is given by $\frac{\Sigma fx}{\Sigma f}$ where x is the value of an item and f is its frequency.
- the **median** is the middle value when they have been arranged in order of size, (when the middle of the list is half-way between two values, the median is the average of these two values)
- the **mode** is the value that occurs most frequently.

For a grouped frequency distribution,
- the **range** is estimated as

    the higher end of the last group – the lower end of the first group
- the **modal group** is the group with the largest number of items in it.
- the **mean value** is estimated as $\dfrac{\Sigma fx}{\Sigma f}$ where x is the midclass value.

Note that Σ means 'the sum of all such terms' so Σf means the sum of all the fs, that is, all the frequencies.

Cumulative frequency

Cumulative frequency is the sum of the frequencies of all values up to and including a particular value.

A *cumulative frequency polygon* is drawn by plotting the cumulative frequencies against the upper ends of the groups and joining the points with straight lines. A *cumulative frequency curve* is obtained by drawing a smooth curve through the points.

The **median** of a grouped distribution of n values is the $\dfrac{n}{2}$th value in order of size and is denoted by Q_2.

The median can be estimated from a cumulative frequency curve.

The **lower quartile** is the value that is $\frac{1}{4}$ of the way through a set of values arranged in order of size and is denoted by Q_1.

The **upper quartile** is the value that is $\frac{3}{4}$ of the way through a set of values arranged in order of size and is denoted by Q_3.

For a grouped distribution, Q_1 is the $\dfrac{n}{4}$th value, and Q_3 is the $\dfrac{3n}{4}$th value. Q_1 and Q_3 can be estimated from a cumulative frequency curve.

The **interquartile range** is the difference between the upper and lower quartiles,

i.e. $Q_3 - Q_1$

We get a **scatter graph** when we plot values of one quantity against corresponding values of another quantity.

When the points are scattered about a straight line, we can draw that line by eye; it is called the **line of best fit**.

We use the word **correlation** to describe the amount of scatter about this line.

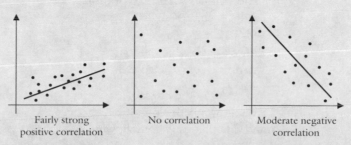

| Fairly strong positive correlation | No correlation | Moderate negative correlation |

PROBABILITY

The probability that an event A happens is $P(A)$ where

$$P(A) = \frac{\text{the number of ways in which } A \text{ can occur}}{\text{the total number of equally likely outcomes}}$$

The probability that an event A does not happen, $P(\bar{A})$, is given by subtracting the probability that it does happen from 1,

i.e. $P(\bar{A}) = 1 - P(A)$.

If p is the probability that an event happens on one occasion, then we expect it to happen np times on n occasions. For example, if we toss an unbiased coin 50 times, we expect $50 \times \frac{1}{2} = 25$ heads.

When we perform experiments to find out how often an event occurs, the **relative frequency** of the event is given by

$$\frac{\text{the number of times the event occurs}}{\text{the number of times the experiment is performed}}$$

Relative frequency is used to give an approximate value for probability.

We **add probabilities** when we want the probability that one or other of two (or more) events will happen, provided that only one of the events can happen at a time.
Events such that only one of them can happen on any one occasion are called **mutually exclusive**.
For example, when one dice is rolled,

$$P(\text{scoring 5 or 6}) = P(\text{scoring 5}) + P(\text{scoring 6})$$

We **multiply probabilities** when we want the probability that two (or more) events both happen, provided that each event has no influence on whether or not the other occurs.
Events such that each has no influence on whether the other occurs are called **independent events**.
For example, when two dice A and B are rolled,

$$P(\text{scoring 6 on A and B}) = P(\text{scoring 6 on A}) \times P(\text{scoring 6 on B})$$

Tree diagrams can be used to illustrate the outcomes when two or more events occur.
This tree, for example, shows the possible outcomes when two coins are tossed.

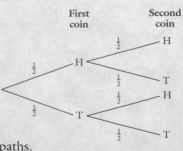

We *multiply* the probabilities when we follow a path along the branches and *add* the results of following several paths.

The exercises that follow are *not* intended to be worked through before starting the main part of this book. They are here for you to use when you need practice on the basic techniques.

**REVISION
EXERCISE 1.1
(Number work)**

Do not use a calculator for any questions in this exercise.

1 Find

a 327×30	**e** 288×73	**i** $256 \div 32$
b 542×52	**f** 492×28	**j** $884 \div 52$
c 479×23	**g** $860 \div 20$	**k** $924 \div 84$
d 716×49	**h** $552 \div 12$	**l** $798 \div 38$

2 Calculate

a $(+5) \times (-2)$	**h** $12 \div (-4)$	**p** $-4 \div \frac{1}{4}$
b $(-4) \div (3)$	**i** $5(-3)$	**q** $2 - (3 - 6)$
c $(-8) \times (-2)$	**j** $-2.4 \div 0.6$	**r** $8 - 2(4 - 7)$
d $6 \times \left(-\frac{1}{3}\right)$	**k** $(-12) \div (-2)$	**s** $(5 - 9) + 3$
e $-3(-4)$	**l** $\frac{3}{8}(-4)$	**t** $3(4 - 7) - 4$
f $(-6) \times (-7)$	**m** $\frac{1}{2} \div \left(-\frac{1}{4}\right)$	**u** $(4 - 12) \div (-2)$
g $6 \times (-3)$	**n** $-4\left(\frac{2}{3}\right)$	**v** $(7 - 3) \div (-2)$

3 a Write these as ordinary numbers.

i 2.3×10^2	**iii** 5.7×10^{-3}	**v** 3.83×10^1
ii 8.6×10^5	**iv** 1.2×10^{-4}	**vi** 4.58×10^{-5}

b Write the following numbers in standard form.

i 0.047	**iii** 5070	**v** 0.000092
ii 0.00008	**iv** 82000000	**vi** 908

4 Express as a single fraction in its simplest form

a $\frac{2}{5} + \frac{3}{4}$	**g** $4\frac{1}{9} + 3\frac{1}{3}$	**m** $\left(\frac{1}{2} - \frac{1}{3}\right) \div \left(\frac{3}{4} - \frac{1}{3}\right)$
b $\frac{3}{4} - \frac{5}{8}$	**h** $3\frac{3}{5} - 1\frac{1}{4}$	**n** $2\frac{1}{2} \div 1\frac{3}{7} + 1\frac{1}{3}$
c $\frac{1}{2} + \frac{2}{3} + \frac{3}{4}$	**i** $6\frac{3}{4} - 4\frac{7}{8}$	**p** $\frac{4}{7} \times \frac{8}{9} \div \frac{16}{21}$
d $3\frac{3}{8} \div 2\frac{1}{4}$	**j** $2\frac{1}{2} \times \frac{3}{5}$	**q** $4\frac{1}{2} - 5\frac{1}{4} + 2\frac{1}{8}$
e $4\frac{1}{7} \times 4\frac{2}{3}$	**k** $3\frac{1}{8} \div 5$	**r** $1\frac{1}{2} + 2\frac{2}{3} \times \frac{3}{4}$
f $1\frac{1}{3} + 2\frac{5}{6}$	**l** $\frac{3}{4} \times 2\frac{1}{3} \div \frac{21}{32}$	**s** $2\frac{2}{5} - \frac{6}{7} \div \frac{5}{14}$

5 Find

a $4.27 + 5.93$	**g** $1.12 \div 0.4$	**m** $0.02 \div 50$
b $16.5 + 2.68$	**h** $53.6 \div 200$	**n** $(0.03)^2$
c $0.05 + 1.23$	**i** 1.6×0.8	**p** $0.008 \div 20$
d $0.49 - 0.009$	**j** $0.001 \div 0.05$	**q** $(0.002)^2$
e $3 - 1.04$	**k** 0.8×0.07	**r** 0.17×60
f $0.045 - 0.0068$	**l** 2.004×0.42	**s** $(0.1)^3$

6 Fill in the blanks (marked with $\square$) in the following calculations.

a $4.9 \times \square = 13.23$	**e** $\square \times 0.65 = 5.343$
b $33.48 \div \square = 5.4$	**f** $\square - 14.25 \div 1.9 = 0$
c $0.725 \times 0.04 = \square$	**g** $0.00234 \div 0.065 = \square$
d $7.1 \div \square = 2.84$	**h** $\square \div 0.55 = 1.7$

7 **a** Give as a fraction   **i** 2^{-3} **ii** 3^{-2} **iii** 5^{-1}

    b Write in the form a^{-b} **i** $\frac{1}{3}$ **ii** $\frac{1}{4}$ **iii** $\frac{1}{27}$

8 Write as a single expression in index form

a $2^4 \times 2^3$	**f** $10^8 \div 10^3$	**k** $p^4 \div p^3$
b $5^4 \times 5^4$	**g** $7^2 \div 7^5$	**l** $2^6 \div 2^2 \times 2^4$
c $3^2 \times 3^5$	**h** $a^8 \div a^4$	**m** $3^2 \times 3^3 \times 3^4$
d $a^2 \times a^4$	**i** $3^3 \div 3^3$	**n** $5^2 \times 5^3 \div 5^4$
e $4^3 \times 4^{-4}$	**j** $b^6 \times b^{-3}$	**p** $\dfrac{4^3 \times 4^2}{4^4}$

9 **a** Illustrate on a number line the range of values of x given by

     i $6 \leqslant x < 10$ **iii** $0 \leqslant x < 0.2$

     ii $-3 < x \leqslant 3$ **iv** $0.04 < x < 0.15$

    b Illustrate on a number line the range of possible values for each of the following corrected numbers.

     i 2.5 correct to 1 d.p.   **iii** 0.06 correct to 2 d.p.

     ii 0.45 correct to 2 d.p.   **iv** 7.2 correct to 1 d.p.

    c To the nearest 1000, there were 42 000 spectators at an international match.
Find the range in which the actual number of spectators lies.

REVISION EXERCISE 1.2
(Using fractions, decimals, ratios and percentages)

1 a Express as a decimal

    i $\frac{21}{25}$ **ii** $\frac{7}{20}$ **iii** 34%   **iv** $12\frac{1}{2}$%

  b Express as a fraction in its lowest terms

    i 75%   **ii** 0.92   **iii** 42%   **iv** 0.375

  c Express as a percentage

    i 0.24   **ii** $\frac{9}{25}$ **iii** 2.46   **iv** $\frac{33}{40}$

  d Express 45% as   **i** a fraction   **ii** a decimal

  e Express $3\frac{3}{4}$ as   **i** a decimal   **ii** a percentage

2 a Put either > or < between each of the following pairs of fractions.

    i $\frac{3}{10}$ $\frac{3}{8}$ **ii** $\frac{4}{5}$ $\frac{2}{3}$ **iii** $\frac{1}{3}$ $\frac{4}{15}$ **iv** $\frac{5}{6}$ $\frac{8}{9}$

  b Change to an improper fraction

    i $3\frac{5}{9}$ **ii** $1\frac{4}{7}$ **iii** $5\frac{2}{5}$ **iv** $4\frac{3}{4}$

  c Give as a mixed number

    i $\frac{21}{5}$ **ii** $\frac{13}{4}$ **iii** $\frac{47}{8}$ **iv** $\frac{28}{9}$

3 a Find

    i 66% of 50 kg   **iii** 8.5% of 640 g   **v** 54% of 25 m

    ii 68% of 550 cm   **iv** 35% of 480 mm   **vi** 95% of £360

  b   **i** Increase £180 by 35%   **v** Increase 550 m^2 by 136%

    ii Decrease £720 by 15%   **vi** Decrease 88 cm^3 by 65%

    iii Increase £99.40 by 15%   **vii** Decrease 198 m by $12\frac{1}{2}$%

    iv Decrease 4.2 m by 8%   **viii** Increase £95 by 72%

  c Find, giving your answer correct to 3 significant figures

    i 43% of 24 m   **iii** $3\frac{3}{4}$% of 558 cm^2 **v** $7\frac{1}{2}$% of 77 cm^3

    ii 77% of 317 cm^2 **iv** $8\frac{1}{4}$% of 87 cm^3 **vi** 19% of 528 m

4 Express

  a 360 mm as a fraction of 50 cm

  b 120 cm as a percentage of 3 m

  c 36 mm as a decimal of 4 cm

  d 2 pints as a fraction of 3 gallons

  e 950 cm^2 as a percentage of 1 m^2

  f 672 cm as a decimal of 12 m

5 **a** Find, correct to the nearest penny, the compound interest on
£460 invested for 2 years at 6%.

b A particular coin increases in value by 15% each year. If it is
bought for £40, what will it be worth in 3 years' time?

c A car bought for £12 000 depreciates in value by 20% each year.
Find its value after 2 years.

6 **a** Give the following ratios in their simplest form.

   i $15:25$ **iii** $232:348$ **v** $\frac{5}{8}:\frac{1}{2}:\frac{3}{4}$

   ii $4:8:20$ **iv** $4.5:3.5$ **vi** $126:56:63$

b Simplify the following ratios.

   i $82\,\text{p}:£2.05$ **iii** $510\,\text{cm}:18\,\text{m}$ **v** $24\,\text{g}:1.5\,\text{kg}$

   ii $0.1\,\text{m}:15\,\text{cm}$ **iv** $700\,\text{mg}:2\,\text{g}$ **vi** $3.3\,\text{t}:220\,\text{kg}$

c Find x if

   i $x:3=5:8$ **iii** $x:4=3:16$ **v** $3:5=5:x$

   ii $x:8=2:9$ **iv** $7:x=8:3$ **vi** $7:2=x:4$

d Express the following ratios in the form $1:n$, giving answers
correct to 3 significant figures where necessary.

   i $2:5$ **iii** $13:18$ **v** $\frac{2}{3}:\frac{3}{4}$

   ii $7:12$ **iv** $7:10$ **vi** $0.65:0.25$

7 **a** **i** Divide 88 cm into 2 parts in the ratio $5:6$.

   ii Divide £135 into 2 parts in the ratio $7:8$.

   iii Divide 4 kg into 3 parts in the ratio $1:3:4$.

   iv Divide 52 litres into 3 parts in the ratio $1:4:8$.

b **i** A sum of money is divided between Kim and David in the ratio
$2:3$. What fraction of the sum of money does Kim receive?

   ii A plank of wood is divided into two pieces whose lengths are
in the ratio $5:7$. What fraction of the length of the plank is
the longer piece?

   iii The chocolates in a box are divided into dark chocolates and
light chocolates in the ratio $4:5$. What fraction of the
chocolates in the box are dark?

8 **a** If $1\,\text{cm}^3$ of copper weighs 8.96 g, what is the weight of

   i $8\,\text{cm}^3$ **ii** $0.6\,\text{cm}^3$?

b If $6\,\text{m}^2$ of carpet costs £74.70 what is the cost of $7\,\text{m}^2$?

c Packets of biscuits are packed in 12 boxes taking 24 packets each.
If the same number of packets are packed in boxes taking
18 packets each, how many boxes would be filled?

d Some sweets are shared equally among 4 children and they get 6 each. How many sweets would each child get if they were shared equally among 12 children?

e At a steady speed of 36 km/h, a journey takes 4 hours. How long would the journey take at a steady speed of 48 km/h?

f A typist types 3990 words in $3\frac{1}{2}$ hours. How long would it take her to type 2850 words at the same rate?

9 In each case find the buying-in price.

a Selling price £84, mark-up 40%

b Selling price £54, loss 40%

c Selling price £484, mark-up 120%

d Selling price £675, loss 55%

e Selling price £56, loss 30%

f Selling price £112, mark-up 75%

g Selling price £11.20, loss 20%

h Selling price £30, mark-up 300%

10 Steve pays £35.25 for a new watch. This includes value added tax at $17\frac{1}{2}$%. Find the price before VAT was added.

REVISION EXERCISE 1.3 (Units, areas and volumes)

1 a **i** Find, giving your answer in metres, $213\,\text{cm} + 1.2\,\text{m} + 642\,\text{mm}$

ii Find, giving your answer in grams, $460\,\text{mg} + 0.42\,\text{kg} + 756\,\text{g}$

iii Find, giving your answer in inches, 2 feet + 7 inches + 3 yards

iv Find, giving your answer in ounces, 2 lb + 6 oz

b Express

i 540 cm in metres

ii 63 mm in cm

iii 36 inches in feet

iv 8 yards in feet

v $10\,\text{cm}^2$ in mm^2

vi $0.4\,\text{m}^2$ in cm^2

vii 8 sq yd in sq ft

viii $7000\,\text{cm}^2$ in m^2

ix 2 sq feet in sq inches

x $80\,000\,\text{mm}^3$ in cm^3

xi $0.005\,\text{m}^3$ in cm^3

xii $3\,000\,000\,\text{cm}^3$ in m^3

xiii 2.5 litres in cm^3

xiv $2\,\text{m}^3$ in litres

2 Give roughly

a the number of pints in 20 litres

b the equivalent in litres of 10 gallons

c 25 hectares in acres

d 5 kg in lb

e 40 miles in km

f 60 yards in metres

g 200 cm in inches

h 10 km in miles

3 a State whether each of the following quantities is a length, an area or a volume.

   i 5 m   **iii** $2.4\,\text{cm}^2$

   ii $35\,\text{mm}^3$ **iv** 3 feet

b State whether each of the following quantities should be measured in length, area or volume units.

   i the space inside a cubical tin

   ii perimeter of a square

   iii the surface area of a cylinder

c If a, b and c represent numbers of length units, A and B represent numbers of area units and V represents a number of volume units, state whether each of the letters W, X, Y and Z used in the following formulas represent numbers of length or area or volume units.

   i $W = \dfrac{3V}{bc}$ **iii** $Y = \dfrac{A}{a}$

   ii $X = 2\pi a^2 b$ **iv** $Z = a^2 + bc$

4 For each shape find **i** the perimeter   **ii** the area.

a

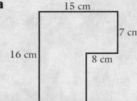

15 cm
7 cm
16 cm
8 cm

c

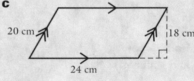

20 cm
18 cm
24 cm

b

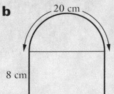

20 cm
8 cm

d

6.25 cm
5 cm
3 cm
3.75 cm

5 a Find, correct to 3 significant figures

   i the circumference of the circle

   ii the length of the minor arc AB

   iii the perimeter of the minor sector OAB

   iv the area of the minor sector OAB.

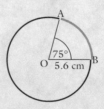

A
75°
O 5.6 cm B

b The area of a circle is $100\,\text{cm}^2$. Find its radius.

6 The diagram shows the cross-section of a wooden prism which is 70 cm long. Find

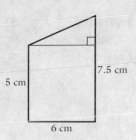

  a the area of the cross-section

  b the volume of the prism

  c the mass of the prism if it is made from wood with a density of 0.85 g/cm^3.

7 Find the volume of each of the following solids.

a

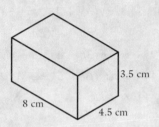

c

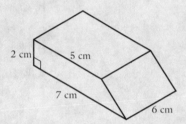

b

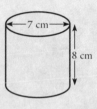

d

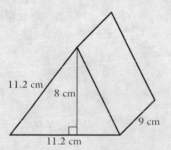

8 **a** A car travels at 45 mph. How long does it take to travel

  i 60 miles   **ii** 195 miles?

  b Ian cycles at 18 km/h. How far will he travel in

  i $2\frac{1}{2}$ hours   **ii** $\frac{3}{4}$ h?

  c Find the average speed in km/h for a journey of

  i 180 km in 3 hr

  ii 30 km in 30 minutes

  iii 9000 m in 45 minutes

  d Kim walks for 1 km at 4 km/h, then jogs for 15 minutes at 10 km/h.

  i How long was Kim walking?

  ii How far did Kim jog?

  iii How far did Kim travel altogether and how long did she take?

  iv What was Kim's average speed for the whole journey?

**REVISION
EXERCISE 1.4
(Algebra)**

Do not use a calculator for any question in this exercise.

1 Expand

a $3(x + 2)$ **d** $5a(b - 2c)$ **g** $(5x - y)(z + 3)$

b $4(a - 3)$ **e** $(a + b)(c - d)$ **h** $(3x + 2)(4 - y)$

c $7x(y + 2z)$ **f** $(2a + b)(4c + d)$ **i** $(4a - b)(c - 3)$

2 Expand

a $(x + 4)(x + 5)$ **g** $(3x + 5)(x + 7)$ **m** $(x - 3)^2$

b $(a + 3)(a + 7)$ **h** $(5x + 2)(2x + 3)$ **n** $(3 + 2x)(1 - x)$

c $(a - 2)(a + 5)$ **i** $(3a + 4)(2a - 5)$ **p** $(x + 4)(3 - x)$

d $(x - 4)(x - 9)$ **j** $(3b - 4)(4a - 1)$ **q** $(4x + 3)(2 - x)$

e $(x - 2)(x - 4)$ **k** $(6c - 5)(c + 3)$ **r** $(3x + 4)(3 - 2x)$

f $(2x + 3)(x + 1)$ **l** $(a + 4)^2$ **s** $(5x + 3)^2$

3 Simplify

a $\dfrac{4x}{12}$ **e** $\dfrac{3}{15x}$ **i** $\dfrac{2a - 6b}{a^2 - 3ab}$

b $\dfrac{ab}{2a}$ **f** $\dfrac{6a^2}{15ab}$ **j** $\dfrac{5p + 10q}{(p - 2q)(p + 2q)}$

c $\dfrac{9p}{3pq}$ **g** $\dfrac{3 + a}{(3 - a)(3 + a)}$ **k** $\dfrac{3a - 3b}{(a + b)(a - b)}$

d $\dfrac{8x}{12xy}$ **h** $\dfrac{p - q}{4(p - q)}$ **l** $\dfrac{2p + 4q}{p^2 + 2pq}$

4 Simplify

a $\dfrac{a}{b} \times \dfrac{b}{c}$ **d** $\dfrac{1}{p^2} \div \dfrac{2}{p}$ **g** $\dfrac{a^2}{b} \div \dfrac{a}{b^2}$

b $\dfrac{ab}{6} \times \dfrac{3}{b^2}$ **e** $\dfrac{x^2}{2y} \div 2x$ **h** $\dfrac{a^3}{8b} \div \dfrac{4a}{b}$

c $a^2b \times \dfrac{b}{c}$ **f** $\dfrac{a^2}{3} \times \dfrac{12}{2ab}$ **i** $\dfrac{3}{p^2} \div \dfrac{2}{p^3}$

5 Simplify

a $\dfrac{2}{a} + \dfrac{3}{b}$ **c** $\dfrac{2}{x} + \dfrac{3}{8x}$ **e** $\dfrac{3x}{4y} + \dfrac{y}{3x}$ **g** $\dfrac{3}{2x} + \dfrac{1}{4x}$

b $\dfrac{2}{x} - \dfrac{3}{2x}$ **d** $\dfrac{1}{3a} - \dfrac{3}{5b}$ **f** $\dfrac{7}{9a} - \dfrac{5}{6b}$ **h** $\dfrac{5}{2a} - \dfrac{2}{5a}$

6 Simplify

a $\dfrac{x+3}{4}+\dfrac{x-1}{5}$ **d** $\dfrac{4x+2}{5}-\dfrac{3x-2}{6}$ **g** $\dfrac{4}{x-2}+\dfrac{5}{x}$

b $\dfrac{x+4}{3}-\dfrac{x+2}{7}$ **e** $\frac{1}{3}(3x-1)-\frac{1}{2}(2x+7)$ **h** $\dfrac{3}{2x+3}-\dfrac{4}{5x}$

c $\dfrac{2x+1}{3}-\dfrac{x+1}{5}$ **f** $\frac{2}{5}(10x-3)-\frac{3}{4}(5-2x)$ **i** $\dfrac{7}{3x}+\dfrac{4}{x-5}$

7 Factorise

a x^2+6x **i** x^2-64 **r** $28-12x-x^2$

b $3x^2-9x$ **j** $3x^2+18x+15$ **s** $2x^2-4x-30$

c $x^2+13x+12$ **k** $32+x^2-18x$ **t** x^2-y^2

d $x^2+17x+30$ **l** x^2-x-20 **u** $2x^2-2x-24$

e $x^2-12x+27$ **m** $x^2+11x-42$ **v** $2x^2-16x+30$

f $x^2-16x+48$ **n** x^2+9-6x **w** $2p^2q-10pq^2$

g x^2+x-12 **p** a^2-4b^2 **x** $8a^2b^3-18a^4b$

h $x^2+2x-15$ **q** $24+5x-x^2$ **y** $9x^3y^2+12xy^4$

REVISION EXERCISE 1.5 (Formulas and equations)

Do not use a calculator for any question in this exercise.

1 If $R=pq-w$ find R when

a $p=4,\ q=3$ and $w=2$ **c** $p=-4,\ q=\frac{1}{2}$ and $w=3$

b $p=3,\ q=5$ and $w=-6$ **d** $p=-1,\ q=-2,\ w=-3$

2 Given that $z=\dfrac{1}{x}+\dfrac{2}{y}$ find z when

a $x=2$ and $y=4$ **c** $x=\frac{1}{2}$ and $y=\frac{1}{4}$

b $x=3$ and $y=5$ **d** $x=0.1$ and $y=0.2$

3 Given that $z=\dfrac{x}{y}$ find

a z when $x=12$ and $y=-3$ **c** z when $x=0.7$ and $y=\frac{1}{2}$

b x when $y=3$ and $z=12$ **d** x when $y=0.6$ and $z=\frac{1}{3}$

4 **a** Write down the first 4 terms and the 10th term of the sequence for which the nth term is $n(n+2)$.

b Find, in terms of n, an expression for the nth term of the sequence 2, 5, 10, 17, ...

5 A number a is equal to the sum of twice a number b and half a number c.

a Find a formula for a in terms of b and c.

b Find a when $b=3$ and $c=6$.

c Make c the subject of the formula.

6 Make the letter in brackets the subject of the formula.

a $a = b + 2c$ (b) **f** $v = u - 10t$ (t)

b $u = v - 6$ (v) **g** $P = 4q - 3s$ (s)

c $p = \frac{1}{2}q$ (q) **h** $a = \frac{1}{4}b + c$ (b)

d $x = 5y$ (y) **i** $z = x - \frac{y}{5}$ (y)

e $C = 2\pi r$ (r) **j** $P = q + 3r$ (r)

7 Solve the equations

a $12x - 23 = 3x + 4$ **g** $\frac{2}{5}x = 15$

b $5x - 7 = 11 - 4x$ **h** $\frac{2x}{5} + \frac{x}{4} = \frac{1}{5}$

c $3x + (5x - 4) = 20$ **i** $\frac{x}{3} - \frac{3}{4} = \frac{5}{12}$

d $\frac{5x}{4} = \frac{3}{8}$ **j** $4x + (3x - 2) = 19$

e $0.6x = 30$ **k** $7x - (5x + 2) = 5$

f $\frac{x}{5} - 2 = 8$ **l** $6x - (x - 3) = 23$

8 Solve the following pairs of simultaneous equations.

a $x + y = 5$ **e** $2p - 5q = 9$ **i** $5x - 4y = 19$
    $3x + y = 11$ $3p - 5q = 11$ $3x + y = 8$

b $x + 2y = 10$ **f** $x - 2y = 7$ **j** $4x - 3y = 17$
    $x + y = 7$ $9x + 2y = 23$ $3x + 4y = -6$

c $7x + 3y = 23$ **g** $3x + y = 5$ **k** $3x + 8y = 23$
    $4x + 3y = 17$ $x + 2y = 5$ $5x + 6y = 9$

d $4x - y = 18$ **h** $x + 2y = 10$ **l** $6x - 5y = 20$
    $3x + y = 10$ $5x - 2y = 14$ $2x + 3y = 16$

9 Solve the following pairs of equations.

a $2x = 2 + y$ **c** $2x - 3y = 14$ **e** $6x - 7 = y$
    $y = 7 - x$ $y = 2x - 10$ $2x = 1 + y$

b $y = 6 + x$ **d** $y + 1 = x$ **f** $3x = y + 1$
    $y = 3x - 2$ $2x - 4 = y$ $x + 2y = 12$

10 Solve the equations

a $x(x+4) = 0$

b $(x+3)(x-7) = 0$

c $(2x-7)(x+2) = 0$

d $x^2 - 5x + 6 = 0$

e $x^2 + 8x + 12 = 0$

f $x^2 - x - 6 = 0$

g $x^2 + 5x - 24 = 0$

h $8x^2 + 5x = 0$

i $7x^2 - 3x = 0$

j $x^2 + x + \frac{1}{4} = 0$

k $x^2 - 12x + 36 = 0$

l $8 = 6x - x^2$

m $12 = 7x - x^2$

n $3x^2 - 6x - 24 = 0$

p $x(x+1) = 6$

q $x(x-5) = 24$

r $(x+6)(x-2) - 9 = 0$

s $(x-3)(x+5) + 7 = 0$

11 Solve the following inequalities and illustrate your solution on a number line.

a $3 < 4 + x$

b $7 - x < 10$

c $7 - x > -6$

d $2 < -x$

e $5 \leqslant 7 - 2x$

f $7 - 3x \geqslant 1$

g $3x + 4 \leqslant 5x + 4$

h $2x + 3 \geqslant 7 - x$

i $x - 6 < 10$

12 a Solve each of the following pairs of inequalities and find the range of values of x which satisfy both of them.

i $6 + x \leqslant 5$ and $5 - x \geqslant 2$ **ii** $2 > 3 - 2x$ and $2x - 7 \leqslant 3$

b Find the range of values of x for which the following inequalities are true.

i $x + 5 > 2x > 4$

ii $4x + 3 < x < 6$

iii $x \leqslant 2x + 3 \leqslant 7$

iv $1 - x < 3x + 1 < 7$

v $2x < x - 4 < 4$

vi $1 + x < 2x < 3 + x$

REVISION EXERCISE 1.6 (Graphs)

Do not use a calculator for any question in this exercise.

1 a Find the y-coordinate of the point on the line $y = -2x$ that has an x-coordinate of

i 3   **ii** -4 **iii** $\frac{3}{2}$

b Find the x-coordinate of the point on the line $y = -\frac{1}{2}x$ that has a y-coordinate of

i 4   **ii** -5 **iii** $\frac{3}{4}$

c The equation of a line is $y = -\frac{1}{4}x$. Determine which of the points $(2, 4), (-2, 4), (4, -1), (-2, -4), (-1, 4)$ and $(2, -4)$ lie

i above the line   **ii** below the line   **iii** on the line.

d Find the gradient of the straight line that passes through the points

i $(2, 6)$ and $(4, 12)$ **ii** $(-4, 2)$ and $(8, -4)$

2 Find the equation of the straight line given on the sketch.

a

b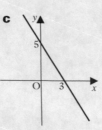

c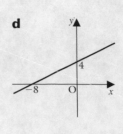

d

3 The equation of the curve could be

A $y = \dfrac{8}{x}$ **C** $y = 9x - x^3$

B $y = x^3 - 9x$ **D** $y = x^2 + 6x - 3$

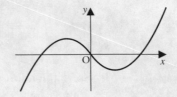

4 The graph represented by the equation $y = x^2 + x - 12$ could be

A 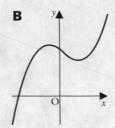   **B** 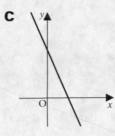   **C** 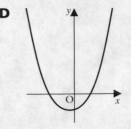   **D**

5 a Use inequalities to describe the region marked **A** in the diagram.

  b Copy the diagram onto squared paper. One region on the diagram is defined by the inequalities

    $x \geqslant 0,\ y \leqslant x,\ y \geqslant -2,\ y \leqslant 2 - x$.

    Shade this region and mark it **B**.

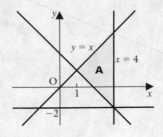

6 Given below are four equations and four graphs. Pair each equation with the appropriate graph.

  a $y = 9 - x^2$ **b** $y = (x + 1)(x - 2)(x - 4)$ **c** $y = \dfrac{12}{x}$ **d** $y = x^2 + 3$

A 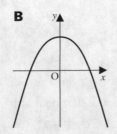   **B** 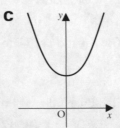   **C**   **D**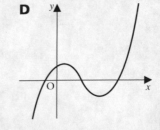

7 You are given the graph of $y = x^2 - 3x - 5$. Give the equation of the other line you need to draw to solve the equation

    a $x^2 - 3x - 9 = 0$ **b** $x^2 - 4x - 1 = 0$ **c** $2x^2 - 7x - 20 = 0$

8

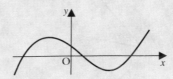

This curve has equation $y = (x + 3)(x - 1)(x - 4)$.

    a What name do we give to this type of equation?

    b How many values of x satisfy the equation $(x + 3)(x - 1)(x - 4) = 0$? What are they?

REVISION EXERCISE 1.7 (Geometry)

Do not use a calculator for any question in this exercise.

1 Find the size of each angle marked with a letter.

a

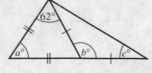

c

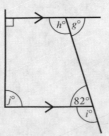

b

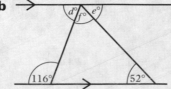

d

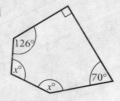

2 **a** Find the size of each interior angle of a regular octagon.

    b How many sides has a regular polygon if each exterior angle is

      i 45°   **ii** 36°?

    c How many sides has a regular polygon if each interior angle is

      i 150°   **ii** 160°?

    d Is it possible for each exterior angle of a regular polygon to be

      i 40°   **ii** 50°   **iii** 60°?

    In those cases where it is possible give the number of sides.

3 State whether or not △s ABC and DEF are similar.

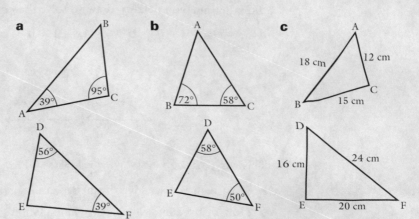

4 a Find YZ.

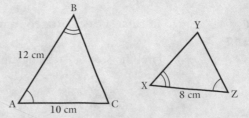

b In △s ABC and DEF, $\widehat{A} = \widehat{E}$ and $\widehat{B} = \widehat{F}$. AB = 8 cm, EF = 10 cm and AC = 10 cm. Find DE.

5 State whether the following pairs of triangles are similar. In each case say which angle, if any, is equal to $\widehat{A}$.

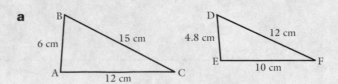

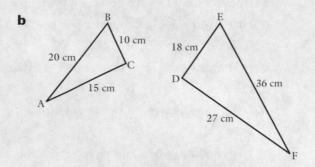

6 Each pair of figures are similar. Find each length marked with a letter.

a

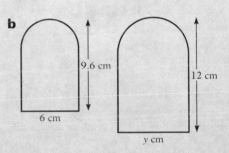

c

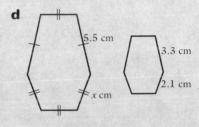

b

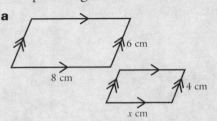

d

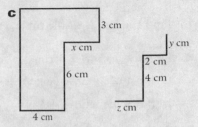

7 Find the marked angles.

a

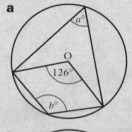

c

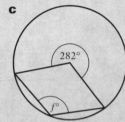

e

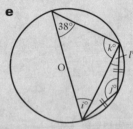

b

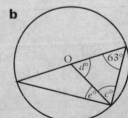

d

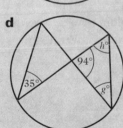

f

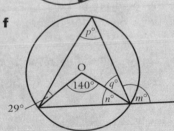

**REVISION
EXERCISE 1.8
(Pythagoras'
theorem and
trigonometry)**

In this exercise give distances that are not exact correct to
3 significant figures.

1 a Find AC.

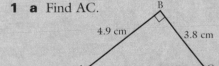

b Find BC.

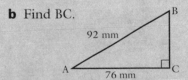

2 a In △ABC, $\widehat{B} = 90°$, AC = 12.6 cm and AB = 9.4 cm.
Find BC.

b In △XYZ, XY = 9.5 cm, XZ = 5.7 cm and YZ = 7.6 cm.
Does this triangle contain a right angle ? If so, which angle is it ?

3 O is the centre of a circle and AB is a chord of length 5.94 cm.
The perpendicular distance of the chord from O is 2.37 cm.
Find the radius of the circle.

4 Find, correct to 1 decimal place

   a the angle whose tangent is   **i** 0.7824   **ii** 1.53   **iii** $\frac{3}{4}$

   b the angle whose sine is   **i** 0.4253   **ii** 0.7216   **iii** $\frac{2}{3}$

   c the angle whose cosine is   **i** 0.9234   **ii** 0.2237   **iii** $\frac{5}{6}$

5 For each triangle find, correct to 1 decimal place, the size of angle A.

   a 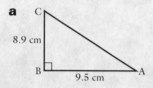   **b** 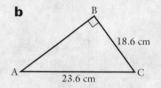   **c**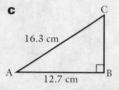

6 For each triangle find the length of BC.

   a 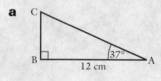   **b** 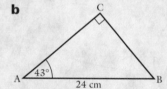   **c**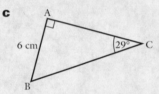

7 In the diagram PQ represents a vertical building and S is a
point on the top of another building which is represented
by SR. $\widehat{SQR} = 26°$ and $\widehat{PSQ} = 43°$. Write down

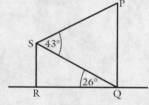

   a the angle of depression of Q from S

   b the angle of elevation of P from S.

8 From my bedroom window P the angle of elevation of the
top A of a tree on level ground directly in front of me is 34°
and the angle of depression of the foot B of the tree is 29°.
Q is the point on the ground vertically below P and
PQ = 4.2 m. Find

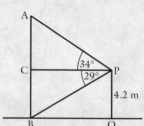

   a the distance from Q to the foot of the tree

   b the height of the tree.

9 In Toomesbury the bearing of the church C from the Post Office P is 325° and the
bearing of the Town Hall H from the Post Office is 292°. From the Town Hall the church
is 500 m away on a bearing of 055°.

   a Draw a sketch to show this information.   **b** Write down the size of each angle in △CPH.

   c Find the distance of the Post Office from   **i** the church   **ii** the Town Hall.

1 Find the mean, mode and median of the following numbers:

$$9, 10, 11, 13, 17, 19, 19$$

2 The ages (in years) of 20 pupils in an athletics team are:

14, 14, 15, 15, 15, 15, 15, 15, 15, 16,
16, 16, 16, 16, 16, 16, 16, 17, 17

The ages (in years) of a different group of pupils (those in the school band) are:

11, 12, 12, 13, 13, 13, 14, 14, 14, 14,
14, 15, 15, 16, 16, 16, 17, 18, 18, 19

a Find the mean and range of the ages in each group.

b Use your answers to part **a** to compare the ages of the two groups.

3 All the pupils in Year 10 at Sumley School sat an English test. Their marks are given in the table.

Mark	0–9	10–19	20–29	30–39	40–49	50–59	60–69	70–79
Frequency	4	14	28	44	29	21	13	9

a Hugh said that at least one pupil must have scored 19. Explain why this may not be true.

b How many pupils scored **i** less than 40   **ii** 30 or more?

c Draw a cumulative frequency curve for these figures. Use 2 cm to represent 10 marks and a cumulative frequency of 20.

d Use your graph to estimate
  i the median
  ii the upper and lower quartiles
  iii the pass mark if 70% of the pupils passed.

4 The height of 110 children are given in the table.

a Find the mean height of these 110 children.

b Explain why your answer to part **a** is only an estimate.

Height, h cm	Frequency
$130 \leqslant h < 135$	5
$135 \leqslant h < 140$	8
$140 \leqslant h < 145$	24
$145 \leqslant h < 150$	23
$150 \leqslant h < 155$	28
$155 \leqslant h < 160$	16
$160 \leqslant h < 165$	4
$165 \leqslant h < 170$	2

5 a An ordinary 6-sided dice is rolled. What is the probability that the number uppermost is

    i 6   **ii** 5 or 6   **iii** 4, 5 or 6   **iv** 7   **v** 1, 2, 3, 4, 5 or 6?

  b What is the probability that the number uppermost is

    i not 6   **ii** not a prime number?

6 a Two 10 p coins are tossed together. Make your own possibility space for the combinations in which they can land. Find the probability of

    i getting 2 heads   **ii** not getting two heads.

  b Two 10 p coins are tossed together 200 times.

    i About how many times would you expect to get 2 heads?

    ii Will you get this number of two heads if you toss two coins 200 times?
Give a reason for your answer.

    iii Explain what your reaction would be if you tossed two 10 p coins 200 times and got 2 heads on just 15 occasions.

7 An ordinary pack of playing cards is cut, reshuffled and cut again. What is the probability that

  a the first card cut is a 2 or a 3

  b the second card cut is a 2 or a 3

  c both cards cut are 2 s?

RATIONAL AND IRRATIONAL NUMBERS

THE NAMING OF NUMBERS

Followers of Pythagoras believed that the only numbers that existed were positive integers. They also believed that all physical phenomena could be described using these numbers. When it was discovered that the ratio of the length of the diagonal of a square to the length of its side could not be expressed using integers, the Pythagoreans did not change their belief, they rejected the idea as being illogical and irrational. (It appears that they also attempted to keep the discovery to themselves; tradition says that one member of the Pythagoreans was drowned for talking about the discovery outside the group.)

The word irrational has stuck as the name of any number that cannot be expressed as the ratio of two integers.

EXERCISE 1A

1 Sketch a square of side a units. Use Pythagoras' theorem to find the length of the diagonal in terms of a. Hence find the ratio of the length of the diagonal of a square to the length of its side. Discuss whether it is possible to express this ratio as a fraction.

2 Discuss whether it is possible to express this fraction exactly

    a using integers   **b** in any other way.

3 **a** Write down the value of $\sqrt{2}$ as a decimal correct to 4 decimal places.

    b Write down the value of $(\sqrt{2})^2$ and also the value of the square of your answer to part **a**. Why are these values not the same? Would the values be the same if $\sqrt{2}$ was written as a decimal correct to 10 decimal places?

IRRATIONAL
NUMBERS

The square roots of all integers that are not perfect squares are irrational numbers.

For example, $\sqrt{2}$, $\sqrt{15}$, ... are irrational numbers, but $\sqrt{4}$, $\sqrt{25}$, ... are not.

There are other irrational numbers such as π, $\sin 25°$, ...

These numbers all have the following property.

> An irrational number cannot be expressed in the form $\dfrac{a}{b}$, where a and b are integers.

> Conversely, any number that can be expressed in the form $\dfrac{a}{b}$, where a and b are integers, is called a *rational number*.

Note that rational and irrational numbers are collectively called *real numbers*, because they can be used to give exact values for real quantities.

We know that some fractions can be expressed as recurring decimals, for example, $\frac{2}{3} = 0.66666\ldots$ which we write as $0.\dot{6}$ to show that the 6 recurs indefinitely. We will also show that any recurring decimal can be expressed as a fraction whose numerator and denominator are integers, that is, recurring decimals are rational numbers.

From this it follows that an irrational number has an infinite number of decimal places with no repeating pattern, hence

> an irrational number cannot be expressed exactly as a decimal.

EXERCISE 1B

1 Which of these numbers are rational?

$$\pi, \ \tfrac{4}{5}, \ 0.01\dot{4}\dot{2}, \ \sqrt{36}, \ (\sqrt{2})^2, \ \sqrt{(\tfrac{1}{5})}, \ \sqrt{5}, \ 1 + \sqrt{5}$$

2 Triangle ABC is equilateral.

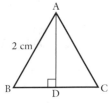

a Copy the diagram and mark on it the lengths of BC, BD and the size of $\widehat{B}$. Calculate the length of AD, leaving the answer in an exact form, and mark this on the diagram.

b Use the information on your diagram to write down, exactly, the values of $\sin \widehat{B}$, $\cos \widehat{B}$, $\tan \widehat{B}$. Which of these trigonometric ratios are irrational?

WRITING
RECURRING
DECIMALS AS
FRACTIONS

Any recurring decimal can be expressed as a fraction whose numerator and denominator are integers.

- Consider the recurring decimal $0.16\dot{2}\dot{5}$.
  First write the decimal without using dots, e.g. $0.16\dot{2}\dot{5} = 0.1\,625\,625\,625\,625\ldots$
- Now multiply both sides by the power of 10 corresponding to the number of figures in the repeating pattern.
  In this case we multiply by 10^3, i.e. $1000 \times 0.16\dot{2}\dot{5} = 162.5\,625\,625\,625\ldots$
- Then subtract the original recurring decimal; the repeating pattern disappears.

i.e.
$$1000 \times 0.16\dot{2}\dot{5} = 162.5\,625\,625\,625\,625\ldots$$
$$- \quad 1 \times 0.16\dot{2}\dot{5} = \quad 0.1\,625\,625\,625\,625\ldots$$
$$999 \times 0.16\dot{2}\dot{5} = 162.4$$

Hence $0.16\dot{2}\dot{5} = \dfrac{162.4}{999} = \dfrac{1624}{9990}$ which can be cancelled down to its lowest terms.

EXERCISE 1C

Express $0.\dot{5}$ as a fraction in its lowest terms.

> There is one figure in the repeating pattern, so multiply both sides by 10.

$$10 \times 0.\dot{5} = 5.555555\ldots$$
$$- \quad 1 \times 0.\dot{5} = 0.555555\ldots$$
$$9 \times 0.\dot{5} = 5$$

> Now subtract the original decimal.

i.e. $\quad 0.\dot{5} = \frac{5}{9}$

Express the following decimals as fractions in their lowest terms.

1 $0.\dot{2}$ **2** $0.\dot{6}$ **3** $0.\dot{8}$ **4** $0.\dot{9}$ (Explain the result.)

Express $0.1\dot{5}$ as a fraction in its lowest terms.

> There is still only one figure in the repeating pattern, so multiply both sides by 10.

$$10 \times 0.1\dot{5} = 1.55555\ldots$$
$$- \quad 1 \times 0.1\dot{5} = 0.15555\ldots$$
$$9 \times 0.1\dot{5} = 1.4$$

so $\quad 0.1\dot{5} = \dfrac{1.4}{9} = \dfrac{14}{90} = \dfrac{7}{45}$

Express the following decimals as fractions in their lowest terms.

5 $0.1\dot{6}$ **6** $0.2\dot{4}$ **7** $0.0\dot{6}$ **8** $0.14\dot{6}$

9 $0.40\dot{7}$ 11 $0.1\dot{5}$ 13 $0.\dot{5}2\dot{5}$ **15** $0.4\dot{5}$

10 $0.0\dot{9}$ 12 $0.11\dot{5}$ 14 $0.06\dot{3}$ **16** $0.1\dot{5}0\dot{5}$

SURDS

When an expression contains irrational numbers such as $\sqrt{2}$, the value can only be given exactly by leaving these irrational numbers in the form $\sqrt{2}$, $\sqrt{3}$, and so on.

Irrational numbers written in the form $\sqrt{2}$, etc. are called *surds*.

Expressions containing surds can often be simplified.

For example, $\sqrt{20}$ can be written in terms of a smaller surd because 20 has a factor 4 which is a perfect square,

i.e. $\sqrt{20} = \sqrt{4 \times 5} = \sqrt{4} \times \sqrt{5} = 2 \times \sqrt{5} = 2\sqrt{5}$

The product of two surds can be expressed as a single surd,

e.g. $\sqrt{2} \times \sqrt{6} = \sqrt{2 \times 6} = \sqrt{12} = \sqrt{4 \times 3} = 2\sqrt{3}$

Alternatively

$$\sqrt{2} \times \sqrt{6} = \sqrt{2} \times \sqrt{2 \times 3} = \sqrt{2} \times \sqrt{2} \times \sqrt{3} = 2\sqrt{3}$$

Fractions whose denominators contain a surd are awkward to work with and there is a way in which a square root can be eliminated from the denominator; the process is called *rationalising the denominator*, and it uses the fact that $(\sqrt{a})^2 = a$.

For example, to rationalise the denominator of $\dfrac{1}{\sqrt{3}}$, we multiply top and bottom by $\sqrt{3}$ to give an equivalent fraction whose denominator is rational,

i.e. $\dfrac{1}{\sqrt{3}} = \dfrac{1 \times \sqrt{3}}{\sqrt{3} \times \sqrt{3}} = \dfrac{\sqrt{3}}{3}$

EXERCISE 1D

Express in terms of the simplest possible surd

1 $\sqrt{8}$ 4 $\sqrt{27}$ 7 $\sqrt{200}$ **10** $\sqrt{500}$

2 $\sqrt{12}$ 5 $\sqrt{50}$ 8 $\sqrt{48}$ **11** $\sqrt{250}$

3 $\sqrt{32}$ 6 $\sqrt{45}$ 9 $\sqrt{72}$ **12** $\sqrt{18}$

Express in the simplest possible form

13 $\sqrt{2} \times \sqrt{3}$ 16 $\sqrt{8} \times \sqrt{2}$ **19** $(\sqrt{5})^2$

14 $\sqrt{3} \times \sqrt{6}$ 17 $(\sqrt{7})^2$ **20** $\sqrt{18} \times \sqrt{3}$

21 $\sqrt{5} \times \sqrt{10}$ 18 $\sqrt{12} \times \sqrt{3}$ **21** $(\sqrt{3})^0$

Expand and simplify $3\sqrt{5}\,(\,\sqrt{10}-\sqrt{5}\,)$

$$3\sqrt{5}\,(\,\sqrt{10}-\sqrt{5}\,) = 3\sqrt{5}\times\sqrt{10}-3\sqrt{5}\times\sqrt{5}$$
$$= 3\times\sqrt{5}\times\sqrt{10}-3\times\sqrt{5}\times\sqrt{5}$$
$$= 3\times\sqrt{50}-3\times\sqrt{25}$$
$$= 3\times\sqrt{25\times2}-15$$
$$= 3\times5\times\sqrt{2}-15$$
$$= 15\sqrt{2}-15$$

It isn't necessary to write out all these steps. Any or all of lines 2, 3 and 4 may be omitted.

Expand and simplify where possible

22 $\sqrt{2}\,(\,2-\sqrt{2}\,)$ **25** $\sqrt{7}\,(\,\sqrt{7}-\sqrt{2}\,)$ **28** $2\sqrt{3}\,(\,3-2\sqrt{3}\,)$

23 $\sqrt{5}\,(\,3+\sqrt{5}\,)$ **26** $\sqrt{3}\,(\,5+\sqrt{27}\,)$ **29** $2\sqrt{2}\,(\,4-\sqrt{18}\,)$

24 $\sqrt{2}\,(\,\sqrt{8}-1\,)$ **27** $\sqrt{5}\,(\,\sqrt{6}-\sqrt{5}\,)$ **30** $4\sqrt{3}\,(\,3\sqrt{3}-\sqrt{27}\,)$

Rationalise the denominators.

31 $\dfrac{3}{\sqrt{2}}$ **34** $\dfrac{2}{\sqrt{10}}$ **37** $\dfrac{4\sqrt{3}}{3\sqrt{2}}$ **40** $\dfrac{3}{\sqrt{3}}$

32 $\dfrac{1}{\sqrt{5}}$ **35** $\dfrac{\sqrt{3}}{\sqrt{2}}$ **38** $\dfrac{3\sqrt{5}}{5\sqrt{3}}$ **41** $\dfrac{2\sqrt{7}}{\sqrt{14}}$

33 $\dfrac{1}{\sqrt{8}}$ **36** $\dfrac{\sqrt{5}}{\sqrt{10}}$ **39** $\dfrac{15}{\sqrt{15}}$ **42** $\dfrac{5\sqrt{6}}{3\sqrt{3}}$

43 Simplify   **a** $\sqrt{12}+\sqrt{3}$ **c** $\sqrt{18}+\sqrt{27}$

               b $4\sqrt{5}-\sqrt{20}$ **d** $3\sqrt{3}-\sqrt{12}$

Rationalise the denominators and simplify.

44 $\dfrac{(\,2-\sqrt{3}\,)}{\sqrt{3}}$ **46** $\dfrac{(\,4-2\sqrt{3}\,)}{\sqrt{2}}$ **48** $\dfrac{(\,5+\sqrt{7}\,)}{2\sqrt{14}}$

45 $\dfrac{(\,1+\sqrt{5}\,)}{\sqrt{5}}$ **47** $\dfrac{(\,1-3\sqrt{2}\,)}{2\sqrt{2}}$ **49** $\dfrac{(\,3\sqrt{2}+2\,)}{3\sqrt{2}}$

50 Simplify

   a $\dfrac{1}{\sqrt{2}}+\sqrt{2}$ **d** $\dfrac{2}{\sqrt{3}}+\sqrt{8}$ **g** $(\,2+\sqrt{3}\,)(\,2-\sqrt{3}\,)$

   b $\dfrac{2}{\sqrt{3}}+\sqrt{3}$ **e** $\dfrac{1}{2\sqrt{5}}+\sqrt{5}$ **h** $(\,1-\sqrt{5}\,)(\,1+\sqrt{5}\,)$

   c $(\,4-\sqrt{2}\,)^{2}$ **f** $(\,2+\sqrt{3}\,)^{2}$ **i** $(\,2+\sqrt{7}\,)(\,2\sqrt{7}-3\,)$

> Simplify $(\sqrt{8})^3$
>
> $(\sqrt{8})^3 = (\sqrt{4 \times 2})^3$
> $= (2 \times \sqrt{2})^3 = 2 \times \sqrt{2} \times 2 \times \sqrt{2} \times 2 \times \sqrt{2}$
> $= 8 \times (\sqrt{2})^2 \times \sqrt{2}$
> $= 8 \times 2 \times \sqrt{2} = 16\sqrt{2}$

51 Simplify   **a** $(\sqrt{12})^3$ **c** $(\sqrt{20})^3$ **e** $(\sqrt{10})^5$
                  b $(\sqrt{3})^5$ **d** $(\sqrt{18})^3$ **f** $(2\sqrt{3})^3$

52 Determine which of the following numbers are rational.

a $(\sqrt{2})(\sqrt{3})$ **d** $(\sqrt{5})(\sqrt{2})$ **g** 2π

b $\dfrac{\sqrt{2}}{\sqrt{8}}$ **e** $\dfrac{\sqrt{27}}{\sqrt{3}}$ **h** $\sqrt{1\frac{11}{25}}$

c $0.01\dot{2}$ **f** $(\sqrt{8})^2$ **i** $(5 - \sqrt{2})(5 + \sqrt{2})$

53 Is the length of AB a rational or an
irrational number?
Justify your answer.

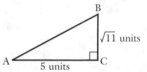

54 Find examples to show that these statements are not true.

a 'The product of two irrational numbers is always irrational.'

b 'The sum of two irrational numbers is always irrational.'

55 Use the information in the diagram to
find $\sin \widehat{A}$ and $\cos \widehat{A}$ leaving your
answers in surd form.

56

The diagram shows a figure with
rotational symmetry of order 6. It is made
from two equilateral triangles of side
3 units. Show that the distance between
opposite vertices is $2\sqrt{3}$ units.

57 Use the information in the diagram to
prove that
$$(\sin \widehat{A})^2 + (\cos \widehat{A})^2 = 1$$

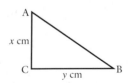

58 Explain why $\sqrt{-4}$ is neither a rational number nor an irrational
number. (It is called an imaginary number.)

CUBE ROOTS

When a number is expressed as the product of three equal factors, the factor is called the *cube root* of the number.

Some numbers have exact cube roots,
e.g. $8 = 2 \times 2 \times 2$ so 2 is the cube root of 8.
These cube roots are rational numbers.

Some numbers do not have exact cube roots; these cube roots are irrational numbers.

We write the 'cube root of 8' as $\sqrt[3]{8}$, i.e. $\sqrt[3]{8} = 2$

Notice that, as $2 \times 2 \times 2 = 2^3$, we have $8 = 2^3 \Leftrightarrow \sqrt[3]{8} = 2$

(The symbol $\Leftrightarrow$ means 'implies and is implied by'.)

Notice also that $(-2)^3 = (-2) \times (-2) \times (-2)$
$$= 4 \times (-2) = -8,$$
i.e. -2 is the cube root of -8

This means that 8 has only one cube root, $+2$; whereas 4 has two square roots, $+2$ and -2.

It also means that -8 has one cube root, -2; whereas -4 has *no* real square roots.

In general

> a positive number has *one* ($+$ve) cube root
> $\qquad\qquad\qquad$ *two* square roots, one $+$ve and one $-$ve,

> a negative number has *one* ($-$ve) cube root
> $\qquad\qquad\qquad$ *no* real square roots.

nth ROOTS

The nth root of a number is the factor such that n of these factors multiplied together gives the number. The nth root of x is written as $\sqrt[n]{x}$.

For example, $\sqrt[4]{16}$ means the 4th root of 16,
and, as $16 = 2^4$, $\sqrt[4]{16} = 2$.

If the nth root of an integer is not itself an integer, it is irrational.

EXERCISE 1E

1 Find

$\quad$ **a** $\sqrt[3]{27}$ $\qquad$ **b** $\sqrt[3]{-27}$ $\qquad$ **c** $\sqrt[3]{64}$ $\qquad$ **d** $\sqrt[3]{-125}$ $\qquad$ **e** $\sqrt[3]{1000}$

2 Find

$\quad$ **a** $\sqrt[4]{81}$ $\qquad$ **b** $\sqrt[5]{32}$ $\qquad$ **c** $\sqrt[4]{625}$ $\qquad$ **d** $\sqrt[5]{100\,000}$ $\qquad$ **e** $\sqrt[6]{64}$

Find $(\sqrt[3]{27})^2$

$(\sqrt[3]{27})^2 = 3^2 = 9$

> Find the cube root first.

3 Find **a** $(\sqrt[3]{-8})^2$ **b** $(\sqrt[5]{-32})^3$ **c** $(\sqrt[4]{10\,000})^3$

4 Which of the following numbers are irrational?

  a $\sqrt[4]{16}$ **b** $\sqrt[3]{3\frac{3}{8}}$ **c** $\sqrt[5]{\frac{1}{32}}$

5 Write those numbers in question **4** which are rational in the form $\frac{a}{b}$, where a and b are integers.

FRACTIONAL INDICES

Consider $2^{\frac{1}{2}} \times 2^{\frac{1}{2}}$.

Using the rule that $a^x \times a^y = a^{x+y}$,

we can see that $2^{\frac{1}{2}} \times 2^{\frac{1}{2}} = 2^1$ i.e. 2

but $\sqrt{2} \times \sqrt{2} = 2$

Therefore we deduce that $2^{\frac{1}{2}} = \sqrt{2}$,

i.e. $2^{\frac{1}{2}}$ means the positive square root of 2.

Similarly, for any number x, $x^{\frac{1}{3}} \times x^{\frac{1}{3}} \times x^{\frac{1}{3}} = x^{\frac{1}{3}+\frac{1}{3}+\frac{1}{3}} = x^1 = x$

but $\sqrt[3]{x} \times \sqrt[3]{x} \times \sqrt[3]{x} = x$,

i.e. $x^{\frac{1}{3}}$ means the cube root of x.

> In general, $x^{\frac{1}{n}}$ means the nth root of x,
>
> i.e. $x^{\frac{1}{n}} = \sqrt[n]{x}$

EXERCISE 1F

Find

1 $9^{\frac{1}{2}}$ **5** $125^{\frac{1}{3}}$ **9** $\left(\frac{1}{8}\right)^{\frac{1}{3}}$ **13** $\left(\frac{1}{9}\right)^{\frac{1}{2}}$

2 $16^{\frac{1}{2}}$ **6** $64^{\frac{1}{3}}$ **10** $\left(\frac{4}{9}\right)^{\frac{1}{2}}$ **14** $49^{\frac{1}{2}}$

3 $36^{\frac{1}{2}}$ **7** $\left(\frac{1}{4}\right)^{\frac{1}{2}}$ **11** $(0.25)^{\frac{1}{2}}$ **15** $(0.01)^{\frac{1}{2}}$

4 $8^{\frac{1}{3}}$ **8** $(0.04)^{\frac{1}{2}}$ **12** $\left(\frac{8}{27}\right)^{\frac{1}{3}}$ **16** $\left(3\frac{3}{8}\right)^{\frac{1}{3}}$

LAWS OF INDICES

We already know that

1 $a^x \times a^y = a^{x+y}$

2 $a^x \div a^y = a^{x-y}$

3 $a^{-x} = \left(\dfrac{1}{a}\right)^x$

Now consider $(a^3)^4$

$$(a^3)^4 = a^3 \times a^3 \times a^3 \times a^3 = a^{3\times4}, \text{ i.e. } a^{12}$$

but
$$(a^4)^3 = a^4 \times a^4 \times a^4 = a^{4\times3}, \text{ i.e. } a^{12}$$

so
$$(a^3)^4 = (a^4)^3$$

Generalising, this gives a fourth law,

4 $(a^x)^y = a^{xy} = (a^y)^x$

This law also applies when x or y are fractions,

e.g. $8^{\frac{2}{3}} = 8^{\frac{1}{3}} \times 8^{\frac{1}{3}} = (8^{\frac{1}{3}})^2 = 2^2 = 4$

Now $(8^{\frac{2}{3}})^3 = 8^{\frac{2}{3}} \times 8^{\frac{2}{3}} \times 8^{\frac{2}{3}} = 8^2$,

so $8^{\frac{2}{3}} = (8^2)^{\frac{1}{3}} = \sqrt[3]{64} = 4$,

i.e. $(8^{\frac{1}{3}})^2 = 8^{\frac{2}{3}} = (8^2)^{\frac{1}{3}}$

Hence $8^{\frac{2}{3}}$ can be evaluated by
either finding the cube root of 8 and then squaring the result
or squaring 8 and finding the cube root of the result.
(The first method is usually easier as it keeps the size of the numbers down.)

EXERCISE 1G

Simplify **a** $4^{\frac{3}{2}}$ **b** $\left(\dfrac{1}{4}\right)^{-\frac{1}{2}}$

a $4^{\frac{3}{2}} = (\sqrt{4})^3 = 2^3 = 8$

> Remember that a negative index means 'take reciprocal',
> i.e. $\left(\frac{1}{4}\right)^{-\frac{1}{2}}$ means (the reciprocal of $\frac{1}{4}$)$^{\frac{1}{2}}$.

b $\left(\dfrac{1}{4}\right)^{-\frac{1}{2}} = (4)^{\frac{1}{2}} = 2$

Simplify

1 $(27)^{\frac{2}{3}}$

2 $\left(\dfrac{1}{8}\right)^{\frac{2}{3}}$

3 $(16)^{\frac{3}{4}}$

4 $(125)^{\frac{2}{3}}$

5 $(0.008)^{\frac{2}{3}}$

6 $(144)^{\frac{3}{2}}$

7 $(0.36)^{\frac{3}{2}}$

8 $81^{\frac{3}{4}}$

9 $32^{\frac{2}{5}}$

10 $(1000)^{\frac{2}{3}}$

11 $(0.0001)^{\frac{3}{4}}$

12 $(100\,000)^{\frac{2}{5}}$

13 $\left(\frac{1}{9}\right)^{-\frac{1}{2}}$ **16** $\left(\frac{8}{27}\right)^{-\frac{1}{3}}$ **19** $(16)^{-\frac{1}{4}}$ **22** $\left(\frac{1}{9}\right)^{-\frac{3}{2}}$

14 $\left(\frac{4}{49}\right)^{-\frac{1}{2}}$ **17** $8^{-\frac{2}{3}}$ **20** $(0.01)^{-\frac{3}{2}}$ **23** $(0.027)^{-\frac{2}{3}}$

15 $(0.04)^{-\frac{1}{2}}$ **18** $(32)^{-\frac{3}{5}}$ **21** $(1000)^{-\frac{2}{3}}$ **24** $(6.25)^{-\frac{1}{2}}$

25 $(x^2)^{\frac{1}{4}}$ **27** $(y^4)^{\frac{1}{2}}$ **29** $(x^8)^{\frac{3}{4}}$ **31** $(x^2 y^6)^{\frac{1}{2}}$

26 $(x^{\frac{1}{3}})^6$ **28** $(a^6)^{\frac{1}{3}}$ **30** $(x^{\frac{2}{3}})^6$ **32** $(p^{-9} q^3)^{\frac{1}{3}}$

33 Express as a power of x

    a $\sqrt[3]{x}$ **b** $\dfrac{1}{\sqrt[3]{x}}$ **c** $(\sqrt[3]{x})^2$ **d** $\dfrac{1}{(\sqrt{x})^3}$

34 $t^{\frac{1}{2}} = 0.4$. Write down the value of   **a** $t^{-\frac{1}{2}}$ **b** $t^{\frac{3}{2}}$ **c** t^2 **d** t^0

Find the value of x for which $8 = 4^x$

> To find the value of an unknown index, first express all numbers as powers of the same base. In this case 8 and 4 are both powers of 2.

$8 = 4^x$, i.e. $2^3 = (2^2)^x$

so $2^3 = 2^{2x}$

i.e. $3 = 2x$ giving $x = \frac{3}{2}$

> Using $(a^x)^y = a^{xy}$ we can see that the powers must be the same.

Find the value of x.

35 $32 = 4^x$ **38** $10^x = 0.1$ **41** $5^x = 0.04$

36 $64 = 2^x$ **39** $0.5 = 2^x$ **42** $16^x = 8$

37 $27 = 9^x$ **40** $0.01^x = 10$ **43** $8^x = 1$

Express 32 as a power of 8.

> We need to find x such that $32 = 8^x$

If $32 = 8^x$, using $32 = 2^5$ and $8 = 2^3$

gives $2^5 = (2^3)^x$ giving $5 = 3x$ so $x = \frac{5}{3}$

i.e. $32 = 8^{\frac{5}{3}}$

---

44 Express each number as a power of 5.

    a 25   **b** 125   **c** $\frac{1}{5}$ **d** $\sqrt{5}$

45 Express each number as a power of 4.

    a 16   **b** 2   **c** 32   **d** 8

46 Copy and complete this table.

Number	Powers of			
	3	9	27	81
1				
3		$9^{\frac{1}{2}}$		
9			$27^{\frac{2}{3}}$	
27	3^3			
81		9^2		81^1

47 Which of the following numbers are irrational?

 a $5^{\frac{1}{2}}$ **b** $25^{\frac{3}{2}}$ **c** $4^{\frac{2}{3}}$ **d** $8^{-\frac{2}{3}}$

48 Simplify

 a $\dfrac{4a^3 \times 6a^4}{48a^2}$ **b** $(2x^2y^5)^3$ **c** $\dfrac{15x^5y}{9x^7 \times 5y^3}$

USING A CALCULATOR

To find the numerical value, to a given number of decimal places, of the nth root of a number, use the $\boxed{\sqrt[x]{}}$ function (this is usually accessed using the $\boxed{\textbf{SHIFT}}$ key or its equivalent).

For example, to find $\sqrt[3]{12}$, press $\boxed{3}$ $\boxed{\sqrt[x]{}}$ $\boxed{1}$ $\boxed{2}$ $\boxed{=}$

This gives $\sqrt[3]{12} = 2.2894 \ldots$
$\qquad\qquad = 2.29$ correct to 3 significant figures.

EXERCISE 1H

Use your calculator to evaluate the following roots, giving your answers correct to 3 significant figures.

 1 $\sqrt[3]{24}$ **4** $\sqrt[5]{216}$ **7** $\sqrt[3]{502}$ **10** $(1.5)^{\frac{1}{5}}$

 2 $(24)^{\frac{1}{2}}$ **5** $\sqrt[3]{0.01}$ **8** $\sqrt[4]{36}$ **11** $\sqrt[6]{0.1}$

 3 $\sqrt[4]{100}$ **6** $(1.8)^{\frac{2}{3}}$ **9** $(0.2)^{\frac{2}{5}}$ **12** $\sqrt[4]{24.2}$

13 The volume of a cube is $18\,\text{cm}^3$. Find, correct to 4 significant figures, the length of an edge of this cube.

14 Find, correct to 3 significant figures, the value of N where
$N = \sqrt[4]{t^2}$ and $t = 0.9$.

MIXED EXERCISE

EXERCISE 1I

1 Simplify

    a $\sqrt{18}+\sqrt{98}$ **b** $\sqrt{12}-\dfrac{1}{\sqrt{3}}$ **c** $(3-\sqrt{7})(3+\sqrt{7})$

2 Express as a fraction in its lowest terms

    a $0.1\dot{2}\dot{1}$ **c** $0.4\dot{7}$

    b $0.0\dot{2}\dot{7}$ **d** $0.\dot{1}0\dot{1}$

3 Simplify

    a 2^{-4} **d** $27^{\frac{2}{3}}$ **g** $(9^{\frac{1}{2}})^{3}$

    b 6^{0} **e** $(y^{2})^{4}$ **h** $8^{-\frac{1}{3}}$

    c $\left(\dfrac{2}{5}\right)^{-1}$ **f** $32^{\frac{2}{5}}$ **i** $\left(5\dfrac{1}{16}\right)^{\frac{3}{4}}$

4 Simplify   **a** $(x^{\frac{1}{2}})^{3}$ **b** $(p^{\frac{1}{3}})^{6}$

5 Express 64 as

    a a power of 2   **b** a power of 4   **c** a power of 16

6 Express 32 as

    a a power of 2

    b a power of 4

    c a power of $\dfrac{1}{2}$

7 Find the value of x when

    a $2^{x}=128$ **b** $16^{x}=32$

8 If $a^{\frac{1}{3}}=0.3$ find the value of

    a a **b** $a^{\frac{2}{3}}$ **c** $a^{-\frac{5}{3}}$

9 Which of the following numbers are rational?

    a $\sqrt{3}-2$ **d** π^{3} **g** $\sqrt{2\frac{7}{9}}$

    b $(\sqrt{3}-2)(\sqrt{3}+2)$ **e** $16^{-\frac{1}{4}}$ **h** $\sqrt[3]{2\frac{2}{3}}$

    c $(\sqrt{3})^{2}-1$ **f** $0.12\dot{3}\dot{4}$ **i** $1-\dfrac{1}{\pi}$

10 Give those numbers in question **9** that are rational as fractions.

INVESTIGATION

Trying to rationalise the irrational

Once mathematicians discovered that numbers such as $\sqrt{2}$ could not be given an exact rational value, the search was on to find rational numbers that would approximate to the value of the irrational number to any degree of accuracy required. Here are two methods for finding approximations to $\sqrt{2}$.

1 The Heronian algorithm

To find rational approximations to $\sqrt{2}$:

- Start with any fraction that is roughly equal to $\sqrt{2}$, say $\frac{7}{5}$
- Next find the fraction which, when multiplied by that fraction ($\frac{7}{5}$) gives 2: $\qquad \frac{10}{7}$
- Then find the mean of these fractions, i.e. $\frac{1}{2}(\frac{7}{5}+\frac{10}{7})$: $\qquad \frac{99}{70}$

This fraction, $\frac{99}{70}$, is a better approximation to $\sqrt{2}$ than $\frac{7}{5}$ is.

a Use your calculator to find the number of decimal places to which $\frac{99}{70}$ agrees with $\sqrt{2}$.

b Now repeat the process starting with $\frac{99}{70}$ and you will get an even better approximation to $\sqrt{2}$.

c Can you discover why this algorithm works?

d Try the process with $\sqrt{3}$ and with some other square roots.

2 Continued fractions

This method gives successively better approximations for $1+\sqrt{2}$.
Start with $2+\frac{1}{2}$ as the first approximation.

The next approximation is $2+\dfrac{1}{2+\frac{1}{2}}$

and the next approximation is $2+\dfrac{1}{2+\dfrac{1}{2+\frac{1}{2}}}$

a Continue the pattern and evaluate each approximation as a decimal to as many decimal places as your calculator allows.

b How many approximations are needed to give the value of $\sqrt{2}$ correct to 7 decimal places?

3 Compare the two methods for finding approximations for $\sqrt{2}$. As part of your comparison you may like to consider which method is easier to set up on a spreadsheet (or other computer software), and which method needs fewer steps to give a particular degree of accuracy.

QUADRATIC EQUATIONS THAT FACTORISE

2

In Book 9A we saw that answers to some problems can be found algebraically by forming quadratic equations of the form $x^2 + bx + c = 0$ and then solving them using factors. A wider range of problems can be dealt with algebraically by extending the methods of solution to equations such as $2x^2 - 95x + 225 = 0$. The following situation leads to such an equation.

Tim lives in Sandfields which is 15 miles from Broadoak. Tim's friend Ian lives in Broadoak. The two friends, who walk at different rates, decided to walk to meet each other.

Tim left Sandfields 1 hour 20 minutes after Ian left Broadoak, and they met after Tim had walked for 2 hours. On another day each boy walked at the same rate as he had on the previous occasion, but this time Tim started $\frac{1}{2}$ hour before Ian. The result was that they met at exactly half-way.

- Tim would like to work out the speed at which each of them walks.
- If Tim walks at x mph he can try to form an equation in x and solve it.

Problems like this often lead to quadratic equations so in this chapter and the next we learn more about constructing and solving such quadratic equations.

1 In solving problems about journeys in cars and coaches John formed the following equations

  a $3x^2 - 152x + 100 = 0$

  b $2x^2 - 75x + 532 = 0$

  c $x^2 - 48x - 96 = 0$

Discuss how these equations differ from the quadratic equations you met in Book 9A.

2 Zoe notices that if the cost of a dozen eggs goes down by 15 p she can buy 2 dozen more for £3.60.
Taking x pence per dozen as the original price of the eggs, Zoe forms the equation $x^2 - 15x - 2700 = 0$, from which she hopes to find the original price of the eggs. This is a quadratic equation, so should give two values for x. Discuss whether or not this equation is satisfied by two values of x which are also solutions to the problem.

Reminder

In Book 9A, Chapter 7, we saw how to factorise expressions of the form $ax^2 + bx + c$ where either a was 1 or a was a common factor. The next exercise gives practice in this work. (Turn over if you need to remind yourself of the pattern.)

Factorise

  1 $x^2 + 8x + 15$ **6** $x^2 - 10x + 24$

  2 $x^2 + 13x + 22$ **7** $x^2 - 15x + 56$

  3 $x^2 + 16x + 63$ **8** $x^2 - 21x + 110$

  4 $x^2 + 13x + 40$ **9** $x^2 - 14x + 45$

  5 $2x^2 - 2x - 24$ **10** $2x^2 - 20x + 18$

  11 $x^2 - 16$ **16** $x^2 - x - 72$

  12 $x^2 - 4x - 21$ **17** $72 + x^2 - 17x$

  13 $x^2 + x - 30$ **18** $42 + x - x^2$

  14 $11x - 12 + x^2$ **19** $8 - 2x^2$

  15 $x^2 + 8x - 33$ **20** $12 - x - x^2$

Factorising quadratic expressions like those in the last exercise reminds us of the following patterns

- If all the terms are + both brackets will have + signs

  e.g. $x^2 + 13x + 36 = (x + 4)(x + 9)$

  (Choose two numbers whose product is 36 and whose sum is 13.)
- If the x^2 term and the number term are +, but the x term is −, both brackets have − signs.

  e.g. $x^2 - 12x + 27 = (x - 3)(x - 9)$

  (The product of −3 and −9 is +27 and their sum is −12.)
- If the x^2 term is + and the number term is −, the signs in the brackets are different

  e.g. $x^2 + 5x - 50 = (x - 5)(x + 10)$

  and $x^2 - 6x - 7 = (x - 7)(x + 1)$
- The terms should be put in order before attempting to factorise,

  e.g. $4x - 45 + x^2 = x^2 + 4x - 45 = (x - 5)(x + 9)$
- Occasionally the x^2 term is negative, in which case end the brackets with $+x$ and $-x$,

  e.g. $4 - 3x - x^2 = (1 - x)(4 + x)$

FURTHER FACTORS

The equation $3x^2 - 152x + 100 = 0$, is given in **Exercise 2A**. To solve equations like this we need to consider factorising the expression $ax^2 + bx + c$ into linear brackets for values of a other than 1.

For example, to factorise $3x^2 + 7x + 2$ the only sensible x terms for the brackets are $3x$ and x.

Since all the signs in the given expression are +, all the signs in the brackets will be +.

The possible number values will be +2 and +1, or +1 and +2.

Trying +2 and +1,

$(3x + 2)(x + 1)$ gives a middle term of $5x$ which is incorrect.

Trying +1 and +2,

$(3x + 1)(x + 2)$ gives a middle term of $7x$ which is correct.

$\therefore$ $\qquad\qquad\qquad 3x^2 + 7x + 2 = (3x + 1)(x + 2)$

Similarly to factorise $5x^2 - 7x + 2$ the brackets start $(5x \quad)(x \quad)$. The number term is +, therefore the brackets have the same sign and since the middle term is − the signs must both be −,

i.e. we have $\qquad\qquad\qquad (5x - \quad)(x - \quad)$

The last term is +2, therefore the numbers must be either −1 and −2, or −2 and −1.

Trying −1 and −2,

$(5x - 1)(x - 2)$ gives a middle term of $-11x$ which is incorrect.

Trying −2 and −1,

$(5x - 2)(x - 1)$ gives a middle term of $-7x$ which is correct.

$\therefore$ $\qquad\qquad\qquad 5x^2 - 7x + 2 = (5x - 2)(x - 1)$

EXERCISE 2C

Factorise and check by expanding your answer.

1 $2x^2 + 3x + 1$ <u>**6**</u> $3x^2 - 8x + 4$

2 $3x^2 - 5x + 2$ <u>**7**</u> $2x^2 + 9x + 4$

3 $4x^2 + 7x + 3$ <u>**8**</u> $5x^2 - 17x + 6$

4 $2x^2 - 7x + 3$ <u>**9**</u> $2x^2 + 11x + 12$

5 $3x^2 + 13x + 4$ <u>**10**</u> $7x^2 - 29x + 4$

11 $2x^2 - 3x - 2$ <u>**16**</u> $7x^2 - 19x - 6$

12 $3x^2 + x - 4$ <u>**17**</u> $6x^2 - 7x - 10$

13 $5x^2 - 13x - 6$ <u>**18**</u> $5x^2 - 19x + 12$

14 $4x^2 + 5x - 6$ <u>**19**</u> $3x^2 - 11x - 20$

15 $3x^2 + 10x - 8$ <u>**20**</u> $4x^2 + 17x - 15$

THE GENERAL CASE

We investigate next the most general case of all; that is when neither bracket is certain to begin with x.

Suppose that we wish to factorise $15x^2 + 26x + 8$
The first terms in the brackets may be

$$(15x \quad)(x \quad) \quad \text{or} \quad (5x \quad)(3x \quad)$$

All the signs must be $+$.

The brackets may end with 8 and 1, 4 and 2, 2 and 4, or 1 and 8.

Try each in turn, until the correct middle term is found.

$(15x + 8)(x + 1)$ middle term $23x$, incorrect
$(15x + 4)(x + 2)$ middle term $34x$, incorrect
$(15x + 2)(x + 4)$ middle term $62x$, incorrect
$(15x + 1)(x + 8)$ middle term $121x$, incorrect

$(5x + 8)(3x + 1)$ middle term $29x$, incorrect
$(5x + 4)(3x + 2)$ middle term $22x$, incorrect
$(5x + 2)(3x + 4)$ middle term $26x$, *correct*

$$\therefore \quad 15x^2 + 26x + 8 = (5x + 2)(3x + 4)$$

After a little practice, you should be able to find the factors without going into so much detail.

EXERCISE 2D

Factorise

1 $6x^2 + 7x + 2$

2 $6x^2 + 19x + 15$

3 $15x^2 + 11x + 2$

4 $12x^2 + 28x + 15$

5 $35x^2 + 24x + 4$

6 $6x^2 - 11x + 3$

7 $9x^2 - 18x + 8$

8 $16x^2 - 10x + 1$

9 $15x^2 - 44x + 21$

10 $20x^2 - 23x + 6$

11 $8x^2 - 10x - 3$

12 $15x^2 - x - 2$

13 $21x^2 + 2x - 8$

14 $80x^2 - 6x - 9$

15 $24x^2 + 17x - 20$

16 $6a^2 - a - 15$

17 $6t^2 - t - 2$

18 $9b^2 - 12b + 4$

19 $5x^2 - 7xy - 6y^2$

20 $4x^2 - 11x + 6$

The next exercise uses the fact that

$$(a+b)(a-b) = a^2 - b^2$$

EXERCISE 2E

> Factorise $4x^2 - 9$
>
> $4x^2 - 9 = (2x)^2 - 3^2$
> $\qquad\quad = (2x + 3)(2x - 3)$

Factorise

1 $4x^2 - 25$

2 $9x^2 - 4$

3 $36a^2 - 1$

4 $16a^2 - b^2$

5 $9x^2 - 25$

6 $4a^2 - 1$

> Factorise $4x^2 - 9y^2$
>
> $4x^2 - 9y^2 = (2x)^2 - (3y)^2$
> $\qquad\qquad = (2x + 3y)(2x - 3y)$

Factorise

7 $16a^2 - 9b^2$

8 $25s^2 - 9t^2$

9 $100x^2 - 49y^2$

10 $9y^2 - 16z^2$

11 $4x^2 - 49y^2$

12 $81x^2 - 100y^2$

13 $9a^2 - 4b^2$

14 $64p^2 - 81q^2$

15 $9M^2 - 4N^2$

Factorise $2 - 18a^2$

$$2 - 18a^2 = 2(1 - 9a^2)$$
$$= 2(1^2 - (3a)^2)$$
$$= 2(1 + 3a)(1 - 3a)$$

Factorise

16 $3a^2 - 27b^2$ **19** $45x^2 - 20$ **22** $2p^2 - 8q^2$

17 $18t^2 - 50s^2$ **20** $5a^2 - 20$ **23** $12 - 3x^2$

18 $27x^2 - 3y^2$ **21** $45 - 5b^2$ **24** $24a^2 - 54b^2$

25 $\frac{1}{2}a^2 - 2b^2$ **27** $27x^2 - \frac{1}{3}y^2$ **29** $\frac{1}{2} - \frac{x^2}{18}$

26 $\frac{a^2}{4} - \frac{b^2}{9}$ **28** $\frac{x^2}{16} - \frac{y^2}{25}$ **30** $\frac{x^2}{8} - \frac{y^2}{2}$

Next in this section we consider the case where taking out a common factor does not make the first term x^2.

EXERCISE 2F

Factorise $8x^2 + 28x + 12$

$$8x^2 + 28x + 12 = 4(2x^2 + 7x + 3)$$
$$= 4(2x + 1)(x + 3)$$

4 is the largest number that divides exactly into 8, 28 and 12.

Factorise

1 $15x^2 + 25x + 10$ **6** $8x^2 + 14x + 6$

2 $4x^2 - 6x - 4$ **7** $25x^2 - 65x - 30$

3 $6x^2 + 9x + 3$ **8** $9x^2 + 3x - 12$

4 $18x^2 - 21x - 30$ **9** $6x^2 + 26x + 8$

5 $8x^2 + 34x - 30$ **10** $15x^2 + 50x - 40$

11 $18x^2 - 36x + 16$

12 $48x^2 - 30x + 3$

13 $12x^2 + 14x + 4$

14 $100x^2 - 115x + 30$

15 $24x^2 - 4x - 8$

16 $21x^2 + 70x - 56$

Factorise $12 + 7x - 10x^2$

$12 + 7x - 10x^2 = (3 - 2x)(4 + 5x)$

Factorise

17 $4 - 5x - 6x^2$

18 $12 + 7x - 12x^2$

19 $21 + 25x - 4x^2$

20 $24 - 16x + 2x^2$

21 $16 - 20x - 6x^2$

22 $9 + 8x - x^2$

23 $12 - 11x - x^2$

24 $8 + 24x + 18x^2$

25 $45 - 30x + 5x^2$

26 $20 + 40x + 15x^2$

**MIXED
QUESTIONS**

Some quadratic expressions such as $4x^2 + 3x + 1$ and $3x^2 + 5$ will not factorise. The next exercise includes expressions that will not factorise.

EXERCISE 2G

Factorise where possible

1 $6x^2 + 5x + 1$

2 $5x^2 + 3x - 2$

3 $12x^2 - 7x + 1$

4 $x^2 - 10x + 21$

5 $6t^2 - 5t - 6$

6 $2x^2 + 7x - 15$

7 $x^2 + x - 90$

8 $8x^2 - 2x - 1$

9 $15p^2 - 22p + 8$

10 $30x^2 - 2x - 4$

11 $28 + 3x - x^2$

12 $30x^2 + 35x + 10$

13 $a^2 - 3a - 18$

14 $6 - 16a + 8a^2$

15 $6x^2 - 19x - 7$

16 $6x^2 + 5x - 4$

17 $4x^2 - 16y^2$

18 $28 - 12x - x^2$

19 $t^2 + 18t + 80$

20 $12x^2 - 17x + 6$

21 $5b^2 - 18b - 8$

22 $7c^2 + 13c - 2$

23 $7a - 10 - a^2$

24 $t + 20 - t^2$

25 $6x^2 - 4x - 16$

26 $3 - 2t - t^2$

27 $12 - 25x + 12x^2$

28 $11x^2 - 35x + 6$

29 $18x^2 + 41x + 20$

30 $6a^2 + 39a + 63$

31 $(a + b)^2 - c^2$

32 $116x^2 - 25x - 1$

33 $a^2 + 23a + 112$

34 $y^4 - y^2 - 2y - 1$

35 $1 + 2x + 4x^2 + 8x^3$

36 $3a^2 + 56 - 31a$

37 $2x^2 - 8x - 154$

38 $4x^2 - (y - z)^2$

39 $a^2b^2 - ab - 342$

40 $2x^4 - x^3 + 4x - 2$

In questions **41** to **48** use your knowledge of factorising to find the value of each expression. Do not use a calculator for these questions.

41 $100^2 - 99^2$

42 $5999^2 - 5998^2$

43 $12\,345\,123\,456^2 - 12\,345\,123\,455^2$

44 $987\,654\,321\,987\,654\,321^2 - 987\,654\,321\,987\,654\,320^2$

45 $0.567\,89^2 - 0.432\,11^2$

46 $9876.543\,212\,3^2 - 9875.543\,212\,3^2$

47 $0.987\,654\,321^2 - 0.012\,345\,679^2$

48 $0.777\,766\,665\,555^2 - 0.222\,233\,334\,445^2$

Without using a calculator show that

49 $12\,345^2 - 12\,346 \times 12\,344 = 1$

50 $123\,456\,789^2 - 123\,456\,790 \times 123\,456\,788 = 1$

QUADRATIC
EQUATIONS

Previously when we were able to solve quadratic equations by forming a product of two linear brackets, the coefficient of x in each bracket was 1. The technique used when the coefficient of x in one or both brackets has any other value is exactly the same, that is, when the product of two expressions is zero, one or other of those expressions must itself be zero.

EXERCISE 2H

Solve the equation $(2x - 3)(3x + 1) = 0$

$$(2x - 3)(3x + 1) = 0$$

Either $\qquad 2x - 3 = 0 \quad$ or $\quad 3x + 1 = 0$

$\Rightarrow \qquad\qquad 2x = 3 \quad$ or $\qquad 3x = -1$

i.e. $\qquad x = \frac{3}{2} = 1\frac{1}{2} \quad$ or $\qquad\quad x = -\frac{1}{3}$

Solve the following equations.

1 $(2x - 5)(x - 1) = 0$ $\qquad$ **11** $(3x - 7)(x - 2) = 0$

2 $(x - 4)(3x - 2) = 0$ $\qquad$ **12** $(3x - 5)(2x - 1) = 0$

3 $(5x - 4)(4x - 3) = 0$ $\qquad$ **13** $x(3x - 1) = 0$

4 $x(4x - 5) = 0$ $\qquad$ **14** $x(7x - 3) = 0$

5 $x(10x - 3) = 0$ $\qquad$ **15** $(2x + 3)(x - 3) = 0$

6 $(5x + 2)(x - 7) = 0$ $\qquad$ **16** $(4x + 3)(2x - 5) = 0$

7 $(6x + 5)(3x - 2) = 0$ $\qquad$ **17** $(10x + 9)(5x - 4) = 0$

8 $(8x - 3)(2x + 5) = 0$ $\qquad$ **18** $(3x - 2)(4x + 9) = 0$

9 $(7x - 8)(4x + 15) = 0$ $\qquad$ **19** $(5x - 12)(2x + 7) = 0$

10 $(4x + 3)(2x + 3) = 0$ $\qquad$ **20** $(5x + 8)(4x + 3) = 0$

SOLUTION BY
FACTORISATION

When a quadratic equation of the form $ax^2 + bx + c = 0$, where $a \neq 1$, can be expressed as the product of two linear factors the equation can be solved by the method used in the previous exercise.

EXERCISE 2I

Solve the equation $5x^2 + 13x - 6 = 0$

$$5x^2 + 13x - 6 = 0$$
$$(5x - 2)(x + 3) = 0$$

∴ either $\qquad 5x - 2 = 0 \quad$ or $\quad x + 3 = 0 \quad \Rightarrow \quad 5x = 2 \quad$ or $\quad x = -3$

i.e. $\qquad\qquad x = \frac{2}{5} \quad$ or $\quad -3$

Solve the equations.

1 $2x^2 - 5x + 2 = 0$

2 $2x^2 - 11x + 12 = 0$

3 $2x^2 - 13x + 20 = 0$

4 $3x^2 + 5x + 2 = 0$

5 $2x^2 + 9x - 35 = 0$

6 $3x^2 - 11x + 6 = 0$

7 $3x^2 - 7x + 2 = 0$

8 $2x^2 + 5x - 12 = 0$

9 $3x^2 + 11x + 6 = 0$

10 $5x^2 + 27x + 10 = 0$

11 $6x^2 - x - 2 = 0$

12 $15x^2 + 14x - 8 = 0$

13 $12x^2 - 7x + 1 = 0$

14 $6x^2 - 13x - 5 = 0$

15 $20x^2 + 19x + 3 = 0$

16 $8x^2 - 18x + 9 = 0$

17 $12x^2 - 20x - 25 = 0$

18 $4x^2 + 8x + 3 = 0$

19 $12x^2 + 17x + 6 = 0$

20 $10x^2 - 29x - 21 = 0$

21 $12x^2 + 25x - 7 = 0$

Solve the equation $4x^2 - 9 = 0$

$$4x^2 - 9 = 0$$
$$(2x - 3)(2x + 3) = 0$$

Either $\qquad\qquad 2x - 3 = 0 \quad$ or $\quad 2x + 3 = 0$

$\Rightarrow \qquad\qquad\qquad 2x = 3 \quad$ or $\qquad 2x = -3$

i.e. $\qquad\qquad\qquad x = \frac{3}{2} \quad$ or $\quad -\frac{3}{2}$

> Alternatively, without factorising, $4x^2 = 9 \quad \Rightarrow \quad x^2 = \frac{9}{4} \quad$ i.e. $\quad x = \pm\frac{3}{2}$

Solve the equations.

22 $16x^2 - 25 = 0$

23 $100x^2 - 81 = 0$

24 $4x^2 - 25 = 0$

25 $9x^2 - 16 = 0$

26 $25x^2 - 144 = 0$

27 $9x^2 - 4 = 0$

28 $81x^2 - 25 = 0$

29 $25x^2 - 4 = 0$

30 $36x^2 - 25 = 0$

Quadratic equations do not always present themselves arranged in the order $ax^2 + bx + c = 0$. When this is the case, we need to rearrange the equation.

EXERCISE 2J

Solve the equation $6 - 7x = 20x^2$

$$6 - 7x = 20x^2$$

i.e. $\qquad 20x^2 = 6 - 7x \qquad$ │ Subtract 6 from each side and add $7x$ to each side. │

$$20x^2 + 7x - 6 = 0$$

$$(5x - 2)(4x + 3) = 0$$

Either $\quad 5x - 2 = 0 \quad$ or $\quad 4x + 3 = 0 \quad$ i.e. $\quad 5x = 2 \quad$ or $\quad 4x = -3$

$\therefore \qquad\qquad x = \frac{2}{5} \quad$ or $\quad -\frac{3}{4}$

Solve the equations.

1 $3x^2 = 11x + 4$

2 $6x^2 = 7x + 3$

3 $7x + 12 = 12x^2$

4 $6 - 35x = 26x^2$

5 $10x^2 = 13x + 3$

6 $3x^2 = 11x - 10$

7 $10x^2 = 1 - 3x$

8 $12x - 1 = 35x^2$

9 $17x = 5x^2 + 6$

Solve the equation $12x^2 + 10x - 12 = 0$

$$12x^2 + 10x - 12 = 0$$

│ Take out the common factor 2. │

$$(2)(6x^2 + 5x - 6) = 0$$

$\therefore \qquad\qquad 6x^2 + 5x - 6 = 0 \qquad$ │ Since 2 is not zero, $6x^2 + 5x - 6$ must be zero. │

i.e. $\qquad (3x - 2)(2x + 3) = 0$

Either $\quad 3x - 2 = 0 \quad$ or $\quad 2x + 3 = 0$

i.e. $\qquad\quad 3x = 2 \quad$ or $\quad 2x = -3$

i.e. $\qquad\quad x = \frac{2}{3} \quad$ or $\quad -\frac{3}{2}$

Solve the equations.

10 $4x^2 - 14x + 6 = 0$

11 $6x^2 - 39x - 21 = 0$

12 $15x^2 - 35x + 10 = 0$

13 $45x^2 - 102x + 45 = 0$

14 $3x + 45 = 18x^2$

15 $18x^2 + 18x - 20 = 0$

16 $30x^2 = 39x + 9$

17 $14x^2 - 36x - 18 = 0$

18 $100x^2 = 115x - 30$

Solve the equation $x(x-3)(x-7)=0$

$$x(x-3)(x-7)=0$$

Any one of the three numbers multiplied together could be zero.

Either $\quad x = 0 \quad$ or $\quad x - 3 = 0 \quad$ or $\quad x - 7 = 0$

i.e. $\qquad\qquad x = 0 \quad$ or $\quad 3 \quad$ or $\quad 7$

Solve the equations

19 $x(x-1)(x-2)=0$ **<u>24</u>** $x(x-6)(x-7)=0$

20 $x(x-3)(x+4)=0$ **<u>25</u>** $x(x+2)(x-5)=0$

21 $x(2x-5)(x-2)=0$ **<u>26</u>** $x(3x+7)(x-5)=0$

22 $x^3 - 2x^2 + x = 0$ **<u>27</u>** $4x^3 - 9x = 0$

23 $2x^3 + 9x^2 + 4x = 0$ **<u>28</u>** $8x = 6x^2 - x^3$

SUMMARY

To solve a quadratic equation by factorising

- collect all terms on one side of the equation and arrange them in the order $ax^2 + bx + c = 0$
- take out any common factors (these may or may not include x)
- complete the factorisation.

MIXED EXERCISE

EXERCISE 2K   Solve the equations.

1 $9x^2 - 1 = 0$ **5** $4 + 11x + 6x^2 = 0$ **9** $5x = 3x^2 - 2$

2 $2x^2 + 3x - 14 = 0$ **6** $14x - 2 = 24x^2$ **10** $6x^2 + 13x - 5 = 0$

3 $2x^2 + 12x + 18 = 0$ **7** $1 - 16x^2 = 0$ **11** $3 + 8x + 4x^2 = 0$

4 $4 = 25x^2$ **8** $2 - x = 6x^2$ **12** $15x^2 + 13x - 20 = 0$

13 $5x - 2x^2 = 0$ **17** $6x^2 = 20 - 2x$ **21** $2x^2 = 18 + 5x$

14 $5x + 2 = 3x^2$ **18** $12x^2 = 17x - 6$ **22** $48 - 12x^2 = 0$

15 $3 - 12x^2 = 0$ **19** $44x = 15 + 32x^2$ **23** $24x^2 = 50x - 24$

16 $2x^2 - 25x + 63 = 0$ **20** $54x^2 + 48x + 8 = 0$ **24** $143x^2 + 2x - 1 = 0$

25 Solve   **a** $3x^2 - 152x + 100 = 0$ **b** $2x^2 - 75x + 532 = 0$
(These are questions 1a and 1b from Exercise 2A.)

EXPRESSING A QUADRATIC EXPRESSION IN THE FORM $ax^2 + bx + c$

$(2x + 3)^2 = 4x^2 + 12x + 9$ is true for every value of x.

For example, if $x = 3$ LHS $= (2 \times 3 + 3)^2 = (6 + 3)^2 = 9^2 = 81$

RHS $= 4 \times 9 + 12 \times 3 + 9 = 36 + 36 + 9 = 81$

and if $x = -4$ LHS $= (2 \times (-4) + 3)^2 = (-8 + 3)^2$

$= (-5)^2 = 25$

RHS $= 4 \times (-4)^2 + 12 \times (-4) + 9$

$= 4 \times 16 - 48 + 9 = 64 - 48 + 9 = 25$

Try any value of your own choice to check the truth of this statement.

It follows that, if $(2x + 3)^2 = ax^2 + bx + c$ for all values of x,
then $4x^2 + 12x + 9 = ax^2 + bx + c$ so $a = 4$, $b = 12$ and $c = 9$
(The coefficient of x^2 is the same on both sides, as is the coefficient of x and the number term.)

IDENTITIES

Two forms of the same expression, such as $(5x - 4)^2 = 25x^2 - 40x + 16$ and $x(x + 1)(x + 2) = x^3 + 3x^2 + 2x$, which are true for all values of x, are called *identities*.

EXERCISE 2L

If $(3x - 2)^2$ can be rewritten as $ax^2 + bx + c$ find the values of a, b and c.

$$(3x - 2)^2 = ax^2 + bx + c$$

i.e. $9x^2 - 12x + 4 = ax^2 + bx + c$

Comparing the coefficients, $a = 9$, $b = -12$ $c = 4$

1 Express $(3x + 4)^2$ in the form $ax^2 + bx + c$ and hence find the values of a, b and c.

2 Express $(7x - 2)^2$ in the form $ax^2 + bx + c$ and hence find the values of a, b and c.

3 Express $(2 - 5x)^2$ in the form $ax^2 + bx + c$ and hence find the values of a, b and c.

4 Expand $(3 + 8x)^2$ and hence find the values of a, b and c if $(3 + 8x)^2 = ax^2 + bx + c$.

5 If $(x + 3)^2 = x^2 + px + q$ for all values of x find the values of p and q.

6 If $(9x + 2)^2 = ax^2 + bx + c$ for all values of x find the values of a, b and c.

Expand $(3x - p)^2$ and hence find the values of p and k if $(3x - p)^2 = 9x^2 + kx + 16$ for all values of x.

$$(3x - p)^2 = 9x^2 - 6px + p^2$$
$$\therefore \qquad 9x^2 - 6px + p^2 = 9x^2 + kx + 16$$

Comparing coefficients: $p^2 = 16$ and $k = -6p$
$$p^2 = 16 \Rightarrow p = 4 \text{ or } -4$$

when $p = 4$ $\qquad k = -6 \times 4 = -24$

and when $p = -4$, $\quad k = -6 \times (-4) = 24$

$\therefore$ either $\quad p = 4$ and $k = -24$ or $p = -4$ and $k = 24$

7 Expand $(2x + k)^2$ and hence find all the possible values of k and p if $(2x + k)^2 = 4x^2 + px + 25$ for all values of x.

8 Expand $(3x - k)^2$ and hence find all the possible values of k and p if $(3x - k)^2 = 9x^2 + px + 16$ for all values of x.

9 If $(2x + p)^2 \equiv ax^2 + 20x + c$ find the values of p, a and c.
(The symbol $\equiv$ means 'identical to'.)

10 If $(3 + kx)^2 \equiv 9 + 12x + ax^2$ find the values of a and k.

11 If $(px + q)^2 \equiv 16x^2 + 56x + 49$ find *all* possible values of p and q.

12 If $(px + q)^2 + r \equiv x^2 + 12x + 36$ find the values of p, q and r.

PROBLEMS

EXERCISE 2M

The sum of two numbers is 13 and the sum of their squares is 97. Find the numbers.

Let one number be x then the other number is $13 - x$

and $\qquad\qquad\qquad (13 - x)^2 + x^2 = 97$
$$169 - 26x + x^2 + x^2 = 97$$
$$2x^2 - 26x + 72 = 0$$
$$2(x^2 - 13x + 36) = 0$$
$$2(x - 4)(x - 9) = 0$$

$x - 4 = 0$ or $x - 9 = 0$ i.e. $x = 4$ or $x = 9$

If $x = 4$, the other number is $13 - x = 9$

If $x = 9$, the other number is $13 - x = 4$

The two numbers are therefore 4 and 9.

1 The sum of two numbers is 14 and the sum of their squares is 106. Find them.

2 The difference between two positive numbers is 2 and the sum of their squares is 20. Find the numbers.

3 The sum of the squares of two consecutive positive numbers is 61. Find the two numbers.

4 One side of a rectangle is 4 cm longer than the other. Find the sides if the area of the rectangle is 45 cm^2.

5 The perimeter of a rectangle is 26 cm and its area is 40 cm^2. Find the lengths of the sides.

6 Two positive whole numbers differ by 3, and the sum of their squares is 89. If the smaller number is x form an equation in x and solve it to find the numbers.

7 The lengths of the sides of a right-angled triangle are x cm, $(x+7)$ cm and $(x+8)$ cm. Find them.

8 A rectangle is 6 cm longer than it is wide. If its area is the same as that of a square of side 4 cm find its dimensions.

9 The lengths of the sides of a right-angled triangle are x cm, $(x-2)$ cm and $(x-4)$ cm. Find them.

10 The hypotenuse of a right-angled triangle is 10 cm. Find the lengths of the other two sides if their sum is 14 cm.

11 The product of two numbers is 84. If these numbers differ by 5, find them.

12 One number is 3 more than another. If their product is 88, find them.

13 The length of a rectangle is 5 cm more than its width. If the area of the rectangle is 36 cm^2 find its dimensions.

14 The base of a triangle is 5 cm more than its perpendicular height. If the area of the triangle is 42 cm^2 find

 a the length of its base

 b its perpendicular height.

15 In a trapezium the parallel sides are of length x cm and $(x+2)$ cm. If the distance between these parallel sides is $\frac{x}{2}$ cm, and the area of the trapezium is 15 cm^2, form an equation in x and solve it to find the dimensions of the figure.

16 The sum of the first n natural numbers is $\dfrac{n(n+1)}{2}$. Find n if the sum of the first n numbers is 300.

17 A straight-sided plane figure with n sides has $\dfrac{n(n-3)}{2}$ diagonals. If such a figure has 54 diagonals how many sides does it have?

18 A stone thrown vertically into the air is h metres above the ground after t seconds where $h = 30t - 5t^2$. When is the stone 40 metres above the ground? Explain the two answers.

19 The area of the page of a book is $300\,\mathrm{cm}^2$. If the length is 5 cm more than the width, find the dimensions of the page.

20 Zoe's problem as stated in **Exercise 2A** question **2**, gave the equation $x^2 - 15x - 2700 = 0$. Solve this equation and hence find the original price of one dozen eggs.

21 The sum of the squares of three consecutive positive whole numbers is 302. Find them.

INVESTIGATION

This investigation is for positive integer values of x, y and a.

a Investigate the possible pairs of values of x and y that satisfy the equation $x^2 - y^2 = 24$.

b Repeat part **a** for the equation $x^2 - y^2 = 151$.

c Investigate whether or not the equation $x^2 - y^2 = a$ always has at least one solution.

d The equation $x^2 - y^2 = a$ has exactly one solution. Investigate whether or not a is a special kind of number. If it is, describe the type of number and give at least three values for a, larger than 100, for which the equation $x^2 - y^2 = a$ has exactly one solution.

THE FORMULA FOR SOLVING QUADRATIC EQUATIONS

We have been able to solve all the quadratic equations we have met so far by factorisation. However, there are some, such as $2x^2 + 7x + 2 = 0$, that cannot be factorised. Many of these can be solved by using a formula.

Consider the equation $x^2 - 6x - 4 = 0$
Now $x^2 - 6x - 4$ does not factorise, but it is possible to solve the equation as follows.

$$x^2 - 6x - 4 = 0$$

Add 4 to each side $\quad x^2 - 6x = 4$

Now add 9 to each side

i.e. $\qquad\qquad x^2 - 6x + 9 = 13$

> We choose 9 because
> $x^2 - 6x + 9 = (x - 3)^2$

This gives $\qquad\qquad (x - 3)^2 = 13$

i.e. $\qquad\qquad x - 3 = \pm\sqrt{13}$

giving $\qquad\qquad x = 3 \pm \sqrt{13}$

(This method is called completing the square.)

- When a similar method is applied to the general quadratic equation $ax^2 + bx + c = 0$, where a, b and c are positive or negative numbers we get

$$x = \frac{-b \pm \sqrt{b^2 - 4ac}}{2a}$$

This is called the *formula* for solving quadratic equations. It gives values of x, or roots of the equation, for any given values of a, b and c (provided that $b^2 - 4ac$ is not negative).

Remember that $\quad a$ is the coefficient of x^2
b is the coefficient of x
c is the constant number term.

Since the two values of x are

$$-\frac{b}{2a} + \frac{\sqrt{b^2 - 4ac}}{2a} \quad \text{and} \quad -\frac{b}{2a} - \frac{\sqrt{b^2 - 4ac}}{2a}$$

the sum of the two roots is always $\left(\dfrac{-b}{2a}\right) + \left(\dfrac{-b}{2a}\right) = -\dfrac{b}{a}$

This provides a useful check that your answers are correct.

EXERCISE 3A

Use the formula to solve the equation $x^2 - 9x - 2 = 0$ giving your answers correct to 2 decimal places.

$$x^2 - 9x - 2 = 0$$
$$a = 1, \quad b = -9, \quad c = -2$$

$$x = \frac{-b \pm \sqrt{b^2 - 4ac}}{2a}$$

$$= \frac{-(-9) \pm \sqrt{(-9)^2 - 4(1)(-2)}}{2 \times 1}$$

$$= \frac{9 \pm \sqrt{81 + 8}}{2} = \frac{9 \pm \sqrt{89}}{2}$$

$$= \frac{9 \pm 9.433\ldots}{2}$$

$$= \frac{18.433\ldots}{2} \quad \text{or} \quad \frac{-0.433\ldots}{2} = 9.216\ldots \quad \text{or} \quad -0.216\ldots$$

$$\therefore \quad x = 9.22 \quad \text{or} \quad -0.22 \quad (\text{correct to 2 d.p.})$$

Check: Sum of roots is $9.22 + (-0.22) = 9$

and $\dfrac{-b}{a} = \dfrac{-(-9)}{1} = 9$ confirming the results.

Note that if we leave the answers as

$$x = \frac{9 + \sqrt{89}}{2} \quad \text{and} \quad x = \frac{9 - \sqrt{89}}{2}$$

they are *exact* answers in surd form. Answers that are given correct to a given number of decimal places are approximate answers.

Use the formula to solve the following equations, giving answers correct to 2 decimal places.

1 $x^2 + 6x + 3 = 0$

2 $x^2 + 7x + 4 = 0$

3 $x^2 + 5x + 5 = 0$

4 $x^2 + 7x - 2 = 0$

5 $x^2 + 4x - 3 = 0$

6 $x^2 + 9x + 12 = 0$

7 $x^2 + 8x + 13 = 0$

8 $x^2 + 10x - 15 = 0$

9 $x^2 + 6x - 6 = 0$

10 $x^2 + 9x - 1 = 0$

11 $x^2 + 3x - 5 = 0$

12 $x^2 + 4x - 7 = 0$

13 $x^2 - 4x + 2 = 0$ **18** $x^2 - 3x + 1 = 0$

14 $x^2 - 7x + 3 = 0$ **19** $x^2 - 9x - 2 = 0$

15 $x^2 - 6x + 6 = 0$ **20** $x^2 - 4x - 9 = 0$

16 $x^2 - 5x - 5 = 0$ **21** $x^2 + 7x - 2 = 0$

17 $x^2 - 5x + 2 = 0$ **22** $x^2 + 3x - 2 = 0$

For questions **23** to **26** give your answers in surd form.

23 $x^2 - 4x - 3 = 0$ **25** $x^2 + 8x + 5 = 0$

24 $x^2 - 7x - 3 = 0$ **26** $x^2 - 2x - 4 = 0$

Solve the equation $3x^2 + 7x - 2 = 0$ giving your answer correct to 2 decimal places.

$$3x^2 + 7x - 2 = 0$$

$$a = 3, \quad b = 7, \quad c = -2$$

$$x = \frac{-b \pm \sqrt{b^2 - 4ac}}{2a}$$

$$= \frac{-7 \pm \sqrt{7^2 - 4(3)(-2)}}{2 \times 3}$$

$$= \frac{-7 \pm \sqrt{49 + 24}}{6} = \frac{-7 \pm \sqrt{73}}{6}$$

$$= \frac{-7 \pm 8.544\ldots}{6}$$

$$= \frac{1.544\ldots}{6} \quad \text{or} \quad \frac{-15.544\ldots}{6}$$

$$= 0.257\ldots \quad \text{or} \quad -2.590\ldots$$

$$= 0.26 \quad \text{or} \quad -2.59 \quad (\text{correct to 2 d.p.})$$

Check: Sum of roots is $0.26 + (-2.59) = -2.33$

and $\dfrac{-b}{a} = \dfrac{-7}{3} = -2.33$ (correct to 2 d.p.)

confirming the results.

Solve the equations, giving answers correct to 2 decimal places.

27 $2x^2 + 7x + 2 = 0$ **32** $3x^2 + 7x + 3 = 0$

28 $2x^2 + 7x + 4 = 0$ **33** $4x^2 + 7x + 1 = 0$

29 $5x^2 + 9x + 2 = 0$ **34** $5x^2 - 9x + 2 = 0$

30 $2x^2 - 7x + 4 = 0$ **35** $3x^2 + 5x - 3 = 0$

31 $4.2x^2 - 7.5x + 1 = 0$ **36** $3.7x^2 + 8.5x - 2 = 0$

37 $5a^2 - 2a - 1 = 0$ **42** $10n^2 + 50n - 3 = 0$

38 $40b^2 + 90b + 21 = 0$ **43** $500p^2 + 75p - 23 = 0$

39 $2S^2 - 4S - 1 = 0$ **44** $\frac{2}{3}x^2 + \frac{3}{4}x + \frac{1}{9} = 0$

40 $\frac{1}{2}x^2 - \frac{1}{3}x - 1 = 0$ **45** $0.2A^2 + A + 0.5 = 0$

41 $0.7R^2 + 1.2R + 0.3 = 0$ **46** $\frac{1}{2}N^2 + 3N - \frac{1}{8} = 0$

47 Use the formula to solve the equation $4x^2 - 12x + 9 = 0$.
Comment on the number of different solutions and on the value
of $b^2 - 4ac$.

48 Repeat question **47** for the equation

a $25x^2 + 10x + 1 = 0$ **b** $9x^2 - 42x + 29 = 0$.

How can you test whether or not a quadratic equation has two
identical solutions?

49 a Use the formula to solve the equation $2x^2 + 9x - 5 = 0$.
What do you notice about the value of $b^2 - 4ac$?

b Solve the equation $2x^2 + 9x - 5 = 0$ by factorising. What can
you conclude about an equation if the value of $b^2 - 4ac$ is a
perfect square?

50 a Use the formula to try to solve the equation $x^2 + 2x + 3 = 0$.

b What is the relationship between the result in part **a** and the
value of $b^2 - 4ac$?

c Use the results of this question and questions **47** to **49** to
deduce a relationship between the number of solutions to a
quadratic equation and the value of $b^2 - 4ac$.

Quadratic equations do not always arise arranged in the order $ax^2 + bx + c = 0$. They should, however, be arranged in this order before the formula is used.

Solve the equation $4x^2 = 7x + 1$ giving your answers correct to 2 decimal places.

$$4x^2 = 7x + 1$$

First arrange the equation in the form $ax^2 + bx + c = 0$

$$4x^2 - 7x - 1 = 0$$
$$a = 4, \quad b = -7, \quad c = -1$$

$$x = \frac{-b \pm \sqrt{b^2 - 4ac}}{2a}$$

$$= \frac{-(-7) \pm \sqrt{(-7)^2 - 4(4)(-1)}}{2 \times 4}$$

$$= \frac{7 \pm \sqrt{49 + 16}}{8} = \frac{7 \pm \sqrt{65}}{8}$$

$$= \frac{7 \pm 8.062\ldots}{8} = \frac{15.062\ldots}{8} \quad \text{or} \quad \frac{-1.062\ldots}{8}$$

$$= 1.882\ldots \quad \text{or} \quad -0.132\ldots$$

$$= 1.88 \quad \text{or} \quad -0.13 \quad (\text{correct to 2 d.p.})$$

Check: Sum of roots is $1.88 + (-0.13) = 1.75$

and $\dfrac{-b}{a} = \dfrac{-(-7)}{4} = \dfrac{7}{4} = 1.75$

confirming the results.

Solve the following equations giving your answers correct to 2 decimal places.

1 $2x^2 = 8x + 11$ **4** $5x^2 = x + 3$

2 $4x^2 = 8x + 3$ **5** $4x^2 + 2 = 7x$

3 $3x^2 = 3 - 5x$ **6** $3x^2 = 12x + 2$

7 $2x^2 = 3x + 1$

8 $4x^2 = 5 - 3x$

9 $3x^2 + 2 = 9x$

10 $6x^2 - 9x = 4$

11 $2x^2 = 5x + 5$

12 $3x^2 + 4x = 1$

13 $4x^2 = 4x + 1$

14 $3x^2 + 7x = 2$

15 $5x^2 = 5x - 1$

16 $8x^2 = x + 1$

17 $3.2x^2 = 5.4x + 1.2$

18 $7.6x^2 = 3.4x + 0.6$

19 $0.8x^2 = 0.5 - 3.1x$

20 $5.9x^2 = 16.8x - 9.6$

In the next exercise, some of the equations can be solved by factorisation. Try this method first. If factors cannot be found, use the formula.

EXERCISE 3C

For questions **1** to **10** solve the equations, giving answers correct to 2 decimal places when necessary.

1 $2x^2 + 3x - 2 = 0$

2 $3x^2 + 6x + 2 = 0$

3 $6x^2 + 7x + 2 = 0$

4 $2x^2 + 3x - 3 = 0$

5 $3x^2 - 8x + 2 = 0$

6 $3x^2 - 8x - 3 = 0$

7 $2x^2 - 3x - 3 = 0$

8 $8x^2 + 10x - 3 = 10$

9 $6x^2 + 7x - 2 = 0$

10 $4x^2 - 3x - 2 = 0$

For questions **11** to **20** solve the equations, giving answers exactly, in surd form when necessary.

11 $7x^2 + 8x - 2 = 0$

12 $5x^2 - 3x - 1 = 0$

13 $3x^2 = 7x - 2$

14 $11x^2 + 12x + 3 = 0$

15 $20x^2 = 3 - 11x$

16 $3x^2 - 14x + 15 = 0$

17 $5x^2 + 8x + 2 = 0$

18 $2x^2 = 7x + 3$

19 $2x^2 + 9x = 5$

20 $6x^2 = 5x + 2$

HARDER
EXPANSIONS
AND EQUATIONS

Solving some problems leads to equations of the form

$$(x+5)\left(\frac{4}{x}-1\right)=7$$

To solve such equations we must first expand the left-hand side.

EXERCISE 3D

Expand $(x+2)\left(\frac{10}{x}-3\right)$

$$(x+2)\left(\frac{10}{x}-3\right)=x\times\frac{10}{x}+x\times(-3)+2\times\frac{10}{x}+2\times(-3)$$

$$=10-3x+\frac{20}{x}-6=4-3x+\frac{20}{x}$$

Expand

1 $(x+5)\left(\frac{6}{x}+1\right)$ 　　　 **4** $(x-7)\left(3-\frac{5}{x}\right)$ 　　　 **7** $\left(\frac{4}{x}-3\right)(5x+1)$

2 $(x+3)\left(\frac{10}{x}-3\right)$ 　　　 **5** $(x-4)\left(\frac{12}{x}-5\right)$ 　　　 **8** $\left(5-\frac{6}{x}\right)(3+2x)$

3 $(x-4)\left(\frac{3}{x}+5\right)$ 　　　 **6** $\left(\frac{5}{x}-2\right)(2x+1)$ 　　　 **9** $\left(3-\frac{2}{x}\right)(x-3)$

Solve the equation $(x-7)\left(\frac{20}{x}+3\right)=100$

$$(x-7)\left(\frac{20}{x}+3\right)=100$$ 　 Expand the brackets.

$$x\times\frac{20}{x_1}+x\times3-7\times\frac{20}{x}-7\times3=100$$

$$20+3x-\frac{140}{x}-21=100$$ 　 Collect like terms on the LHS.

$$3x-\frac{140}{x}-1=100$$ 　 Subtract 100 from both sides.

$$3x-\frac{140}{x}-101=0$$ 　 Multiply every term by x.

$$3x^2-140-101x=0$$ 　 Arrange in the form $ax^2+bx+c=0$

$$3x^2-101x-140=0$$ 　 Factorise 　 $\Rightarrow$ 　 $(3x+4)(x-35)=0$

Either 　　 $3x+4=0$ or $x-35=0$ 　　 $\Rightarrow$ 　 $3x=-4$ or $x=35$

i.e. 　　　　　 $x=-\frac{4}{3}$ or 35

Solve the equations.

10 $(x-5)\left(\dfrac{8}{x}-9\right)=0$ **14** $(x+7)\left(\dfrac{12}{x}-5\right)=0$

11 $(x+5)\left(\dfrac{14}{x}-5\right)=0$ **15** $(2x+7)\left(\dfrac{20}{x}+9\right)=0$

12 $(x+5)\left(\dfrac{6}{x}+1\right)=24$ **16** $(x-4)\left(\dfrac{12}{x}-5\right)=96$

13 $(x+4)\left(\dfrac{120}{x}-3\right)=144$ **17** $(x-3)\left(\dfrac{12}{x}-7\right)=70$

---

a Rewrite the equation $\dfrac{6}{x}+\dfrac{3}{x+1}=4$ in the form $ax^2+bx+c=0$

b Hence solve the equation $\dfrac{6}{x}+\dfrac{3}{x+1}=4$

a $$\dfrac{6}{x}+\dfrac{3}{x+1}=4 \qquad \boxed{\text{Multiply each term by x and by } x+1}$$

$$\dfrac{6}{x}\times x\times(x+1)+\dfrac{3}{x+1}\times x\times(x+1)=4\times x\times(x+1)$$

$$\Rightarrow \qquad\qquad 6x+6+3x=4x^2+4x$$

$$9x+6=4x^2+4x$$

$$0=4x^2-5x-6$$

$$4x^2-5x-6=0$$

b Factorising $\quad 4x^2-5x-6=0\quad$ gives $\quad(4x+3)(x-2)=0$

Either $4x+3=0\quad$ or $\quad x-2=0$

$$4x=-3\quad\text{or}\quad x=2\Rightarrow x=-\tfrac{3}{4}\quad\text{or}\quad 2$$

In questions **18** to **23**
a Express each equation in the form $ax^2+bx+c=0$
b Solve the given equation.

18 $x-\dfrac{12}{x}=1$ **20** $x-\dfrac{5}{x}=3$ **22** $\dfrac{2}{x}+\dfrac{1}{x+1}=4$

19 $x+\dfrac{2}{x}=11$ **21** $x+\dfrac{2}{x}=7$ **23** $\dfrac{5}{x}-2x=5$

Solve the equation $\dfrac{1}{x+1} + \dfrac{2}{x-3} = 4$ giving your answers correct to 2 decimal places.

$$\frac{1}{x+1} + \frac{2}{x-3} = 4$$

> Multiply both sides by $(x+1)(x-3)$

$$\frac{(x+1)(x-3)}{x+1} + \frac{2(x+1)(x-3)}{x-3} = 4(x+1)(x-3)$$

$$(x-3) + 2(x+1) = 4(x+1)(x-3)$$
$$x - 3 + 2x + 2 = 4(x^2 - 2x - 3)$$
$$3x - 1 = 4x^2 - 8x - 12$$

i.e. $\qquad 4x^2 - 11x - 11 = 0$

$$a = 4, \quad b = -11, \quad c = -11$$

$$x = \frac{-b \pm \sqrt{b^2 - 4ac}}{2a}$$

$$= \frac{11 \pm \sqrt{121 + 176}}{8} = \frac{11 \pm \sqrt{297}}{8}$$

$$= \frac{11 \pm 17.233\ldots}{8} = \frac{28.233\ldots}{8} \quad \text{or} \quad \frac{-6.233\ldots}{8}$$

$$= 3.529\ldots \quad \text{or} \quad -0.779\ldots$$

i.e. $\quad x = 3.53 \quad$ or $\quad -0.78 \quad$ (correct to 2 d.p.)

Solve the following equations; give answers correct to 2 decimal places where necessary.

24 $\dfrac{3}{x-1} + \dfrac{2}{x+2} = \dfrac{7}{2}$ $\qquad$ **28** $\dfrac{4}{x-4} + \dfrac{4}{x-2} = 3$

25 $\dfrac{4}{x} + \dfrac{5}{x+2} = 1$ $\qquad$ **29** $\dfrac{1}{x-3} - \dfrac{1}{x-1} = \dfrac{1}{4}$

26 $\dfrac{2}{x-3} + \dfrac{4}{x+6} = 1$ $\qquad$ **30** $\dfrac{4}{x+1} + \dfrac{2}{3x-2} = 1$

27 $\dfrac{3}{x-1} + \dfrac{2x}{x-2} = 0$ $\qquad$ **31** $\dfrac{2x}{x+20} - \dfrac{1}{x+1} = 0$

32 $\dfrac{3}{x+2} - \dfrac{1}{x+4} = 2$

34 $\dfrac{3}{x-1} - \dfrac{2}{x+3} = 1$

33 $\dfrac{2}{x+5} + \dfrac{3}{x-2} = 4$

35 $\dfrac{1}{x-3} + \dfrac{5}{x+3} = 1$

PROBLEMS

EXERCISE 3E

A rectangular lawn measuring 20 m by 15 m is surrounded by a path x m wide. If the area of the path is $74\,\text{m}^2$ form an equation in x and solve it to find the width of the path.

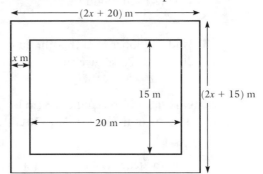

The lawn and path together form a rectangle measuring $(2x+20)$ m by $(2x+15)$ m

$\therefore$ area of lawn and path together $= (2x+20)(2x+15)\,\text{m}^2$

while the area of the lawn is $20 \times 15\,\text{m}^2 = 300\,\text{m}^2$

$\therefore$ area of path is $(2x+20)(2x+15) - 300\,\text{m}^2$

But the area of the path is given as $74\,\text{m}^2$.

> Equating the two values for the area of the path gives the equation

$$(2x+20)(2x+15) - 300 = 74$$

i.e. $\quad 4x^2 + 30x + 40x + 300 - 300 = 74$

$$4x^2 + 70x - 74 = 0 \qquad \boxed{\text{Divide each term by 2.}}$$

$$2x^2 + 35x - 37 = 0$$

$$(2x+37)(x-1) = 0$$

i.e. either $2x + 37 = 0$ or $x - 1 = 0$

$\qquad\qquad 2x = -37 \quad$ or $\quad x = 1$

$\qquad\qquad x = -\frac{37}{2} \quad$ or $\quad 1$

Since the width of the path must be positive the only acceptable solution is $x = 1$

$\therefore$ the width of the path is 1 m

> Check by reading the question and seeing if a path of width 1 m fits the information given.

The following questions may lead to quadratic equations that do not factorise but always check first whether a quadratic equation will factorise before using the formula. If the answer is not rational give it correct to 3 significant figures.

1 The sum of two numbers is 10 and the sum of their squares is 80. Find them.

2 The sum of two numbers is 9 and the difference between their squares is 60. Find them.

3 Find a number such that the sum of the number and its reciprocal is 20. In this case give the answers correct to 2 decimal places.

4 One side of a rectangle is 3 cm longer than another. Find the sides if the area of the rectangle is $20\,\text{cm}^2$.

5 Find the length of the hypotenuse of a right-angled triangle whose sides are $x\,\text{cm}$, $(x+1)\,\text{cm}$ and $(x+3)\,\text{cm}$.

6 The parallel sides of a trapezium are $(x-2)\,\text{cm}$ and $(x+4)\,\text{cm}$ long. If the distance between the parallel sides is $x\,\text{cm}$ and the area of the trapezium is $42\,\text{cm}^2$ find its dimensions.

7 A rectangular block is 2 cm wider than it is high and twice as long as it is wide. If its total surface area is $190\,\text{cm}^2$ find its dimensions.

8 Sally is x years old. Her mother's age is (x^2-4) years and her father is 6 years older than her mother. If the combined age of all three is 76 years, form an equation in x and solve it. How old is her father?

9

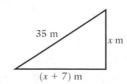

The lengths of the three edges of a triangular flower bed are given on the diagram. The length of the longest side is 35 m and the triangle is right-angled. Find the lengths of the sides containing the right angle.

10 A square of side x cm is removed from a rectangular piece of cardboard measuring $(3x+1)$ cm by $(x+2)$ cm. If the area of card remaining is $62\,\text{cm}^2$ form an equation in x and solve it to find the dimensions of the original card.

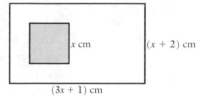

x cm $(x+2)$ cm

$(3x+1)$ cm

11 N is the midpoint of the base BC of a triangle ABC. If $AN = x$ cm, $BC = (2x+14)$ cm, $AC = (x+8)$ cm and $AB = AC$, form an equation in x and solve it. Hence find the length of the base and height of the triangle ABC.

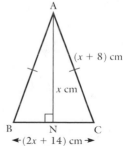

12 Mrs Brown bought x grapefruit for £4.20. If the price of each grapefruit is increased by 5 p she can buy 2 fewer grapefruit for the same money.

  a Express the price, in pence, of one grapefruit in terms of x.

  b Use your answer to part **a** to write down the price, in terms of x, of a grapefruit at the increased price.

  c Hence show that x satisfies the equation $\left(\dfrac{420}{x}+5\right)(x-2) = 420$

  d Solve the equation to find the number of grapefruit bought and the price of each one.

13 Alan bought x copies of a reference book for £240. If he had waited for the summer sale, when the books were reduced by £2 each, he could have bought 4 more books for the same amount.

  a Express the original price of a book in terms of x.

  b Express the sale price of a book in terms of x.

  c Express the number of books that could be bought at the sale price in terms of x.

  d Use your answers to parts **b** and **c** to form the equation $(x+4)\left(\dfrac{240}{x}-2\right) = 240$

  e Solve the equation given in part **d**. How many books did Alan buy and how much did each one cost?

14 The sides of a square of side x cm are all extended by 4 cm so that their extremities, when joined, form another square. The area of this square is five times the area of the original square. Form an equation in x and solve it to find the length of a side of the original square.

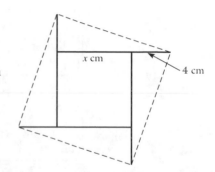

x cm   4 cm

A coach is due to reach its destination 30 kilometres away at a certain time. Its start is delayed by 18 minutes, but by increasing the average speed by 5 km/h the driver arrives on time. How long did the journey actually take? What was the intended average speed?

Let the intended average speed be x km/h.

> The information can then be set out in table form taking care to work in compatible units.

	Speed in km/h	Distance in km	Time in hours
Intended journey	x	30	$\dfrac{30}{x}$
Actual journey	$x + 5$	30	$\dfrac{30}{x + 5}$

Since the actual time is 18 minutes, i.e. $\frac{3}{10}$ hour, shorter than the intended time, then

$$\frac{30}{x} - \frac{30}{x + 5} = \frac{3}{10}$$

> Multiply both sides by $10x(x + 5)$

$$\frac{30 \times 10x(x + 5)}{x} - \frac{30 \times 10x(x + 5)}{x + 5} = \frac{3 \times 10x(x + 5)}{10}$$

$$300(x + 5) - 300x = 3x(x + 5)$$

$$100(x + 5) - 100x = x^2 + 5x$$

$$100x + 500 - 100x = x^2 + 5x$$

$$0 = x^2 + 5x - 500$$

i.e. $\qquad x^2 + 5x - 500 = 0$

$$(x + 25)(x - 20) = 0$$

$\therefore \qquad\qquad x = -25 \quad \text{or} \quad 20$

But -25 is unacceptable as the average speed has to be positive.

$\therefore \qquad\qquad x = 20$

i.e. the intended speed is 20 km/h and the time actually taken is $\dfrac{30}{20 + 5}$ hours $= \dfrac{30}{25}$ hours i.e. 1 hour 12 minutes.

15 When its average speed increases by 10 mph the time taken for a car to make a journey of 105 miles is reduced by 15 minutes. Find the original average speed of the car.

16 Find the price of potatoes per kilogram if, when the price rises by 5 p per kg, I can buy 1 kg less for £2.10.

17 Tickets are available for a concert at two prices, the dearer ticket being £3 more than the cheaper one. Find the price of each ticket if a youth group can buy ten more of the cheaper tickets than the dearer tickets for £180.

18 From a piece of wire 42 cm long, a length $10x$ cm is cut off and bent into a rectangle whose length is one and a half times its width. The remainder is bent to form a square. If the combined area of the rectangle and square is 63 cm^2 find their dimensions.

19 The members of a club hire a coach for the day at a cost of £210. Seven members withdraw which means that each member who makes the trip must pay an extra £1. How many members originally agreed to go?

20 Find the original price of oranges if, when the price of each orange rises by 4 p, Jean can buy 5 fewer oranges for £6.

21 Two footpaths connect Antley and Berry. The distance between the two villages along one footpath is 15 miles while the distance between them along the other path is 18 miles. Len takes the shorter route and, while walking at x mph, takes $\frac{1}{2}$ hour longer than Mandy. Mandy takes the longer route and walks at 1 mph faster than Len. Find the speed at which each walks and the time each of them takes.

22 George walks at x km/h, which is 2 km per hour faster than Liam, and in consequence takes 40 minutes less to walk 8 km. Find the speed at which each walks.

PUZZLE

A bird table is 3 m from one corner, 4 m from another corner and 5 m from a third corner of a square patio. Find the length of an edge of the patio.

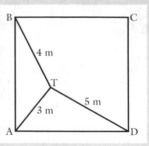

INVESTIGATION

a Use the formula to try to find solutions to the equation $x^2 - 4x + 8 = 0$. Explain why the method breaks down. What can you deduce about the equation $x^2 - 4x + 8 = 0$?

b Is there another method, not using the formula, from which you can reach the same deduction about the equation $x^2 - 4x + 8 = 0$?

c Repeat parts **a** and **b** for the equation $2x^2 + 3x + 4 = 0$.

d Make a deduction about any quadratic equation of the form $ax^2 + bx + c = 0$ when a is positive and c is negative.

e Find a simple test that will show whether a quadratic equation has two different roots or the same root twice (these are called repeated roots) or no real roots.

FORMULAS

Kevin is using the special theory of relativity in a series of experiments. The theory states that a mass m is equivalent to a quantity of energy E, given by the formula $E = mc^2$
where c m/s is the speed of light and $c = 2.998 \times 10^8$.

In one set of experiments, he needs to use the formula to calculate the energy equivalent to some very large masses.

In another set of experiments, Kevin wants to find the mass associated with different amounts of energy.

- To find the energy equivalent to a mass of 5.075×10^6 kg, Kevin has to calculate $(5.075 \times 10^6) \times (2.998 \times 10^8)^2$, that is, he needs to know how to work with numbers in standard form.
- To find the mass equivalent to 1.87×10^{-3} joules of energy, requires finding the value of m from the equation $1.87 \times 10^{-3} = m(2.998 \times 10^8)^2$. When a calculation such as this needs to be performed several times, it is more efficient to rearrange the formula as $m = \dfrac{E}{c^2}$, that is, to make m the subject of the formula, as m can then be found directly.

EXERCISE 4A **1** The formula

$$f = \frac{1}{2\pi} \sqrt{\frac{k}{m}}$$

can be used to find the frequency of vibrations in, for example, tuning forks.

With $k = 135$ and $m = 1.5 \times 10^5$, Jason calculated f as 0.5×10^{-4}.

Gill looked at his answer and said 'That is not right.'

Discuss what you need to be able to do in order to recognise that an answer to such a calculation is obviously wrong.

2 The 'weight' of sheet paper is given in terms of grams per square metre.

The weight of a book therefore depends on the size of the pages, the number of pages and the 'weight' of paper used.

A publisher has to consider how changing any one of these quantities affects the others.

Discuss how this can be done.

USING NUMBERS IN STANDARD FORM

Calculations involving numbers in standard form can be done on a calculator.

For example, to enter 1.738×10^{-6}, the number 1.738 is entered normally followed by the **EXP** button and then the power of 10.

Hence, to calculate $(1.738 \times 10^{-6}) \times (4.093 \times 10^{-4})$, we enter

```
1 . 7 3 8  EXP  (–) 6  ×  4 . 0 9 3  EXP  (–) 4  =
```

giving 7.114×10^{-10} corrected to 4 significant figures.
(Check your manual to find the key equivalent to EXP on your calculator.)

However, as with all calculations, it is important to know whether the answer is about right; this means that we need to be able to estimate results using non-calculator methods.

Now
$(1.738 \times 10^{-6}) \times (4.093 \times 10^{-4})$
$\approx 2 \times 10^{-6} \times 4 \times 10^{-4}$
$= 8 \times 10^{-10}$

> Numbers can be multiplied in any order,
> i.e. $2 \times 10^{-6} \times 4 \times 10^{-4} = 2 \times 4 \times 10^{-6} \times 10^{-4}$
> and $10^{-6} \times 10^{-4} = 10^{-6+(-4)} = 10^{-10}$

so the answer given above is reasonable.

EXERCISE 4B

If $a = 1.2 \times 10^{-2}$ and $b = 6 \times 10^{-4}$, find

a ab **b** $\dfrac{a}{b}$ **c** $a + b$

a $ab = (1.2 \times 10^{-2}) \times (6 \times 10^{-4})$
$= 7.2 \times 10^{-6}$

b $\dfrac{a}{b} = \dfrac{1.2 \times 10^{-2}}{6 \times 10^{-4}} = \dfrac{1.2}{6} \times 10^{-2-(-4)}$

$= 0.2 \times 10^2 = 2 \times 10^1$

c Multiplication must be done before addition, so each number must be written in full.

$a + b = 1.2 \times 10^{-2} + 6 \times 10^{-4}$
$= 0.012 + 0.0006$
$= 0.0126$
$= 1.26 \times 10^{-2}$

Do not use a calculator for questions **1** to **6**.

1 Write down the value of ab in standard form if

  a $a = 2.1 \times 10^2$, $b = 4 \times 10^3$

  b $a = 5.4 \times 10^4$, $b = 2 \times 10^5$

  c $a = 7 \times 10^{-2}$, $b = 2.2 \times 10^{-3}$

  d $a = 5 \times 10^{-4}$, $b = 2.3 \times 10^{-2}$

  e $a = 1.6 \times 10^{-2}$, $b = 2 \times 10^4$

  f $a = 6 \times 10^5$, $b = 1.3 \times 10^{-7}$

2 Write down the value of $\dfrac{p}{q}$ in standard form if

  a $p = 6 \times 10^5$, $q = 3 \times 10^2$

  b $p = 1.4 \times 10^8$, $q = 2 \times 10^3$

  c $p = 9 \times 10^3$, $q = 3 \times 10^5$

  d $p = 7 \times 10^{-3}$, $q = 5 \times 10^2$

  e $p = 1.8 \times 10^{-3}$, $q = 6 \times 10^{-4}$

  f $p = 2.5 \times 10^4$, $q = 2 \times 10^{-4}$

3 Write down the value of $x + y$ in standard form if

   a $x = 2 \times 10^2$, $y = 3 \times 10^3$

   b $x = 3 \times 10^{-2}$, $y = 2 \times 10^{-3}$

   c $x = 2.1 \times 10^4$, $y = 3.1 \times 10^5$

   d $x = 1.3 \times 10^{-4}$, $y = 4 \times 10^{-3}$

   e $x = 1.9 \times 10^{-3}$, $y = 2.4 \times 10^{-2}$

   f $x = 3 \times 10^5$, $y = 2.5 \times 10^6$

4 If $x = 1.2 \times 10^5$ and $y = 5 \times 10^{-2}$ find, in standard form, the value of

   a xy **b** $x \div y$ **c** $x + 1000y$ **d** $\dfrac{x - y}{y}$

5 If $m = 7.2 \times 10^{-7}$ and $n = 1.2 \times 10^{-5}$ find, in standard form, the value of

   a mn **b** $m \div n$ **c** $n - m$ **d** $\dfrac{n + m}{n}$

6 If $u = 2.6 \times 10^5$ and $v = 5 \times 10^{-3}$ find, in standard form, the value of

   a uv **b** $u \div v$ **c** $\dfrac{u}{100} + 100v$ **d** $\dfrac{u}{10} - 1000v$

For questions **7** to **13**, first estimate the answer and then use a calculator to give the answer correct to 3 significant figures.

7 The special theory of relativity states that a mass m is equivalent to a quantity of energy, E, where

$$E = mc^2.$$

c m/s is the speed of light and $c = 2.998 \times 10^8$.

Find E when $m = 1.66 \times 10^{-27}$.

8 The quantity of nitrate in one bottle of mineral water is 1.5×10^{-3} g. The quantity of nitrate in another bottle of mineral water is 7.3×10^{-4} g.

The two bottles are emptied into the same jug. How much nitrate is there in the water in the jug?

9 The planet Xeron is 5.87×10^7 km from its sun.
The planet Alpha is 2.71×10^8 km from the same sun.

a Light travels at 3.0×10^5 km/s. Find, to the nearest minute, the time that light takes to travel to Alpha from its sun.

b Find the difference between the distances of Xeron and Alpha from their sun.

c Explain why the answer to part **b** does not give the distance between Xeron and Alpha.

10 Two planets A and B are respectively 1.8×10^{11} km and 8.9×10^{10} km from the Sun.

a How much further is one planet from the Sun than the other?

b Find the ratio of the distances of A and B from the Sun in the form $1 : n$.

c If light travels at 3.00×10^5 km/s, find how long it takes to travel from the Sun to the more distant planet.

11 The formula

$$f = \frac{1}{2\pi} \sqrt{\frac{k}{m}}$$

can be used to find the frequency of vibrations.
Calculate f when $k = 135$ and $m = 1.5 \times 10^5$.

12 A cylinder of radius r units and length h units has a total surface area, A square units, given by

$$A = 2\pi r^2 + 2\pi rh$$

The individual links in a chain are gold-plated cylinders of radius 2×10^{-4} m and length 8×10^{-4} m.
Find the surface area of gold-plating on

a one link   **b** 20 000 links.

13 When an amount of money, £P, is invested, the formula

$$A = P\left(1 + \frac{r}{100}\right)^t$$

is used to predict the value, £A, of the investment after t years at compound interest of $r\%$ p.a.
The trustees of a pension fund invest £1.37×10^8.
Use the formula to predict the value of this fund after 10 years with interest assumed constant at 7.8% p.a.

CONSTRUCTING FORMULAS

An instruction to find one quantity in terms of other quantities may be described in words. Sometimes such a relationship is implied by the context. In **Exercise 4A**, question **2**, for example, we are given the following information.

> The 'weight' of sheet paper is given in terms of grams per square metre. The weight of a book therefore depends on the size of the pages, the number of pages and the 'weight' of paper used.

To be able to work mathematically with this information it is necessary to translate it into mathematical symbols, that is to construct a formula.

- The first step is to allocate a letter to the number of units of each unknown quantity.
  In this example, we can use
  W grams for the weight of the book,
  n for the number of pages,
  w mm by b mm for the size of the pages
  d g/m^2 for the 'weight' of the paper used.
- We then use the information given and other relevant information known to us to form a relationship between these letters.

  In this case we know that if the book has n pages, there are $\dfrac{n}{2}$ sheets

  of paper (one sheet has two sides, that is gives 2 pages).
  Each sheet has an area of wb mm^2,

  so the total area of paper used is $\dfrac{n}{2} \times wb$ mm^2.

  As the 'weight' is given in terms of grams/square metre, we express

  total area of paper in square metres, i.e. $\dfrac{n}{2} \times wb \times 10^{-6}$ m^2.

> Remember that 1 m$^2 = 1000 \times 1000$ mm^2, so we divide by 10^6, i.e. multiply by 10^{-6}.

Then the weight of paper used is $d \times \dfrac{n}{2} \times wb \times 10^{-6}$ grams,

i.e. $W = d \times \dfrac{n}{2} \times wb \times 10^{-6}$

which we can tidy up to give $W = 5dnwb \times 10^{-7}$

EXERCISE 4C

If you cannot see how to construct a formula, first think what you would do if numbers were given in place of letters.

1 The sum of three numbers, a, b and c, is T. Give a formula for

  a T in terms of a, b and c.

  b a in terms of T, b and c.

2 Six exercise books cost p pence each and 8 pencils cost q pence each. Give a formula for C if C pence is the total cost of books and pencils.

3 A ladder has N rungs. The rungs are 20 cm apart and the top and bottom rungs are 20 cm from the ends of the ladder. If the length of the ladder is y cm, give a formula for y in terms of N. (Draw a diagram to help.)

4 The sum of two numbers is x. One of the numbers is 6.

   a What is the second number in terms of x?

   b The product of the two numbers is P. Give a formula for P in terms of x.

5 A furniture shop buys chairs at £C each and sells them for £S each. N chairs are sold for a total profit of £T. Give a formula for T in terms of C, S and N.

6 A room measures x cm by y cm. The area of the floor is A m^2. Give a formula for A in terms of x and y.

7 A sequence of numbers begins 4, 7, 10, 13, …

   a Find the eighth number in the sequence.

   b The nth term is x. Find a formula for x in terms of n. (Check your formula by using $n = 8$ and comparing the result with your answer to part **a**.)

8 The diagram shows a rectangular piece of card measuring 40 cm by 30 cm, from which the four shaded squares each of side x cm have been cut. The remaining piece is folded up to form an open box.

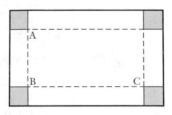

   a Give the lengths of AB and BC in terms of x.

   b If the volume of the box is V cm^3, give a formula for V in terms of x.

9 Two opposite sides of a rectangular field are each of length x metres. The perimeter of the field is 600 m.

   a Find the area of the field in terms of x.

   b If the area is 21 600 m^2, find the dimensions of the field.

10 A cube of edge x cm has a hole of cross-sectional area 5 cm^2 cut through it in a direction perpendicular to one pair of faces.

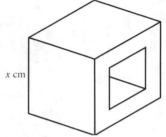

x cm

   a Find in terms of x the remaining area of each of these faces.

   b Find in terms of x the volume of the remaining solid.

   c If the volume is also equal to $\frac{4}{5}x^3$, find the value of x.

11 The volume of a rectangular box is 288 cm^3. The base of the box measures x cm by $2x$ cm.

   a Find the height of the box in terms of x.

   b If the height is $4\frac{1}{2}$ cm, find the other dimensions of the box.

12 The number of diagonals of an n-sided polygon is $\frac{1}{2}n(n-3)$. If the number of diagonals is 35, find the number of sides of the polygon.

13 A clock shows the time to be exactly 2 o'clock. A few minutes later the hour hand has moved through x degrees.

   a Through what angle, in terms of x, has the minute hand moved?

   b What angle does each hand make with the vertical line from the centre through 12?

   c If the minute hand is exactly over the hour hand, what is the value of x?

14 If x and y are positive integers such that $(x+y)$ is divisible by 4, show why $(5x+y)$ is also divisible by 4.

In the remaining questions, start by allocating a letter to the number of units of each unknown quantity and state clearly what each letter represents.

15 A rectangular gasket has a square hole in it. The gasket is made from cork which can vary in thickness. Find a relationship between the volume of cork in the gasket and the dimensions of the gasket.

16 The dose rate of a drug is given in terms of milligrams per kilogram of body weight. Find a formula that can be used to work out the dose needed for any one person.

SIMPLIFYING FRACTIONS

A formula is easier to use if it is in as simple a form as possible.

For example, the formula $S = \dfrac{n}{n-1} + \dfrac{n-3}{n^2 - 1}$ is easier to use to find S for a given value of n if the right-hand side is expressed as a single fraction. When this is done, the formula simplifies to $S = \dfrac{n+3}{n+1}$.

The second worked example in **Exercise 4D** shows how this simplification is achieved. In general, remember that algebraic fractions follow the same rules as arithmetic fractions; if you need to revise basic simplification use Summary 1 together with Revision Exercise 1.4 for practise.

EXERCISE 4D

Express $\dfrac{2}{x^2 - 9} - \dfrac{3}{x+3}$ as a single fraction.

> Factorise the denominators whenever this is possible; it is then easier to see the simplest common denomninator.

$$\dfrac{2}{x^2 - 9} - \dfrac{3}{x+3} = \dfrac{2}{(x+3)(x-3)} - \dfrac{3}{(x+3)}$$

> The common denominator is $(x+3)(x-3)$

$$= \dfrac{2 - 3(x-3)}{(x+3)(x-3)}$$

$$= \dfrac{2 - 3x + 9}{(x+3)(x-3)}$$

$$= \dfrac{11 - 3x}{(x+3)(x-3)}$$

Express as a single fraction

1 $\dfrac{3}{x+1} + \dfrac{2}{x^2 - 1}$

2 $\dfrac{5}{x^2 - 4} + \dfrac{3}{x+2}$

3 $\dfrac{3}{x^2 - 16} - \dfrac{4}{x-4}$

4 $\dfrac{4}{x-3} - \dfrac{1}{x^2 - 9}$

5 $\dfrac{2}{x+2} - \dfrac{x-4}{x^2 - 4}$

6 $\dfrac{7}{x^2 - 1} + \dfrac{2}{x-1}$

7 $\dfrac{3}{x+5} - \dfrac{2}{x^2-25}$

10 $\dfrac{1}{2x} + \dfrac{x-3}{x^2-2x}$

8 $\dfrac{5}{x^2-49} - \dfrac{9}{x-7}$

11 $\dfrac{2}{3x} + \dfrac{x-5}{x(x+3)}$

9 $\dfrac{4}{x+4} + \dfrac{3}{x^2-16}$

12 $\dfrac{3}{x^2-9} + \dfrac{5}{x+3}$

When reducing several fractions to a single fraction, the result can sometimes be simplified further because there is a factor, common to the numerator and the denominator, which can be cancelled.

Reduce $\dfrac{n}{n-1} - \dfrac{n-3}{n^2-1}$ to a single fraction in its lowest terms.

$$\dfrac{n}{n-1} + \dfrac{n-3}{n^2-1} = \dfrac{n}{n-1} + \dfrac{n-3}{(n+1)(n-1)}$$

Factorising n^2-1 first.

$$= \dfrac{n(n+1)+n-3}{(n+1)(n-1)}$$

Using $(n+1)(n-1)$ as the common denominator.

$$= \dfrac{n^2+2n-3}{(n+1)(n-1)}$$

Expanding and simplifying the numerator. Next we factorise the numerator.

$$= \dfrac{(n+3)(n-1)}{(n+1)(n-1)}$$

Now we can see that $(n-1)$ is a factor common to both top and bottom, so we can cancel it.

$$= \dfrac{n+3}{n+1}$$

Reduce to a single fraction in its lowest terms

13 $\dfrac{1}{x+1} + \dfrac{2}{x^2-1}$

16 $\dfrac{6}{x^2-9} + \dfrac{1}{x+3}$

14 $\dfrac{1}{2+x} + \dfrac{2x}{4-x^2}$

17 $\dfrac{1}{x-3} + \dfrac{1}{x^2-7x+12}$

15 $\dfrac{6}{x^2-2x-8} + \dfrac{1}{x+2}$

18 $\dfrac{3}{x^2-x-2} + \dfrac{1}{x+1}$

19 $\dfrac{3}{x^2 + 5x + 4} + \dfrac{1}{x + 4}$

24 $\dfrac{1}{x^2 - 4x + 3} + \dfrac{1}{x^2 - 1}$

20 $\dfrac{2}{x + 1} + \dfrac{4}{x^2 - 1}$

25 $\dfrac{9}{x^2 + x - 2} - \dfrac{3}{x - 1}$

21 $\dfrac{1}{x - 1} - \dfrac{x + 2}{2x^2 - x - 1}$

26 $\dfrac{10}{2x^2 - 3x - 2} - \dfrac{2}{x - 2}$

22 $\dfrac{8}{x^2 - 2x - 15} - \dfrac{1}{x - 5}$

27 $\dfrac{x}{x^2 + 6x + 8} + \dfrac{1}{x + 2}$

23 $\dfrac{2}{x^2 + 4x + 3} - \dfrac{1}{x^2 + 5x + 6}$

28 $\dfrac{1}{x^2 + 9x + 20} + \dfrac{2}{x^2 + 6x + 8}$

The remaining questions involve a mixture of operations. In each case express as a single fraction in its lowest terms.

29 $\dfrac{3x + 2}{3} + \dfrac{x + 1}{4}$

36 $\dfrac{3}{x^2 - 2x - 8} - \dfrac{5}{x^2 - 5x + 4}$

30 $\dfrac{5x - 3}{5} - \dfrac{3x - 2}{4}$

37 $\dfrac{2}{x + 5} + \dfrac{14}{x^2 + 3x - 10}$

31 $\dfrac{1}{a} \times \dfrac{1}{b}$

38 $\dfrac{8pq}{r^2} \times \dfrac{r}{q^2}$

32 $1 \div \dfrac{a}{b}$

39 $\dfrac{T(T - 1)}{T + 2} \times \dfrac{3(T + 2)}{T}$

33 $\dfrac{5}{6d} - \dfrac{2}{3d}$

40 $\dfrac{1}{x^2 - 7x + 12} + \dfrac{1}{x^2 - 5x + 6}$

34 $\dfrac{n - 1}{4} \times \dfrac{3}{n - 1}$

41 $\dfrac{p^2}{p - 5} \div \dfrac{2p}{p - 5}$

35 $\dfrac{6}{s - 2} - \dfrac{4}{s^2 - 4}$

42 $\dfrac{1}{2m^2 + 3m - 2} - \dfrac{1}{3m^2 + 7m + 2}$

43 The nth term of one sequence is $\dfrac{1}{n}$.

The nth term of a second sequence is $\dfrac{1}{n + 2}$.

The corresponding terms of the two sequences are added to form a third sequence.

Find a formula for u_n, the nth term of this third sequence.

CHANGING THE
SUBJECT OF A
FORMULA

On page 88 we obtained the formula $W = 5dnwb \times 10^{-7}$ for the total weight, W grams, of a book with n pages each measuring w mm by b mm when the paper used has 'weight' $d\,\mathrm{g/m^2}$.

If n, w and b have fixed values, say 300, 212 and 155 respectively, the formula becomes

$$W = 4.929 \times d$$

This can be used to find W for a variety of values of d.

However, to find d for several different values of W requires an extra step each time, namely solving the resulting equation for d. In such circumstances it is quicker to start by rearranging the formula as

$$d = \frac{W}{4.929}$$

so that d can be found directly for each different value of W.

By rearranging $W = 4.929 \times d$ as $d = \dfrac{W}{4.929}$, we have changed the subject of the formula from W to d.

In Book 9A, we changed the subject of formulas where only one or two operations were needed. We now extend the process to formulas requiring more operations.

Remember that changing the subject of a formula is like solving an equation so, if you cannot see how to proceed, it may help to replace all the letters, except the one to be made the subject, by numbers.

Remember also that when solving an equation, first multiply out any brackets; the same applies to changing the subject of a formula.

EXERCISE 4E

In questions **1** to **6** find x in terms of the other letters or numbers.

1 $2(x+1) = 5$

4 $a(2x+m) = y$

2 $a(x+b) = c$

5 $2(4-x) = b$

3 $2(2x-5) = 1$

6 $p(1+5x) = 4$

Make b the subject of the formula $A = 2L(b+c)$

$A = 2L(b+c)$

$A = 2Lb + 2Lc$

$A - 2Lc = 2Lb$

$\dfrac{A - 2Lc}{2L} = b$

First multiply out the bracket.
Next isolate the term containing b on one side, i.e. take $2Lc$ from both sides.
Finally divide both sides by $2L$.

In questions **7** to **16**, make the letter in the bracket the subject of the formula.

7 $p(q+r) = 1$ (q)

12 $x(y-z) = 2$ (y)

8 $3(P-Q) = 2$ (P)

13 $m - pr = mr$ (p)

9 $X = 5Y(c-2)$ (c)

14 $A = \frac{1}{2}h(a+b)$ (a)

10 $L = D(A-B)$ (A)

15 $C = 2\pi(r+R)$ (R)

11 $S(2T-1) = v-2$ (T)

16 $A = b(\frac{1}{2}h+1)$ (h)

17 The height, h cm, of an adult and the length, l cm, of the humerus (upper arm bone) are related approximately by the formula

$$h = 3(l + 30)$$

a Make l the subject of the formula.

b Most two-year-old children are between 80 cm and 110 cm tall. Explain why it is impossible to use this formula to find the length of the upper arm of a two-year-old.

18 If $A = 3n(a+l)$

a find a when $A = 72$, $n = 6$ and $l = 6$

b make a the subject of the formula and use your result to check your answer to part **a**.

19 A firework is shot vertically upwards with velocity u m/s. The velocity, v m/s, of the firework t seconds later is given by

$$v = u - gt$$

a Make t the subject of the formula.

b Use your result from part **a** to find t when $v = 5$, $u = 250$ and $g = 9.81$.

c Describe how you can check your answer to part **b**.

20 The formula

$$N = \tfrac{1}{2}n(n-3)$$

gives the number of diagonals, N, of a polygon with n sides.

a Find n when $N = 20$.

b Make n the subject of the formula and use your result to check your answer to part **a**.

FORMULAS INVOLVING SQUARES AND SQUARE ROOTS

Remember that if $x^2 = 4$ then x has *two* values, i.e. $x = \pm 2$.

Similarly, if $x^2 = a$ then $x = \pm\sqrt{a}$

Remember also that only the positive square root is denoted by $\sqrt{a}$.

EXERCISE 4F

Find x if   **a** $4x^2 = 9$ **b** $ax^2 = b$ **c** $2(x-a)^2 = p$

> Isolate the squared term involving x then take the square root of each side.

a $4x^2 = 9$

$$x^2 = \frac{9}{4}$$

$$x = \pm\frac{3}{2}$$

b $ax^2 = b$

$$x^2 = \frac{b}{a}$$

$$x = \pm\sqrt{\frac{b}{a}}$$

c $2(x-a)^2 = p$

$$(x-a)^2 = \frac{p}{2}$$

$$x - a = \pm\sqrt{\frac{p}{2}}$$

$$x = a \pm\sqrt{\frac{p}{2}}$$

Find x in terms of the other letters or numbers.

1 $6x^2 = 24$

2 $9x^2 = 25$

3 $3x^2 + 4 = 9$

4 $x^2 = p$

5 $px^2 = q$

6 $px^2 = q^2$

7 $x^2 = p + q$

8 $\dfrac{ax^2}{b} = c$

9 $(x-4)^2 = 9$

10 $(x-a)^2 = b$

11 $4 = 9(x-3)^2$

12 $s = t(x-5)^2$

13 $A = \tfrac{1}{2}t(x-2)^2$

14 $\tfrac{1}{3}P = 4(2x-a)^2$

15 $2(a-x)^2 = R$

Make x the subject of the formula

a $a = b\sqrt{x}$ **b** $a = \sqrt{b+x}$ **c** $a = b + \sqrt{x}$

> First isolate the term containing the square root then square both sides.

a $a = b\sqrt{x}$

$\dfrac{a}{b} = \sqrt{x}$

$\dfrac{a^2}{b^2} = x$

i.e. $x = \dfrac{a^2}{b^2}$

b $a = \sqrt{b+x}$

$a^2 = b + x$

$a^2 - b = x$

i.e. $x = a^2 - b$

> Note that $\sqrt{b+x}$ is *not* $\sqrt{b} + \sqrt{x}$
> Similarly $(\sqrt{b} + \sqrt{x})^2$ is *not* $b + x$;
> $(\sqrt{b} + \sqrt{x})^2 = b + 2\sqrt{bx} + x$

c $a = b + \sqrt{x}$

$a - b = \sqrt{x}$

$(a - b)^2 = x$

i.e. $x = (a - b)^2$

Find x in terms of the other letters or numbers.

16 $\sqrt{x} = 4$ **20** $p\sqrt{x} = q$ **24** $\sqrt{x} + 3 = 10$

17 $3\sqrt{x} = 2$ **21** $\sqrt{px} = r$ **25** $a = b + \sqrt{x}$

18 $\sqrt{3x} = 9$ **22** $\sqrt{x} = p\sqrt{q}$ **26** $\sqrt{x-1} + 4 = 7$

19 $\sqrt{x} = a$ **23** $\sqrt{x+a} = 4$ **27** $s = t + \sqrt{x-t}$

In questions **28** to **39** make the letter in the bracket the subject of the formula.

28 $4p^2 = q$ (p) **32** $\sqrt{A+B} = C$ (A)

29 $a = 2\sqrt{p}$ (p) **33** $D = \sqrt{\dfrac{3h}{2}}$ (h)

30 $\sqrt{x+a} = b$ (a) **34** $\sqrt{z} = \sqrt{a+b}$ (a)

31 $a^2 + b = c$ (a) **35** $\sqrt{x^2 + a^2} = b$ (x)

36 $R = s(m - Q)^2$ (m) **38** $2a + \sqrt{a - b} = c$ (b)

37 $a + \sqrt{x} = p$ (x) **39** $r^2 = l(p - r)^2$ (r)

40 If $z = 2(x^2 + y^2)$

  a find x when $z = 26$ and $y = 2$

  b make x the subject of the formula and use the result to check
    your answer to part **a**.

41 If $P = \sqrt{Q + R}$

  a find Q when $P = 5$ and $R = 5$

  b make Q the subject of the formula and use the result to check
    your answer to part **a**.

**FORMULAS
INVOLVING
FRACTIONS**

When solving fractional equations or changing the subject of a formula
involving fractions, all fractions should be removed *as soon as possible* by
multiplying by the appropriate number or letters.

EXERCISE 4G

Make x the subject of the formula

a $\dfrac{x}{a} + \dfrac{x}{b} = c$ **b** $\dfrac{x}{a - b} = c$

a $\dfrac{x}{a} + \dfrac{x}{b} = c$

> Multiply both sides by ab

$$ab \times \frac{x}{a} + ab \times \frac{x}{b} = ab \times c$$

$$bx + ax = abc$$

$$x(b + a) = abc$$

$$x = \frac{abc}{a + b}$$

b $\dfrac{x}{a - b} = c$

> Multiply both sides by $(a - b)$

$$(a - b) \times \frac{x}{a - b} = (a - b) \times c$$

$$x = c(a - b)$$

In questions **1** to **12**, find x in terms of the other letters or numbers. Remember to eliminate fractions first.

1 $\dfrac{x}{6} = 4$ **5** $\dfrac{x}{p} = q$ **9** $\dfrac{x}{a} + b = c$

2 $\dfrac{2x}{3} = 5$ **6** $\dfrac{x}{p} - \dfrac{x}{q} = 1$ **10** $\dfrac{x+a}{b} = \dfrac{x-b}{a}$

3 $\dfrac{x}{2} + \dfrac{x}{3} = \dfrac{4}{3}$ **7** $\dfrac{ax}{p} = r$ **11** $\dfrac{x}{a} = \dfrac{x+b}{a+b}$

4 $\dfrac{2x}{3} - \dfrac{x}{4} = 1$ **8** $\dfrac{x}{p+q} = r$ **12** $\dfrac{x}{a} + \dfrac{x}{b} = \dfrac{c}{a}$

In each question from **13** to **24**, make the letter in the bracket the subject of the formula.

13 $I = \dfrac{PTR}{100}$ (R) **19** $\dfrac{s}{x} = \dfrac{r}{x} + t$ (x)

14 $A = \dfrac{n}{2}(a+1)$ (n) **20** $a = 2\sqrt{\dfrac{p}{q}}$ (q)

15 $P = \dfrac{Q+R}{4}$ (Q) **21** $T = 2\pi\sqrt{\dfrac{l}{g}}$ (l)

16 $\dfrac{a}{3} = \dfrac{b}{2} - \dfrac{c}{4}$ (b) **22** $t = \dfrac{2Hh}{H+h}$ (H)

17 $\dfrac{1}{x} = \dfrac{1}{a} + \dfrac{1}{b}$ (x) **23** $a^2 + \dfrac{b}{X} + \dfrac{c}{bX} = 0$ (X)

18 $\dfrac{p}{x} + \dfrac{q}{x} + \dfrac{r}{x} = 1$ (x) **24** $\dfrac{L}{M} = \dfrac{2a}{B-b}$ (B)

The remaining questions give practice on a variety of formulas. In each question, make the letter in the bracket the subject of the formula.

25 $v = u + at$ (t) **30** $A = \frac{1}{2}(a+b)h$ (h)

26 $A = \frac{1}{2}bh$ (h) **31** $\dfrac{1}{v} + \dfrac{1}{u} = \dfrac{1}{f}$ (f)

27 $a^2 = b^2 + c^2$ (c) **32** $A = \frac{1}{2}(a+b)h$ (a)

28 $s = \dfrac{t}{2}(u+v)$ (v) **33** $\dfrac{1}{v} + \dfrac{1}{u} = \dfrac{1}{f}$ (u)

29 $s = \dfrac{t}{2}(u+v)$ (t) **34** $v^2 = u^2 + 2as$ (a)

35 $A = \pi r^2 + \pi r h$ (h)

36 $v^2 = u^2 + 2as$ (u)

37 $v = \omega\sqrt{a^2 - x^2}$ (a)

38 $A = \pi r\sqrt{h^2 + r^2}$ (h)

39 $s = ut + \frac{1}{2}at^2$ (u)

40 $s = ut + \frac{1}{2}at^2$ (a)

41 $A = \frac{1}{2}pq \sin R$ (p)

42 $E = \frac{1}{2}m(v^2 - u^2)$ (u)

43 $T = 2\pi\sqrt{\dfrac{l}{g}}$ (g)

44 $A = P + \dfrac{PTR}{100}$ (R)

45 A computer is bought in for £C and sold for £S. The percentage gain is p%.

  a Find a formula for p in terms of C and S.

  b Make C the subject of the formula.

SUBSTITUTION

A number of different sized circular rugs are shop-soiled. They are entered in the stock-list by their circumferences.

Tony has to order enough cleaning powder to clean all the rugs and he has to find the area of each rug in order to work out the quantity of cleaning powder to apply.

We know that the circumference of a circle is given by $C = 2\pi r$ and that the area of a circle is given by $A = \pi r^2$.

Tony can use the formula $C = 2\pi r$ to find the value of r. He can then find the area by substituting this value for r in the formula $A = \pi r^2$.

As Tony has to work out the areas of several circular rugs of different sizes, he can do it directly by first expressing A in terms of C. This can be done by making r the subject of $C = 2\pi r$, and then substituting the expression obtained for r in the formula $A = \pi r^2$, i.e. $C = 2\pi r$ gives $r = \dfrac{C}{2\pi}$

Substituting $\dfrac{C}{2\pi}$ for r in the formula $A = \pi r^2$ gives

$$A = \pi \times \left(\frac{C}{2\pi}\right)^2$$

$$A = {}'\pi \times \frac{C^2}{4\pi^2}{}_\pi$$

$$A = \frac{C^2}{4\pi}$$

In general when two formulas both contain the same letter, this letter can be eliminated by

- making that letter the subject of the simpler formula
- substituting the expression found for that letter in the second formula.

EXERCISE 4H

> Given that $a = x + y$ and $b = x^2 + y^2$, find a formula for b in terms of a and x.
>
> > To find b in terms of a and x, we need to eliminate y from the pair of formulas. We will use $a = x + y$ to find y in terms of a and x as it is the simpler formula.
>
> $a = x + y$ gives $y = a - x$
> Substituting $(a - x)$ for y in $b = x^2 + y^2$ gives
>
> $b = x^2 + (a - x)^2$ > > This can now be simplified by expanding the bracket and collecting like terms.
> $b = x^2 + a^2 - 2ax + x^2$
> $b = 2x^2 - 2ax + a^2$

1 If $p = a - b$ and $q = a + ab$ find q in terms of p and a.

2 Given that $T = s + 2v$ and $U = s(s - v)$, find U in terms of s and T.

3 Given that $E = \frac{1}{2}nF$ and $V = \frac{1}{3}nF$, use the relationship $F = E - V + 2$ to find a formula for F in terms of n.

4 The formula for the volume of a cylinder is $V = \pi r^2 h$ and the formula for the curved surface area of a cylinder is $A = 2\pi rh$. Find a formula for V in terms of A and r.

5 Use the formulas $v = u + at$ and $s = ut + \frac{1}{2}at^2$ to find a formula for s in terms of v, u and a.

6 Water from a dripping radiator is forming a circular pool on the floor. The radius of this pool is r cm and is increasing so that t seconds after the drips started, $r = 2\sqrt{t}$.

a Write down the formula for the area, A cm^2, of the pool in terms of r.

b Find a formula for A in terms of t and hence find the area of the pool when the radiator has been dripping for one minute.

7 The temperature of a gas oven is set using the Gas Mark scale.
The formula $T = 25G + 250$ is used to convert Gas Mark G to $T°$ Fahrenheit.
The formula $t = 14G + 121$ is used to convert Gas Mark G to $t°$ Celsius.
Use these two formulas to find T in terms of t.

8 a Use the equations $x + y = 3$ and $x^2 + y^2 = 17$ to find an equation in x only, by substituting an expression for y obtained from the first equation into the second equation.

b Solve this equation and hence find the values of x and y that satisfy both the original equations.

9 a Explain why the equations $x^2 + y^2 = 5$ and $x + y = 3$ cannot be solved simultaneously by addition or subtraction.

b Use a method similar to that described in question **8** to solve the equations $x^2 + y^2 = 5$ and $x + y = 3$.

10 Use substitution to solve the following pairs of equations simultaneously.

a $2xy + y = 10$
$\quad x + y = 4$

b $x^2 - 2xy = 32$
$\quad y + x = 2$

c $x + y = 7$
$\quad xy = 12$

11 The solid shown is a cube of edge x cm with a hole, whose cross-section is a square of side 4 cm, cut through it perpendicular to two faces.

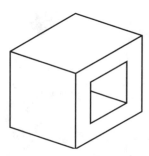

a The volume of the solid is V cm^3.
Find a formula for V in terms of x.

b The external surface area of the solid is A cm^2.
Find a formula for A in terms of x.

c Use your results from parts **a** and **b** to find the volume of the solid when $A = 132$ cm^2.

12 The curved surface area of the cone shown is given by $A = \pi r l$.

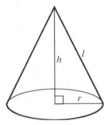

a Find l in terms of r and h.

b Find A in terms of r and h.

c Given that the volume, V cubic units, is given by $V = \frac{1}{3}\pi r^2 h$,

find V in terms of A and r.

13 The table shows how the terms of two sequences relate to their position in the sequence.

n	1	2	3	4	5	...	n	...
nth term of sequence P, p_n	1	$\frac{1}{2}$	$\frac{1}{3}$	$\frac{1}{4}$	$\frac{1}{5}$			
nth term of sequence Q, q_n	2	5	10	17	26			

a Find expressions for p_n and q_n in terms of n.

b Hence find q_n in terms of p_n.

MIXED EXERCISE

EXERCISE 4I

1 Find, in standard form without using a calculator, the value of

a $(1.2 \times 10^{-4}) \times (1.5 \times 10^{-5})$

b $(1.2 \times 10^{-4}) \div (1.5 \times 10^{-5})$

2 At a time when Jupiter, Pluto and the Sun are in line, the distances of Jupiter and Pluto from the Sun are respectively 7.88×10^8 km and 5.95×10^9 km.

What is the distance between Jupiter and Pluto when the two planets and the Sun are in line with

a the planets on opposite sides of the Sun

b the planets on the same side of the Sun?

3 Express as a single fraction in its lowest terms.

a $\dfrac{6}{x-2} - \dfrac{4}{x^2-4}$

c $\dfrac{M}{M^2-4} + \dfrac{M}{M^2-5M+6}$

b $\dfrac{6}{x-2} \div \dfrac{4}{x^2-4}$

d $\dfrac{1}{2x^2+3x-2} \div \dfrac{1}{3x^2+7x+2}$

4 A pendulum of length l metres takes T seconds to swing from one side to the other and back again.

The formula for T is $T = 2\pi\sqrt{\dfrac{l}{g}}$ where $g\,\text{m/s}^2$ is the acceleration due to gravity.

a How long does it take for a pendulum 6 metres long to swing from one side to the other side and back again when $g = 9.8$?

b Make l the subject of the formula.

5 The length, d cm, of the diagonal of the cuboid shown is given by the formula

$$d = \sqrt{a^2 + b^2 + c^2}$$

a How long is the diagonal of a cuboid measuring 2 m by 2.5 m by 80 cm?

b The diagonal of a cuboid is 25 cm long. The cuboid is 8 cm long and 12 cm wide. What is its depth?

c Make c the subject of the formula.

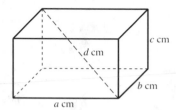

INVESTIGATIONS

1 How accurate are calculators?

a Use your calculator to perform these instructions.
Enter 5×10^{-20} on your calculator.
Now add 2.
Next subtract 1.
Multiply the result by 10^{20}.

b Repeat the instruction given in part **a** without using a calculator. Comment on the results.

c For this part, you will need to use a calculator on which you can enter more than 8 figures. (A graphics calculator will cope with this.)
Find the value of $\sqrt{100\,000\,000} - \sqrt{99\,999\,999}$
How many significant figures are there in your answer?
It is possible to use such a calculator to evaluate $\sqrt{100\,000\,000} - \sqrt{99\,999\,999}$ to 11 significant figures. Can you discover how to do this?

d A basic scientific calculator, on which you cannot enter more than eight figures, can be used to enter the numbers $\sqrt{100\,000\,000} - \sqrt{99\,999\,999}$ by first writing them in another form. How can this be done? Try it and comment on the result.

2 The number 495

  a Choose any three digits, not all the same, and then arrange them to make the largest possible three-figure number.

  b Now reverse the digits to give another three-figure number and subtract it from the first number.

  c Using the digits of the number given in part **b**, repeat the process until you find a pattern. (The title of this investigation gives a clue.)

  d The object of this investigation is to find out whether what you find in part **c** always happens whatever number is chosen to start with. One method is to try all the possible numbers, but there are a lot of them! Another method is to find a general formula for the first number and then apply the process to this formula: suppose that the digits, in descending order of size are a, b, c. Remembering that not more than two digits can be the same, what conditions apply to a, b and c?

  e Write down a formula for the first number, n_1, in terms of a, b and c.

  f Write down a formula for the second number, n_2, in terms of a, b and c.

  g Now find a formula for the third number, $n_1 - n_2$, in terms of a, b and c.

  h Use the formula found in part **g** together with the conditions for a, b and c, to find the possible numbers given by the first subtraction. Now investigate these as the numbers to start with.

GRAPHS

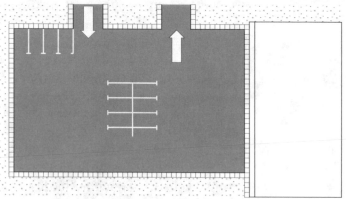

The planning consent for a new store requires that at least 50 parking spaces are provided. When constraints such as the shape of the plot, road access and so on are taken into account, it is found that the number of possible parking spaces, x, is such that $x^2 - 120x + 3200 \leqslant 0$.

- This means that the possible number of parking spaces, x, has to satisfy the inequalities $x \geqslant 50$ and $x^2 - 120x + 3200 \leqslant 0$.
  In order to find out the number of spaces that are possible, we need to be able to solve the inequality $x^2 - 120x + 3200 \leqslant 0$.

EXERCISE 5A

This exercise is intended for group discussion and is based on the following problem.

Open tins with square bases can be made from square sheets of metal of side 50 cm. Smaller squares are removed from each of the corners, and the sides are bent up and the edges then soldered. The only constraint on these tins is that they must each have a capacity greater than one litre. The problem is to find the possible sizes of the squares that are cut from the sheet of metal.

1 What can you do to help you understand how the tins are made?

2 What steps are needed in order to find a mathematical relationship between the capacity of a tin and the size of the squares removed from the sheet?

3 How can you visualise how the capacity of the tin changes with the size of the squares removed from the sheet?

4 The problem is changed so that, instead of having a capacity greater than one litre, the tins have to hold exactly two litres. How does this change the mathematical nature of the problem to be solved?

SKETCHING CURVES

The problem at the start of this chapter involves the inequality
$$x^2 - 120x + 3200 \leqslant 0$$
There are many values of x that satisfy this inequality (and many that do not).

Clearly the value of the expression $x^2 - 120x + 3200$ depends on the value of x and we can 'see' how these values are related by drawing the graph of
$$y = x^2 - 120x + 3200$$
In general we can get this 'picture' without making an accurate plot; we can draw a sketch by using known and easily obtained facts.

A sketch graph should show the shape of the curve and its position on the axes. The axes do not need to be scaled but the values where the curve crosses the axes should be shown. The sketch should not be too small and, unless you can draw straight lines freehand, it is a good idea to use a ruler to draw the axes.

In the case of $y = x^2 - 120x + 3200$ we know that the curve is a U-shaped parabola.
We can position the curve on the axes by finding where it crosses the y-axis and the x-axis.

This curve cuts the y-axis where $x = 0$, i.e. where $y = 3200$,

and   cuts the x-axis where $y = 0$, i.e. where
$$x^2 - 120x + 3200 = 0$$
$$\Rightarrow \qquad (x - 80)(x - 40) = 0$$
$$\Rightarrow \qquad x = 80 \text{ and } x = 40$$

We now have enough information to sketch the graph.

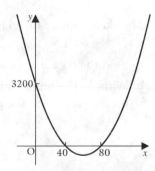

The following exercise involves quadratic, cubic or reciprocal curves. If you need reminding about the shapes of these curves, refer to Summary 1 at the front of this book.

1 Draw a sketch of the curve given by the equation

a $y = (x-1)(x-6)$ **f** $y = x^2 + 5$

b $y = (x+4)(x+7)$ **g** $y = 4 - x^2$

c $y = x^2 - 2x - 3$ **h** $y = (4-x)(5+x)$

d $y = x^2 + 8x + 12$ **i** $y = (x+9)(6-x)$

e $y = x(4-x)$ **j** $y = (5-x)(x-2)$

2 The sketch shows the graph of
$y = x^2 - 5x + 6$

  a Find the coordinates of A, B and C.

  b Find the equation of the straight line joining A and C.

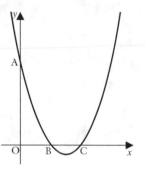

3 The equation of the curve shown in the sketch is
$y = x^2 + px + q$

Find   **a** p and q

       b the coordinates of A.

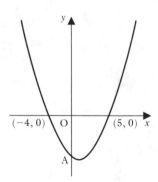

4 The sketch shows the graph of
$y = x^2 + 6x + 9$

  a Find the coordinates of A and B.

  b Without plotting points sketch, on the same axes, the graph of
$y = x^2 - 6x + 9$

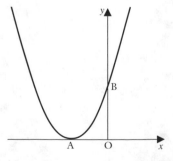

5 Sketch, on the same axes, the graphs of $y = x^2 - 1$, $y = x^2$ and $y = x^2 + 2$, clearly distinguishing between them.

6 On the same axes sketch the graphs of $y = x^2$ and $y = -x^2$. Describe a transformation that maps the first curve to the second.

7 Sketch, on the same axes, the graphs of $y = x^2 - 4$ and $y = -x^2 + 4$ Describe a transformation that maps the first curve to the second.

8 The sketch shows the graph of $y = 9 - x^2$

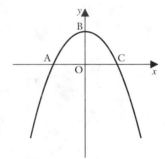

  a Find the coordinates of A, B and C.

  b Without plotting points, sketch on the same axes the graph of $y = x^2 - 9$

Sketch the cubic graph given by the equation $y = x^3 - 4x$

> The x^3 term is positive and therefore the shape of the curve is either
>
> $\sim$ or $\diagup$
>
> $$y = x^3 - 4x$$
> $$= x(x^2 - 4)$$
> $$= x(x+2)(x-2)$$
>
> The curve crosses the x-axis when $y = 0$, i.e. when $x = 0$, $x = -2$ and $x = 2$.

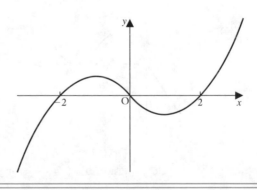

---

9 Draw a sketch of the curve given by the equation

  a $y = (x-1)(x-3)(x-5)$ **d** $y = 9x - x^3$

  b $y = (x+1)(x-2)(x+7)$ **e** $y = 3x(4 - 2x^2)$

  c $y = (x+1)(x+3)(x+6)$ **f** $y = x^3 - 2x^2 + x$

10

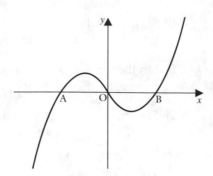

The sketch shows the graph of $y = x^3 - x^2 - 12x$ Find the coordinates of A and B.

11

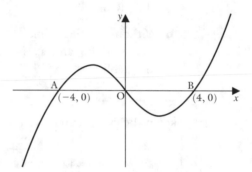

The equation of the cubic curve shown in the sketch is $y = x^3 + ax^2 + bx$ If the curve passes through the points A($-4, 0$) and B($4, 0$) find the values a and b.

12

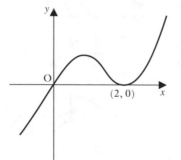

Find the equation of the cubic curve shown in the diagram.

13 Sketch the graph of $y = \dfrac{10}{x}$ for values of x between 1 and 10.

14 Sketch the graph of $y = \dfrac{-12}{x}$ showing clearly the two parts of the curve.

15 Sketch the graph of $y = \dfrac{2}{x}$.

In questions **16** to **19** several possible answers are given. Write down the letter that corresponds to the correct answer.

16 The graph of $y = x^2 + 6x + 8$ could be

A 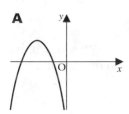 **B** 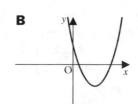 **C** 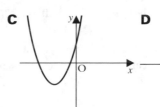 **D**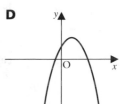

17 The graph of $y = x(x^2 - 9)$ could be

A 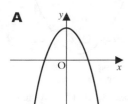 **B** 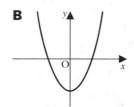 **C** 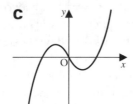 **D**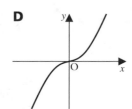

18 The graph of $y = -\dfrac{15}{x}$ could be

A 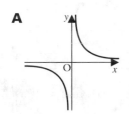 **B** 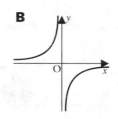 **C** 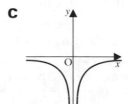 **D**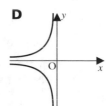

19

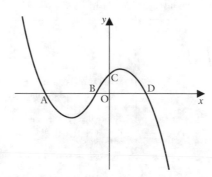

The sketch shows the graph of $y = (x + 5)(x + 1)(4 - x)$ The coordinates of C are

A $(0, 5)$ **B** $(0, 1)$ **C** $(0, 4)$ **D** $(0, 20)$

USING SKETCH GRAPHS TO SOLVE INEQUALITIES

At the start of this chapter we saw that the planning consent for a new store and the shape of the plot on which it is to be built dictate that the possible number of parking spaces, x, has to satisfy the inequalities

$$x \geqslant 50 \quad \text{and} \quad x^2 - 120x + 3200 \leqslant 0$$

For $y = x^2 - 120x + 3200$, the values of x for which $x^2 - 120x + 3200 \leqslant 0$ correspond to the values of y for which $y \leqslant 0$, i.e. the values of y that are negative. These values are those for which the curve is below the x-axis and they can be seen clearly on the sketch of the graph.

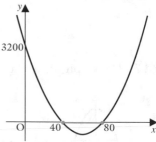

Now we can see that

$$x^2 - 120x + 3200 \leqslant 0 \quad \text{for} \quad 40 \leqslant x \leqslant 80$$

When we add the condition that $x \geqslant 50$, we see that between 50 and 80 parking spaces will satisfy all the constraints placed on the development.

There are several graphs printed in this book from which you need to take readings. To avoid drawing on the book we suggest you use a clear plastic ruler on the graph, or use tracing paper.

EXERCISE 5C

1 Find the range of values of x for which

a $x^2 - 4 \leqslant 0$ **b** $x^2 - 25 \leqslant 0$ **c** $x^2 - 3x + 2 \leqslant 0$

Find the values of x for which $x^2 > 3x$

> First rearrange the inequality so that the RHS is zero, i.e. $x^2 - 3x > 0$.
> (Remember that adding or subtracting the same quantity on each side of an inequality does not alter its truth.)
> Now consider the curve $y = x^2 - 3x$; this is a parabola that crosses the x-axis where $x^2 - 3x = 0$,
> i.e. where $x(x - 3) = 0 \Rightarrow x = 0$ and $x = 3$.
> Now we can draw a sketch of the curve.

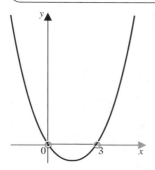

> When $x^2 - 3x > 0$, $y > 0$. This applies to those parts of the curve that are above the x-axis.
> The corresponding values of x are $x < 0$ and $x > 3$.
> Notice that $y = 0$ is not included in the inequality, therefore neither are $x = 0$ nor $x = 3$. This is shown by open circles at 0 and 3.

$x^2 > 3x$ when $x < 0$ and $x > 3$

2 Find the range of values of x for which

a $x^2 > 36$ **d** $x^2 - 6x + 10 \leqslant 2$

b $x^2 < 7x$ **e** $x^2 \geqslant 16$

c $x^2 - 4x < 5$ **f** $3 - 2x < x^2$

3 a Use the formula to find the values of x for which
$x^2 + x - 3 = 0$, leaving your answers in square root form.

  b Hence find the values of x for which $x^2 + x - 3 < 0$

4

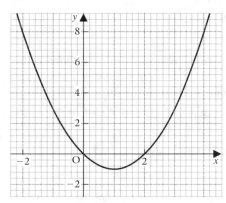

The diagram shows the graph of the curve $y = x^2 - 2x$

  a Use the graph to write down the solutions of the equations

    i $x^2 - 2x = 4$ **ii** $x^2 - 2x = 1$

  b Hence find the range of values of x for which

    i $x^2 - 2x < 4$ **ii** $x^2 - 2x \geqslant 1$

  c Explain why there are no values of x for which $x^2 - 2x < -2$

5

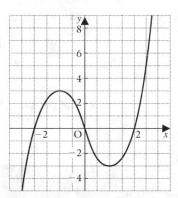

The diagram shows the graph of the curve $y = x^3 - 4x$

  a Use the graph to solve the equations

    i $x^3 - 4x = 0$ **ii** $x^3 - 4x = 2$

  b Hence find the ranges of values of x for which

    i $x^3 - 4x > 0$ **ii** $x^3 - 4x < 2$

6 In a triangle ABC,
$AB = x$ cm, $AC = (x + 2)$ cm, and $BC = (x + 5)$ cm.

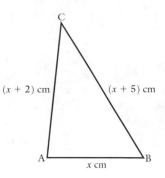

(x + 2) cm   (x + 5) cm

x cm

  a Write down, in terms of x, a relationship that is satisfied if $B\widehat{A}C$ is 90°.
     Find, correct to 3 significant figures, the values of x for which $B\widehat{A}C$ is 90°.

  b Write down, in terms of x, a relationship that is satisfied if $B\widehat{A}C < 90°$.
     Find the values of x for which $B\widehat{A}C < 90°$.

7 A path of width x metres is to be built round two sides of a building. The width of the path has to be more than 1.5 metres, and the area of the path must be such that x satisfies the condition $x^2 - 3x - 4 < 0$.
Find the range for the possible widths of the path.

8 The terms of a sequence are $1, 4, 9, 16, \ldots$

  a Find, in terms of n, an expression for the nth term of this sequence.

  b The size of the terms of this sequence obviously increase as the sequence progresses and eventually they are going to be larger than 10 000.
     Find, in terms of n, a relationship that is satisfied by the terms that are greater than 10 000.
     Hence find which term of this sequence is the first that is greater than 10 000.

9 **a** Sketch the curve $y = x(x - 2)(x - 3)$

  b Hence find the ranges of values of x for which $x(x - 2)(x - 3) < 0$

  c The width of a box is x inches and it has to satisfy the condition that

$$x(x - 2)(x - 3) < 0$$

  Find the range in which the width of the box lies.

10 The diagram shows a sequence of patterns made from blue and grey tiles.

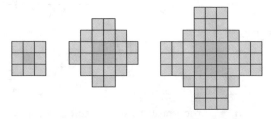

  a Write down, in terms of n, the number of blue tiles in the nth pattern of this sequence.

  b Which is the highest number pattern that has less than 1000 blue tiles in it?

11 A cannon ball is fired into the air and t seconds later it is s metres above the ground where

$$s = 45t - 5t^2$$

a Find the range of values of t for which $s > 40$.

b Find the time for which the cannon ball is more than 40 metres above the ground.

12 The nth term of a sequence is $\dfrac{10}{n}$. Find the values of n for which $\dfrac{10}{n} > 1$.

Hence write down the terms of this sequence that are greater than 1.

13 A car rally is in two stages. The first stage is 110 miles and the second stage is 180 miles. The rally has to be completed in 4 hours or less. Kay judges that she can average 10 mph more on the second section than she can average on the first section.

a If Kay drives the first section at an average speed of x mph, write down

  i her time for the first section

  ii her average speed for the second section

  iii her time for the second section.

b Explain why x is such that $x > 0$ and show that, in order to complete the rally within the time limit, x must satisfy the inequality

$$2x^2 - 125x - 550 \geqslant 0$$

c The first section of the rally is on public roads so the maximum average speed over this section is 70 mph. Find the range in which Kay's average speed must lie on this section in order to finish the rally within the time limit.

SOLVING QUADRATIC INEQUALITIES ALGEBRAICALLY

Instead of drawing a sketch graph to solve an inequality, we can use a table. Consider the inequality $x^2 < 7x$

As before we rearrange the inequality to give zero on the right-hand side,

i.e. $x^2 - 7x < 0$

First we find where $x^2 - 7x$ is zero.

i.e. we solve the equation $x^2 - 7x = 0$,

$$\Rightarrow x(x - 7) = 0, \quad \Rightarrow \quad x = 0 \text{ and } x = 7$$

Then we need to find whether $x^2 - 7x$ is greater than or less than zero (that is, +ve or −ve) for each of the ranges $x < 0, \ 0 < x < 7, \ x > 7$

This can be done in a table:

	$x < 0$	$0 < x < 7$	$x > 7$
$x^2 - 7x$	+	−	+

> To find whether $x^2 - 7x$ is +ve or −ve for a range of values of x, substitute any value of x in that range,
> e.g. for $x < 0$, try $x = -1$, giving $(-1)^2 - 7(-1) = 1 + 7$ which is +ve.

Now we can see that $x^2 - 7x < 0$ when $0 < x < 7$

EXERCISE 5D

Use an algebraic method to solve the inequalities.

1 $x^2 < 6x$ **4** $x^2 - 5x + 4 > 0$ **7** $x^2 + 9x > 0$

2 $x^2 + 5x < 0$ **5** $2x^2 > 9x - 9$ **8** $2x^2 < 3x$

3 $x^2 < 49$ **6** $x^2 < 6x + 7$ **9** $3x^2 + 2x - 1 > 0$

10 Find, algebraically, the range of values of x for which

$$x(x - 2)(x + 5) < 0$$

11 Explain why there are no values of x for which $x^2 + 1 < 0$.

INTERSECTING GRAPHS

In the previous exercises we have solved equations and inequalities by drawing a graph and finding either where the graph crossed the x-axis or where it had a particular value of y.

Sometimes it is easier to draw the simplest graph, e.g. $y = x^2$, together with a suitable straight line graph.

Suppose that we draw the graphs of $y = x^2$ and $y = 2x + 3$ on the same axes.

At the points where these graphs intersect their y-values are the same.

Hence the value of y on the curve (which is x^2) is equal to the value of y on the line (which is $2x + 3$),
i.e. at the points of intersection of the graphs,
$$x^2 = 2x + 3$$
which can be arranged as $x^2 - 2x - 3 = 0$

The values of x at the points of intersection must therefore be the values of x that satisfy the equation $x^2 - 2x - 3 = 0$.

This method can be used to solve any given quadratic equation.

For example, to solve $x^2 - 3x - 7 = 0$
we rearrange the equation as $x^2 = 3x + 7$.

Then we draw, on the same axes, the graphs of $y = x^2$ and $y = 3x + 7$.

At the points where these graphs intersect, the y-values are equal,
i.e. $x^2 = 3x + 7$

Therefore the x-values at the points of intersection are the solutions of the equation $x^2 - 3x - 7 = 0$.

EXERCISE 5E

> What equation can be solved by finding where the graph of
> $y = 5x - 2$ intersects the graph of $y = x^2$?
>
> When the graphs intersect their y-values are equal
> i.e. $\qquad\qquad x^2 = 5x - 2$
> $\Rightarrow \qquad\quad x^2 - 5x + 2 = 0$
> The values of x at the points of intersection must therefore be
> the solutions of the equation $x^2 - 5x + 2 = 0$

1 What equation can be solved by finding where the graph
of $y = x^2$ intersects the graph of the straight line with the
following equation?

    a $y = x + 7$ **d** $y = 5 - 3x$

    b $y = 2x + 5$ **e** $y = -3x - 2$

    c $y = 6x - 4$ **f** $y = \frac{1}{2}x + 3$

2 What straight line graphs should be drawn to intersect the graph of
$y = x^2$ in order to solve the following quadratic equations?

    a $x^2 - 2x - 1 = 0$ **c** $x^2 + 6x + 4 = 0$

    b $x^2 - 7x + 2 = 0$ **d** $2x^2 + 7x + 2 = 0$

3 Sketch on the same axes the graphs of $y = x^2$ and $y = x + 4$ for
values of x in the range -4 to 4.
Estimate the values of x at the points of intersection of the two
graphs.
What equation has these values of x as roots?

4 Sketch the graphs of $y = x^2$ and $y = 5x + 20$ for values of x
from -6 to 9.
Estimate the values of x at the points where the two graphs intersect.
What equation is satisfied at these points?

5 Sketch the graphs of $y = x^2 + 1$ and $y = x + 1$ for values of x
from $x = -2$ to $x = 4$.
Estimate the values of x at the points where the graphs intersect.
What equation has these values as solutions?

6 Sketch the graphs of $y = 1 - x^2$ and $y = 2x$ for values of x from
$x = -3$ to $x = 3$.
Estimate the values of x at the points where the graphs intersect and
write down the equation for which these values are the solutions.

The graph of $y = x^2 + 5x + 4$ is given below.

a Use the graph to find the lowest value of $x^2 + 5x + 4$ and the corresponding value of x.

b Draw on the same axes the graph of $y = x + 6$. Find, in its simplest form, the equation for which the values of x at the points of intersection of the two graphs are the roots. Give the roots of this equation.

c What line should be drawn on this graph to solve the equation $x^2 + 2x - 1 = 0$?

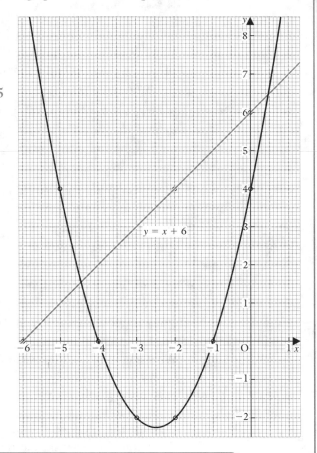

a From the graph, the lowest value of $x^2 + 5x + 4$ (i.e. of y) is -2.2 and it occurs when $x = -2.5$

b

> The graph of $y = x + 6$ is a straight line so we need take only three values of x and find the corresponding values of y.

x	-6	-2	0
$y(= x + 6)$	0	4	6

The graphs intersect where the values of y for the curve and the straight line are equal, i.e. where $x^2 + 5x + 4 = x + 6$ giving $x^2 + 4x - 2 = 0$
This occurs where $x = -4.45$ and $x = 0.45$
The roots of the equation are -4.45 and 0.45

c

> To use the graph of $y = x^2 + 5x + 4$ to solve the equation $x^2 + 2x - 1 = 0$, we arrange the equation so that the LHS is $x^2 + 5x + 4$; we do this by adding $3x + 5$ to both sides.

$$x^2 + 2x - 1 = 0$$
$$\Rightarrow \quad x^2 + 2x + 3x - 1 + 5 = 3x + 5$$
i.e. $\quad x^2 + 5x + 4 = 3x + 5$

LHS = RHS where the graphs $y = x^2 + 5x + 4$ and $y = 3x + 5$ intersect.
Therefore we need to draw the graph of $y = 3x + 5$

7 **a** Make your own copy of the graph of $y = 12 - x^2$ given below. Use graph paper and a scale of 2 cm for 1 unit for x and 1 cm for 1 unit for y.

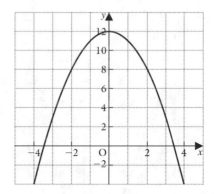

  b Use your graph to solve the equation $12 - x^2 = 0$

  c On the same axes draw the graph of $y = 2x + 7$

  d What equation is satisfied by the values of x at the points of intersection of the graphs drawn?
  Give the solutions of this equation.

  e What line needs to be added to your graph to solve the equation

$$x^2 - x - 10 = 0?$$

  Add this line and hence give the roots of the equation.

8 *Sketch* the graph of $y = x^3$ for values of x from -2 to 2.

  a Add to your sketch the line needed to solve the equation

$$x^3 = 2x$$

  b Estimate the solutions of the equation $x^3 = 2x$.

  c Use a different sketch graph to show the solutions of the equation $x^3 = x^2$.

9 *Sketch* the graph of $y = \dfrac{10}{x}$ for values of x from 1 to 10.

  a Add to your sketch the line needed to solve the equation

$$\frac{10}{x} = x + 1$$

  b Explain why your sketch cannot be used to find all the solutions of the equation $\dfrac{10}{x} = x + 1$.

What line should be used, together with the graph of $y = x^2$, to find the range of values of x for which $2x^2 - x - 3 < 0$?
Sketch the two graphs and hence find the range of values of x for which $2x^2 - x - 3 < 0$

> Rearrange $2x^2 - x - 3 < 0$ so that x^2 is on the LHS.

$2x^2 - x - 3 < 0 \implies 2x^2 < x + 3$, i.e. $x^2 < \frac{1}{2}x + \frac{3}{2}$

Therefore the line $y = \frac{1}{2}x + \frac{3}{2}$ should be used.

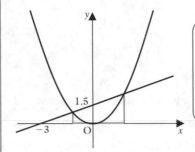

> From the sketch we see that y-values on the curve (i.e. values of x^2) are less than y-values on the line (i.e. values of $\frac{1}{2}x + \frac{3}{2}$) for values of x between the points where the line and the curve intersect. These values are where $x^2 = \frac{1}{2}x + \frac{3}{2}$.

$x^2 = \frac{1}{2}x + \frac{3}{2}$ gives $2x^2 - x - 3 = 0$
$$(2x - 3)(x + 1) = 0$$
$$x = \frac{3}{2} \text{ and } x = -1$$
Therefore $2x^2 - x - 3 < 0$ for $-1 < x < \frac{3}{2}$

10 What graph should be used, together with the graph of $y = x^2$, to solve the equation $2x^2 - x - 12 = 0$?
Sketch the two graphs for values of x in the range -4 to 4.
Use your sketch to estimate the solutions of the equation $2x^2 - x - 12 = 0$.

11 What graph should be used, together with the graph of $y = x^2$, to solve the equation $2 - 5x - x^2 = 0$?
Sketch the two graphs for values of x in the range -6 to 2.
Use your sketch to estimate the solutions of the equation $2 - 5x - x^2 = 0$.

12 What graph should be used, together with $y = x^2$, to solve $x^2 + x - 6 < 0$?
Sketch the graphs and use your sketch to determine the range of values of x for which $x^2 + x - 6 < 0$.

13 Draw the graph of $y = \dfrac{16}{x}$, taking unit intervals for x in the range 1 to 16.

Take 1 cm as unit on both axes. Draw on the same axes the graph of $x + y = 12$

a Write down the value(s) of x at the point(s) where the graphs intersect.

b What equation has these x-values as its roots?

c Write down the range of values of x for which $12 - x \geqslant \dfrac{16}{x}$

14 a Draw the graph of $y = x + \dfrac{1}{x}$ for values of x from $\frac{1}{2}$ to 4, taking the x-values at half-unit intervals. Take 4 cm as 1 unit on both axes.

b Draw, on the same axes, the graph of $x + y = 4$

c Write down the value of x at the point where the graphs intersect.

d Write down, and simplify, the equation which is satisfied by this value of x.

15 A subsidiary of a large company produces electric switchboards. When it produces x thousand switchboards it makes a profit of y thousand pounds, where $y = 7x - (x^2 + 2)$

Corresponding values of x and y are given in the following table.

x	0	1	2	3	4	5	6
y	−2	4	8	10	10	8	4

Draw a graph to represent this data using 4 cm as the unit for x and 1 cm as the unit for y. You may find it helps to plot additional points.

Use your graph to find

a the maximum profit the company can make and the number of switchboards it must produce to give this profit

b the minimum number of switchboards the company must produce in order at least to break even.

c The parent company decides that the subsidiary must make a minimum profit of £6000 to remain in production. Within what range must the number of switchboards lie in order to achieve this?

16 a Draw the graph of $y = x^2 + \dfrac{1}{x}$ for values of x from 0.1 to 3.

If possible use a graphics calculator, otherwise take values of x at half-unit intervals, adding extra values where you need them to help clarify the shape of the curve.

b Add the appropriate line to your graph so that it can be used to solve the equation $3x^2 + \dfrac{3}{x} = 2x + 9$.

c Write down the roots of $3x^2 + \dfrac{3}{x} = 2x + 9$ giving them corrected to 1 decimal place if you plot the graph, or corrected to 2 decimal places if you use a graphics calculator.

17 A farmer has a roll of wire 140 metres long, and wishes to make a rectangular enclosure using a straight wall as one side.

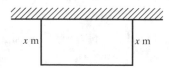

x m x m

If the rectangle is x metres wide, find its length in terms of x, and hence show that the area of the enclosure, $A\,\text{m}^2$, is given by

$$A = 2x(70 - x).$$

Complete the following table to find the values for A corresponding to the given values for x.

x	0	10	20	30	40	50	60	70
$A = 2x(70 - x)$	0	1200		2400		2000	1200	

Draw the graph of $A = 2x(70 - x)$ for values of x from 0 to 70. Take 1 cm to represent 5 units for x and 1 cm to represent 100 units for A.

Use your graph to find

a the width of the enclosure when its area is $1500\,\text{m}^2$

b the maximum area that the farmer can enclose and the corresponding value of x

c the area enclosed when the width of the enclosure is 56 m

d the area enclosed when the length of the enclosure is 56 m.

18

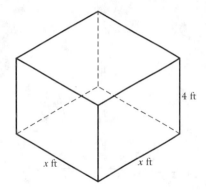

The diagram shows a four-foot-deep water tank with a square base of side x feet.

a Show that the capacity of the tank, C cubic feet, is given by the formula

$$C = 4x^2.$$

b Complete the table below which shows the value of C for various values of x.

x	0.5	1	1.3	1.7	2	2.3	2.7	3	3.3	3.6	4
C	1	4	6.76	11.56			29.2	36	43.6	51.8	64

c Draw the graph of $C = 4x^2$ for values of x from 0 to 4.
Take 4 cm as 1 unit on the x-axis and choose your own scale for the C-axis.

d What value for x will give a capacity of 40 ft^3?

e A householder needs a new tank with a capacity between 30 ft^3 and 40 ft^3.
To fit the tank into the available space the side of the base must be less than 3 feet.
What range of values for x will satisfy these conditions?

19 Sketch the graph of $y = x^2$ for values of x from -3 to 3.

a What line needs to be added to the sketch in order to estimate the solutions of the equation

$$x^2 + 6x + 10 = 0?$$

b Add this line and hence explain why the equation

$$x^2 + 6x + 10 = 0$$

has no solutions.

**PRACTICAL
WORK**

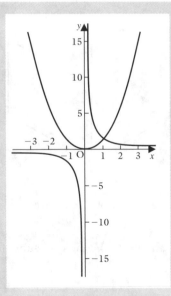

The diagram shows how the graph of $y = x^2 + \dfrac{1}{x}$ can be sketched from sketches of the graphs of $y = x^2$ and $y = \dfrac{1}{x}$ by adding the y-coordinates of points with the same x-coordinates.

First copy the left-hand graph and use it to produce your own sketch of the graph of $y = x^2 + \dfrac{1}{x}$ as shown below.

These graphs can also be combined by subtraction, multiplication and division to give further graphs.

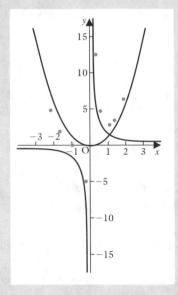

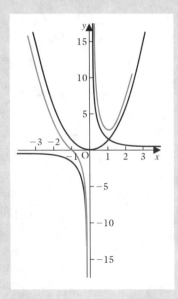

Make three further copies of the top diagram.
Use your copies and the method of combining the y-coordinates to obtain the graph of

a $y = x^2 - \dfrac{1}{x}$ **b** $y = x^2 \times \dfrac{1}{x}$ **c** $y = x^2 \div \dfrac{1}{x}$

You can easily check whether your graphs for parts **b** and **c** are correct – how?

INVESTIGATION

You will need a graphics calculator.

a Investigate the relationship between the graph of $y = x^2$ and the graphs of $y = x^2 + a$ for different values of a, including some negative values.

Describe the relationship as simply as possible.

b Repeat part **a** for the relationship between the graph of $y = x^2$ and the graph of

i $y = (x + a)^2$ **ii** $y = ax^2$

SUMMARY 2

RATIONAL NUMBERS

A rational number can be written in the form $\dfrac{a}{b}$ where a and b are integers.

RECURRING DECIMALS

A recurring decimal is a rational number that has an infinite number of decimal places that contain a repeating pattern; for example,
$$0.\dot{1}2\dot{3} = 0.123\,123\,123\,123\,123\ldots$$

IRRATIONAL NUMBERS

An irrational number cannot be expressed in the form $\dfrac{a}{b}$ where a and b are integers, nor can it be expressed exactly as a decimal; it has an infinite number of decimal places with a non-repeating pattern. Examples of irrational numbers are $\sqrt{2}$, π.

SURDS

The square root of an integer that is not a perfect square is an irrational number and when it is written in square root form, it is called a surd; $\sqrt{2}$, $\sqrt{3}$, and so on, are surds.

THE nth ROOT OF A NUMBER

The nth root of a number is the factor such that n of these factors multiplied together gives the number.
The nth root of x is written as $\sqrt[n]{x}$
For example, $\sqrt[4]{16}$ means the 4th root of 16,
and, as $16 = 2 \times 2 \times 2 \times 2$, $\sqrt[4]{16} = 2$

FRACTIONAL INDICES

$x^{\frac{1}{n}}$ means the nth root of x, i.e. $x^{\frac{1}{n}} = \sqrt[n]{x}$

For example, $8^{\frac{1}{3}} = \sqrt[3]{8} = 2$

LAWS OF INDICES

The four laws of indices are

1 $a^x \times a^y = a^{x+y}$, e.g. $2^3 \times 2^4 = 2^7$

2 $a^x \div a^y = a^{x-y}$, e.g. $2^3 \div 2^4 = 2^{-1}$

3 $a^{-x} = \left(\dfrac{1}{a}\right)^x$, e.g. $2^{-3} = \dfrac{1}{2^3}$

4 $(a^x)^y = a^{xy} = (a^y)^x$, e.g. $(2^2)^3 = 2^6$

QUADRATIC EQUATIONS

To solve a quadratic equation, first arrange the equation in the form

$$ax^2 + bx + c = 0,$$

then, if the left-hand side factorises, use the fact that one or other of the factors is zero.
If the left-hand side does not factorise, use the formula

$$x = \frac{-b \pm \sqrt{b^2 - 4ac}}{2a}$$

CHANGING THE SUBJECT OF A FORMULA

When the letter to be made the subject of a formula is squared, 'solve' the formula for the square and then remember that,

if $x^2 = a$, then $x = \pm\sqrt{a}$

For example, to make a the subject of $b = a^2 + c^2$,
first 'solve' for a^2, giving $a^2 = b - c^2$,
then take the square root of both sides, i.e. $a = \pm\sqrt{b - c^2}$

When a formula contains square roots, first isolate the square root and then square both sides.
For example to make m the subject of $h = 3 - \sqrt{m + n}$,
first 'solve' for $\sqrt{m + n}$ giving $\sqrt{m + n} = 3 - h$
then square both sides, i.e. $m + n = (3 - h)^2$, so $m = (3 - h)^2 - n$

GRAPHS

A *sketch* graph should show the shape of the curve and its position on the axes. The axes do not need to be scaled but the values where the curve crosses the axes should be shown.

To solve a *quadratic inequality* graphically, arrange it in the form
$ax^2 + bx + c <$ or > 0 as appropriate, then sketch the curve
$y = ax^2 + bx + c$
$ax^2 + bx + c < 0$ for the values of x for which the curve is below the
x-axis,
$ax^2 + bx + c > 0$ for the values of x for which the curve is above the
x-axis.

REVISION EXERCISE 2.1 (Chapters 1 and 2)

1 a Which of these numbers are irrational?

i $\frac{3}{5}$ **ii** $\sqrt{3}$ **iii** $0.\dot{7}14\,28\dot{5}$ **iv** $(\sqrt{7})^2$ **v** π

b Express as a fraction in its lowest terms

i $0.\dot{4}$ **ii** $0.00\dot{3}$ **iii** $0.0\dot{7}$ **iv** $0.\dot{2}\dot{3}$

2 Express in terms of the simplest possible single surd

a $\sqrt{100}$ **b** $\sqrt{252}$ **c** $\sqrt{3} \times \sqrt{5}$ **d** $\sqrt{18} \times \sqrt{12}$

3 Simplify

a $\sqrt{3}(2 + 3\sqrt{27})$ **b** $\sqrt{27} + \sqrt{12}$ **c** $\sqrt{75} - \sqrt{48}$

4 Rationalise the denominator

a $\dfrac{4}{\sqrt{2}}$ **b** $\dfrac{2 + \sqrt{3}}{\sqrt{3}}$ **c** $\dfrac{2 + 3\sqrt{2}}{2\sqrt{5}}$

5 a Find

i $\sqrt[4]{16}$ **ii** $\sqrt[3]{-64}$ **iii** $100^{-\frac{1}{2}}$ **iv** $81^{\frac{3}{2}}$

b Find x if **i** $32 = 2^x$ **ii** $10^x = 0.01$

6 Factorise

a $3x^2 - 11x - 4$ **c** $20x^2 - 23x + 6$

b $9x^2 - 4$ **d** $4x^2 - 15x + 14$

7 Solve the equation

a $(3x - 5)(x - 2) = 0$ **d** $6x^2 + 10 = 19x$

b $x(5x - 1) = 0$ **e** $9x^2 + 9x = 4$

c $(2x + 5)(3x + 7) = 0$ **f** $10x^2 + 14 = 39x$

8 a Expand $(2x - 7)^2$ and hence find the values of a, b and c if $(2x - 7)^2 = ax^2 + bx + c$

b Find, without using a calculator, the value of $199^2 - 99^2$

9 The lengths of the sides of a right-angled triangle are $x\,\text{cm}$, $(x + 2)\,\text{cm}$ and $(x - 14)\,\text{cm}$. Find them.

10

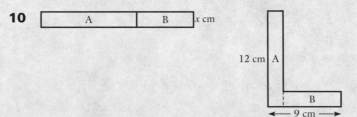

A strip of card of area $54\,\text{cm}^2$ and width $x\,\text{cm}$ is cut into two rectangles which are arranged to form a letter L.

a Use the dimensions given on the diagram to form a quadratic equation in x and solve it.

b Hence find the dimensions of the original strip.

11 Do not use a calculator when answering this question.
All working must be shown.
Simplify each of the following, indicating in each case whether your answer is rational or irrational.

    a $\dfrac{6}{\sqrt{3}} + \sqrt{48}$ **b** $(3 - \sqrt{2})^2$ **c** $25^{\frac{1}{2}} \times 3^{-2}$ (WJEC)

12 **a** Which of the these are rational?

      i $1 + \sqrt{2}$ **ii** π^2 **iii** $3^0 + 3^{-1} + 3^{-2}$

    b When p and q are two different irrational numbers, $p \times q$ can be rational.
Write down one example to show this.

    c Write down a fraction which is equal to the recurring decimal $0.036\,\dot{3}\dot{6}$.   (SEG)

13 Factorise

    a $6p - 12p^2$ **b** $12t^2 - 17t + 6$ (MEG)

14 **a** Calculate the value of $\sqrt{9 \times 10^{-2}}$, giving your answer in standard form.

    b Simplify $(a^2 \times b^{-4})^{\frac{1}{2}}$, writing your answer without negative indices.   (MEG)

**REVISION
EXERCISE 2.2
(Chapters 3
to 5)**

1 **a** Solve the equation $x^2 + 7x + 5 = 0$, giving your answers correct to 2 decimal places.

    b Solve the equation $x^2 + 10x - 3 = 0$, giving your answers in surd form as simply as possible.

2 **a** Expand $(x - 6)\left(\dfrac{4}{x} + 2\right)$

    b Hence solve the equation $(x - 6)\left(\dfrac{4}{x} + 2\right) = 5$

3 One side of a rectangle is 2 cm shorter than another.

    a If the length of a shorter side is x cm write down, in terms of x, an expression for the length of a longer side.

    b The area of the rectangle is 48 cm². Form an equation in x and solve it. Find the lengths of the sides of the rectangle.

4 When the price of satsumas increases by 5 p each, I can buy 3 fewer for £1.80.

    a If the original price is x pence each find, in terms of x, the number of satsumas I can buy for £1.80.

    b Find, in terms of x, the number I can buy for £1.80 when the price of each satsuma increases by 5 p.

    c Form an equation in x and solve it. What was the original price of one satsuma?

5 If $p = 3.2 \times 10^4$ and $q = 8 \times 10^2$, write down in standard form

    a pq **b** $\dfrac{p}{q}$ **c** $p + 100q$

6 Express as a single fraction in its lowest terms

    a $\dfrac{4}{x^2 - 4} - \dfrac{3}{x + 2}$ **c** $\dfrac{9}{x^2 - x - 20} - \dfrac{2}{x^2 - 8x + 15}$

    b $\dfrac{2}{x - 2} - \dfrac{2}{x^2 - 6x + 8}$ **d** $\dfrac{2}{a^2 - 9} + \dfrac{1}{a + 3}$

7 Make the letter in brackets the subject of the formula

    a $4(P + Q) = 3$ (P) **c** $c = \sqrt{a^2 - b^2}$ (a)

    b $A = 2\pi r^2 + 2\pi rh$ (h) **d** $p = 2q + \sqrt{r}$ (r)

8 Draw a sketch of the curve given by the equation

    a $y = (x - 3)(x + 7)$ **b** $y = 9 - x^2$

9 **a** Sketch, on the same axes, the graphs of $y = x^2 - 2$ and $y = 2 - x^2$

    b Write down, in surd form, the coordinates of the points where these two curves cross.

    c Describe a transformation that

      i maps the first curve onto the second

    ii maps the second curve onto the first.

10 **a** Sketch the graph of $y = \dfrac{8}{x}$ for values of x between 1 and 8.

    b Draw a sketch of the curve given by the equation

      i $y = 4x - x^3$ **ii** $y = (x + 2)(x - 2)(x - 3)$

11 A possible points system for the high jump event in athletics is given by

$$P = a(M - b)^2$$

M is the height jumped in cm, P is the number of points awarded and a and b are non-zero positive constants.

a Zero points are scored for a height jumped of 75 cm. What is the value of the constant b?

b Express M in terms of P, a, and b. (SEG)

12 $y = x^3 - 4x - 1$

a Complete the table of values.

x	−2	−1	0	1	2	3
y		2				

b On a grid, draw the graph of $y = x^3 - 4x - 1$

c By drawing a suitable straight line on the grid, solve the equation

$$x^3 - 4x - 3 = -2$$

(London)

13 Solve the equation

$$\frac{3}{x} + \frac{2}{x-1} = 5$$

giving your answers correct to two decimal places. (WJEC)

REVISION EXERCISE 2.3 (Chapters 1 to 5)

Do not use a calculator for any question in this exercise.

1 a Express the following recurring decimals as fractions in their lowest terms.

   i $0.\dot{2}$ **ii** $0.\dot{2}\dot{7}$ **iii** $0.0\dot{8}$

b Simplify   **i** $(\sqrt{8})^3$ **ii** $(\sqrt{3})^6$ **iii** $(\sqrt{5})^5$ **iv** $(0.001)^{\frac{2}{3}}$

2 a Rationalise the denominator $\dfrac{1 + 4\sqrt{2}}{2\sqrt{2}}$

b Expand and simplify   **i** $(\sqrt{5} + 2)(2\sqrt{5} + 3)$ **ii** $(3 - \sqrt{5})^2$

c If $p^{\frac{1}{3}} = 0.8$ write down the value of

   i $p^{-\frac{1}{3}}$ **ii** $p^{\frac{2}{3}}$ **iii** $p^{\frac{2}{3}} \div p^{-\frac{1}{3}}$

3 a Factorise where possible

i $18x^2 + 17x - 3$ **ii** $3x^2 + 10x + 3$ **iii** $27a^2 - 3b^2$

b Solve the equation

i $(x+7)(4x-1) = 0$ **ii** $x(x-6) = 0$ **iii** $9x = 2 - 5x^2$

4 a If $(x-9)^2 = x^2 + px + q$ find the values of p and q.

b The perimeter of a rectangle is 30 cm and its area is 54 cm². Find the sides.

$$\boxed{\quad 54\text{ cm}^2 \qquad} \; x\text{ cm}$$

5 a Solve the equation $4x^2 - 5x - 7 = 0$, giving your answers in surd form.

b Solve the equation $2x^2 - 6x - 1 = 0$, giving exact answers.

6 Solve the equation $(x-5)\left(\dfrac{2}{x}+3\right) = 16$

7 a If $a = 8 \times 10^3$ and $b = 1.5 \times 10^{-3}$ find, in standard form

i ab **ii** $\dfrac{a}{b}$ **iii** $a + 100\,000b$

b Express as a single fraction in its lowest terms

i $2 \div \dfrac{3a}{2b}$ **ii** $\dfrac{2}{x^2 - 16} - \dfrac{3}{x+4}$

8 a If $\dfrac{x-a}{b} = \dfrac{x+b}{a}$ find x in terms of the other letters.

b Make a the subject of the formula

i $A = a^2 + bc$ **ii** $\sqrt{x-a} = 4$

9 Find the values of x for which $x^2 - 7x + 15 < 3$

10 What straight line graph should be drawn to intersect the graph of $y = x^2$ in order to solve the equation

a $x^2 - 3x + 1 = 0$ **b** $2x^2 + 8x - 3 = 0$?

REVISION EXERCISE 2.4 (Chapters 1 to 5)

1 a Which of these are irrational? $(\sqrt{3})^4$, $\dfrac{\sqrt{24}}{\sqrt{2}}$, $\sqrt[3]{3\tfrac{3}{8}}$, $\sqrt{\dfrac{12}{5}}$

b Express as the simplest possible single surd

i $\sqrt{300}$ **ii** $\sqrt{28} \times \sqrt{2}$ **iii** $\sqrt{12} \times \sqrt{15}$

2 a Use a calculator, giving your answers correct to 3 significant figures, to find

i $\sqrt[3]{72}$ **ii** $(2.5)^{\frac{3}{5}}$ **iii** $\sqrt[4]{60}$

b Find **i** $(\sqrt[3]{-8})^2$ **ii** $(a^{\frac{1}{2}})^4$ **iii** x if $10^x = 0.001$

3 Factorise   **a** $6x^2 + 11x + 3$ **c** $3x^2 - 12y^2$

                 b $4x^2 + 22x + 10$ **d** $3 + 2x - x^2$

4 Solve the equation   **a** $(4x - 3)(2x + 3) = 0$ **c** $3x = 10 - 4x^2$

                      b $2x^2 - 17x + 21 = 0$ **d** $x(x - 4)(x + 2) = 0$

5 Solve the following equations. Give all answers correct to 2 decimal places.

    a $6x^2 - x - 8 = 0$ **b** $3x^2 = 9x + 2$

6 Solve the equation $\dfrac{1}{x - 1} + \dfrac{2}{x - 2} = 4$ giving your answers correct to 2 decimal places.

7 Make the letter in brackets the subject of the formula

    a $A = \dfrac{(a + b)h}{2}$ (a) **c** $\dfrac{1}{u} + \dfrac{1}{v} = \dfrac{1}{f}$ (f)

    b $a = b + \sqrt{c}$ (c) **d** $(a - b)^2 = 5$ (a)

8 a Given that $c = a - 2b$ and that $d = 2a(a + 2b)$ find d in terms of a and c.

    b A rectangular rug is x cm wide and $3x$ cm long. The area of the rug is A cm^2.
       Give a formula for   **i** A in terms of x **ii** x in terms of A.

9 The equation of the curve shown in the sketch
is $y = x^2 + bx + c$ Find

    a b and c

    b the coordinates of B

    c the coordinates of the point where the curve crosses the
       y-axis.

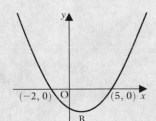

10 a The graph of $y = \dfrac{12}{x}$ could be

A   B   C   D

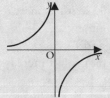 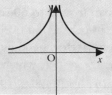 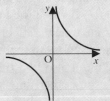 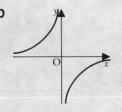

    b A straight line is added to the graph of $y = \dfrac{12}{x}$ to solve the equation $\dfrac{12}{x} - x = 0$.
       What is the equation of the line?

TANGENTS AND AREAS

An outside tap is left dripping and the water from it forms a circular puddle on the ground.

The graph shows how the radius of the puddle changes as time passes.

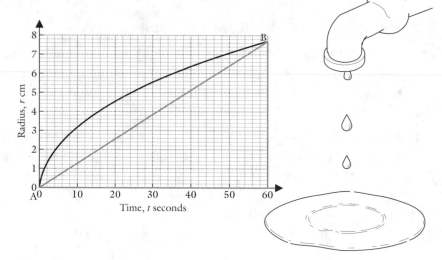

The graph shows that the radius of the puddle continues to increase as the tap drips. Looking at the shape of the curve, we see that the curve is steepest at the start and continues to get flatter as time passes. This means that the radius is increasing most rapidly when the tap starts to drip and the rate of increase of the radius slows down over the 60 second time span.

- Reading from the graph, we can see that the radius has increased from 0 to 7.7 cm in the time span from 0 to 60 seconds, so it has increased at an average rate of $\frac{7.7}{60}$ cm per second over this time span. This corresponds to the gradient of the line joining A and B.
- We can also find the average rate at which the radius has increased for any other time span on this graph. It is not, however, immediately obvious how to find the rate at which the radius is changing at any particular instant, for example, exactly 5 seconds after the tap started dripping. The next exercise investigates how this may be done.

EXERCISE 6A

1 Copy the graph opposite and use your copy to answer the questions.

a Find the points on the curve where $t = 5$ and where $t = 50$ and label them C and D respectively. Draw the line *through* C and D (extend it beyond both C and D). Find

  i the increase in r over this time span

  ii the average rate of increase in r over this time span.

Explain the relationship between the answer to part **ii** and the gradient of the line through C and D.

b Mark the point E on the curve where $t = 30$ and repeat part **a** for the points C and E.

c Mark the point F on the curve where $t = 10$ and repeat part **a** for the points C and F.

d Mark the point G on the curve where $t = 6$ and repeat part **a** for the points C and G.

e Use your results from parts **a** to **d** to give an estimate of the rate at which the radius is increasing when $t = 5$. Discuss the relationship between your estimate and the gradients of the lines.

f Discuss how an improved estimate for the rate of increase of r when $t = 5$ can be found.

2 This is the graph of the curve whose equation is
$$y = x(x - 2)(x - 4)$$

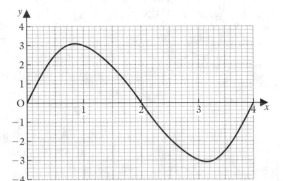

a Discuss how y changes as x increases from $x = 0$ to $x = 3$.

b Find the gradient of the line joining the points $(1, 3)$ and $(2, 0)$ on this curve and discuss the meaning of the gradient in relation to how y is changing with respect to values of x from $x = 1$ to $x = 2$.

c Discuss how you could estimate the change in y with respect to x at the point on the curve where $x = 2$.

TANGENTS TO CURVES

This graph shows the curve whose equation is

$$y = \tfrac{1}{2}x(5 - x)$$

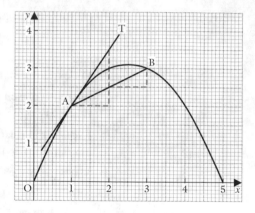

A line joining two points on a curve is a *chord*.
The line AB is a chord of the curve shown.

A line which touches a curve at a point is a *tangent* to the curve at the point. In the diagram, AT is a tangent to the curve at A.

When moving along a curve, the gradient changes continuously. Imagine moving along the curve in the diagram, starting from O. When you get to A imagine that you stop following the curve and move on in a constant direction: you will move along the tangent AT.

Therefore   the gradient of a curve at a point is defined as the gradient of the tangent to the curve at this point.

In the diagram, the gradient of the tangent AT is $\tfrac{3}{2}$, therefore the gradient of the curve at A is $\tfrac{3}{2}$.

Finding a gradient by drawing and measurement means that the curve must be accurately drawn and then the tangent must be positioned carefully. Using a transparent ruler helps and, as a rough guide, the tangent should be approximately at the same 'angle' to the curve on each side of the point of contact.

Discussion from **Exercise 6A** shows that, at a particular point on a curve, we can estimate the rate at which values of y are increasing as values of x increase by finding the gradient of a chord from that point. This estimate is improved by making the chord as short as possible.

From this we deduce that

the gradient of the tangent to the curve at a point gives the rate at which values of y are increasing as values of x increase at this point.

We also saw that the gradient of a chord gives the *average* rate of increase of y-values for the values of x between the ends of the chord.

EXERCISE 6B

1 Draw x- and y-axes from -6 to $+6$ using a scale of 1 cm for 1 unit on both axes. Plot the points A(1, 1), B(3, 2), C($-4, -1$), D($-5, 1$), E(1, 6), F(4, -5).

Find the gradient of

a AB   **b** BC   **c** DE   **d** EF   **e** AD

Explain why it is not possible to give a value for the gradient of AE.

2 Copy and complete the table for $y = \dfrac{x^2}{10}$

x	0	1	2	3	4	5	6	7	8
y	0	0.1	0.4						

Use a scale of 2 cm for 1 unit on both axes and draw the curve.

a P is the point on the curve where $x = 2$ and Q is the point on the curve where $x = 4$. Draw the chord PQ and find its gradient.

b Draw, as accurately as possible, the tangents to the curve at the points where $x = 1$, $x = 4$ and $x = 6$.

c Find the gradients of the tangents to the curve at the points where $x = 1$, $x = 4$ and $x = 6$.

3 Copy and complete the table for $y = \dfrac{10}{x}$ giving values of y correct to 1 decimal place.

x	1	1.5	2	3	4	5	6	7	8
y	10	6.7	5	3.3	2.5				

Use a scale of 2 cm for 1 unit on both axes and draw the curve for values of x from 1 to 8.

a A is the point on the curve where $x = 1$ and B is the point on the curve where $x = 4$. Find the gradient of the chord AB.

b Find the gradients of the tangents to the curve at A and B.

c Find the gradient of the tangent to the curve at the point where $x = 3$.

4 Draw the graph of $y = x^3$ for values of x from 0 to 3.5 using a scale of 2 cm for 1 unit on both axes.

Find the gradient of the curve at the points where

a $x = 1$ **b** $x = 3$

In the many practical applications of graphs it is rarely possible to have the same scales on both axes.

When the scales are not the same, care must be taken to read vertical measurements from the scale on the vertical axis and horizontal measurements from the scale on the horizontal axis.

The table shows the girth, w cm, of a pumpkin, n days after being fed with fertiliser.

n	1	2	3	4	5	6	7
w	15	17	20	24	29	35	41

Use a scale of 2 cm for 1 day and 2 cm for 10 cm of girth to draw the graph illustrating this information.

a Find the gradient of the chord joining the points where $n = 3$ and $n = 7$ and interpret the result.

b Find the gradient of the tangent at the point where $n = 3$ and interpret the result.

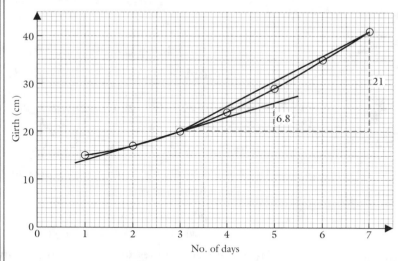

a Gradient of chord $= \frac{21}{4} = 5.25$

This shows that the girth of the pumpkin is increasing by an average of 5.25 cm per day over the four-day period.

b Gradient of tangent $\approx \frac{6.8}{2} = 3.4$

This shows that the girth of the pumpkin is increasing by 3.4 cm per day at the time of measurement on the third day.

5 The number of ripe strawberries on a particular strawberry plant were counted on Monday, Wednesday, Friday, Saturday and Sunday during one week. The results were recorded and plotted to give the following graph.

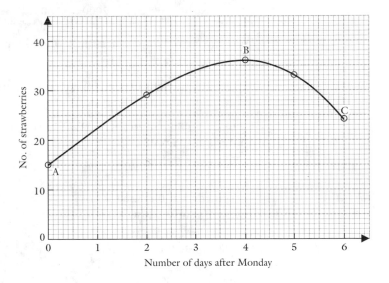

a How many ripe strawberries were there on

  i Wednesday   **ii** Saturday?

b How many strawberries were probably ripe on Thursday?

c Find the gradient of the chord joining the points A and B and interpret the result.

d Find the gradient of the chord joining B and C and interpret the result.

6 The table shows the population of an island at 10-year intervals from 1900 to 1980.

Date, D	1900	1910	1920	1930	1940	1950	1960	1970	1980
No. of people, N	500	375	280	210	160	120	90	65	50

Using a scale of $2\,\text{cm} \equiv 10$ years and $2\,\text{cm} \equiv 50$ people, draw the graph illustrating this information.

a Find the gradient of the chord joining the points on the curve where $D = 1910$ and $D = 1940$. Interpret your result.

b Find the gradient of the tangent to the curve where $D = 1910$ and interpret the result.

7 The table shows the sales of 'Jampot' jam for 5 months following an advertising campaign.

Month, M	1	2	3	4	5
Sales (Number of jars)	2000	2500	3500	5000	7000

Using a scale of $2\,\text{cm} \equiv 1$ month and $2\,\text{cm} \equiv 1000$ jars draw the graph illustrating this information.

a Find the gradient of the tangent to the curve where $M = 2$ and interpret the result.

b Find the gradient of the tangent to the curve where $M = 4$ and interpret the result.

AREAS BOUNDED BY CURVES

The curved edge of this shelf is formed by the curve whose equation is $y = \frac{1}{2}x(5-x)$. The top of the shelf is veneered and to find the cost of the veneer, we need first to find the area of the top surface.

The graph shows the part of the curve used for the curved edge. The shaded part corresponds to the area of the top surface of the shelf.

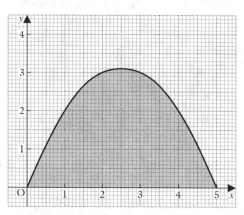

EXERCISE 6C

1 The shaded area shown above can be estimated by counting squares.

a Discuss how the accuracy of an estimate obtained this way compares with the size of the squares that are counted.

b Discuss how the accuracy of the estimate compares with the time taken to obtain it.

2

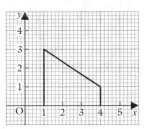

The diagram shows the area enclosed by the line whose equation is $y = \frac{1}{3}(11 - 2x)$, the x-axis and the lines $x = 1$ and $x = 4$.

a Can this area be found accurately or is it possible only to find an estimate?

b Find the area explaining, with reasons, whether your answer is an estimate or not.

3 a Sketch a diagram to show the part of the line $y = 2x - 3$ for values of x from $x = 2$ to $x = 4$ and the part of the line $y = 9 - x$ for values of x from $x = 4$ to $x = 9$.

b Find the area enclosed by the two lines, the x-axis and the line $x = 2$.

c On your sketch, draw a curve through the points $(2, 1), (4, 5)$ and $(9, 0)$. Consider the area between this curve, the x-axis and the line $x = 2$. How good an estimate do you consider your answer to part **b** to be for this area? Discuss whether it is possible to improve this estimate and how.

4 Discuss whether, when equations are known, it is necessary to draw an accurate graph to find an estimate for the area enclosed by straight lines on a graph.

AREAS UNDER GRAPHS

Discussion from the last exercise shows that when the area between a graph and the x-axis is bounded by straight lines whose equations we know, this area can be calculated accurately.

When we have an area bounded by the x-axis and a curve whose equation is known, we can estimate the value of the area without plotting the curve accurately.

THE TRAPEZIUM RULE

A curve can be approximated to by a series of straight lines.

To find the area between a curve and the x-axis, the area is divided into a convenient number of vertical strips. A chord is drawn across the top of each strip to give a set of trapeziums.

The sum of the areas of these trapeziums is then found and this is approximately equal to the required area.

Consider the area between the curve in the diagram, the x- and y-axes and the line $x = 12$.

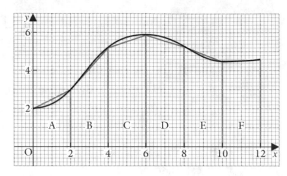

The area under this curve is divided into six strips each of width 2 units. Drawing the chords across the top of each strip gives six trapeziums.

Reading from the graph,
for trapezium A, the lengths of the parallel sides are 2 units and 3 units and the distance between them is 2 units,

therefore

$$\text{area A} = \tfrac{1}{2}(\text{sum of parallel sides}) \times (\text{distance between them})$$
$$= \tfrac{1}{2}(2 + 3) \times (2) \text{ sq units} = 5 \text{ sq units}$$

Finding the sum of the areas of all six trapeziums gives the total area as

$$5 + 8.2 + 11.1 + 11.2 + 9.8 + 9.1 \text{ sq units}$$
$$= 54.4 \text{ sq units}$$

Notice that all the strips are the same width.
This method for finding the area under a curve is called the *trapezium rule*.

The rule can be generalised.

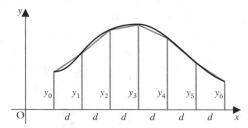

Consider the area shown in the diagram.
The area under the curve is divided into six strips each of width d.
The lengths of the parallel sides of the first trapezium are y_0 and y_1, so its area is $\tfrac{1}{2}(y_0 + y_1) \times d = \tfrac{1}{2}d(y_0 + y_1)$

Similarly, the area of the second trapezium is $\frac{1}{2}d(y_1 + y_2)$, and so on. The sum of the areas of all the trapeziums is

$$\frac{1}{2}d(y_0 + y_1) + \frac{1}{2}d(y_1 + y_2) + \frac{1}{2}d(y_2 + y_3) + \frac{1}{2}d(y_3 + y_4)$$
$$+ \frac{1}{2}d(y_4 + y_5) + \frac{1}{2}d(y_5 + y_6)$$
$$= \frac{1}{2}d(y_0 + y_1 + y_1 + y_2 + y_2 + y_3 + y_3 + y_4 + y_4 + y_5 + y_5 + y_6)$$
$$= \frac{1}{2}d(y_0 + 2y_1 + 2y_2 + 2y_3 + 2y_4 + 2y_5 + y_6)$$

and this gives an estimate for the area under the curve.

We can generalise further.

> If the area under a curve is divided into n strips, each of width d, the area is estimated as
>
> $$\frac{1}{2}d(y_0 + 2y_1 + \ldots + 2y_{n-1} + y_n)$$
>
> where $y_0, y_1, \ldots$ are the lengths of the vertical sides of the strips.

It is not necessary to remember the general form of the rule; problems can usually be worked out from a simple diagram like the one opposite.

EXERCISE 6D

Use the trapezium rule to find the area between each of the following curves and the x-axis. Use the given number of *equal width* strips.

1

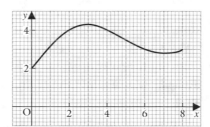

Use **a** two strips **b** four strips.
Explain whether your estimates are more or less than the area and which is more accurate.

2 Use five strips and explain whether your estimate is more or less than the actual area.

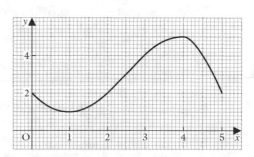

Use five strips to find, approximately, the area under the curve passing through the points given in the table for values of x from 1 to 11.

x	1	3	5	7	9	11
y	2	10	20	25	20	15

An accurate plot of this curve is not needed. A sketch is sufficient to give the necessary information.

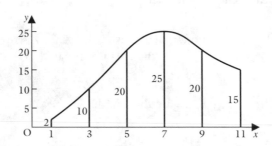

Area $\approx \frac{1}{2}(2+10)\times 2 + \frac{1}{2}(10+20)\times 2 + \frac{1}{2}(20+25)\times 2$

$$+ \tfrac{1}{2}(25+20)\times 2 + \tfrac{1}{2}(20+15)\times 2 \text{ sq units}$$

$$= 12 + 30 + 45 + 45 + 35 \text{ sq units} = 167 \text{ sq units}$$

3 A curve goes through the points given in the table.

Draw a rough sketch of the curve.
Use four strips to find the area under the curve.
Is your answer greater than or less than the true value?

x	0	1	2	3	4
y	10	6	4	6	10

4 A curve passes through the points given in the table.

Use four strips to find approximately the area between this curve and the x-axis.

x	0	1	2	3	4
y	1	2	4	4	2

5 Sketch the graph of the parabola $y = 3x^2$ from $x = 0$ to $x = 3$.

a Divide the area under the curve into three strips and mark the values of the ordinates on your sketch. Hence find, approximately, the area under your curve.

b Repeat part **a** using six strips.

6 A river is 40 metres wide and its depth was measured from one bank to the other bank at 5-metre intervals across its width. The values obtained are shown in the table.

Distance from bank (m)	0	5	10	15	20	25	30	35	40
Depth (m)		2	5	6	6.5	6	5	4	2.5	1.5

a Draw a rough sketch of the cross-section of the river.

b Use eight strips to estimate the area of the cross-section.

c The speed of the water in the river is measured as 0.25 m/s. How many litres of water (to the nearest 10 litres) pass through this cross-section in one second?

d How many litres of water flow through the cross-section in one hour? Give your answer to the nearest 1000 litres.

INVESTIGATION

The graph shows the curve whose equation is $y = x^2$.

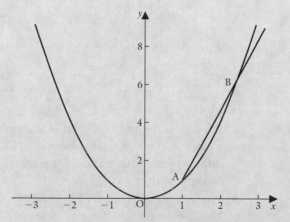

a A is the point on the curve where $x = 1$. B is the point on the curve where $x = 1 + h$. Find the gradient of AB in terms of h.

b Find the gradient of AB when $h = 2$, $h = 1$, $h = 0.5$, $h = 0.25$, $h = 0.1$. Investigate the sequence of values obtained for the gradient of AB as h gets smaller. What value do these appear to approach? Justify your conclusion. What does this value represent in relation to the curve?

c Repeat parts **a** and **b** when A is the point on the curve where $x = 2$. Try finding the gradient of the curve at the point where $x = -3$. Find a relationship between the gradient of the curve at a point and the x-coordinate of the point.

d Try a similar method for finding the relationship between the gradient at a point on the curve $y = x^3$ and its x-coordinate.

TRAVEL GRAPHS

The graph shows the speed of a police car plotted against time during a chase.

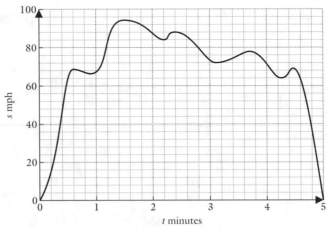

- We can read quite a lot of information about the behaviour of the car from this graph; it started from rest, its speed increased most rapidly during the first 0.6 minutes, it reached a maximum speed of about 95 mph, and so on.
- We cannot, however, read how far the car travelled during the chase. Nor can we tell whether the car travelled just one way down a road – it may have made a U-turn at some point. In this chapter we develop the work on travel graphs so that they can be used to find such quantities.

EXERCISE 7A

1 These two graphs each illustrate the journey of a car between two sets of traffic lights.

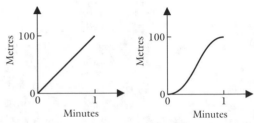

a Which of these graphs is a more realistic representation of the car's journey? Explain your answer.

b Find the average speed, in m/s, of the car between the two sets of lights. Is it possible to use either graph to work this out? Explain your answer.

2 A car driver takes the wrong exit from a roundabout so he continues to the next roundabout where he turns round and comes back along the same road.

The car travels at a steady 30 mph in both directions.

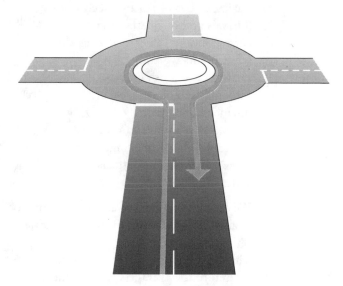

These two graphs are attempts to illustrate the journey of the car along this road.

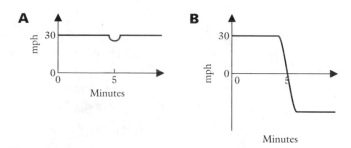

a Discuss whether, from graph **A**, you can tell in which direction the car is travelling along the road. What do you think the dip in the line in graph **A** attempts to show?

b Discuss what graph **B** attempts to show. Include in your discussion the speed shown after 5 minutes.

CURVED
DISTANCE–TIME
GRAPHS

When an object moves with constant speed, the distance–time graph representing its motion is a straight line. However, when an object moves so that its speed is constantly changing (for example, a car or a big-dipper) then the distance–time graph representing its motion is a curved line. To draw such a graph, we need a relation between the time and the distance travelled.

Consider, for example, a rocket fired from the ground so that its distance, d metres, from the launching pad after t seconds is given by

$$d = 80t - 5t^2$$

Taking values of t at two-second intervals and calculating the corresponding values of d gives a set of points which we can plot. Drawing a smooth curve through the points gives this distance–time graph.

From this graph we can see that 3 seconds after launching, the rocket is 195 m above the launch pad.

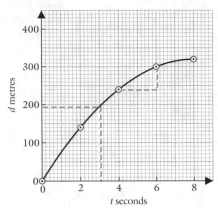

We can also find the average speed of the rocket over any interval of time. Consider, for example, the motion during the fifth and sixth seconds (from $t = 4$ to $t = 6$).

The rocket moves $(300 - 240)$ m, i.e. 60 m, in these 2 seconds. Therefore the average speed for the interval from $t = 4$ to $t = 6$ is $\frac{60}{2}$ m/s $= 30$ m/s

Notice that the chord joining the points on the curve where $t = 4$ and $t = 6$, has a gradient of $\frac{60}{2} = 30$.

This confirms what we expect; in Chapter 6 we saw that the gradient of a chord gives the average rate of increase of the quantity on the vertical axis with respect to the quantity on the horizontal axis. In this case, the gradient of a chord gives the rate of increase of distance with respect to time, that is, metres per second.

EXERCISE 7B

1 A car moves away from a set of traffic lights. The table shows the distance, d metres, of the car from the lights after t seconds.

t	0	1	2	3	4	5
d	0	2	8	18	32	50

Draw the distance–time graph using scales of $1\,\text{cm} \equiv \frac{1}{2}$ second and $1\,\text{cm} \equiv 5\,\text{m}$.

From your graph find

a the distance of the car from the lights after $2\frac{1}{2}$ seconds

b the average speed of the car during the 2nd second

c the average speed of the car during the first five seconds.

2 A rocket is launched and the table shows the distance travelled, d metres, after a time t seconds from lift-off.

t	0	1	2	3	4	5
d	0	5	40	135	320	625

Draw the distance–time graph using scales of $2\,\text{cm} \equiv 1$ second and $1\,\text{cm} \equiv 100\,\text{m}$.

Use your graph to find

a the distance of the rocket from the launch pad $4\tfrac{1}{2}$ seconds after lift-off

b the average speed of the rocket for the first 4 seconds of its journey

c the average speed of the rocket during the fourth second.
(Keep this graph; it is needed for question **1**, **Exercise 7d.**)

3 This distance–time graph illustrates the motion of a ball thrown upwards from the ground.

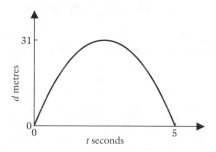

a How far does the ball go above the ground?

b What is the average speed of the ball on its way up?

c What is the average speed of the ball on its way down?

d Copy the diagram and draw the chord whose gradient represents

    i the answer to part **b**   **ii** the answer to part **c**.

e How far does the ball travel from when it leaves the ground until it returns and for how long is it in the air?

f What is the average speed for the whole of the motion shown?

g What is the gradient of the chord joining the points representing the start of the motion and the end of the motion?

h Discuss the meaning of your answers to parts **f** and **g**.

i Explain why this situation did not arise in questions **1** and **2**.

VELOCITY

Discussion from **Exercise 7A** shows that when an object is moving along a straight line, the speed of the object gives no indication of the direction of its movement.

Consider a bead threaded on a straight wire AB.

If we are told that the bead is moving along the wire at 5 m/s, we know something about the motion of the bead but we do not know which way the bead is moving.

If we are told that the bead is moving from A to B at 5 m/s we know *both* the direction of motion *and* the speed of the bead.

> *Velocity* is the name given to the quantity that includes
> *both* the speed *and* the direction of motion.

When an object moves along a straight line, like the bead, there are only two possible directions of motion. In this case a positive sign is used to indicate motion in one direction and a negative sign is used to indicate motion in the opposite direction.

Taking the direction A to B as positive, we can illustrate velocities of +5 m/s and −5 m/s on a diagram.

A 5 m/s B	A 5 m/s B
Velocity = +5 m/s	Velocity = −5 m/s

EXERCISE 7C

1 For each of the following statements state whether it is the velocity or the speed of the object that is given.

a A train travels between London and Watford at 70 km/h.

b A train travels from London to Watford at 70 km/h.

c A ball rolls down a hill at 5 m/s.

d A ball rolls along a horizontal groove at 3 m/s.

e A lift moves between floors at 2 m/s.

f A lift moves up from the ground floor at 2 m/s.

2 A bead moves along a horizontal wire AB. Taking the direction from A to B as positive, draw a diagram to illustrate the motion of the bead if its velocity is

a −2 m/s   **b** 4 m/s   **c** −10 m/s   **d** 0

3 The graph illustrates the motion of a bead along a straight wire AB as the bead moves from A to B, stops at B, and moves back to A again. Taking the direction from A to B as a positive, find

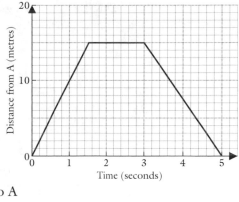

a the speed of the bead as it moves from A to B

b the velocity of the bead as it moves from A to B

c the speed of the bead as it moves from B to A

d the velocity of the bead as it moves from B to A

e the average speed for the whole motion.

4 The graph illustrates the motion of a ball rolling in a straight line along horizontal ground. Taking the direction of the first part of the motion as positive, describe the motion of the ball, giving its velocity for each section of the motion.

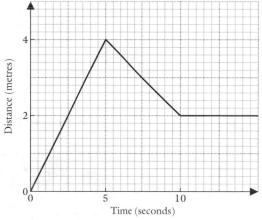

5 The graph illustrates the motion of a lift which travels from the ground floor to the first floor and then returns to the ground floor. Taking the upward direction as positive, state which of the following statements *must* be true.

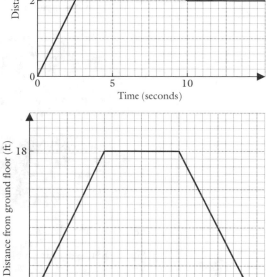

a The velocity of the lift is the same on both the upward and downward journeys.

b On the downward journey the speed is 6 ft/s.

c The average speed of the lift between leaving the ground floor and returning to it, is zero.

d On the upward journey the velocity of the lift is 6 ft/s.

e The velocity of the lift is zero for three seconds.

FINDING VELOCITY FROM A DISTANCE– TIME GRAPH

This distance–time graph illustrates the motion of a ball thrown upwards from the ground.

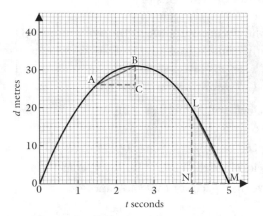

Taking the upward direction as positive we see that, up to the point where $t = 2.5$, the distance of the ball from the ground is increasing, i.e. the ball has a positive velocity (the ball is going up).

From $t = 2.5$ to $t = 5$, the distance of the ball from the ground is decreasing,
i.e. the ball has a negative velocity (the ball is going down).

> *Average velocity* is defined as $\dfrac{\text{increase in distance}}{\text{time taken}}$

Therefore the average velocity of the ball in the interval from $t = 1.5$ to $t = 2.5$ is

$$\frac{\text{increase in distance from } t = 1.5 \text{ to } t = 2.5}{2.5 - 1.5} \text{ m/s}$$

$$= \frac{5}{1} \text{ m/s} = 5 \text{ m/s}$$

On the graph this is represented by the gradient of the chord AB.

Similarly the average velocity of the ball from $t = 4$ to $t = 5$ is

$$\frac{\text{increase in distance in this time}}{5 - 4} \text{ m/s} = -20 \text{ m/s}$$

On the graph this is represented by the gradient of the chord LM.

> In a distance–time graph, the gradient of a chord gives the average velocity over the time interval spanned by the chord

The average velocity during any time interval can now be found using this fact, as the following example shows.

From $t = 1.5$ to $t = 4$ the average velocity is given by the gradient of the chord AL,

i.e. $$\frac{-6}{2.5} \; m/s = -2.4 \, m/s$$

VELOCITY AT AN INSTANT

This is the distance–time graph first shown opposite.

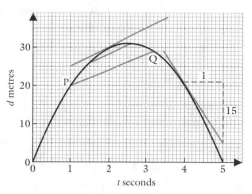

Suppose that we want to find the velocity of the ball at the instant when $t = 2$.

We can get an approximate value for this velocity by finding the average velocity from, say, $t = 1$ to $t = 3.2$, i.e. by finding the gradient of the chord PQ.

A better approximation is obtained by taking a smaller interval of time, say from $t = 1.5$ to $t = 2.6$, that is by making the ends of the chord closer together.

The best answer is obtained when the interval of time is as small as possible, that is when the ends of the chord coincide. When this happens the chord becomes a tangent to the curve at the point where $t = 2$.

Therefore the velocity of the ball at the instant when $t = 2$ is given by the gradient of the tangent to the curve at the point where $t = 2$.
By drawing and measurement, the velocity is $5 \, m/s$.

Similarly, at the point where $t = 4$, the gradient of the tangent is found to be -15. Therefore the velocity when $t = 4$ is $-15 \, m/s$. (Both results are estimates because they were obtained from a graph.)

This confirms what we expect; in Chapter 6 we saw that the gradient of a tangent to a curve gives the rate of increase of the quantity on the vertical axis with respect to the quantity on the horizontal axis at that point on the curve. In this case, the gradient of a tangent gives the rate of increase of distance with respect to time, that is, the velocity.

> In a distance–time graph, the gradient
> of a tangent to the curve gives the velocity at that instant.

EXERCISE 7D

1 Use the graph drawn for question **2** in **Exercise 7B** to estimate

a the average velocity of the rocket during the time from $t = 2$ to $t = 4$

b the average velocity of the rocket over the interval $t = 2$ to $t = 3$

c the velocity of the rocket when **i** $t = 2$ **ii** $t = 2.5$.

2 The table shows the distance, d metres, of a ball from its starting position, t seconds after being thrown into the air.

t	0	1	2	3	4	5	6
d	0	25	40	45	40	25	0

Using scales of $2\,\text{cm} \equiv 1$ second and $1\,\text{cm} \equiv 5\,\text{m}$, draw the graph of d against t. From your graph estimate

a when the ball returns to the starting point

b the average velocity of the ball from $t = 1$ to $t = 2$

c the average velocity of the ball from $t = 1$ to $t = 1.5$

d the velocity of the ball when **i** $t = 1$ **ii** $t = 4$ **iii** $t = 5$.

3 Use the graph on page 152 to estimate

a the velocity when $t = 1$

b the average velocity during the first second

c the average velocity during the first four seconds

d the greatest height of the ball

e the average velocity for the time between $t = 3$ and $t = 5$.

4 A particle moves in a straight line so that t seconds after leaving a fixed point O on the line, its distance, d metres, from O is given by

$$d = 8t - 2t^2$$

a Copy and complete the following table.

t	0	1	2	3	4
d	0	6			

b Use scales of $2\,\text{cm} \equiv 1$ second and $1\,\text{cm} \equiv 2\,\text{m}$ and draw the distance–time graph.

c From your graph estimate the velocity of the particle when $t = 2$ and when $t = 3$.

d What is the greatest distance of the particle from its starting point?

ACCELERATION

When the velocity of a moving object is changing we say that the object is accelerating.

Velocity includes speed and direction; we are concerned here with objects that move in just one direction so the changes in velocity involve only changes in speed.

If a train moves away from a station A and accelerates from rest so that its speed increases by 2 m/s each second then

1 second after leaving A the train has a speed of 2 m/s
2 seconds after leaving A the train has a speed of 4 m/s
3 seconds after leaving A the train has a speed of 6 m/s.

The train is said to have an acceleration of 2 m/s per second, i.e. 2 m/s/s and this is written as $2 \, \text{m/s}^2$.

If the speed of the train decreases it is said to be decelerating.

Suppose that the speed of the train decreases by 1 m/s each second, then we say that the deceleration is 1 m/s per second or $1 \, \text{m/s}^2$.

We can also say that the train has an acceleration of $-1 \, \text{m/s}^2$, i.e. a deceleration is a negative acceleration.

Consider a car that accelerates from rest at $5 \, \text{m/s}^2$ for 10 seconds and then decelerates at $2 \, \text{m/s}^2$ back to rest.
An acceleration of $5 \, \text{m/s}^2$ means that the speed of the car increases by 5 m/s each second. Therefore after 10 seconds its speed is 50 m/s. A deceleration of $2 \, \text{m/s}^2$ means that the speed of the car reduces by 2 m/s each second. Therefore, the speed of 50 m/s is reduced by 2 m/s each second, and this means that the car takes 25 seconds to stop.

EXERCISE 7E

1 A train accelerates from rest at $1 \, \text{m/s}^2$ for 30 seconds. How fast is the train moving at the end of the 30 seconds?
If the train now decelerates back to rest at $0.5 \, \text{m/s}^2$ how long does it take for the train to stop?

2 A train accelerates from rest at $0.2 \, \text{m/s}^2$. How fast is the train moving after

a 2 seconds   **b** 30 seconds   **c** 1 minute?

3 A bus moves away from rest at a bus stop with an acceleration of $0.4 \, \text{m/s}^2$ for 5 seconds; it then has to decelerate to rest at $0.2 \, \text{m/s}^2$. How long after leaving the bus stop is the bus again stationary?

4 The speed of a lift increases from 6 m/s to 20 m/s in 7 seconds. Find the acceleration.

5 A train accelerates from rest at $0.5\,\text{km/minute}^2$.
How fast (in km/h) is the train moving after

  a 3 minutes   **b** 10 minutes   **c** 45 seconds?

6 The speed of a car increases from $10\,\text{km/h}$ to $80\,\text{km/h}$ in 5 seconds.
Find the acceleration.

7 Find, in m/s^2, the acceleration of a motor bike when its speed
increases from $10\,\text{km/h}$ to $50\,\text{km/h}$ in 4 seconds.

**VELOCITY–TIME
GRAPHS**

A car accelerates from rest at $5\,\text{m/s}^2$ for 6 seconds and then travels at a
constant speed for 10 seconds after which it decelerates to rest at $3\,\text{m/s}^2$.
This information can be shown on a graph by plotting velocity against
time. This is called a velocity–time graph.

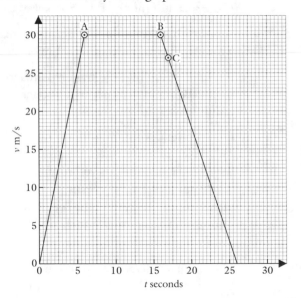

After 6 seconds, the car is moving at $30\,\text{m/s}$, so we draw a straight line
from the start to the point A, where $t = 6$ and $v = 30$.
Notice that the gradient of this line represents the acceleration (i.e. the
rate of increase of velocity with respect to time).

The line AB (zero gradient) represents the car moving at constant speed.

The last section of the journey is represented by the line drawn from B
through C to the time axis, where C is 1 unit along the time axis and 3
units down the velocity axis from B. Notice that the gradient of BC
is -3 and this represents the deceleration of $3\,\text{m/s}^2$.

> Acceleration is represented by the gradient of the
> velocity–time graph.

EXERCISE 7F

1 This velocity–time graph illustrates the journey of a car between a set of traffic-lights and a zebra crossing.

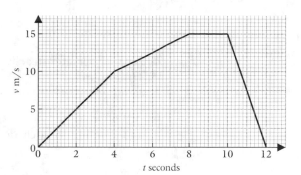

a What is the car's acceleration for the first 4 seconds?

b What happens when $t = 4$?

c For how long is the car moving at a constant speed?

d For how long is the car braking?

e What is the deceleration of the car?

f For how long is the car moving?

2 This velocity–time graph illustrates the first 7 minutes of the flight of a rocket.

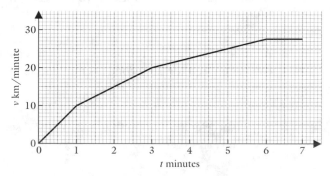

a What is the initial acceleration of the rocket?

b What is the speed of the rocket 2 minutes after its launch?

c What steady speed is obtained by the rocket?

d What is the acceleration of the rocket during the fourth minute of its flight?

3 This velocity–time graph illustrates the journey of a train between two stations.

a What is the acceleration for the first 2 minutes?

b What is the greatest speed of the train?

c For how long is the train travelling at constant speed?

d What is the acceleration during the third minute?

e What is the deceleration of the train?

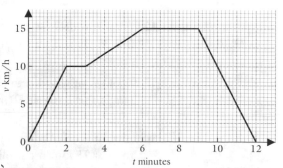

Draw a velocity–time graph to illustrate the following journeys.
Use scales of 1 cm ≡ 2 seconds and 1 cm = 5 m/s.

4 A car accelerates steadily from rest reaching a speed of 12 m/s in 10 seconds.

5 A train accelerates from rest reaching a speed of 8 m/s in 5 seconds and then immediately decelerates to rest in 4 seconds.

6 A motorbike accelerates from rest to a speed of 20 m/s in 4 seconds, maintains this steady speed for 8 seconds and then decelerates to rest in 5 seconds.

Sketch a velocity–time graph for each of the following journeys.

7 A bullet is fired into a block of wood at 100 m/s and comes to rest 3 seconds later.

8 A car accelerates from rest at 2 m/s^2 for 5 seconds, then moves with constant speed for 15 seconds before decelerating back to rest at 4 m/s^2.

9 A train accelerates from rest at 1 m/s^2 for 3 seconds, 2 m/s^2 for 3 seconds and then 5 m/s^2 for 5 seconds.

10 A car accelerates from rest at 10 m/s^2 for 2 seconds, 5 m/s^2 for 5 seconds and then 2 m/s^2 for 3 seconds. The car then travels at constant speed for 10 seconds before decelerating at 8 m/s^2 back to rest.

11 A bullet is fired at 50 m/s into sand which retards the bullet at 30 m/s^2.

12 A car travels at 30 m/s for 5 seconds, then decelerates at 4 m/s^2 for 3 seconds and travels at constant speed for another 10 seconds.

13 A block of wood is thrown straight down into the sea. The wood enters the water at 50 m/s and sinks for 6 seconds.

14 A train accelerates from rest at 5 km/h per minute for 5 minutes, then at 15 km/h per minute for 5 minutes and then maintains its speed for 10 minutes.

FINDING THE DISTANCE FROM A VELOCITY–TIME GRAPH

This graph shows a car travelling at a steady 15 m/s for 20 seconds.

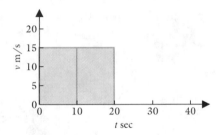

The distance travelled by the car in this time is given by speed × time, i.e. distance travelled = 15 × 20 metres.

Now the area of the shaded rectangle is also 15 × 20 square units, so the distance travelled is represented by the area under the velocity–time graph.

Now consider this velocity–time graph which represents a car accelerating at a constant rate from a speed of 5 m/s to a speed of 20 m/s in 10 seconds.

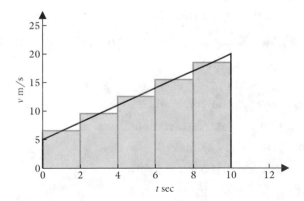

The changing speed can be approximated by considering a car moving at a constant speed of 6.5 m/s for 2 seconds, 9.5 m/s for 2 seconds, and so on, as shown by the green lines on the graph.

The distance travelled by the car is then represented by the sum of the areas of the rectangles shown on the graph.

Now, because the parts of the rectangles above the line are equal in area to the white parts under the black line, the sum of the areas of these rectangles is equal to the area under the black line.

Hence

the distance travelled is equal to the area under the velocity–time graph.

EXERCISE 7G

The velocity–time graph illustrates a train journey between two stations.

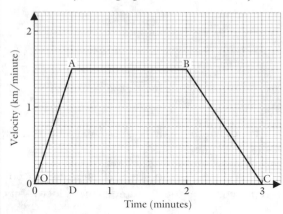

a What is the maximum speed of the train in km/h?

b What is the train's acceleration in the first half-minute?

c How far does the train travel in the first 30 seconds?

d What is the distance between the stations?

a From the graph, the maximum speed is $1.5\,\text{km/min} = 1.5 \times 60\,\text{km/h}$
$$= 90\,\text{km/h}$$

b The acceleration is given by the gradient of OA, which is $\dfrac{1.5}{0.5} = 3$

Therefore the acceleration is $3\,\text{km/minute}^2$.

c The distance travelled in the first 30 seconds is given by the area of $\triangle$OAD.
Area $\triangle$OAD $= \frac{1}{2}(\,\text{OD}\,) \times (\,\text{AD}\,)$
$$= 0.5 \times (\,0.5\,) \times (\,1.5\,) = 0.375$$
Therefore the train travels $0.375\,\text{km}$ in the first 30 seconds.

d The distance between the stations is represented by the area of trapezium OABC.
Area OABC $= \frac{1}{2}(\,\text{OC} + \text{AB}\,) \times \text{AD}$
$$= 0.5(\,3 + 1.5\,) \times 1.5$$
$$= 3.375$$
Therefore the distance between the stations is $3.375\,\text{km}$.

1 The velocity–time graph represents a car journey between two sets of traffic lights.

a What is
  i the acceleration
  ii the deceleration of the car?

b For how long does the car accelerate?

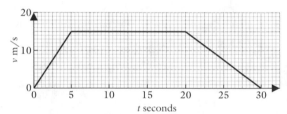

c How many metres does the car travel while braking?

d Find the distance between the two sets of lights.

2 Use the graphs for questions **1, 2** and **3** of **Exercise 7F** to find

   a the distance covered by the car in question **1**

   b the distance travelled by the rocket in the first 3 minutes in question **2**

   c the distance travelled by the train in the first 2 minutes in question **3**. (Be careful with the units.)

3 The velocity–time graph represents a missile fired into a 'wall' made up of a layer of sand followed by a layer of wood and then a layer of brick.

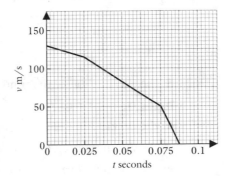

   a Find the deceleration of the missile as it passes through the layer of sand.

   b Find the depth of the sand.

   c Find the deceleration of the missile as it passes through the layer of wood.

   d Find the depth of the layer of wood.

   e What retardation of the missile does the layer of brick cause?

   f Find the depth to which the missile penetrates the brick.

4 The graph represents a two-minute section of a car journey.

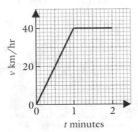

Find

   a the acceleration, in m/s^2, of the car during the first minute

   b the distance, in metres, travelled by the car during the two minutes.

5 A cross-country runner covers three sections of the course in succession. The first is a downhill sweep, then there is a level section followed by a hill climb. The graph below shows the speed, v m/s, of the runner over the three sections.

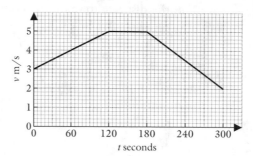

Find

a the acceleration of the runner on the downhill section

b the constant speed over the level section

c the deceleration of the runner during the hill climb

d the distance covered on the level section

e the distance covered on the hill climb.

6 The graph represents the journey made by a bus between two bus stops.

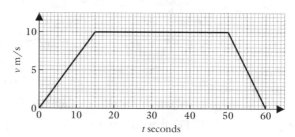

a What is the acceleration of the bus?

b What is the deceleration of the bus?

c What distance does the bus cover while accelerating?

d What distance does the bus cover while decelerating?

e What is the distance between the two bus stops?

CURVED VELOCITY–TIME GRAPHS

When acceleration is not constant, the velocity–time graph is a curved line.

For example, suppose that a ball rolls along the ground in such a way that, t seconds after starting, its velocity is v m/s where

$$v = t(10 - t)$$

Using this information we can draw the following velocity–time graph.

From the graph we see that the speed of the ball increases for 5 seconds, that is, the ball accelerates for 5 seconds. Then the speed decreases for 5 seconds, that is, the ball decelerates for 5 seconds.

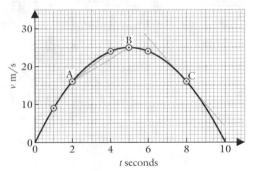

The maximum speed is 25 m/s and occurs 5 seconds after the start.

The *average acceleration* over an interval of time is the steady acceleration that gives the same final velocity.

In the interval of time from $t = 2$ to $t = 5$, a steady increase in velocity is represented by the straight line AB. Hence the average acceleration over this interval of time is represented by the gradient of the chord AB.

Now consider acceleration at an instant. On the graph, the gradient of the tangent at the point C represents the rate at which v is changing at the instant when $t = 8$,
i.e. the acceleration at the instant when $t = 8$. Hence

> acceleration at an instant is represented by the gradient of the tangent to the velocity–time curve at that instant.

Consider the *distance travelled* in an interval of time. When the acceleration is constant, the velocity–time graph is a straight line and the distance is represented by the area under the straight line. Now a curve can be represented approximately by a succession of short straight lines; the diagram shows an approximation to the curve between A and B.

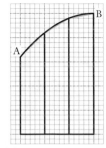

The sum of the areas under each of these straight lines gives a very good approximation for the distance covered in the interval from $t = 2$ to $t = 5$. Hence

> the distance covered in an interval of time is represented by the area under the velocity–time graph for that interval.

EXERCISE 7H

The graph represents the first five minutes of the journey of a train.

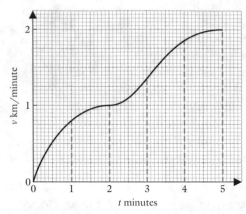

Estimate **a** the times at which the acceleration is zero

b the distance covered by the train in the 5 minutes.

a The tangent has zero gradient where $t = 2$ and where $t = 5$.

The acceleration is zero when $t = 2$ and $t = 5$.

b Using five strips each of width 1 unit gives five trapeziums.
Therefore the area is approximately

$\frac{1}{2}(0 + 0.8)(1) + \frac{1}{2}(0.8 + 1)(1) + \frac{1}{2}(1 + 1.35)(1) + \frac{1}{2}(1.35 + 1.85)(1) + \frac{1}{2}(1.85 + 2)(1)$

$= 0.4 + 0.9 + 1.175 + 1.6 + 1.925 = 6$

Distance covered $\approx 6\,\text{km}$

1 The graph illustrates the motion of a ball rolled along the ground.

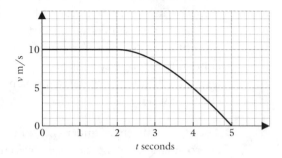

a Find the velocity of the ball when $t = 4$.

b Is the ball accelerating or decelerating from $t = 2$ to $t = 5$?

c Find the distance the ball moves before it stops. (Use five strips each of width 1 unit.)

2 The graph illustrates a five-second interval of a car journey.

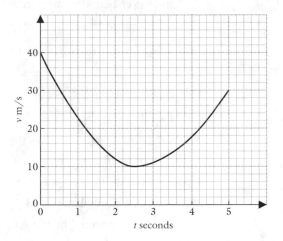

a Find the distance covered by the car in these five seconds.

b The following statements about this graph are either true or false. If the statement is true write T, if it is false write F.

  i The car is accelerating when $t = 4$.

  ii The car comes momentarily to rest when $t = 2.5$.

  iii The car changes direction halfway through this interval of time.

  iv The car's speed is decreasing for the first 2 seconds.

3 A rocket is fired and its velocity, v km/minute, t minutes after firing is given by

$$v = t^3$$

Copy and complete the following table.

t	0	1	2	3	4
v	0		8		

Use scales of $2\,\text{cm} \equiv 1\,\text{minute}$ and $1\,\text{cm} \equiv 10\,\text{km/min}$ to draw the velocity–time graph. From your graph estimate

a the acceleration 2 minutes after firing

b the velocity after $2\frac{1}{2}$ minutes

c the time when the velocity is $20\,\text{km/min}$

d the distance covered in the first 3 minutes

e the distance covered in the fourth minute.

4 The table shows the velocity, v m/s, of a helium filled balloon t seconds after being released in the air on a calm day.

t	0	1	2	3	4	5	6
v	0	5	8	9	8	5	0

Use scales of 1 cm ≡ 1 second and 1 cm ≡ 1 m/s to draw the velocity–time graph. From your graph estimate

a the maximum velocity of the balloon and the time when this occurs

b the velocity after $1\frac{1}{2}$ seconds

c the acceleration 1 second after release

d the acceleration when $t = 3$

e the distance covered by the balloon in these 6 seconds.

5 The graph is given on page 146. If we assume that it shows the *velocity* of a police car plotted against time during a chase, use the graph to estimate

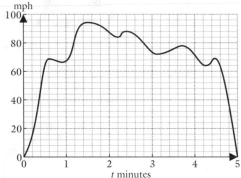

a the greatest acceleration

b the greatest deceleration

c the time for which the car was travelling at more than 70 mph

d the distance covered in this time.

The graph is given on page 146.

MIXED EXERCISE

EXERCISE 7I

Each question is followed by several alternative answers. Write down the letter that corresponds to the correct answer.

1

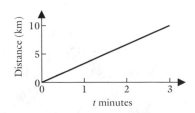

The graph shows an object moving at

A 10 km/min   **B** $3\frac{1}{3}$ km/min   **C** $\frac{3}{10}$ km/min   **D** 30 km/min

2

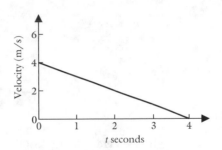

The graph shows an object which in 4 seconds covers a distance of

A 1 m   **B** 8 m   **C** 16 m   **D** −8 m

3 The acceleration of the object whose motion is given in question **2** is

A 1 m/s^2 **B** 4 m/s^2 **C** 16 m/s^2 **D** −1 m/s^2

4

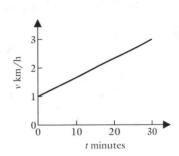

From the graph the distance covered in the thirty minutes is

A 60 km   **B** 1 km   **C** 2 km   **D** 4 km

5

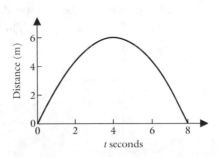

The graph shows an object

A whose velocity is constant
B whose speed when $t = 0$ is zero
C which continues to move away from its initial position
D which returns to its initial position after 8 seconds.

6

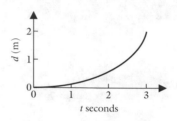

The average velocity from $t = 0$ to $t = 3$ is

A $2\,\mathrm{m/s}$ **B** $1\,\mathrm{m/s}$ **C** $\frac{2}{3}\,\mathrm{m/s}$ **D** $1\frac{1}{2}\,\mathrm{m/s}$

7 Deducing from the shape of the graph in question **6**, the acceleration when $t = 2$ could be

A $-1\,\mathrm{m/s}^2$ **B** zero   **C** $20\,\mathrm{m/s}^2$ **D** $1\,\mathrm{m/s}$

8 The distance–time graph representing the motion of a stone dropped from a cliff top could be

A   **B**   **C**

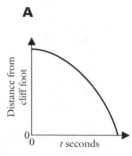
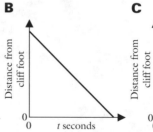
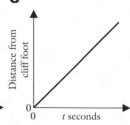

9 A bead moves along a straight wire with a constant speed for 2 seconds and then its speed decreases at a constant rate to zero. The velocity–time graph illustrating this could be

A   **C**

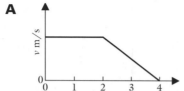
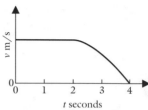

B   **D**

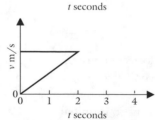
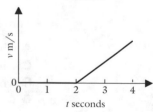

10

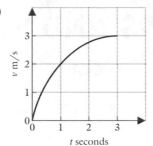

From the graph the distance covered in 3 seconds could be

A 6 m

B 8 m

C 9 m

D 6 km

PUZZLE

A car was tested on a race track.

Graph **A** purports to show the velocity of the car plotted against the distance (as the crow flies) between the car and its starting point.

Graph **B** purports to show the speed of the car plotted against its distance (as the crow flies) from the starting point.

A

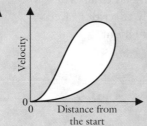

B

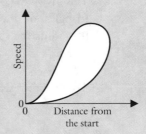

Both graphs look impossible, but one of them is possible.

Which one and why?

CONSTRUCTIONS AND TRANSFORMATIONS

Sometimes a construction has to be done without the aid of a protractor or set square. Here is a reminder of the most useful 'ruler and compasses only' constructions.

In these diagrams, the positions where the point of the compasses has to be placed are marked P_1, P_2, ... for the first, second, ... positions.

To construct an angle of 60° at A

This involves constructing an equilateral triangle but drawing only two sides. Keep the radius the same throughout.

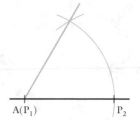

To bisect angle ACB

Keep the radius the same throughout.

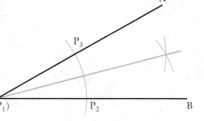

To construct and angle of 30° at A

Construct an angle of 60° at P_1 and then bisect it. Keep the radius the same throughout.

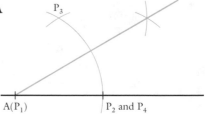

To construct and angle of 90° at A

Bisect an angle of 180° at P_1. Enlarge the radius for the arcs drawn from P_2 and P_3.

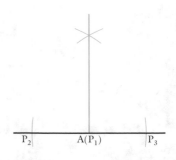

To construct and angle of 45° at A

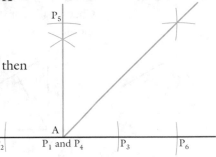

Construct an angle of 90° at A and then
bisect it.

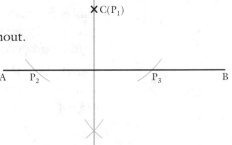

To draw a perpendicular from C to the line AB

Keep the radius the same throughout.

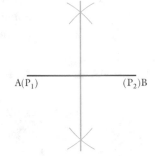

To bisect a line AB

Keep the radius the same throughout.

ACCURACY

When they are done properly, ruler and compasses constructions give
more accurate results than those using the protractors and set squares
commonly available. That accuracy depends, however, on

- using compasses that are reasonably stiff (a loose joint means that the
  radius will change in use)
- using a *sharp* pencil, preferably an H, and keeping it sharp
- making the construction as large as is practical, in particular *not* using
  too small a radius on the compasses. (Aim for a minimum radius of
  about 5 cm and do not rub out any arcs.)

EXERCISE 8A

Construct the following figures using only a ruler and a pair of compasses. Check your construction by measuring the length marked x. Your result should be within 1 mm of the value given in the Answers.

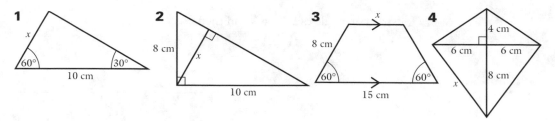

SKETCHES

In the last exercise, a sketch was given of the shape to be drawn accurately. Sometimes however, only a description of the figure is given. In this case it is essential to draw a sketch first because it gives some understanding of the shape and properties of the accurate drawing that has to be produced.

A sketch should be drawn freehand, but neatly. It should be big enough for essential information to be marked. Sometimes a first attempt at a sketch does not fit the given information. When this happens make another sketch.

SCALES

The construction of a scale drawing usually requires the choice of a scale and the calculation of lengths to be used. The next exercise gives practice in producing useful sketches and getting information from them. Some of the questions also involve using scales and interpreting information from scale drawings.

EXERCISE 8B

1 a Sketch a quadrilateral ABCD in which $AB = 10$ cm, $BC = 8$ cm, $BD = 10$ cm and $A\widehat{B}C = B\widehat{C}D = 90°$.

b What other properties of ABCD can you deduce from your sketch? Justify your answer.

2 ABCD is an equilateral triangle of side 6 cm. The line which bisects $\widehat{B}$ cuts AC at D and BD is produced to E so that $DE = BD$.

a Sketch the quadrilateral ABCE.

b What type of quadrilateral is ABCE? Give reasons.

3 Draw a base line AC about 16 cm long. Mark B on AC so that $AB = 8$ cm. Show on a sketch the position of D if $D\widehat{A}C = 30°$ and $D\widehat{B}C = 60°$.

a Write down the sizes of the angles in $\triangle ABD$.

b What type of triangle is $\triangle ABD$?

c Construct the diagram and measure BD. Does its length confirm your answer to part **b**?

4 A first-floor window A is 4 m above ground level and overlooks a level garden with a tree PQ standing in front of the window. From A the angle of depression of Q, the foot of the tree, is 30° and the angle of elevation of P, the top of the tree, is 60°.

a Draw a sketch to represent this data. Mark B the point on the ground vertically beneath A, and C the foot of the perpendicular from A to PQ.

b Construct this figure with AB = 4 cm. What scale has been used to represent the real-life situation described above?

c Use your diagram to find

   i the distance from B to the foot of the tree   **ii** the height of the tree.

5 A quadrilateral PQRS is to be drawn to scale. PQ = 92 m and QR = 76 m.

a Find what the lengths of PQ and QR should be if the scale is

   i 1 cm to 10 m   **ii** 1 cm to 8 m.

b On a drawing using a scale of 1 cm to 10 m, the measured length of PR is 6.8 cm. What is the real length of PR?

c On a drawing using a scale of 1 cm to 8 m, the measured length of QS is 7.2 cm. What is the real length of QS?

d Which scale was easier to use? Would a scale of 1 cm to 5 m be easier to use than 1 cm to 8 m? Give your reasons.

6

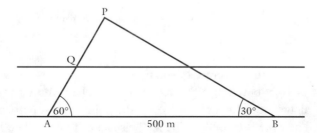

Tom stands on a river bank and sees a pylon P in a field on the opposite bank. A and B are two points on his river bank which are 500 m apart. From A he measures $P\hat{A}B$ as 60° and from B he measures $P\hat{B}A$ as 30°.

a Using ruler and compasses only and using a scale of 1 cm to represent 50 m, make a scale drawing to show this data. Leave all construction lines clearly visible.

b Measure the shortest distance from the pylon to the river bank on which Tom is standing.

c Calculate, using trigonometry, the shortest distance from the pylon to the river bank on which Tom is standing.

d Discuss how reliably accurate the answers to parts **b** and **c** can be.

e If the point Q at which AP crosses the opposite river bank is the midpoint of AP, find the width of the river.

TRANSFORMATIONS

The transformations we have considered in previous books are:

reflection in a mirror line, rotation, translation, and enlargement using positive and negative scale factors. To revise this work refer to Summary 1 on page 17.

We found the image of a shape when it was rotated about a given centre but, unless it was obvious, we could not find the centre of rotation from the original position of a shape and its image. We now determine how this can be done.

FINDING THE CENTRE OF ROTATION

When an object is rotated we can quite often locate the centre of rotation simply by looking at the object and its image. This is not always possible, however, and then we use the fact that the centre of rotation is the same distance from a point on the object and from the image of that point.

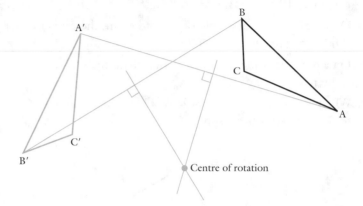

To locate the centre of rotation in this diagram, first we find the point midway between A and its image A′. Then, through this point, a line is drawn at right angles to AA′. Any point on this perpendicular bisector is equidistant from A and A′. (This fact can be checked by measurement.) This process is repeated with either B and B′ or C and C′. The perpendicular bisectors meet at the centre of rotation.

EXERCISE 8C

In each diagram the blue shape is the image by rotation of the black shape. Trace the diagram and find the centre of rotation and the angle of rotation.

1

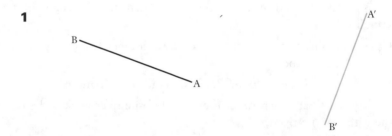

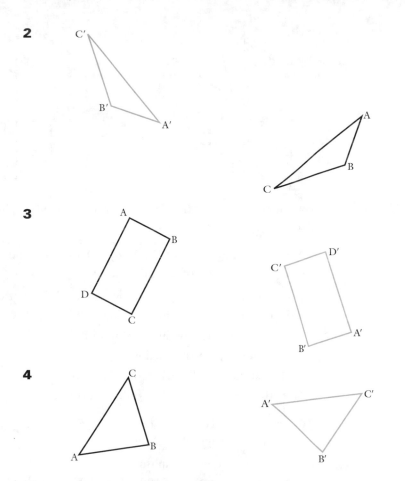

Reflections, translations, enlargements and rotations all appear in the remaining questions in this exercise.

In questions **5** to **8** name the transformation that maps the black shape to the blue one (A′ is the image of A, etc.). Describe each transformation as fully as possible; for example, if the transformation is a rotation give the centre and angle of rotation.

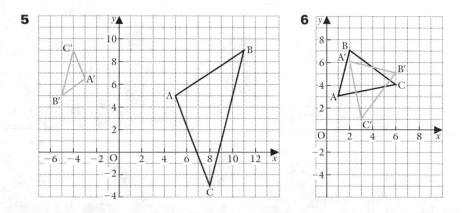

7

8

For questions **9** and **10** draw x- and y-axes, each for values from -6 to 6. Use 1 cm for 1 unit.

9 Draw $\triangle PQR$ with $P(-1, 2)$, $Q(-1, 5)$ and $R(-3, 2)$.
Draw the image of $\triangle PQR$

    a under a reflection in the line $y = x$. Label it $\triangle P_1 Q_1 R_1$

    b under a reflection in the y-axis. Label it $\triangle P_2 Q_2 R_2$

    c under a reflection in the x-axis. Label it $\triangle P_3 Q_3 R_3$.

Describe the transformation

    d that maps $\triangle P_2 Q_2 R_2$ onto $\triangle P_3 Q_3 R_3$

    e that maps $\triangle P_3 Q_3 R_3$ onto $\triangle P_1 Q_1 R_1$.

10 Draw $\triangle LMN$ with $L(3, 2)$, $M(5, 2)$ and $N(5, 5)$.
Draw the image of $\triangle LMN$

    a under a reflection in the line $y = -x$. Label it $\triangle L_1 M_1 N_1$

    b under a rotation of $180°$ about $(0, 2)$. Label it $\triangle L_2 M_2 N_2$

    c under a translation described by the vector $\begin{pmatrix} -4 \\ 1 \end{pmatrix}$. Label it $\triangle L_3 M_3 N_3$.

What is the image of $\triangle LMN$ under a rotation of $360°$ about O?

11

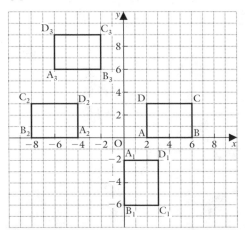

    a Give the transformation that maps rectangle ABCD to

        i $A_1 B_1 C_1 D_1$

        ii $A_2 B_2 C_2 D_2$

        iii $A_3 B_3 C_3 D_3$

    b $A_1 B_1 C_1 D_1$ is mapped to $A_3 B_3 C_3 D_3$ by a rotation. Copy the diagram and use it to find the centre of rotation.

12 P is the point (3, 3) and Q is (1, 2).
Find the coordinates of the point to which P is mapped under

a an enlargement, centre Q, scale factor 2

b an enlargement, centre Q, scale factor -1

c a clockwise rotation of $90°$ about Q.

13 A translation maps the point (6, 2) to the point (7, 5) and the mirror line of a reflection is the line $x + y = 2$.
Find the image of the point (1, 2) under

a the translation   **b** the reflection.

14

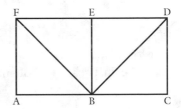

ABEF and BCDE are squares.

a Under a rotation, $\triangle$CDB is mapped to $\triangle$ABF. Give the centre of rotation and the angle of rotation.

b Under a reflection, $\triangle$CDB is mapped to $\triangle$AFB. Give the mirror line.

c Under another rotation, square CDEB is mapped to FABE. Give the centre of rotation and the angle of rotation.

15

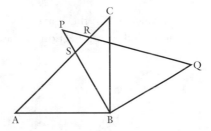

In $\triangle$ABC, AB $=$ BC and $\widehat{ABC} = 90°$. $\triangle$ABC is mapped to $\triangle$PBQ by a rotation of $60°$ clockwise about B.

a Name all the lengths equal to   **i** AB   **ii** AC.

b Through what angle has BC rotated in this transformation?
What is the size of $\widehat{CBQ}$?

c Through what angle has AC rotated? What is the size of $\widehat{ARP}$?

d Calculate $\widehat{CSB}$.

e If AB $= 6$ cm, give the length of CQ.

COMPOUND
TRANSFORMATIONS
If we reflect any object in the x-axis and then rotate it by $180°$ about P, we are carrying out one example of a compound transformation.

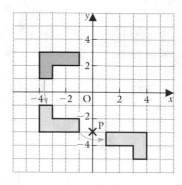

EXERCISE 8D

In this exercise copy the diagram and carry out the compound transformation.

Label the final image P. You may find it worthwhile to use tracing paper.

1

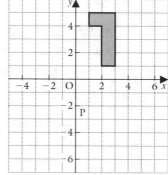

A reflection in the x-axis followed by a reflection in the y-axis

3

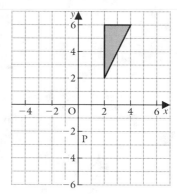

A reflection in the y-axis followed by a reflection in the x-axis

2

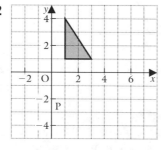

A rotation of $90°$ clockwise about the point $(3, 2)$ Followed by a reflection in the x-axis

4

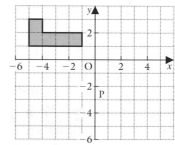

A reflection in the x-axis followed by a rotation of $90°$ clockwise about the origin

5

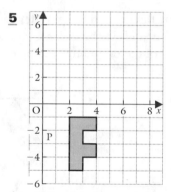

A reflection in the *x*-axis
Followed by a translation
defined by the vector $\begin{pmatrix} 4 \\ 1 \end{pmatrix}$

6

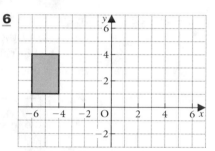

A reflection in the *y*-axis followed
by a rotation of 90° anticlockwise
about the point (4, 1)

USING A
COMPUTER

The shape labelled **A** can be drawn on a
computer screen using a drawing program.

A particular drawing program has two commands to transform a shape:

Flip <u>T</u>op-bottom   and   <u>R</u>otate 90° clockwise

The Flip <u>T</u>op-bottom transforms a shape by reflecting in the horizontal line
through the centre of the bounding rectangle. The <u>R</u>otate 90° clockwise
rotates the shape about the centre point of the bounding rectangle.

If this Flip <u>T</u>op-bottom command is used becomes

The <u>R</u>otate 90° clockwise command changes to

If the Flip <u>T</u>op-bottom command is followed by the <u>R</u>otate 90° clockwise
command then

 becomes becomes

This shows how a compound transformation can be achieved by using a
computer program.

EXERCISE 8E   In questions **1** to **6** copy the given shape and draw its image after carrying out the two commands in the order given. All commands operate about the centre of the bounding rectangle. Where you draw the image is not important.

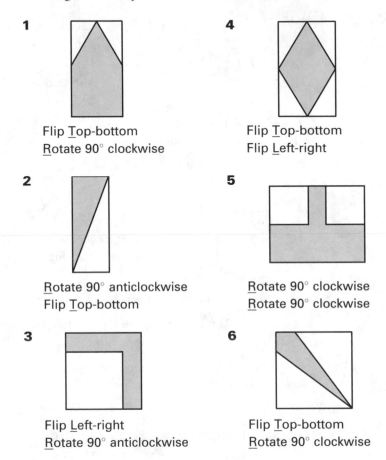

1

Flip <u>T</u>op-bottom
<u>R</u>otate 90° clockwise

4

Flip <u>T</u>op-bottom
Flip <u>L</u>eft-right

2

<u>R</u>otate 90° anticlockwise
Flip <u>T</u>op-bottom

5

<u>R</u>otate 90° clockwise
<u>R</u>otate 90° clockwise

3

Flip <u>L</u>eft-right
<u>R</u>otate 90° anticlockwise

6

Flip <u>T</u>op-bottom
<u>R</u>otate 90° clockwise

In questions **7** to **10** what single transformation, selected from the four transformations listed below, will move the design on the tile from the position shown in **A** to the position shown in **B** ?

Reflection in the horizontal line through the centre of the tile.
Reflection in the vertical line through the centre of the tile.
Rotation about the centre of the tile 90° clockwise.
Rotation about the centre of the tile 90° anticlockwise.

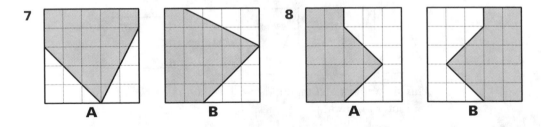

7

A   **B**

8

A   **B**

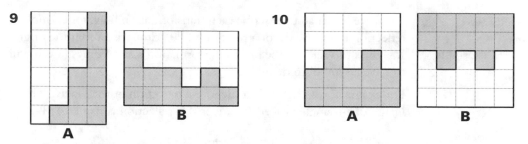

In questions **11** to **14** describe, in the correct order, two transformations selected from the four given above questions **7** to **10**, that map the design on the tile from the position shown in **A** to the position shown in **B**.

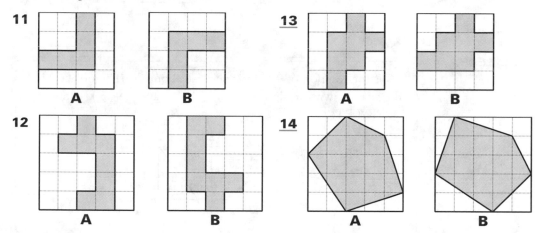

15 On a computer drawing program Leah has two commands

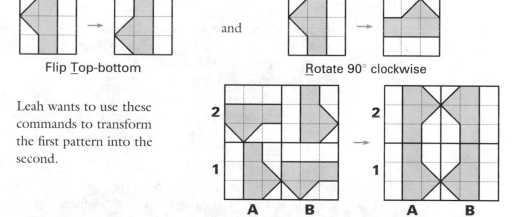

Flip <u>T</u>op-bottom   and   <u>R</u>otate 90° clockwise

Leah wants to use these commands to transform the first pattern into the second.

Copy and complete the commands so that the four tiles are transformed to their required positions. *Remember* you can only Flip Top-bottom or Rotate 90° clockwise.

Tile **A1** Already in the correct position
Tile **A2** Flip Top-bottom, ...
Tile **B1** . . . .
Tile **B2** . . . .

NOTATION
FOR
TRANSFORMATIONS

So far we have had to describe each transformation fully, for example, a reflection in the *x*-axis, or a rotation of 90° clockwise about the origin. If we wish to refer to the same transformation several times, it is useful to have a symbol to denote it.

For example, we can use Y to denote a reflection in the *y*-axis. The image of a triangle (called P) under this reflection is named Y(P).

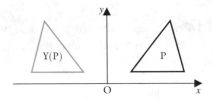

EXERCISE 8F

R₁ is the rotation of 90° anticlockwise about O. The object P is the triangle with vertices (1, 1), (4, 1) and (4, 5). Draw P and R₁(P).

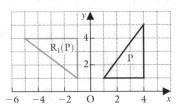

In this exercise

R₁ is a rotation of 90° anticlockwise about O
R₂ is a rotation of 180° about O
R₃ is a rotation of 90° clockwise about O
X is a reflection in the *x*-axis
Y is a reflection in the *y*-axis
T is a translation defined by the vector $\begin{pmatrix} 2 \\ 3 \end{pmatrix}$.

For each question, draw *x*- and *y*-axes, each scaled from −6 to 6.

1 P, Q and R are the points (1, 2), (1, 5) and (3, 5) respectively. Draw △PQR and label it A. Draw and label the following images.

a R₁(A)   **b** R₂(A)   **c** R₃(A)

2 P is the triangle with vertices (−5, 0), (−3, 0) and (−3, 2). Q is the triangle with vertices (1, 0), (3, 0) and (1, 2). R is the triangle with vertices (−2, −6), (0, −6) and (0, −4).

Draw and label **a** T(P)   **b** T(Q)   **c** T(R)

3 A, B, C and D are the points (−2, 1), (−4, 1), (−4, 5) and (−2, 5) respectively. Draw rectangle ABCD and label it Q.

Draw and label the images **a** X(P) **b** Y(Q)

4 Q is the quadrilateral with vertices (1, −1), (3, −1), (5, −3) and (2, −4). Draw and label **a** R_2(Q) **b** Y(Q) **c** X(Q)

5 L is a reflection in the line $x + y = 1$ and M is a reflection in the line $y = x + 1$. The object A is the triangle with vertices (2, 1), (5, 0) and (4, 3). Find **a** L(A) **b** M(A) **c** Y(A)

6 N is a rotation of 90° anticlockwise about (1, 1). R is a rotation of 90° clockwise about (0, −1). The object B is the triangle with vertices (−2, 1), (−5, 1) and (−2, 2).

Find **a** N(B) **b** R(B)

NOTATION FOR COMPOUND TRANSFORMATIONS

If we reflect the object P in the *x*-axis and then reflect the resulting image in the *y*-axis, we are carrying out a compound transformation. The letters defined at the beginning of the previous exercise can be used to describe the final image.

In the diagram below, the first image is X(P). The second image is Y(X(P)) but the outer set of brackets is not usually used so it is written YX(P).

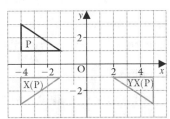

Notice that the letter X, denoting the transformation used first, is nearer to the object P. We always work outwards from the bracket containing the object.

In the diagram below, YT(P) means 'translate P first and then reflect the image in the *y*-axis', whereas TY(P) means 'reflect P in the *y*-axis and then translate the image'.

Notice that YT(P) is not the same as TY(P).

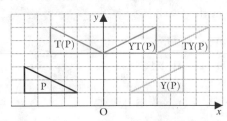

EXERCISE 8G   In this exercise, R_1 is a rotation of 90° anticlockwise about O

R_2 is a rotation of 180° about O

R_3 is a rotation of 90° clockwise about O

X is a reflection in the x-axis

Y is a reflection in the y-axis

T is a translation defined by the vector $\begin{pmatrix} 4 \\ 3 \end{pmatrix}$.

A, B and C are the points $(4, 1)$, $(6, 1)$ and $(6, 4)$.

Draw △ABC and label it P.

Draw and label $R_1(P)$, $XR_1(P)$ and $YR_1(P)$.

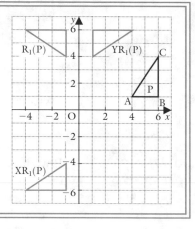

In each of the following questions draw x- and y-axes, each for values from -6 to 6.

1 P, Q and R are the points $(1, 3)$, $(3, 3)$ and $(1, 6)$. Draw △PQR and label it A.

  a Draw and label   **i** $R_3(A)$ **ii** $XR_3(A)$ **iii** $X(A)$ **iv** $R_3X(A)$

  b Describe the single transformation that will map A to $R_3X(A)$.

2 L, M and N are the points $(-2, 1)$, $(-4, 1)$ and $(-2, 5)$. Draw △LMN and label it P.

  a Draw and label   **i** $R_1(P)$ **ii** $R_2R_1(P)$ **iii** $R_3R_1(P)$

  b What is the single transformation that will map
    i P to $R_2R_1(P)$ **ii** $R_2R_1(P)$ to $R_1(P)$?

3 A, B and C are the points $(-5, 2)$, $(-2, 2)$ and $(-5, 4)$. Draw △ABC and label it P.

  a Draw and label   **i** $X(P)$ **ii** $YX(P)$ **iii** $R_2(P)$ **iv** $Y(P)$ **v** $XY(P)$

  b Is $YX(P)$ the same triangle as $XY(P)$?

  c Is $R_2(P)$ the same triangle as $XY(P)$?

  d What single transformation is equivalent to a reflection in the x-axis followed by a reflection in the y-axis?

4 L, M and N are the points $(-3, 0)$, $(-1, 0)$ and $(-1, 3)$. Draw △LMN and label it Q.

  a Find   **i** $T(Q)$ **ii** $XT(Q)$ **iii** $X(Q)$ **iv** $TX(Q)$

  b Describe the single transformation that will map
    i $X(Q)$ to $XT(Q)$ **ii** $XT(Q)$ to $TX(Q)$.

**EQUIVALENT
SINGLE
TRANSFORMATIONS**

We have seen that if we reflect an object P in the x-axis and then reflect the image X(P) in the y-axis we get the same final image as if we had rotated P through $180°$ about O. YX(P) is the same as R_2(P) and the effect of YX is the same as the effect of R_2.

We can write   YX(P) = R_2(P)   referring to the images

and   YX = R_2 referring to the transformations.

In the following exercise notice that X^2 = XX, that is, the transformation X is used twice in succession.

EXERCISE 8H

In each question draw x- and y-axes, each for values from -6 to 6.

1 A is a reflection in the line $x = -1$ and B a reflection in the line $y = 2$. Z is the triangle with vertices (1, 4), (4, 6) and (1, 6).

a Find A(Z), B(Z), AB(Z) and BA(Z).

b Describe the single transformations given by AB and BA. Is AB equal to BA?

c Find A^2(Z) and B^2(Z).

2 T is a reflection in the line $x = 1$.
U is a reflection in the line $y = 2$.
V is a rotation of $180°$ about the point (1, 2).
A is the triangle with vertices (1, 1), (3, 1) and (3, -2).

a Draw T(A), U(A), TU(A) and UT(A).

b Are TU and UT the same transformation?

c Is it true that V = TU?

3 R_1 is a rotation of $90°$ anticlockwise about O.
R_2 is a rotation of $180°$ about O.
R_3 is a rotation of $90°$ clockwise about O.
P is the triangle with vertices (1, 2), (4, 2) and (1, 4).

a Draw R_1(P), $R_1{}^2$(P), R_2(P), R_2R_1(P) and R_3(P).
Complete the following statements

i $R_1{}^2 =$ **ii** $R_2R_1 =$

b Draw whatever images are needed and complete the following statements

i $R_3{}^2 =$ **ii** $R_2R_3 =$ **iii** $R_3R_2 =$

THE IDENTITY TRANSFORMATION

If an object is rotated through 360° or translated using the vector $\binom{0}{0}$, the final image turns out to be the same as the original object. We are back where we started and might as well not have performed a transformation at all. This operation is called the *identity transformation* and is usually denoted by I.

INVERSE TRANSFORMATION

The inverse of a transformation reverses the effect of that transformation, for example, the inverse of a rotation of 90° anticlockwise is a rotation of 90° clockwise about the same point (or a rotation of 270° anticlockwise).

EXERCISE 8I

In this exercise

R_1 is a rotation of 90° anticlockwise about O
R_2 is a rotation of 180° about O
R_3 is a rotation of 90° clockwise about O
A is a reflection in the x-axis
B is a reflection in the y-axis
C is a reflection in the line $y = x$
D is a reflection in the line $y = -x$
I is the identity transformation.

P is the triangle with vertices $(2, 1)$, $(5, 1)$ and $(2, 3)$.
Find $B(P)$ and $B^2(P)$. Name the single transformation which is equal to B^2.

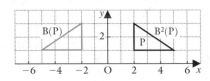

$$B^2(P) = P \qquad \therefore \ B^2 = 1$$

For each question draw x- and y-axes, each for values from -6 to 6.

1 P is the triangle with vertices $(2, 1)$, $(5, 1)$ and $(5, 5)$.

a Find $R_1(P)$, $R_2(P)$, $R_3(P)$, $R_1R_3(P)$ and $R_3R_1(P)$. Name the single transformation which is equal to both R_1R_3 and R_3R_1.

b Complete the following statements with a single letter.

i $R_2{}^2 =$ **ii** $R_2R_3 =$ **iii** $R_1R_2 =$

2 Q is the triangle with vertices $(-2, 1)$, $(-5, 1)$ and $(-4, 5)$.

a Find $A(Q)$, $B(Q)$, $AB(Q)$, $R_2(Q)$ and $B^2(Q)$.

b Complete the following statements with a single letter.   **i** $B^2 =$ **ii** $AB =$

3 N is the triangle with vertices $(1, 3)$, $(1, 6)$ and $(5, 6)$.

a Find $C(N)$, $DC(N)$, $C^2(N)$, $AC(N)$, $BC(N)$ and $IC(N)$.

b Complete the following statements with a single letter.

   i $DC =$ **ii** $C^2 =$ **iii** $AC =$ **iv** $BC =$ **v** $IC =$

4 M is the triangle with vertices $(3, 2)$, $(5, 2)$ and $(5, 6)$.

a Find $R_1(M)$, $A(M)$, $A^2(M)$, $AR_1(M)$ and $R_1A(M)$.

b Complete the following statements with a single letter.

   i $A^2 =$ **ii** $AR_1 =$ **iii** $R_1A =$

c Is the statement $AR_1 = R_1A$ true or false?

5 L is the triangle with vertices $(3, 1)$, $(4, 4)$ and $(1, 4)$.

a Find $I(L)$, $AI(L)$, $BI(L)$, $IA(L)$ and $IB(L)$.

b Simplify AI, BI, IA and IB.

6 The diagram shows a set of transformations of trapezium P.

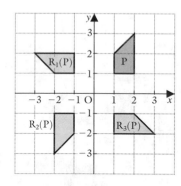
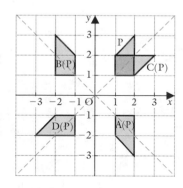

a The tables show several single transformations that give the same result as each of the pairs. Copy and complete both tables.

		Second transformation			
		A	B	C	D
First transformation	A	I	R_2	R_1	R_3
	B	R_2	I	R_3	R_1
	C	R_3			
	D	R_1			

		Second transformation			
		I	R_1	R_2	R_3
First transformation	I	I	R_1	R_2	R_3
	R_1				
	R_2				R_1
	R_3				

b Use the tables from part **a** to write down the inverse of each transformation.

Transformation	I	A	B	C	D	R_1	R_2	R_3
Inverse	I	A				R_3		

The inverse of A is A but the inverse of R_1 is R_3. Explain why some transformations in the table are their own inverses whereas others are not.

MIXED EXERCISE

EXERCISE 8J

1 Construct a quadrilateral ABCD in which AB $= 12$ cm, AD $= 10$ cm, $B\widehat{A}D = 90°$, $A\widehat{B}C = 60°$ and $A\widehat{D}C = 60°$. Construct the bisector of $B\widehat{C}D$ to meet AB in E. Construct the perpendicular from D to EC to meet EC at H. Measure HC.

2 Copy the diagram and draw the image when A is transformed by a rotation of 90° anticlockwise about the origin followed by a translation defined by the vector $\begin{pmatrix} 3 \\ -6 \end{pmatrix}$ followed by an enlargement, centre O and scale factor $\frac{1}{2}$.
Mark the final image P.

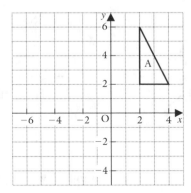

3 Copy the diagram and draw the image of P when it is transformed by a reflection in the x-axis followed by a rotation of 180° about the point $(2, 0)$. Mark the final image Q.

Describe the single transformation that maps Q onto P.

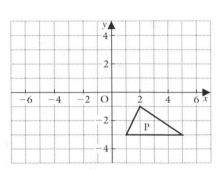

4 Describe, in the correct order, two transformations that will move the
design on the tile from the position shown in **A** to the position
shown in **B**. You can select the transformations from these four:

P: Reflection in the horizontal line through the centre of the tile.
Q: Reflection in the vertical line through the centre of the tile.
R: Rotation about the centre of the tile by 90° clockwise.
S: Rotation about the centre of the tile by 90° anticlockwise.

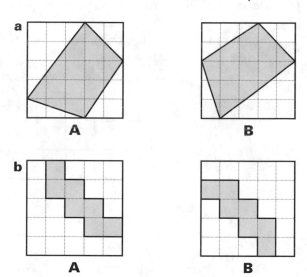

5 Draw x- and y-axes, each from -6 to 6.

R_1 is a rotation 90° anticlockwise about O
R_2 is a rotation of 180° about O
R_3 is a rotation 90° clockwise about O
I is the identity transformation.
A is a reflection in the x-axis
B is a reflection in the y-axis
C is a reflection in the line $y = x$
D is a reflection in the line $y = -x$

P is the triangle with vertices $(2, 1)$, $(4, 1)$ and $(4, 4)$.

a Find

i $R_1(P)$ **ii** $R_2(P)$ **iii** $R_3(P)$ **iv** $C(P)$ **v** $C^2(P)$ **vi** $DI(P)$

b Name the single transformation that maps

i $R_1(P)$ onto $C(P)$ **ii** $C(P)$ onto $R_3(P)$.

c Name the single transformation that is equivalent to

i R_2R_1 **ii** R_1R_3

a Make a pattern by following these instructions:

From any starting point, S, and facing up the page
go 1 square forward and turn 90° clockwise
next go 2 squares forward and turn 90° clockwise
and then go 4 squares forward and turn 90° clockwise.

Repeat these three instructions until you get back to your starting point.

This is called pattern 124 because it follows the instructions using the digits 1, 2, 4 in that order.

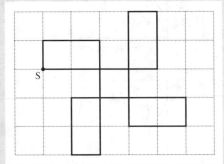

b Does this shape have line symmetry? If so, draw the mirror line.

c Does this shape have rotational symmetry? If so, state the order of rotational symmetry.

d Repeat parts **a** to **c** but putting the same three digits in a different order. For example, 2, 4, 1 or 4, 2, 1.
How many different shapes do you get?

e Repeat parts **a** to **d** for other triples of digits, for example 252, 243, 267, ...

f Some sets of digits lead to shapes that have both line symmetry and rotational symmetry.

  i List those sets you have found.

  ii Some set of digits lead to shapes that have rotational symmetry only. List those sets.

  iii Find a rule about the digits which allows you to forecast the symmetry of the shapes, and test it on new sets of digits.

LENGTHS, AREAS AND VOLUMES

Gino works as a designer for a packaging company. The latest project he has been working on involves designing boxes for transporting and displaying tennis balls. The boxes are to be manufactured from flat sheets of card and must take from three to six tennis balls. His brief is to use the smallest amount of card per ball and have as little wasted space in each box as possible. Some of the shapes he has come up with are shown below.

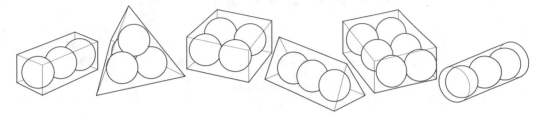

To move ahead with this project Gino needs to know

- how much card is used to make each shape he designs
- the capacity of each box
- the volume of a spherical object
- how to calculate the amount of unused space in each box.

This chapter, together with Chapter 10, shows us how to solve this and similar problems. In this chapter we concentrate on rectilinear shapes, that is shapes whose edges are straight lines and whose faces are flat.

<table>
<tr><td>GREATEST AND
SMALLEST
VALUES</td><td>In Book 9A, Chapter 1 we studied rounded numbers. We found that if the length of a nail is 25 mm, correct to the nearest millimetre, then if l mm is the actual length of the nail, $24.5 \leqslant l < 25.5$.
24.5 is called the lower bound of l and 25.5 is called the upper bound of l.
The largest value of l that is less than 25.5 is 25.499999999 ... and when this is corrected to any number of decimal places it becomes 25.5.</td></tr>
</table>

We shall therefore assume that, for practical purposes, the greatest possible value any quantity can have is the same as its upper bound.

In this section we extend upper and lower bounds to the areas and volumes of shapes and solids and apply this knowledge to everyday problems.

EXERCISE 9A

The area of a rectangle measuring 12 cm by 8 cm is A cm^2, each dimension being given correct to the nearest whole number.

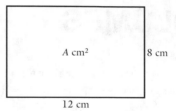

a Find the value of A when it has

i the greatest value possible   **ii** the smallest value possible. Do not round the answers.

b How much larger is the greatest possible value of the area than the smallest value?

a

> A will have its greatest value when the dimensions of the rectangle are as large as possible. The greatest possible value of the length is **12.5** cm and the greatest possible value of the width is **8.5** cm.

i Greatest area = 12.5×8.5 cm^2
$= 106.25$ cm^2

i.e. the greatest possible value of A is 106.25

ii Smallest area = 11.5×7.5 cm^2
$= 86.25$ cm^2

i.e. the smallest possible value of A is 86.25

b From part **a** the difference between the greatest possible area and the smallest possible area is
$(106.25 - 86.25)$ cm^2 i.e. 20 cm^2

1

The page of a book measures 22 cm by 16 cm. Each measurement is correct to the nearest centimetre.

a What is the upper bound for the area of the page?

b What is the lower bound?

2 A rectangular kitchen unit is 32 cm wide and 54 cm deep, each dimension being correct to the nearest centimetre. Kevin measures the gap into which the unit is to be fitted and finds it is 32 cm, correct to the nearest centimetre.

a When Kevin attempts to fit the unit into the gap he finds that it will not go. Explain why this is so.

b Calculate the smallest possible value for the area of the top surface of the unit.

c By how much is the largest possible value for the area of the top surface greater than the smallest possible value?

3 A square concrete paving slab is to measure 50 cm by 50 cm by 48 mm, where each dimension must be correct to the nearest whole number. Calculate the percentage saving in the volume of concrete used if the company is able to produce slabs with the smallest acceptable dimensions rather than with the greatest acceptable dimensions.

4 The dimensions of this rectangular carton are correct to one decimal place.

a Find the upper bound for the area of one of the vertical sides.

b What is the lower bound for the area of shelf one of these cartons stands on?

c How many litres of tomato juice must be available to be sure that 3000 cartons can be filled?

d How many extra cartons could be filled if every carton was made to the minimum acceptable dimensions?

5 A gold ingot in the form of a cuboid measures

$$8.2 \text{ cm} \times 5.7 \text{ cm} \times 3.5 \text{ cm}$$

Each measurement is correct to 1 decimal place. If 1 cm^3 of gold has a mass of 19.3 g find the largest possible mass for an ingot satisfying the given dimensions.

How much greater is this than the mass of an ingot with the smallest acceptable dimensions?

6

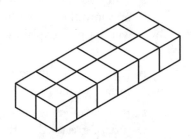

A cardboard box is to hold 12 child's blocks arranged in two rows of 6. Each block is a cube of edge 3.4 cm, correct to 1 decimal place.

a What is the shortest possible length that the box must have to be certain that the 12 blocks will fit into it?

b Find the lower bound of the mass of the box and blocks if the density of the wood used to make the blocks is 0.65 g/cm^3 and the mass of the box is 35 g, both values being correct to two significant figures.

7

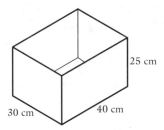

25 cm

30 cm   40 cm

The base of an open rectangular water tank measures 40 cm by 30 cm externally and the tank is 25 cm deep on the outside. It is made from plastic 4 mm thick.

All the dimensions are correct to the nearest whole number.

a Find the largest possible value for the depth of the tank.

b What is the least horizontal area needed if the tank is to be placed on the ground?

c Find the largest amount of water that a tank satisfying the above data could hold.

Give your answer in litres correct to 3 significant figures.

So far we have dealt with problems where corrected numbers have been either added or multiplied; in those cases the maximum value of the calculation occurs when the individual numbers have their maximum values and vice versa. We now consider calculations involving subtraction or division.

If $a \div b \left(= \dfrac{a}{b} \right)$ is to be as large as possible then, a must have its maximum possible value and b must have its minimum possible value.

Similarly $\dfrac{a}{b}$ is least when a is as small as possible and b is as large as possible.

The same reasoning is true for $a - b$.

A rectangular carton holds 75 centilitres of juice, correct to the nearest centilitre. The dimensions of its base are 10 centimetres by 6 centimetres, both correct to the nearest whole number. Find the largest and smallest possible values for the height of the carton. Round each value to 1 decimal place.

$$\text{Capacity} = \text{length} \times \text{breadth} \times \text{height}$$

$$\therefore \qquad \text{height} = \frac{\text{capacity}}{\text{length} \times \text{breadth}}$$

> The largest value of a quotient occurs when the numerator is as large as possible and the denominator is as small as possible. Note that $1 \, \text{cl} = 10 \, \text{cm}^3$.

Greatest possible height

$$= \frac{\text{greatest possible capacity}}{\text{smallest possible length} \times \text{smallest possible breadth}}$$

$$= \frac{755}{9.5 \times 5.5} \, \text{cm} = 14.449 \ldots \text{cm}$$

$$= 14.4 \, \text{cm} \ (\text{correct to 1 d.p.})$$

Similarly, smallest possible height

$$= \frac{\text{smallest possible capacity}}{\text{largest possible length} \times \text{largest possible breadth}}$$

$$= \frac{745}{10.5 \times 6.5} \, \text{cm} = 10.915 \ldots \text{cm}$$

$$= 10.9 \, \text{cm} \ (\text{correct to 1 d.p.})$$

8 The volume of a rectangular tank is $3\,\text{m}^3$ and the area of the base is $2\,\text{m}^2$, both measurements being correct to 1 significant figure. Which of these gives the least value for the depth of the tank?

A $\dfrac{3.5}{1.5}\,\text{m}$ **B** $\dfrac{2.5}{1.5}\,\text{m}$ **C** $\dfrac{2.5}{2.5}\,\text{m}$ **D** $\dfrac{3.5}{2.5}\,\text{m}$

Justify your answer.

9 A length of 2 m is cut from a plank of wood 5 m long. If both measurements are correct to 1 significant figure, the longest remaining length is

A $(5 - 1.5)\,\text{m}$ **C** $(5.5 - 1.5)\,\text{m}$
B $(5.5 - 2.5)\,\text{m}$ **D** $(4.5 - 2.5)\,\text{m}$

10 The dimensions in the diagram are both correct to 1 decimal place. The largest value of $\tan\widehat{A}$ is

A $\dfrac{1.25}{0.95}$ **C** $\dfrac{1.15}{0.85}$

B $\dfrac{1.15}{0.95}$ **D** $\dfrac{1.25}{0.85}$

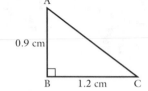

11 The area of a rectangle is $30\,\text{cm}^2$ and its length is $6\,\text{cm}$, both values being correct to the nearest whole number. Find the greatest and least values for the width of the rectangle.

12 In a right-angled triangle ABC, $\widehat{B} = 90°$, $AB = 9.8\,\text{cm}$ and $BC = 6.3\,\text{cm}$. If each length is correct to the nearest tenth of a centimetre find the greatest and least possible values for the length of the third side.

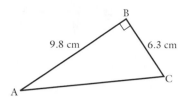

13 In a right-angled triangle ABC, $\widehat{C} = 90°$, $AB = 8.6\,\text{cm}$ and $BC = 5.2\,\text{cm}$, each length being correct to 2 significant figures. Find the greatest and least possible values for the size of the angle A. Give your values correct to the nearest tenth of a degree.

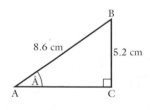

14 The sketch shows the end wall of a lean-to shed. $\widehat{BAC} = 30°$ (correct to the nearest degree) and $BC = 1.6\,m$ (correct to 1 d.p.). Find the difference between the greatest and least possible values for the length of AC. Give your answer rounded to 2 significant figures.

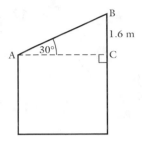

15 A rectangular carton has a volume of $1000\,cm^3$. The area of the base, correct to the nearest whole number, is $85\,cm^2$. Find the greatest and least possible values for the height of the carton.

16

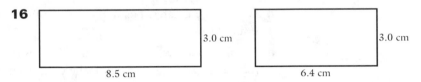

Tracey cuts two rectangular pieces of card, one **8.5** cm long, the other **6.4** cm long, from a strip of card that is **3.0** cm wide. All dimensions are correct to 1 decimal place.

a The two pieces are placed edge to edge as shown.

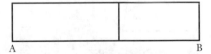

For the distance AB find
  i its largest possible value
  ii its smallest possible value.

b The two pieces are rearranged to form a symmetrical letter **T**.

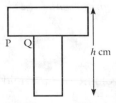

  i What is the smallest possible value for the length PQ ?
  ii Find the upper bound for the height, h cm, of this **T**-shape.

17 Liz bought several cartons of orange squash for Kelvin's birthday party. She also bought a supply of plastic cups. Each carton holds 85 centilitres of squash, and each cup will hold 12 centilitres, each quantity being correct to the nearest centilitre.

a Write down the upper and lower bounds for the contents of a carton.

b Write down the upper and lower bounds for the amount that a plastic cup will hold.

c How many cups can Liz definitely fill from one carton?

d What is the greatest possible number of cups Liz could fill from 1 full carton?

e Liz fills 5 cups from 1 full carton. What is the difference between the most that could remain in the carton and the least?

PYRAMIDS

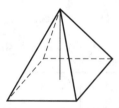
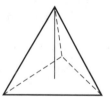
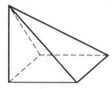

Each of these solids is a pyramid; its shape is given by drawing lines from a single point to each corner of the base.

The first solid has a square base and is called a square-based pyramid.

The second one has a triangular base and is called a triangular pyramid. It is also called a *tetrahedron*: a special name that applies only to this shape.

In a *right pyramid* the vertex is directly above the middle point of the base.

VOLUME OF A PYRAMID

The volume of a pyramid is given by

$$\text{Volume} = \tfrac{1}{3} \text{ area of base} \times \text{perpendicular height}$$

The surface area of any pyramid is found by adding the area of the base
to the sum of the areas of the sloping sides.

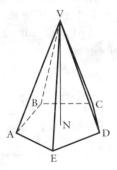

Drawing a net often helps in finding the total surface area of a pyramid.
This makes it clear what distances and areas are needed and where the
right angles are.

For example, the net for a right pyramid with a rectangular base is shown
below. It is easy to see that the equal sloping sides occur in pairs.

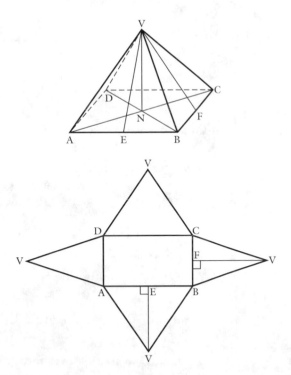

E is the middle point of AB and F is the middle point of BC.

Total surface area of this pyramid

= area base ABCD + 2 × area △VAB + 2 × area △VBC

EXERCISE 9B

A right pyramid stands on a square base ABCD of side 6 cm and its height is 4 cm. The distance from its vertex E to the midpoint F of BC is 5 cm. Find

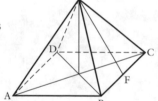

a the volume of the pyramid

b its total surface area.

First draw a net to show the actual shapes of the base and sloping sides. On it mark all the distances you need.

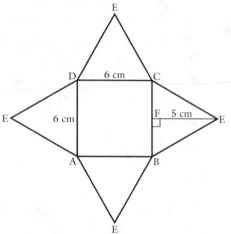

a Area of base $= 6 \times 6$ cm^2

$\qquad\qquad\quad = 36$ cm^2

Volume of pyramid

$\qquad = \frac{1}{3}$ area of base $\times$ perpendicular height

$\qquad = \frac{1}{3} \times 36 \times 4$ cm^3

$\qquad = 48$ cm^3

b Length of FE $= 5$ cm

Area of one sloping side $= \frac{1}{2} \times 6 \times 5$ cm^2

$\qquad\qquad\qquad\qquad\qquad = 15$ cm^2

$\therefore$ area of the four sloping sides $= 4 \times 15$ cm^2

$\qquad\qquad\qquad\qquad\qquad\qquad = 60$ cm^2

Total surface area of pyramid

$\qquad = $ area of the base $+$ area of the four sloping sides

$\qquad = (36 + 60)$ cm^2

$\qquad = 96$ cm^2

Find the volumes of the pyramids in questions **1** to **4**.

1

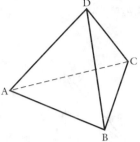

The base of the pyramid is △ABC whose area is 52 cm². The height of the pyramid is **6.8** cm.

2

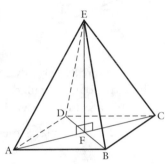

The base ABCD is a rectangle. AB = 8 cm, BC = **4.5** cm and EF = 6 cm.

3

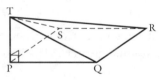

The base PQRS is a rectangle. PQ = 20 cm, QR = 12 cm and TS = 8 cm.

4

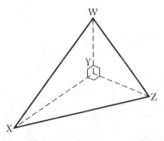

The base is triangle XYZ. XY = 10 cm, YZ = 8 cm and WY = 8 cm.

5 The volume of a pyramid is **76.8** cm³ and the area of its base is **32.0** cm².

    a Find the height of the pyramid.

    b If the measurements given are correct to 3 significant figures, what is the least possible value for the height?

6 A solid copper pyramid with a square base of side 9 cm has a mass of 1780 g. If the mass of 1 cm^3 of copper is 8.9 g find

a the volume of the pyramid

b its height.

7

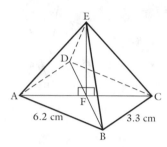

The base of a right pyramid is a rectangle ABCD where AB = 6.2 cm and BC = 3.3 cm. The vertex of the pyramid is E and EF = 5.8 cm. Each measurement is given correct to 1 decimal place.

a Write down, correct to 2 decimal places the greatest and least values for

   i the length of AB
  ii the area of the rectangle ABCD
 iii the volume of the pyramid.

b By what percentage, correct to the nearest whole number, is the largest possible volume greater than the smallest possible volume?

8

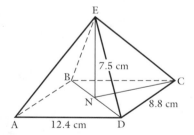

The dimensions of a right pyramid with a rectangular base are shown on the diagram. Each dimension is given correct to 1 decimal place. Find

a the largest possible value for the area of the base

b the smallest possible value for the volume of the pyramid

c the largest possible number of pyramids that have a total volume that is less than 10 000 cm^3.

PROBLEMS IN THREE DIMENSIONS

To find angles or lengths in solid figures, a right-angled triangle containing the unknown quantity has to be identified. To find a suitable triangle often means drawing a section through a solid or, if it is a prism, its cross-section.

If a plane cuts a solid into two parts the shape that is revealed by the plane is called a *section*.

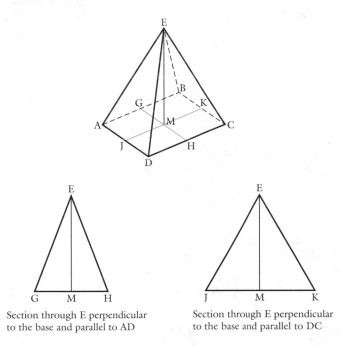

Section through E perpendicular to the base and parallel to AD

Section through E perpendicular to the base and parallel to DC

Some solids (called prisms) are such that the section is the same wherever the solid is cut by a plane perpendicular to its axis. These sections are called *cross-sections*.

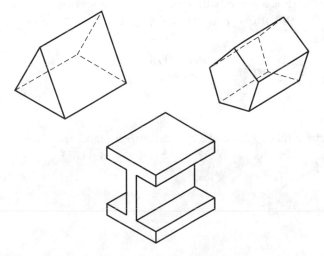

Each shape is a prism with a uniform cross-section.

EXERCISE 9C

The figure is a pyramid on a square base ABCD.
The edges of the base are 30 cm long and the
height EH of the pyramid is 42 cm.

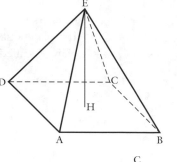

Find   **a** the length of AC

       b the angle $E\widehat{A}H$

a

> First identify a right-angled triangle with AC as one of its sides, then
> draw this triangle. AC is a diagonal of the square base ABCD so we
> will use △ABC.

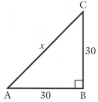

Using △ABC, $\widehat{B} = 90°$, AB = BC = 30 cm
$$AC^2 = AB^2 + BC^2 \quad (\text{Pythag. theorem})$$
$$\therefore \qquad x^2 = 900 + 900 = 1800$$
$$x = 42.42\ldots$$
$$\therefore \qquad AC = 42.4 \text{ cm} \quad (\text{correct to 3 s.f.})$$

b

> $E\widehat{A}H$ is in △AHE, in which $\widehat{H} = 90°$ and AH $= \frac{1}{2}$AC $= 21.21\ldots$cm.

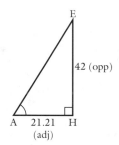

$$\tan \widehat{A} = \frac{\text{opp}}{\text{adj}} = \frac{42}{21.21\ldots} = 1.979\ldots$$
$$\therefore \qquad \widehat{A} = 63.20\ldots°$$
$$\text{i.e.} \ \ E\widehat{A}H = 63.2° \ (\text{correct to 1 decimal place})$$

1 ABCDEF is a prism with a triangular cross-section.
$A\widehat{B}C = 90°$, BC = 8 m, AB = 6 m and CD = 20 m.
Find   **a** AC   **c** $A\widehat{C}B$

        b BD   **d** $A\widehat{D}B$

        e the surface area of the prism.

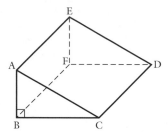

2 In the cuboid, AB = 12 cm, BF = 6 cm and BC = 8 cm.
Find   **a** FC   **b** AF   **c** DB   **d** $H\widehat{B}D$

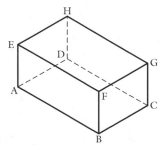

3 ABCD is a pyramid on an equilateral triangular base ABC of side 15 cm. AD is perpendicular to AC and AB, and is also 15 cm long. E is the midpoint of BC.

Find   **a** AE   **b** A$\hat{B}$D   **c** A$\hat{E}$D   **d** DE

        e the total surface area of the pyramid.

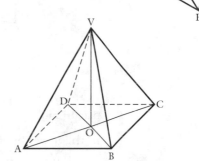

4 VABCD is a square-based pyramid with V vertically above O, the centre of the square ABCD.

If AB = 15 cm and VO = 20 cm find

a AC   **c** AV

b V$\hat{A}$O   **d** V$\hat{A}$B

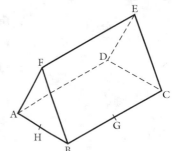

5 ABCDEF is a prism with cross-section an equilateral triangle of side 2 cm. BC = 5 cm, G is the midpoint of BC and H is the midpoint of AB.

Find   **a** FG   **b** B$\hat{F}$G   **c** A$\hat{G}$B   **d** F$\hat{G}$H

Sketch the solid whose vertices are F, H, G and B.

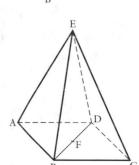

6 The diagram shows a square-based pyramid. Its base is horizontal and E is vertically above F, the centre of the base. AB = 8 cm and EF = 10 cm.

a Sketch section EBD. What type of triangle is it? Find BD and the area of the section.

b Sketch the vertical section through EF, parallel to BC. Find its area.

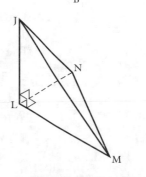

7 The base of a pyramid is triangle LMN. N$\hat{L}$M = 90°, LN = 11 cm, LM = 12 cm and J$\hat{M}$L = 32°

a Find   **i** JL   **ii** the volume of the pyramid.

b The pyramid is turned over so that triangle JNM is its base which is resting on a table. Find the total surface area of the pyramid that is now visible.

8

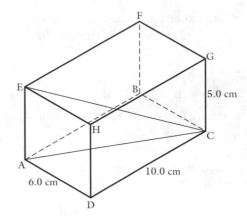

In the diagram each dimension of the cuboid is correct to 1 decimal place. Find

a the upper bound for the value of

i EA   **ii** AC

b the lower bound for the value of

i EA   **ii** AC

c Use your answers to parts **a** and **b** to find the upper bound for the angle ECA.

Give your answer correct to 1 decimal place.

9 The base, ABCD, of a right pyramid is a rectangle measuring 18 cm by 10 cm, and the height of the pyramid, EF, is 12 cm. If H is the midpoint of AB and G is the midpoint of BC find

a the lengths of FG and EG

b the lengths of HF and EH

c the volume of the pyramid

d its total surface area.

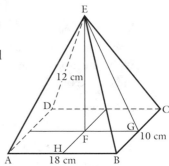

10 The base of a wooden pyramid is a horizontal square PQRS. The diagonals of the square meet at T.
The vertex U is vertically above T. PQ = 8 cm and PU = 12 cm.

a Find, in surd form, the exact length of

i PR   **ii** TR   **iii** UT

b If the density of the wood is 0.74 g/cm^3 find the mass of the pyramid.

Give your answer correct to 3 significant figures.

11 The base of a right pyramid is a regular hexagon ABCDEF. G is vertically above the centre, H, of the hexagon, and I is the midpoint of BC. If $GI = 13\,cm$ and $GH = 12\,cm$ find

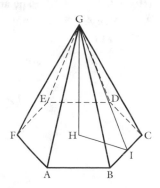

   a HI

   b BC

   c the area of a sloping side

   d the area of the hexagonal base

   e the total surface area of the pyramid.

12 The diagram shows a cube of edge 6 inches. P is the midpoint of AB. An insect starts from P and crawls to G over the surface of the cube.

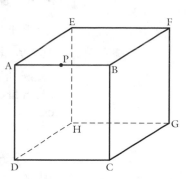

   a Find the length of the shortest route it can take crossing the edge BF. Find also the angle with the horizontal at which the insect is crawling when it is on the vertical face BCGF.

   b Show that there is an alternative shortest route from P to G. What angle does this route make with the horizontal when the insect is on the vertical face BCGF?

13

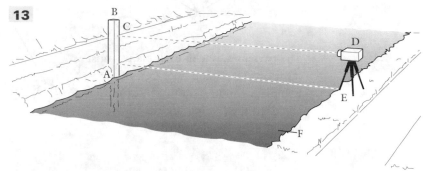

The width of a canal is to be measured from the side EF, the opposite bank being inaccessible. Measuring tapes are available: also a theodolite which can measure angles of depression and elevation, and the angle of rotation in a horizontal plane (so that, for example, $B\widehat{D}C$ and $E\widehat{A}F$ can be measured).

Describe as neat a method as possible for finding the width of the canal and the height of the pole AB.

**THE ANGLE
BETWEEN A LINE
AND A PLANE**

The angle between the line PQ and the plane ABCD is defined as the angle between PQ and its projection on the plane ABCD.

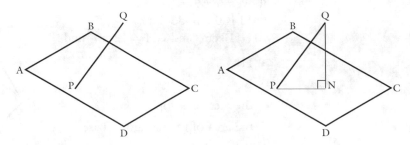

Draw a perpendicular, QN, from Q to the plane. (N is called the foot of the perpendicular.) Join P to N.

The required angle is QP̂N. (This angle is tucked under the line.)

The line PN is called the *projection* of the line PQ on the plane.

(Note: if the plane does not look horizontal, it may help you to see which line is the perpendicular if you turn the page and look at the diagram from a different angle.)

**THE ANGLE
BETWEEN TWO
PLANES**

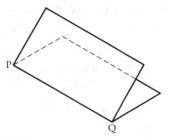

To find the angle between two planes we need to find two lines to act as the arms of the angle.

The two lines, one in each plane, must meet on the joining line, PQ, of the two planes and each must be at right angles to the joining line.
One possible angle is AR̂C.

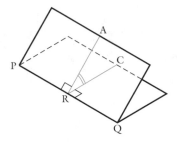

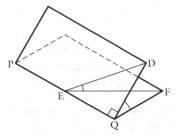

Notice that there are any number of pairs of lines that meet at a given point on the joining line but only a pair at right angles to PQ gives the required angle. DÊF is *not* a possible angle but DQ̂F is possible.

It can be helpful to use a section through a solid when trying to identify the angle between two of its faces. The section, or cut, must be made at right angles to the edge where the two faces meet, cutting this edge at P, say. Then the angle between the faces is the angle at P in the section. For example, in a right pyramid, the angle between the base and a sloping face can be found from a section formed by a cut through the vertex perpendicular to the base.

EXERCISE 9D

ABCD is a right pyramid of height 5 cm.
Its base ABCD is a rectangle in which
AB = 6 cm and BC = 8 cm.

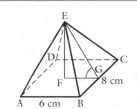

a Find the angle between EA and the plane ABCD.

b Find the angle between the planes EBC and ABCD.

a

> EF is the perpendicular from E to ABCD. EÂF is the required angle, so we draw △EAF.

$AF = \frac{1}{2}AC$

In △ABC, AC = 10 cm (3, 4, 5△)

∴ AF = 5 cm

∴ EÂF = 45° (rt-angled isos. △)

The angle between EA and ABCD is 45°.

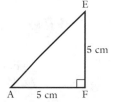

b

> BC is the joining line for the planes. From symmetry, EG and FG are both perpendicular to BC at G.
> EĜF is the required angle, so we draw △EGF

In △EFG, F̂ = 90°

$\tan G = \dfrac{\text{opp}}{\text{adj}} = \dfrac{5}{3} = 1.666\,66\ldots$

EĜF = 59.0°

The angle between the planes is 59.0° (correct to 1 decimal place)

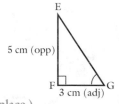

Questions **1** to **3** are concerned with identifying angles, questions **4** onwards require the sizes of the angles to be calculated.

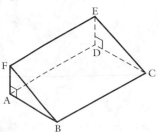

1 For this wedge, sketch and label a triangle containing the angle between

  a FB and the base ABCD   **d** the planes BCEF and ABCD

  b FC and the base ABCD   **e** the planes FAC and FAB.

  c BE and the base ABCD

2

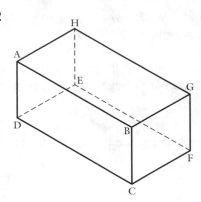

For this cuboid, sketch and label a triangle containing the angle between

a AC and the base CDEF

b AC and the face ADEH

c HC and the face EFGH

d the planes CDHG and CDEF

e the planes ACFH and CDEF

f the planes ABFE and EFGH.

3

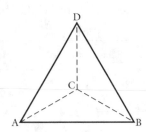

For this regular tetrahedron (each face is an equilateral triangle), sketch and label a triangle containing the angle between

a AD and the base ABC

b CD and the base ABC

c AB and the face ACD

d the planes ABC and DBC.

4 The height of this pyramid is 10 m and its base is a square.

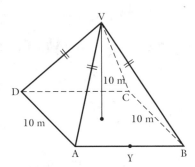

a Calculate the length of DB.

b Calculate the length of VB.

c Find the angle that VB makes with the base ABCD.

d Calculate the length of VY, where Y is the midpoint of AB.

e Draw the section containing the angle between VY and the face ABCD.

f Calculate the angle described in part **e**.

g Write down the angle between the planes VAB and ABCD.

5

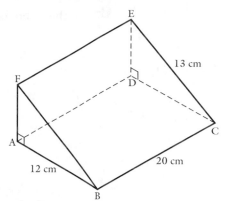

For this metal wedge,

a calculate the lengths of AF and FC

b draw the section containing the angle between the diagonal FC and the base ABCD

c find the size of the angle that FC makes with the base ABCD

d find the size of the angle between the planes FBCE and ABCD

e find the mass of the wedge if the density of the metal from which it is made is 7.9 g/cm³.

6

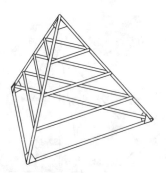
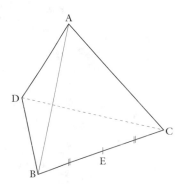

This is a sketch of a playground climbing structure. The basic shape is a pyramid with each face an equilateral triangle of side 3 m. It is possible to climb to the top in various ways.

a Find the distance from the bottom to the top, starting at
   i a corner   **ii** the midpoint of a side.

b Find and sketch a section that contains both the angle that AD makes with the base and the angle that AE makes with the base.

c Using a scale of 4 cm to 1 m, draw this section accurately.

d By taking measurements from your drawing find the angles described in part **b** and the height of the structure.

e When not in use the climbing frame is covered by a canvas sheet that fits exactly over it. How much canvas has been used to make the cover? Neglect any overlaps.

7 In this cuboid, AB = 7 cm, AE = 6 cm and BC = 10 cm.

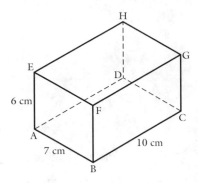

6 cm

7 cm

10 cm

Find the size of the angle between

a EC and the plane ABCD

b FD and the plane ABFE

c the planes EBCH and AEHD

d the planes EFCD and CDHG.

e If each dimension is correct to the nearest centimetre find the upper bound of the angle between the line EC and the plane ABCD.

8

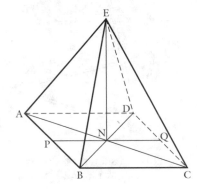

The great pyramid of Cephren at Gizeh in Egypt has a square base of side 215 m and is 225 m high. In the diagram E is the vertex of the right pyramid and ABCD is its base. The diagonals of the base intersect at N; P and Q are the midpoints of AB and DC respectively.

a A tunnel runs from the entrance P to the burial chamber at N. Find PN. How far is N from A?

b How far is it **i** from P to the top **ii** from A to the top?

c A climber wishes to climb from the base of the pyramid to the top. Where should he start

 i to make the shortest climb

 ii to climb in one straight line at the smallest angle to the horizontal?

9

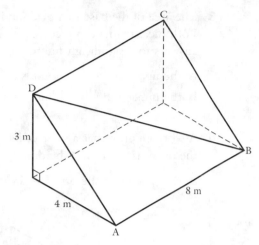

The diagram shows a part of a sea wall whose constant cross-section is a right-angled triangle.

The road is at the level of the top, DC, and the beach starts at AB.

Jim clambers from the road to the beach straight down the path DA whereas Pete goes along the path DB. Find

a the length of the each path

b the inclination to the horizontal of each path.

MIXED EXERCISE

EXERCISE 9E   **1**

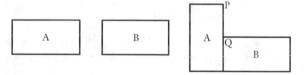

Two identical rectangular cards, A and B, each measure 8.3 cm by 5.7 cm. Each dimension is correct to 1 decimal place. The cards are placed together as shown in the diagram. Find

a the upper bound of the length PQ

b the lower bound of the perimeter of the L-shape

c the upper bound of the area of the shape.

2 The base of a pyramid is a horizontal rectangle ABCD. The vertex E is vertically above A, AB = 15 m, BC = 16 m and AE = 12 m. Find

a the length of EB

b the volume of the pyramid

c the total surface area of the pyramid.

3 The area of the base of a pyramid is $44\,\text{cm}^2$ and it is $5.8\,\text{cm}$ high. Both measurements are correct to 2 significant figures. Find, giving answers to 3 significant figures,

   a the upper and lower bounds for the area of the base

   b the upper and lower bounds for the volume of the pyramid.

4 A wooden prism has a mass of $54\,\text{g}$. The area of the cross-section of the prism is $9\,\text{cm}^2$ and the density of the wood is $0.75\,\text{g/cm}^3$. Find

   a the volume of the prism   **b** its length.

5

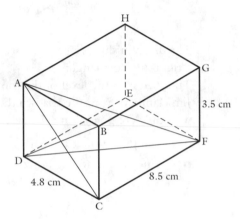

Use the information given in the diagram to find the angle between

   a DF and CF

   b AF and the face DEFC

   c AC and AF

   d the planes ACF and BCFG.

6

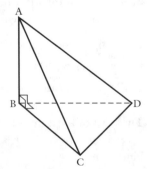

The diagram shows a corner block for a concrete edging system. $AB = BC = BD = 60\,\text{mm}$. Find the angle that the sloping face, ACD, makes with the horizontal base, BCD.

PUZZLE

It is easy to divide a circle into 3 equal parts by drawing 3 lines of equal length. Divide a circle into 4 parts of equal area using 3 lines or curves that do not cross, that are of equal length.

INVESTIGATION

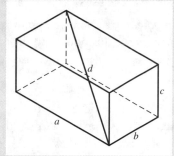

An open rectangular box is a units long, b units wide and c units deep. The length of the longest straight stick that will fit into this box, without projecting outside it is d units.

Find a relationship between d^2 and a, b and c.

Investigate the possible values of a, b, c and d if all four lengths are whole numbers.

SUMMARY 3

CURVES

A line joining two points on a curve is a *chord*.
The *gradient of a chord* gives the average rate at which y-values increase for the values of x between the ends of the chord.

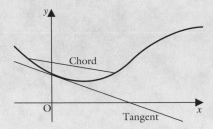

A line which touches a curve at a point is a *tangent* to the curve at that point.

The *gradient of a curve* at a point is defined as the gradient of the tangent to the curve at this point and gives the rate at which values of y are increasing as values of x increase at this point.

THE TRAPEZIUM RULE

When the area under a curve is divided into n strips, each of width d, the area is estimated as

$$\tfrac{1}{2}d(y_0 + 2y_1 + \ldots + 2y_{n-1} + y_n)$$

where $y_0, y_1, \ldots$ are the lengths of the vertical sides of the strips.

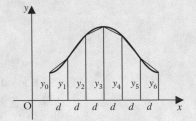

TRAVEL GRAPHS

Velocity
Velocity is the speed *and* the direction of motion of a moving object.

In a *distance–time graph*,

the gradient of a chord gives the *average velocity* over the time interval spanned by the chord,

the gradient of a tangent to the curve gives the *velocity* at that instant.

Acceleration is the rate at which velocity increases.

Negative acceleration is called *deceleration*.

In a *velocity–time graph*,

acceleration is represented by the gradient of the graph when the velocity–time graph is a straight line,

acceleration at an instant is represented by the gradient of the tangent to a curve at that instant,

the *distance covered* in an interval of time is represented by the area under the velocity–time graph for that interval.

**THREE–
DIMENSIONAL
OBJECTS**

A *right pyramid* has its vertex directly above
the centre of its base.

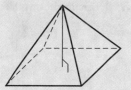

The *volume of any pyramid* is given by

Volume = $\frac{1}{3}$ area of base × perpendicular height

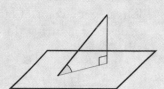

To find the *angle between a line and a
plane* we draw a perpendicular from the
top of the line to the plane, and join the
foot of that perpendicular to the base of
the line. The angle between this join
and the line is the angle we want.

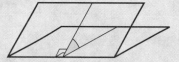

The *angle between two planes* is the
angle between two lines, one in each
plane, that are perpendicular to the
line joining the planes.

**REVISION
EXERCISE 3.1
(Chapters 6
and 7)**

1 Find, in square units, the area enclosed by the x-axis, the line whose
equation is $y = 5x + 10$ and the lines at $x = 1$ and $x = 4$.

2 Copy and complete the table for the equation $y = \frac{1}{8}x^3$. Give values
of x correct to 1 decimal place.

x	0	1	2	3	3.5	4	4.5	5
y		0.1	1	3.4	5.4		11.4	

Using a scale of 4 cm for 1 unit on the x-axis and 1 cm for 1 unit on
the y-axis draw the graph of $y = \frac{1}{8}x^3$ from $x = 0$ to $x = 5$.

a P is the point on the curve where $x = 2$ and Q is the point on
the curve where $x = 5$. Draw PQ and find its gradient.

b Draw, as accurately as possible, the tangents to the curve at the
points where **i** $x = 1$ **ii** $x = 3$ **iii** $x = 4$

c Find the gradients of the tangents to the curve for the values of x
given in part **b**.

3 Copy and complete the table for $y = 3x(4 - x)$

x	0	1	2	2.5	3	4
y	0	9				

Using a scale of 2 cm for 1 unit on the x-axis and 1 cm for 1 unit on the y-axis draw the graph of $y = 3x(4 - x)$

Use the graph to find the gradient of the tangent to the curve where

a $x = 2$ **b** $x = 2.5$ **c** $x = 3$

4 A model aeroplane flies in a circle at a constant speed for 4 minutes. Its speed then decreases at a constant rate until it comes to rest. Which of the following velocity–time graphs best illustrates this motion?

A
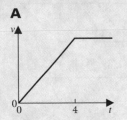

B
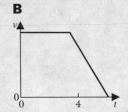

C
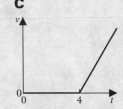

D
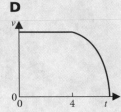

5
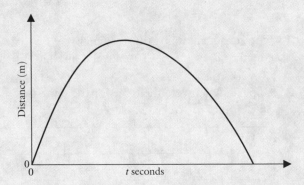

This graph shows the distance of an object from its starting point at different times. Which of these statements are true?

A The velocity of the object is greatest at the beginning of the journey.

B The object returns to its starting point.

C The velocity is zero at the start and increases to a maximum in less than half the time.

D The velocity increases from zero at the start to a maximum at the end of the journey.

6

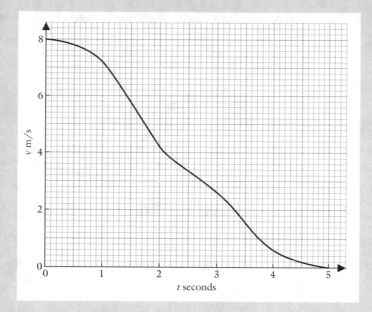

The graph represents 5 seconds in the journey of a skier in a downhill race.

a Are these 5 seconds at the beginning, during or after the end of the race?

b Estimate the distance the skier travels during the 5 seconds.

c Is the skier's acceleration zero at any time? If so, when?

7 When Becky goes to school she sometimes gets a lift part of the way with her father in the car, sometimes she catches the school bus all the way and at other times she walks all the way.

a Which of the following graphs cannot represent Becky's journey?
Give a reason for your answer.

b Which graph could show Becky's journey when she catches the school bus?

c Suggest how she went to school on the other two occasions,
i.e. was it by car, on the bus or on foot, or a combination of these?

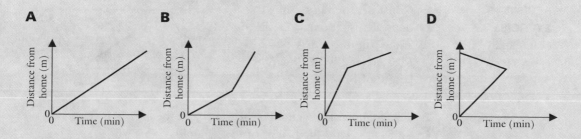

8 The table shows the number of pairs of manx shearwaters on an island at yearly intervals.

Date, D	1985	1986	1987	1988	1989	1990	1991	1992	1993	1994	1995	1996	1997
Number of pairs, n	390	375	365	360	360	365	375	390	410	435	470	530	620

Using a scale of $1\,\text{cm} \equiv 1$ year and $2\,\text{cm} \equiv 100$ pairs draw a graph to illustrate this information.

a Find the gradient of the chord joining the points on the curve where $D = 1990$ and $D = 1993$. Interpret the result.

b Estimate the gradient of the tangent to the curve where $D = 1993$ and interpret the result.

9 Here is a velocity–time graph of a car travelling between two sets of traffic lights.

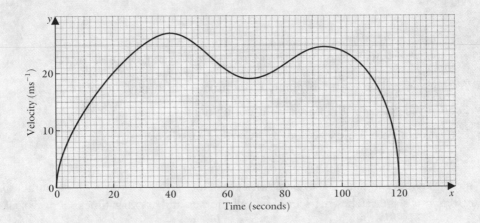

a Calculate an estimate for the acceleration of the car when the time is equal to 20 seconds.

b Calculate an estimate for the total distance travelled by the car.

(London)

REVISION EXERCISE 3.2 (Chapters 8 and 9)

1 Construct the figure shown opposite using only a ruler and a pair of compasses. Measure and write down the length of BD.

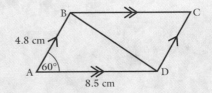

2 The volume of a pyramid is $84.5\,\text{cm}^3$ and the area of its base is $32.5\,\text{cm}^2$. Find the height of the pyramid.

3 From a point P on the sea, 30 m from the foot of a vertical cliff, the angle of elevation of the base of a lighthouse is 30° and the angle of elevation of the top of the lighthouse is 50°.

   a Draw a sketch to represent this data. Mark the foot of the cliff A, the base of the lighthouse B and the top of the lighthouse C.

   b Construct this figure with PA = 15 cm. What scale is used to represent real-life distances?

   c Use your diagram to find

     i the height of the cliff

     ii the height of the lighthouse

     iii the vertical distance from the top of the lighthouse to sea level.

4 Describe as fully as possible the transformation that maps △ABC onto △A′B′C′.

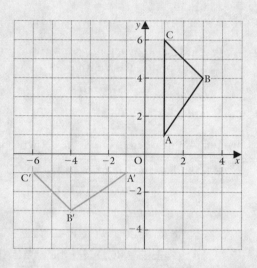

5 Draw △PQR with P(−5, 5), Q(−4, 1) and R(−2, 2). Draw the image of △PQR

   a under a reflection in the line $y = x$. Label it $P_1Q_1R_1$.

   b under a reflection in the x-axis. Label it $P_2Q_2R_2$.

   c under a reflection in the y-axis. Label it $P_3Q_3R_3$.

Describe the transformation that

   d maps $\triangle P_2Q_2R_2$ onto $\triangle P_3Q_3R_3$

   e maps $\triangle P_1Q_1R_1$ onto $\triangle P_2Q_2R_2$.

6 My patio is rectangular and measures 10 m by 8 m, each measurement being correct to the nearest metre.

   a What is the upper bound for the area of the patio?

   b What is the lower bound for the area of the patio?

7 Copy the given tile and draw its image after carrying out the two commands in order about the centre of the square. Its position on the page is not important.

a

Rotate 90° clockwise
Reflect in a horizontal line

b

Reflect in a horizontal line
Rotate 90° anticlockwise

c

Reflect in a horizontal line
Reflect in a vertical line

8 The diagram shows an open metal box in the form of a cuboid.
AB = 15 cm, BC = 9 cm and EA = 8 cm.

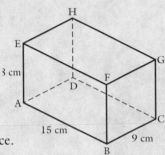

a Find, giving your answer in surd form where appropriate, the length of

i AF   **ii** BG   **iii** AC

b Find EĈA giving your answer correct to 1 decimal place.

9 For the wooden door wedge shown opposite

a calculate the length of

i DE   **ii** AC   **iii** AE

b find the angle between

i the line BE and the base ADEF

ii the plane ABCD and the plane ADEF

c draw the vertical section containing the angle between AC and the base ADEF. Find this angle.

d find the mass of the wedge if the density of the wood from which it is made is 0.78 g/cm^3.

10 A company makes rectangular sheets of tinplate for use in cans.

DIMENSIONS OF RECTANGULAR SHEETS

Thickness	Length	Width
0.15 mm	830 mm	635 mm

The length and width are given to the nearest mm, and the thickness to the nearest 0.01 mm

Calculate the percentage saving in volume to the company if it produces the sheets to minimum dimensions rather than maximum dimensions.   (SEG)

11 Three triangles, ABC, LMN and PQR have been drawn on the graph paper below.

a Copy the diagram and on the same axes:

   i Enlarge triangle ABC by a scale factor of 3, centre the origin. Label the new triangle $A_1B_1C_1$.

   ii Reflect triangle LMN in the y-axis. Label the new triangle $L_1M_1N_1$.

   iii Rotate triangle ABC $90°$ anticlockwise about $(1, 0)$. Label the new triangle $A_2B_2C_2$.

b Write down the vector representing the translation which maps triangle ABC onto triangle LMN.

c Which single transformation maps triangle $L_1M_1N_1$ onto triangle PQR? (WJEC)

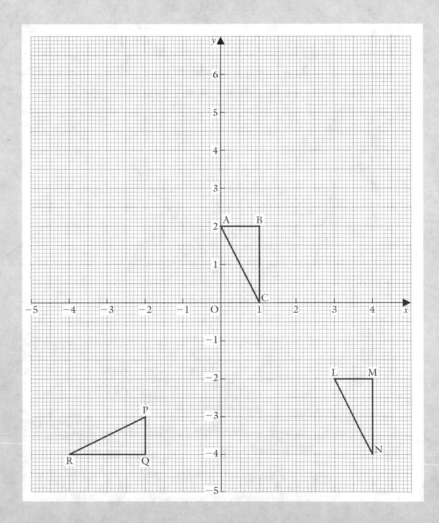

1 Find, in square units, the area enclosed by the x-axis, the line whose
equation is $y = 12 - 2x$ and the ordinates at $x = 0$ and $x = 5$.

2 Copy and complete the table for $y = \dfrac{12}{x}$

x	1	2	4	6	8	10	12
y		6			1.5		

Using a scale of 1 cm to 1 unit on both axes draw the graph of $y = \dfrac{12}{x}$
for value of x from 1 to 12.

a Draw the tangent to the curve at the point where $x = 4$ and find
its gradient.

b P is the point on the curve where $x = 2$ and Q is the point on
the curve where $x = 8$. Find the gradient of PQ.

3 a A car travels at 99 km/h for 5 minutes. How far does it travel?

b A ball rolls 3 m in $1\frac{1}{2}$ seconds. Find its average speed in km/h.

4

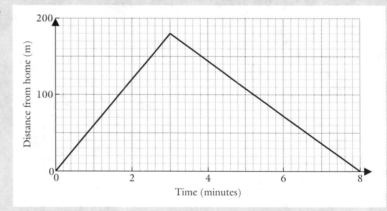

The graph illustrates Ray's journey from his home to the post box at
the end of his street. Taking Ray's velocity on the outward journey as
positive, find

a his speed from his home to the post office

b his velocity from his home to the post office.

c his speed from the post box to his home

d his velocity from the post box to his home.

5 Which of the following distance–time graphs could represent the motion of a cricket ball thrown into the air?

A

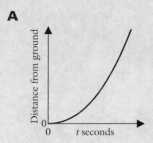

C

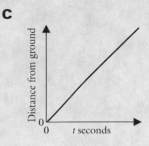

B

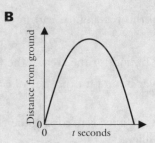

D

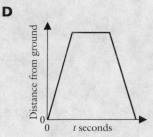

6 Describe the rotation that maps the black shape onto the green shape. Which point maps onto P? Write down the coordinates of the centre and angle of rotation.

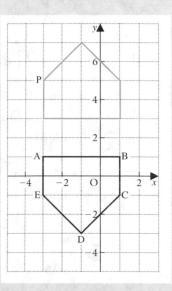

7 A translation maps the point $(2, 3)$ onto the point $(4, -1)$ and the mirror line of a reflection is the line $x + y = 3$. Find the image of the point $(3, 2)$ under

a the translation   **b** the reflection.

8

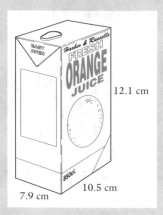

12.1 cm

10.5 cm

7.9 cm

The dimensions of this rectangular carton of orange juice are correct to 1 decimal place.

a Find the upper bound for the area of the base.

b What is the lower bound for the area of one of the smaller vertical sides?

c How much orange juice is needed to be certain that 100 of these cartons can be filled?

d Jo has 6 glasses, each of which can hold 125 ml of juice. Can she be certain that one full carton of juice is enough to fill all 6 glasses?

9 A pyramid stands on a rectangular base measuring 8 cm by 5 cm and is 9 cm high.

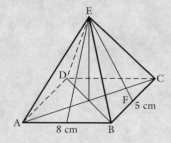

a Find the volume of the pyramid.

b F is the midpoint of BC. Find, correct to 2 decimal places, the length of EF.

c Find the area of one of the large sloping sides of the pyramid.

10 The diagram shows a cube with edge 5 cm. Find the angle between

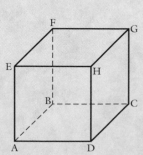

a ED and the base ABCD

b EC and the base ABCD

c the plane EHCB and the plane BCGF.

**REVISION
EXERCISE 3.4
(Chapters 1 to 9)**

Do not use a calculator for any question in this exercise.

1 **a** Which of these numbers are irrational?

    i $\left(\sqrt{8}\right)^3$ **ii** $\sqrt{1\frac{7}{9}}$ **iii** $\left(\sqrt{12}\right)^3$

  b Find x if   **i** $27^x = 9$ **ii** $8^x = 4$ **iii** $16^x = 64$

2 **a** Factorise

    i $5x^2 + 27x - 18$ **ii** $21x^2 - 29x + 10$ **iii** $15a^2 + 7a - 4$

  b Solve the equation   **i** $(7x - 2)(3x + 4) = 0$

                        ii $25x^2 - 16 = 0$

                        iii $x(x - 3)(x + 5) = 0$

3 **a** If $(px + q)^2 = 4x^2 + 20x + 25$ for all values of x, find the positive values of p and q.

  b The sum of the squares of three consecutive positive whole numbers is 245. If the smallest number is x form an equation in x and solve it. What are the three numbers?

4 The height of a triangle is 3 cm less than the length of its base. The area of the triangle is $20\,\text{cm}^2$. Find the length of its base.

5 **a** Express as a single fraction in its lowest terms

    i $\dfrac{1}{a - b} - \dfrac{1}{a^2 - b^2}$ **ii** $\dfrac{6}{x^2 - 4} + \dfrac{1}{x + 2}$

  b **i** Make b the subject of the formula $s = \frac{1}{2}(a + b + c)$

    ii Make $\cos \widehat{A}$ the subject of the formula $a^2 = b^2 + c^2 + 2bc \cos \widehat{A}$

6 Sketch the graph of $y = x(x - 2)(x - 4)$

7 The table shows the number of units produced per day in a new factory building during the first six months of its occupation.

Number of months building has been open, N	1	2	3	4	5	6
Number of units produced, P	15	40	80	140	235	400

Using a scale of $2\,\text{cm} \equiv 1$ unit on the N-axis and $2\,\text{cm} \equiv 100$ units on the P-axis, draw a graph to represent this information.

  a Find the gradient of the curve when $N = 2$ and interpret this result.

  b Find the gradient of the curve when $N = 5$ and interpret this result.

8 For each object state whether it is the speed or the velocity of the object that is given.

    a Sally walks between home and school at 5 km/h.

    b Sally cycles from her home to the Post Office at 12 km/h.

    c When Ken hits a tennis ball it travels at 80 mph.

    d A tennis ball rolls toward the umpire at 2 m/s.

9 R_1 is a rotation of 90° anticlockwise about O
    R_2 is a rotation of 180° about O
    R_3 is a rotation 90° clockwise about O
    A is a reflection in the x-axis
    B is a reflection in the y-axis
    C is a reflection in the $y = x$
    D is a reflection in the line $y = -x$

On squared paper draw the rectangle with vertices $(2, -1), (2, -3),$ $(5, -1)$ and $(5, -3)$. Mark it P.

    a Draw   **i** $R_1(P)$ **ii** $AR_1(P)$ **iii** $R_2(P)$ **iv** $AR_2(P)$

    b Name the single transformation that maps

        i AR_1 onto R_2 **ii** AR_2 onto P

    c Name the single transformation that is equivalent to

        i $R_2 R_3$ **ii** AB

10 A metal prism has a mass of 768 g. The prism is 8 cm long and the density of the metal is 6.4 g/cm^3. Find

    a the volume of the prism   **b** the area of its cross-section.

REVISION
EXERCISE 3.5
(Chapters 1 to 9)

1 a Simplify to the smallest possible surd

    i $\sqrt{27}$ **ii** $\sqrt{500}$

  b Rationalise the denominator

    i $\dfrac{18}{\sqrt{12}}$ **ii** $\dfrac{8 - 3\sqrt{2}}{\sqrt{2}}$

2 a Factorise

    i $15x^2 - 29x - 14$ **ii** $15 + 7x - 2x^2$ **iii** $16x^2 - 81y^2$

  b Solve the equation

    i $(x - 2)(3x - 4) = 0$

   ii $12 + 5x = 2x^2$

  iii $9x^3 - 25x = 0$

3 Solve the equation $3x^2 + 10x - 4 = 0$ giving your answers correct to 2 decimal places.

4 If $a = 1.6 \times 10^{-4}$ and $b = 8 \times 10^{-6}$ find, in standard form

  a ab **b** $\dfrac{a}{b}$ **c** $a + b$ **d** $10a + 1000b$

5 The sum of the first n natural numbers is $\dfrac{n(n+1)}{2}$.

  Starting with 1 how many consecutive natural numbers must be added together to give a total of   **a** 210   **b** 1326

6

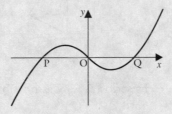

The sketch shows the graph of $y = x^3 + 3x^2 - 10x$
Find the coordinates of P and Q .

7 Use five strips to find approximately, the area under the curve that passes through the points given in the table for values of x from 0 to 10. (You do not need to draw an accurate graph.)

x	0	2	4	6	8	10
y	25	14	9.5	8	9.5	12.5

8

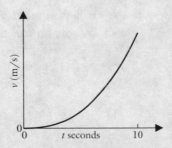

The graph shows the motion of a particle over 10 seconds. Which of the following statements are true ?

  A The acceleration of the particle is always increasing.

  B The acceleration of the particle is constant.

  C The velocity of the particle is always increasing.

  D The acceleration of the particle decreases for part of the motion.

9

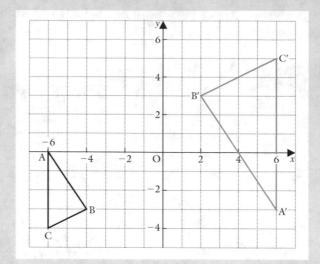

Describe as fully as possible the transformation that maps △ABC onto △A′B′C′.

10 The dimensions of a right pyramid with a square base are given on the diagram.
If each dimension is correct to 1 decimal place find

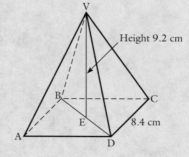

a the smallest possible value for the area of the base

b the largest possible value for the volume of the pyramid

c the smallest number of the largest possible pyramids that have a total volume greater than 5000 cm³.

CYLINDERS, CONES AND SPHERES

10

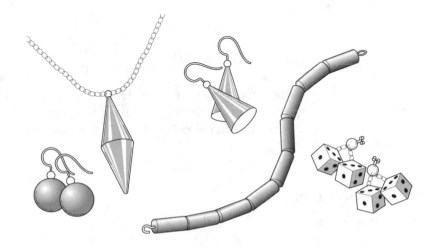

Rose is employed by a large jewellery manufacturer as their 'metals' buyer. Her job includes buying precious metals. She can buy precious metals either in rectangular sheets or in rectangular solid blocks called ingots.

In the workshop the craftsmen often need to cut the sheets into squares, rectangles or circular discs. From time to time they have to cut out sectors of circles so that they can be bent to form an open cone. On other occasions they need small solid cylinders, cones and spheres. These can be made by melting down ingots and recasting them to the desired shapes. Since the metal is expensive, the firm intends only to buy what they need so Rose is given detailed dimensions of every new item as soon as it has been designed.

Rose has to calculate accurately the amount of metal used for each shape so that she can order the exact amount that is needed. To do this Rose needs to know formulas for finding the surface area and volume of each of these shapes.

The work that follows introduces these formulas.
Remember to check calculations by making a rough estimate.

ARCS AND
SECTORS

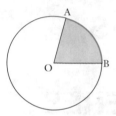

In Book 9A, Chapter 13 we found the following facts for the length of an arc AB of a circle, centre O, and the area of the sector AOB.

$$\text{Length of arc AB} = 2\pi r \times \frac{\text{A}\widehat{\text{O}}\text{B}}{360°}$$

and $\quad$ area of sector AOB $= \pi r^2 \times \dfrac{\text{A}\widehat{\text{O}}\text{B}}{360°}$

In the next exercise we revise this work and extend it to include questions where the length of an arc or the area of a sector are given and we have to find the radius of the circle or the angle at the centre.

EXERCISE 10A

In each question from **1** to **4** find

a the length of the arc $\qquad$ **b** the area of the sector.

1 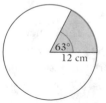 $\qquad$ **2** 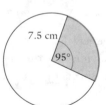 $\qquad$ **3** 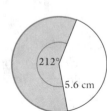 $\qquad$ **4**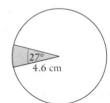

Find the angle at the centre of a circle of radius 10 cm subtended by an arc of length 5 cm.

θ is a greek letter pronounced 'theta'.

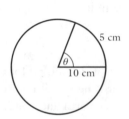

$$\frac{\text{Arc length}}{\text{Circumference}} = \frac{\theta°}{360°}$$

$$\frac{5}{2\pi r} = \frac{\theta}{360}$$

$$\frac{\overset{18}{\cancel{360}} \times 5}{\underset{1}{\cancel{2}} \times \pi \times \cancel{10}} = \theta$$

$$\theta = 28.64\ldots°$$

The angle at the centre is 28.6° correct to 1 d.p.

In each question from **5** to **7** find the angle subtended at the centre of the circle.

5 Arc length 7 cm, radius of circle 6 cm

6 Arc length 60 cm, radius of circle 80 cm

7 Arc length 3.2 cm, radius of circle 12 cm

In each question from **8** to **10** find the radius of the circle.

8 Arc length 3 cm, angle at the centre $20°$

9 Arc length 7 cm, angle at the centre $45°$

10 Arc length 9 m, angle at the centre $150°$

11 Do not use a calculator for this question.
   The length of the arc AB is π cm and the radius is 5 cm.
   Find, in terms of π
   a $A\hat{O}B$ **b** the area of the shaded sector.

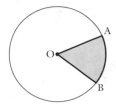

The area of the sector AOB is $10\,\text{cm}^2$ and the radius of the
circle is 7 cm. Find

a the angle at the centre of the circle, $A\hat{O}B$

b the length of the perimeter of the sector.

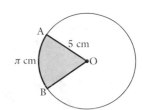

a Using the formula: Area of the sector $= \pi r^2 \times \dfrac{A\hat{O}B}{360°}$ gives

$$10 = \pi \times 7 \times 7 \times \frac{A\hat{O}B}{360°}$$

$$360° \times 10 = 49 \times \pi \times A\hat{O}B$$

$$A\hat{O}B = \frac{3600°}{49 \times \pi} = 23.38\ldots° = 23.4° \ (\text{correct to 3 s.f.})$$

b Length of arc AB $= 2\pi r \times \dfrac{A\hat{O}B}{360°}$

$$= 2\pi \times 7 \times \frac{23.38\ldots°}{360°} = 2.857\ldots \text{ cm}$$

$$= 2.86 \text{ cm} \ (\text{correct to 3 s.f.})$$

Perimeter of sector $=$ OA $+$ OB $+$ arc AB $= 7 + 7 + 2.857\ldots$ cm

$$= 16.85\ldots \text{ cm} = 16.9 \text{ cm} \ (\text{correct to 3 s.f.})$$

12 The area of the sector AOB is $20\,\text{cm}^2$ and the length of a
   radius OA is 4.5 cm.
   Find   **a** angle AOB
       b the length of the arc AB.

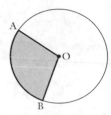

13 The area of the sector of a circle is $100\,\text{cm}^2$. The angle in the sector at the centre of the circle is $83°$. Find

   a the radius of the circle

   b the perimeter of the sector.

14 The area of the shaded sector is $212\,\text{cm}^2$ and the radius of the circle is $17.5\,\text{cm}$. Find

   a angle AOB

   b the perimeter of the sector.

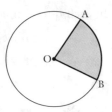

15 A cone made of cardboard has a slant height of $6\,\text{cm}$ and a base of radius $2\,\text{cm}$.

   a Find the circumference of the base circle.

   b The curved surface of the cone is flattened out into a sector of a circle. Draw a diagram and mark in its measurements.

   c Find the angle of the sector.

   d Find the area of the sector.

   e Find the total surface area of the cone including the base.

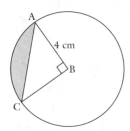

16

Using the data given in the diagram, find

   a the area of $\triangle ABC$

   b the area of the shaded segment.

17 A pattern is formed by painting a white circle of radius $15\,\text{cm}$ with four sectors of angle $27°$ each. Two are painted red and two yellow. Find the total area of

   a the white parts

   b the red parts.

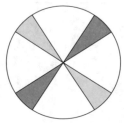

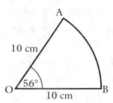

The two radii forming a sector of a circle are 10 cm in length and contain an angle of 56°. If both figures are given correct to the nearest whole number, find

a the upper bound for the length of the arc AB

b the smallest possible area for the sector OAB.

a

> The upper bound for the length of the arc AB occurs when both the angle AOB and the radius are as large as possible.

Upper bound of $A\hat{O}B = 56.5°$
and the upper bound of the radius is 10.5 cm

Using $\qquad$ arc length $= 2\pi r \times \dfrac{A\hat{O}B}{360°}$

Upper bound of arc AB $= 2\pi \times 10.5 \times \dfrac{56.5°}{360°}$

$$= 10.354\ldots \text{cm}$$

$$= 10.4 \text{cm (correct to 3 s.f.)}$$

b

> The smallest area of the sector occurs when both the angle and the radius are as small as possible i.e. when $r = 9.5$ and $A\hat{O}B = 55.5°$.

Smallest area $= \pi \times 9.5^2 \times \dfrac{55.5°}{360°}$

$$= 43.71\ldots \text{cm}^2 = 43.7 \text{cm}^2 \text{ (correct to 3 s.f.)}$$

18 The angle at the centre, O, of a circle of radius 24 cm, subtended by the arc AB is 110°. If both numbers are correct to the nearest whole number find

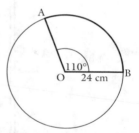

a the upper bound of the radius

b the lower bound of the arc AB

c the lower bound of the area of the sector.

19 In a circle centre O, the minor arc $AB = 18\,\text{cm}$ and $A\widehat{O}B = 68°$. Both numbers are correct to the nearest whole number. Find the largest possible value for the area of the sector.

20 Silver ear-rings are to be made in the shape of a sector of a circle of radius 15 mm such that the angle between the radii is 40°. Both measurements must be correct to the nearest whole number. The sheet silver used to make the ear-rings costs £25 per square centimetre.

a Find the cost of silver used in a pair of ear-rings that are made to the minimum acceptable size. Give your answer correct to the nearest 10 p rounded up.

b How much less is this than if they were made to the largest acceptable size?

VOLUME OF A CYLINDER

The formula for the volume of a cylinder (circular prism) is

$$V = \pi r^2 h$$

where V cubic units is the volume, r units is the radius of the circular cross-section and h units is its height or length.

We have previously used this formula to find the volume of a cylinder for given values of r and h, but in the next exercise we use it to find r or h when V is given.

EXERCISE 10B

Find the radius of a cylinder of volume $72\,\text{cm}^3$ and height 9 cm.

$$V = 72 \qquad h = 9$$

$$V = \pi r^2 h$$

$$72 = \pi \times r^2 \times 9$$

$$\frac{72}{\pi \times 9} = r^2 \qquad \boxed{\text{Estimate: } r^2 \approx \frac{72}{3 \times 9} \approx 3}$$

$$r^2 = 2.546\ldots \quad \Rightarrow \quad r = 1.595\ldots$$

The radius is 1.60 cm correct to 3 s.f.

In each question from **1** to **6**, find the missing measurement of the cylinder.

	Radius	Height	Volume
1	3.1 cm		72 cm^3
2	11 cm		1024 cm^3
3		1.6 m	15 m^3

	Radius	Height	Volume
4		0.7 m	9.83 m^3
5	3.8 cm		760 cm^3
6		0.12 cm	0.56 cm^3

7 The diameter of a cylinder is equal to its height. If the volume of the cylinder is 30 cm^3 find its diameter.

THE CURVED SURFACE AREA OF A CYLINDER

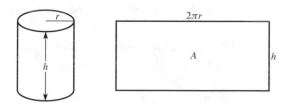

If we have a cylindrical tin with a paper label covering its curved surface, we can take off the label and flatten it out to give a rectangle whose length is equal to the circumference of the tin.

Therefore the area A of the curved surface is given by $2\pi r \times h$

i.e.

$$A = 2\pi rh$$

EXERCISE 10C

In each question from **1** to **8**, find the curved surface area of the cylinder whose measurements are given. Remember to make sure that units are compatable.

1 Radius 4 cm, height 6 cm   **5** Radius 0.06 m, height 32 cm

2 Radius 30 cm, height 2 cm   **6** Radius 5.2 cm, height 7.8 cm

3 Radius 6.2 cm, height 5.8 cm   **7** Radius 72.6 cm, height 30 cm

4 Radius 2 m, height 82 cm   **8** Radius 4.2 m, height 98 cm

9 A closed cylinder has radius 6 cm and height 10 cm.

Find **a** the area of its curved surface

b the area of its base

c the total surface area.

10 A closed cylinder has radius 3.2 cm and height 4.8 cm.

Find **a** the area of its curved surface

b the total surface area.

11 Find the area of the paper label covering the side of a cylindrical soup tin of height 9.6 cm and radius 3.3 cm. The label has an overlap of 1 cm.

12 What area of card is needed to make a cylindrical tube of length 42 cm and radius 3.2 cm? The card overlaps by 2 cm.

13 A garden roller is in the form of a cylinder of radius 0.25 m and width 0.7 m. What area of lawn does the roller cover in four revolutions?

14 Find the total area of sheet metal used to make a cylindrical oil drum with radius 24 cm and height 85 cm.

15 The diameter of a cylindrical buoy is 60 cm and its height is 150 cm. Find its total surface area.

---

50 litres of water are poured into a cylindrical tank of radius 0.3 m. Find the depth of water in the tank in centimetres.

$$\text{Volume} = 50 \, \text{litres}$$
$$= 50\,000 \, \text{cm}^3$$
$$V = 50\,000, \, r = 0.3 \times 100 = 30$$
$$V = \pi r^2 h$$
$$50\,000 = \pi \times 30^2 \times h$$
$$\frac{50\,000}{\pi \times 30^2} = h$$
$$h = 17.68\ldots$$

The depth of water is 17.7 cm correct to 3 s.f.

---

16 1 m³ of water fills a cylindrical drum of radius 50 cm. Find the height of the drum.

17 Water from a full rectangular tank measuring 1 m by 2 m by 0.5 m is emptied into a cylindrical tank and fills it to a depth of 1.2 m.

Find **a** the volume of water involved

   b the diameter of the cylindrical tank.

18 A solid bronze cylinder of height 4.3 cm has a mass of 200 g. If the density of bronze is 8.96 g/cm³ find the diameter of the cylinder.

19 A cylindrical water butt has a diameter of 80 cm and a height of 1 m. It is half full of water. If a further 20 100 cm³ of water are poured in, find the new depth of water.

20 Water pours out of a cylindrical pipe at the rate of 1 m/s. The diameter of the pipe is 3 cm.
How much water comes out in 1 minute?

VOLUME OF A CONE

We have already stated that the volume of a pyramid is given by

$$\tfrac{1}{3} \times \text{area of base} \times \text{perpendicular height}$$

where a pyramid is a solid with a flat base and which comes up to a point called the vertex.

The formulas we quote for pyramids, cones and spheres cannot be proved at this stage.

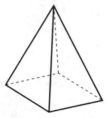  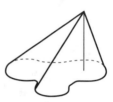

This definition applies to a cone so the volume of a cone is given by

$$\text{Volume} = \tfrac{1}{3} \times \text{area of circular base} \times \text{perpendicular height}$$

i.e.

$$V = \tfrac{1}{3}\pi r^2 h$$

A cone whose vertex is directly above the centre of the base is called a *right* circular cone; this is the only type that we deal with in this book.

EXERCISE 10D

> Find the volume of a cone of base radius 3.2 cm and of height 7.2 cm.
>
> $r = 3.2,$ $h = 7.2,$ $V = \tfrac{1}{3}\pi r^2 h$
>
> $$= \frac{\pi \times (3.2)^2 \times 7.2}{3} = 77.20\ldots$$
>
> The volume is 77.2 cm³ correct to 3 s.f.

In each question from **1** to **6** find the volume of the cone whose dimensions are given.

1 Base radius 9 cm, height 20 cm

2 Base radius 2.2 cm, height 5.8 cm

3 Base diameter 26.8 cm, height 104 cm

4 Base radius 0.6 cm, height 1.4 cm

5 Base diameter 4.2 cm, height 5.9 cm

6 Base diameter 0.62 m and height 106 cm. Give the volume in cubic metres.

7 A tower of a toy fort is formed by placing a cone on top of a cylinder. The total height of the tower is 20 cm, the common radius is 5 cm and the height of the cone is 8 cm. Find the volume of the tower.

8

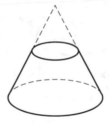

A *frustum* of a cone is formed by cutting the top off a cone. The original cone has base radius 6 cm and height 10 cm. The part cut off has base radius 3 cm and height 5 cm. Find the volume of the frustum.

9

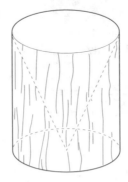

A cylindrical piece of wood of radius 3.6 cm and height 8.4 cm has a conical hole cut in it. The cone has the same radius and the same height as the cylinder.

a Find the volume of the remaining solid.

b The mass of this solid is 1254 g. Find the density of the wood.

SURFACE AREA OF A CONE

The curved surface area of a cone is given by

$$A = \pi r l$$

where *l* units is the *slant* height.

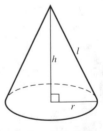

EXERCISE 10E

In each question from **1** to **4** find the area of the curved surface of the cone whose measurements are given.

1 Radius 4 cm, slant height 10 cm.

2 Radius 0.6 m, slant height 2.2 m.

3 Radius 9.2 cm, slant height 15 cm.

4 Radius 67 mm, slant height 72 mm.

5 Find the total surface area of a cone of base radius 4 cm and with slant height 9 cm.

6 The radius of a cone is 6 cm and its perpendicular height is 8 cm. Find
  a the volume of the cone
  b its slant height
  c its curved surface area.

7

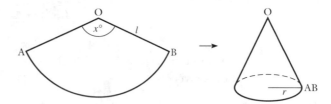

The sector OAB is formed into the cone as shown.
  a Find the length of the arc AB in terms of π, l and x.
  b Find the circumference of the base of the cone in terms of π and r.
  c Hence show that $\dfrac{r}{l} = \dfrac{x}{360}$
  d Find the area of the sector in terms of π, l and x. Hence show that the area, A, of the curved surface of the cone is given by $A = \pi r l$.

**VOLUME OF A
SPHERE**

The volume of a sphere is given by the formula

$$V = \tfrac{4}{3}\pi r^3$$

EXERCISE 10F

In each question from **1** to **6** find the volume of the sphere whose radius is given.

1 3 cm	**3** 1.8 m	**5** 38 cm
2 7.2 cm	**4** 0.62 cm	**6** 13 mm

7 Find the volume of a hemisphere (half a sphere) of radius 5 cm.

8 Twenty lead spheres of radius 1.2 cm are melted down and recast into a cuboid of length 8 cm and width 4 cm.

  a Find the volume of lead involved.

  b How high is the cuboid ?

9 Find, in terms of π, the volume of a sphere of radius $1\frac{1}{2}$ cm. (Do not use a calculator.)

10 Kingsley has a supply of lead pellets which are small spherical spheres. Each pellet has a nominal diameter of 2.0 mm correct to 1 decimal place. If the density of lead is 11.4 g/cm^3 what is the minimum number of pellets, to the nearest 1000, that Kingsley must have to be certain that their total mass will exceed 1 kg ?

SURFACE AREA OF A SPHERE

The surface area, A, of a sphere of radius r is given by the formula

$$A = 4\pi r^2$$

EXERCISE 10G

In each question from **1** to **4** find the surface area of the sphere whose radius is given.

1 9 cm   **2** 4.5 mm   **3** 41 cm   **4** 0.9 m

5 Find the curved surface area of a hemisphere of radius 23 cm.

6 240 spheres of radius 0.22 m are to be painted. Each pot of paint contains enough to cover 26 m^2. How many pots of paint are needed ?

7 The surface area of a sphere is 100 cm^2.
Find **a** the radius of the sphere   **b** its volume.

The next exercise involves a variety of problems concerning volumes and surface areas of cylinders, cones and spheres.

EXERCISE 10H

1 The radius of a spherical ball-bearing is 0.2 cm. How many ball-bearings can be made from 20 cm^3 of metal ?

2

A toy is formed from a cone and a hemisphere. The radius of the hemisphere is 5.2 cm and the total height of the toy is 15 cm. Find the total volume.

3 Which has the greater volume, a cone of radius 3.5 cm and a perpendicular height of 12 cm or a sphere of radius 3.5 cm? What is the difference in volume?

4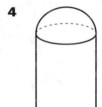

A concrete bollard is in the shape of a cylinder surmounted by a hemisphere. The radius of the hemisphere and of the cylinder is 25 cm and the total height of the bollard is 130 cm. Find its volume.

5 A hollow metal sphere has an outer radius of 16 cm and its walls are 1 cm thick. Find

    a the inner radius   **b** the volume of metal.

6

Three glasses are in the shape of a cone, a cylinder and a hemisphere respectively. The radius of each is 4 cm and the depth of the cone and of the cylinder is also 4 cm.

Find, in terms of π, the capacity of **a** the cone shaped glass

                                    b the cylindrical glass

                                    c the hemispherical glass

7 Find in terms of π, the volume of

    a a sphere of radius 2 cm

    b a sphere of radius 8 cm.

The larger sphere is made of metal. It is melted down and made into spheres of radius 2 cm.

    c How many of the smaller spheres can be made from the larger sphere?

8 Which has the greater surface area, a cone of radius 3.5 cm and slant height 9 cm or a sphere of radius 3.5 cm? What is the difference between the areas?

9 Find the total surface area of a hemisphere of radius 7 cm.

10

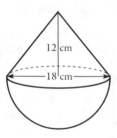

A solid is formed from a cone joined to a hemisphere as shown in the diagram. Find

a the slant height of the cone

b the total surface area of the solid.

11 A sphere of radius 1.2 m and a solid cone of radius 1.2 m and slant height 2.6 m are being painted for a funfair. The tin of paint available contains enough paint to cover 30 m². Is there enough paint for the purpose?
Give details of the extra amount needed or the amount of paint left over.

12

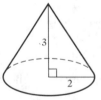

The radius of the base of a cone is 2 units and the height of the cone is 3 units.
Find, as irrational numbers, exact forms for

a the curved surface area   **b** the volume.

13

The diagram shows an egg-timer. It is symmetrical and is made from hollow cones, cylinders and hemispheres which are joined together as shown. When the timer starts, the depth of the sand in the upper container is 3 cm. Find

a the depth of sand in the lower container after it has all flowed through.

b the rate, in cm³/min, at which the sand flows from the one container to the other if the total time taken is 3 minutes.

14 A container is made of sheet metal in the form of an open cone joined to an open-ended cylinder. The radius of the cylinder and of the base of the cone is 8.6 cm, the depth of the cylinder is 4 cm and the slant height of the cone is 10.9 cm. Find the area of sheet metal used.

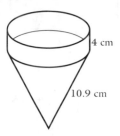

15

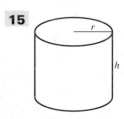

Write down, in terms of π, r and h, the formula for V, the volume of the cylinder and the formula for A, the curved surface area of the cylinder. Hence show that $2V = Ar$.

MIXED EXERCISE

EXERCISE 10I

1 A sector of a circle has an area of $750 \, \text{cm}^2$ and the angle at the centre is $254°$. Find

a the radius of the circle

b the length of the major arc AB.

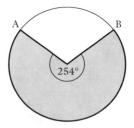

2 The diameter of a circular flower bed is 14 ft, correct to the nearest whole number. A gardener orders 600 bulbs for this bed. If each bulb requires an area of $0.25 \, \text{ft}^2$ decide whether or not

a the gardener has definitely ordered enough bulbs

b he may have ordered enough bulbs

c he has definitely not ordered enough bulbs.

3 A solid cylinder of gold has a radius of 2.5 cm and a height of 2.2 cm. One cubic centimetre of gold has a mass of 19.3 g.

Find **a** the volume of the cylinder

b the mass of the gold.

4 A cylindrical metal rod of radius 1 cm and length 80 cm is melted down and recast into a cylindrical rod of radius 2 cm. How long is the new rod?

5 A solid wooden spinning top consists of a cone of base radius 2 cm, height 5 cm and a hemisphere that fits exactly over the base of the cone.

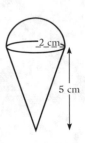

a Find the volume of the top.

b Calculate its total surface area.

c If the mass of the top is 25 g find the density of the wood from which it is made.

In the remaining questions several alternative answers are given. Write down the letter that corresponds to the correct answer. Do not use a calculator. Remember that using $\pi \approx 3$ gives a quick estimate.

6 The circumference of a circle of radius 10 cm is

    A 18.8 cm   **B** 31.4 cm   **C** 62.8 cm   **D** 314 cm

7 The circumference of a circle is 15 cm. Its diameter is

    A 50.3 cm   **B** 4.77 cm   **C** 2.38 cm   **D** 9.54 cm

8 The area of a circle is 60 cm^2. Its radius is

    A 4.37 cm   **B** 9.55 cm   **C** 19.1 cm   **D** 3.09 cm

9 A sector of a circle of radius 8 cm contains an angle of 45°. Its area is

    A 25.1 m^2 **B** 12.6 cm^2 **C** 50.3 cm^2 **D** 25.1 cm^2

10 An arc of a circle of radius 4 cm subtends an angle of 36° at the centre of the circle. The length of the arc is

    A 50.3 cm   **B** 1.25 cm   **C** 5.03 cm   **D** 2.51 cm

11 A cylinder has radius 2 cm and height 5 cm. The area of its curved surface is

    A 62.8 cm^2 **B** 31.4 cm^2 **C** 126 cm^2 **D** 98.7 cm^2

12 A cylinder has radius 2 cm and height 9 cm. Its volume is

    A 509 cm^3 **B** 113 cm^3 **C** 56.5 cm^3 **D** 226 cm^3

13 A cylinder has radius 10 cm and height 10 cm. The area of its curved surface is

    A $100\pi \, cm^2$ **B** $1000\pi \, cm^2$ **C** $400\pi \, cm^2$ **D** $200\pi \, cm^2$

14 400 cm³ of water fills a cylindrical container of radius 4 cm. The height of the container is

    A 63.7 cm   **B** 31.8 cm   **C** 7.96 cm   **D** 15.9 cm

15 A cylinder has radius 3 cm and height 5 cm. Its volume is

    A $30\pi \, cm^3$ **B** $45\pi \, cm^3$ **C** $30\pi \, cm^2$ **D** $48\pi \, cm^3$

16 The diameter of a sphere is 6 cm. Its volume is

    A $18\pi \, cm^3$ **B** $27\pi \, cm^3$ **C** $36\pi \, cm^3$ **D** $288\pi \, cm^3$

17 The radii of two glasses, one conical, the other cylindrical, are 2.5 cm and both glasses are 8 cm deep. The number of times that the conical glass can be filled from a full cylindrical glass is

    A 1   **B** 2   **C** 3   **D** 4

INVESTIGATIONS

1 A cylindrical can with a capacity of 400 cm³ is to be designed. Find the diameter of its base for at least ten different heights. Investigate the dimensions of the can such that the least amount of sheet metal is used to make it.

Do the standard cans that you find in the supermarket, and which hold about 400 g, use the minimum amount of sheet metal necessary?

Investigate which foods are stored and transported in cylindrical cans, and why. Include in your report an explanation of why cubical or rectangular containers are not used instead (after all, they would pack into cartons without wasting any space).

2 At the beginning of the previous chapter we considered the possible different shapes that boxes used to store tennis balls could have. Investigate which shapes (including those mentioned) use the least amount of cardboard per ball for a box that contains four tennis balls. Ignore the lip on the lid of the box. (You do not need to know the exact diameter of a tennis ball to do this but if it helps to use figures assume that its radius is 3 cm).

3 A factory produces three-metre lengths of copper tubing which has a external diameter of 2 cm.

The lengths are stored in boxes whose internal dimensions are $3\,\text{m} \times 40\,\text{cm} \times 16\,\text{cm}$ and they are arranged in the boxes as shown in the diagram.

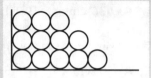

An employee suggests that they can get more lengths into the same box if they arrange things differently. Do you agree? What is the greatest number of 3 m lengths that can be packed into a box of this size?

SINE AND COSINE FORMULAS

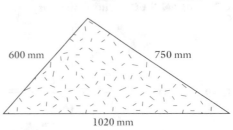

11

The diagram, which is not
drawn to scale, shows
a piece needed to fill in
an awkward corner
in a kitchen worktop.

600 mm   750 mm

1020 mm

To cut this exactly, it would be useful to know the angles of this
triangle.

- The triangle is not right-angled so the angles can be found by making
  a scale drawing but we know from experience that this method is slow
  and not very accurate. There are, however, formulas that can be used
  to find sides and angles in non-right-angled triangles and these are
  introduced in this chapter.

Many triangles, such as the one above, contain obtuse angles, so we start
by investigating the sines and cosines of obtuse angles.

1 a Copy and complete the following table.
   Use a calculator to find each value of $\sin x°$ correct to 2 decimal
   places

x	0	15	30	45	60	75	90	105	120	135	150	165	180
$\sin x°$													

b Using scales of 1 cm for 15 units on the horizontal axis and 1 cm
   for 0.2 on the vertical axis, plot these points on a graph and draw a
   smooth curve through the points.

c This curve has a line of symmetry. About which value of x is the
   curve symmetrical?

d From your graph, find the two angles for which

   i $\sin x° = 0.8$ **ii** $\sin x° = 0.6$ **iii** $\sin x° = 0.4$.

   Find, in each case, a relationship between the two angles.

2 Use a calculator to complete the following statements,

a $\sin 30° = \square$, $\sin 150° = \square$, $150° = \square - 30°$

b $\sin 40° = \square$, $\sin 140° = \square$, $140° = \square - 40°$

c $\sin 72° = \square$, $\sin 108° = \square$, $108° = \square - 72°$

SINES OF OBTUSE ANGLES

The results from **Exercise 11A** demonstrate that, when two angles are supplementary (i.e. they add up to $180°$) their sines are the same.

$$\sin x° = \sin (180° - x°)$$

EXERCISE 11B

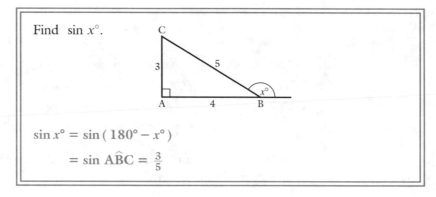

Find $\sin x°$.

$\sin x° = \sin (180° - x°)$

$= \sin \widehat{ABC} = \frac{3}{5}$

In questions **1** to **6**, find $\sin x°$.

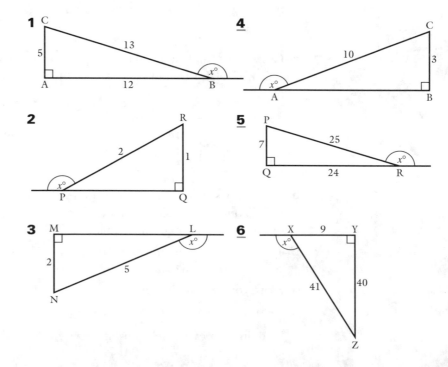

In questions **7** to **12**, $x°$ is an acute angle. Find x.

7 $\sin x° = \sin 165°$

10 $\sin x° = \sin 100°$

8 $\sin x° = \sin 140°$

11 $\sin x° = \sin 175°$

9 $\sin x° = \sin 152°$

12 $\sin x° = \sin 91°$

In the next exercise we investigate the cosines of obtuse angles.

EXERCISE 11C

1 a Copy and complete the following table. Use a calculator to find each value of $\cos x°$ correct to 2 decimal places.

x	0	15	30	45	60	75	90	105	120	135	150	165	180
$\cos x°$													

b Using scales of 1 cm for 15 units on the horizontal axis and 1 cm for 0.2 on the vertical axis, plot these points on a graph and draw a smooth curve through them.

c This curve has a point of rotational symmetry. What is the value of x at this point?

d What do you notice about the sign of the cosine of an obtuse angle?

e From your graph find the angles for which

i $\cos x° = 0.8$ **ii** $\cos x° = -0.8$

What is the relationship between these two angles?

2 Use a calculator to complete the following statements.

a $\cos 30° = \square$, $\cos 150° = \square$, $150° = \square - 30°$

b $\cos 50° = \square$, $\cos 130° = \square$, $130° = \square - 50°$

c $\cos 84° = \square$, $\cos 96° = \square$, $96° = \square - 84°$

COSINES OF OBTUSE ANGLES

The results from the last exercise demonstrate that
the cosine of an obtuse angle is negative,
the numerical value (i.e. ignoring the sign) of the cosines of supplementary angles is the same.

$$\cos x° = -\cos (180° - x°)$$

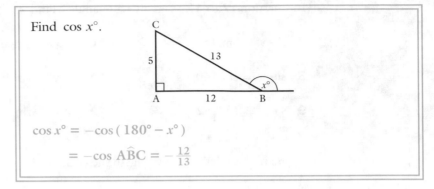

Find $\cos x°$.

$\cos x° = -\cos(180° - x°)$

$\qquad = -\cos \widehat{ABC} = -\frac{12}{13}$

In questions **1** to **4**, find $\cos x°$.

1

3

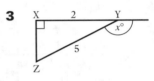

2

4

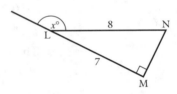

5 Find $\widehat{A}$ if   **a** $\cos \widehat{A} = -\cos 20°$ **b** $\cos \widehat{A} = -\cos 50°$

TRIGONOMETRIC RATIOS AS FRACTIONS

For an angle A in a right-angled triangle, if one of $\sin \widehat{A}$, $\cos \widehat{A}$ or $\tan \widehat{A}$ is given as a fraction, we can draw a right-angled triangle and mark in the lengths of two sides.

For example, if $\sin \widehat{A} = \frac{3}{5}$, this triangle can be drawn.

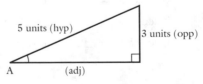

Then, using Pythagoras' theorem, the length of the third side can be calculated. In this case it is of length 4 units.

Now the cosine of angle A can be written down as a fraction,

ie. $\cos \widehat{A} = \frac{4}{5}$

Similarly $\tan \widehat{A} = \frac{3}{4}$

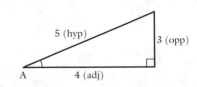

EXERCISE 11E

If $\cos \widehat{P} = \frac{12}{13}$, draw a suitable right-angled triangle and hence find $\sin \widehat{P}$ and $\tan \widehat{P}$.

$QR = 5$

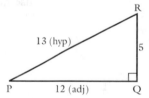

> Using Pythagoras' theorem or recognising a 5, 12, 13 triangle.

Therefore

$\sin \widehat{P} = \frac{5}{13}$

and

$\tan \widehat{P} = \frac{5}{12}$

1 If $\sin \widehat{A} = \frac{7}{25}$ find $\cos \widehat{A}$ and $\tan \widehat{A}$.

2 If $\cos \widehat{A} = \frac{5}{13}$ find $\sin \widehat{A}$ and $\tan \widehat{A}$.

3 If $\tan \widehat{P} = \frac{3}{4}$ find $\sin \widehat{P}$ and $\cos \widehat{P}$.

4 If $\cos \widehat{D} = \frac{3}{5}$ find $\tan \widehat{D}$ and $\sin \widehat{D}$.

5 If $\sin \widehat{X} = \frac{9}{41}$ find $\cos \widehat{X}$ and $\tan \widehat{X}$.

6 If $\tan \widehat{A} = 1$ find $\sin \widehat{A}$ and $\cos \widehat{A}$.

(Remember that $1 = \frac{1}{1}$ and leave the square root in your answer.)

7 ABC is an equilateral triangle of side 2 units. D is the midpoint of AC.

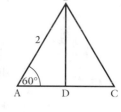

    a Show that $AD = 1$ unit and $BD = \sqrt{3}$ units.

    b Find the value, in surd form where necessary, of

        i $\sin 60°$ **ii** $\cos 60°$ **iii** $\tan 60°$

    c Find in surd form the value of

        i $\sin 30°$ **ii** $\cos 30°$ **iii** $\tan 30°$

8 In $\triangle ABC$, $AB = BC = 1$ unit and $A\widehat{B}C = 90°$.

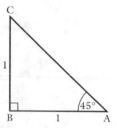

    a Show that $CA = \sqrt{2}$ units.

    b Find, in square root form where necessary, the value of

        i $\sin 45°$ **ii** $\cos 45°$ **iii** $\tan 45°$

TRIGONOMETRIC RATIOS OF 30°, 45° AND 60°

As we have seen from questions **6** to **8** in the last exercise, it is possible to give the trig ratios of 30°, 45° and 60° in an exact form as surds.

It is useful to gather the results together in a table.

	sin	cos	tan
30°	$\frac{1}{2}$	$\frac{\sqrt{3}}{2}$	$\frac{1}{\sqrt{3}}$
45°	$\frac{1}{\sqrt{2}}$	$\frac{1}{\sqrt{2}}$	1
60°	$\frac{\sqrt{3}}{2}$	$\frac{1}{2}$	$\sqrt{3}$

EXERCISE 11F

1 If $\sin \widehat{A} = \frac{1}{2}$ and $\widehat{A} < 90°$ find $\cos \widehat{A}$.

Hence find, in surd form, the value of

a $2 \sin \widehat{A} \cos \widehat{A}$ **b** $2(\cos \widehat{A})^2 - 1$

2 Use the table given in the text to write down the values of $\sin 30°$, $\cos 30°$, $\sin 60°$ and $\cos 60°$.

  a Hence find, in square root form, the value of

    i $\sin 30° \cos 60° + \cos 30° \sin 60°$

    ii $\sin 60° \cos 30° - \cos 60° \sin 30°$

  b What angle has a sine equal in value to your answer to part **a i**?

  c What angle has a sine equal in value to your answer to part **a ii**?

The remaining questions use all the work considered so far in this chapter.

3 Write down, as a fraction

  a $\cos x°$ **b** $\sin x°$

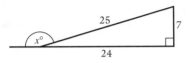

4 Find two angles each with a sine of 0.5.

5 If $\cos 59° = 0.515$ what is $\cos 121°$?

6 Find an obtuse angle whose cosine is equal to $-\cos 72°$.

7 If $\sin x° = \frac{4}{5}$, find as a fraction

  a $\sin (180° - x°)$ **b** $\cos x°$ **c** $\cos (180° - x°)$

**TRIANGLE
NOTATION**

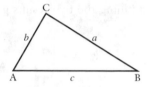

In a triangle ABC, the sides can be referred to as AB, BC and CA. It is convenient, however, to use a single letter to denote the number of units in the length of a side and the standard notation uses

a for the side opposite angle A
b for the side opposite angle B
c for the side opposite angle C.

In this triangle, for example,

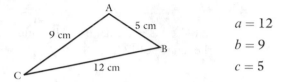

$a = 12$

$b = 9$

$c = 5$

THE SINE RULE

Consider a triangle ABC in which there is no right angle.

If a line is drawn from C, perpendicular to AB, the original triangle is divided into two right-angled triangles ADC and BDC as shown.

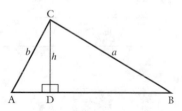

In $\triangle$ADC $\qquad \sin \widehat{A} = \dfrac{h}{b} \quad \Rightarrow \quad h = b \sin \widehat{A}$

In $\triangle$BDC $\qquad \sin \widehat{B} = \dfrac{h}{a} \quad \Rightarrow \quad h = a \sin \widehat{B}$

Equating the two expressions for h gives

$$a \sin \widehat{B} = b \sin \widehat{A}$$

Hence $\qquad \dfrac{a}{\sin \widehat{A}} = \dfrac{b}{\sin \widehat{B}} \qquad$ (dividing both sides by $\sin \widehat{A} \sin \widehat{B}$)

Now if we were to divide $\triangle$ABC into two right-angled triangles by drawing the perpendicular from A to BC the similar result would be $\qquad \dfrac{b}{\sin \widehat{B}} = \dfrac{c}{\sin \widehat{C}}$

Combining the two results gives

$$\frac{a}{\sin \widehat{A}} = \frac{b}{\sin \widehat{B}} = \frac{c}{\sin \widehat{C}}$$

This result is called the *sine rule* and it enables us to find angles and sides of triangles which are *not* right-angled.

The sine rule is made up of three equal fractions, but only two of them can be used at a time. When using the sine rule we choose the two fractions in which three quantities are known and only one is unknown.

In all the following exercises, unless instructed otherwise, give angles correct to 1 decimal place and lengths to 3 significant figures.

EXERCISE 11G

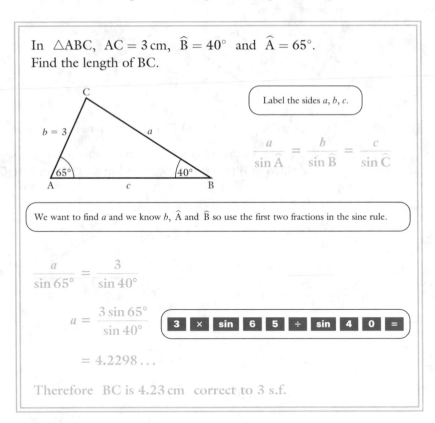

In $\triangle ABC$, $AC = 3\,\text{cm}$, $\widehat{B} = 40°$ and $\widehat{A} = 65°$.
Find the length of BC.

Label the sides a, b, c.

$$\frac{a}{\sin \widehat{A}} = \frac{b}{\sin \widehat{B}} = \frac{c}{\sin \widehat{C}}$$

We want to find a and we know b, $\widehat{A}$ and $\widehat{B}$ so use the first two fractions in the sine rule.

$$\frac{a}{\sin 65°} = \frac{3}{\sin 40°}$$

$$a = \frac{3 \sin 65°}{\sin 40°}$$

3 × sin 6 5 ÷ sin 4 0 =

$$= 4.2298\ldots$$

Therefore BC is $4.23\,\text{cm}$ correct to 3 s.f.

1 Find BC.

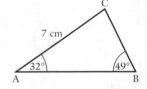

2 Find PQ.

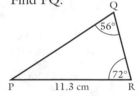

3 Find XZ.

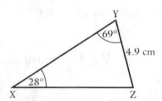

4 Find AB.

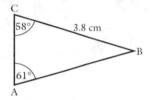

5 In △LMN, LM = 17.7 cm, $\widehat{N} = 73°$ and $\widehat{L} = 52°$. Find MN.

The sine rule can be used when one angle is obtuse.

In △ABC, AB = 6 cm,
$\widehat{B} = 25°$ and $\widehat{C} = 110°$.
Find AC.

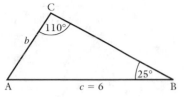

From the sine rule

$$\frac{a}{\sin \widehat{A}} = \boxed{\frac{b}{\sin \widehat{B}} = \frac{c}{\sin \widehat{C}}}$$

$$\frac{b}{\sin 25°} = \frac{6}{\sin 110°}$$

$$b = \frac{6 \sin 25°}{\sin 110°}$$

| 6 | × | sin | 2 | 5 | ÷ | sin | 1 | 1 | 0 | = |

$$= 2.698\ldots$$

Therefore AC = 2.70 cm correct to 3 significant figures.

6 Find AB.

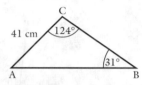

8 Find MN.

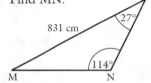

7 Find PR.

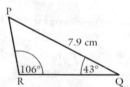

9 Find DE.

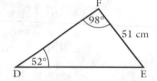

Sometimes the third angle must be found before a suitable pair of fractions can be selected from the sine rule.

In △ABC, AC = 4 cm, $\widehat{A} = 35°$ and $\widehat{C} = 70°$. Find BC.

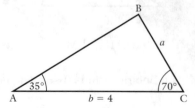

The two sides involved are a and b so we must use $\widehat{A}$ and $\widehat{B}$ in the sine rule; first we must find $\widehat{B}$.

$$\widehat{B} = 180° - (35° + 70°) = 75°$$

$$\boxed{\frac{a}{\sin \widehat{A}} = \frac{b}{\sin \widehat{B}}} = \frac{c}{\sin \widehat{C}}$$

$$\frac{a}{\sin 35°} = \frac{4}{\sin 75°}$$

$$a = \frac{4 \sin 35°}{\sin 75°}$$

$$= 2.375\ldots$$

Therefore BC is 2.38 cm correct to 3 s.f.

10 Find AB.

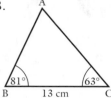

11 Find QR.

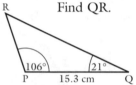

12 Find LM.

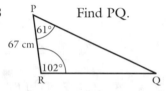

13 Find PQ.

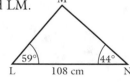

14 In triangle ABC, given in question **10**, the length of BC is given correct to the nearest centimetre and angles B and C are given correct to the nearest degree. Find the smallest possible value for the length of AB.

15 In triangle ABC, $\hat{A} = 60°$,
$\hat{B} = 45°$ and $BC = 10$ cm.
Find the length of AC, giving
your answer as an irrational
number in surd, i.e. square root,
form.

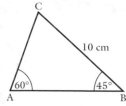

16 In triangle ABC, $\sin\hat{A} = \frac{2}{3}$ and $\sin\hat{C} = \frac{2}{5}$.
Find, without using a calculator,
the length of BC.

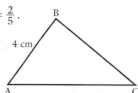

USING THE SINE RULE TO FIND AN ANGLE

The sine rule can be used to find an angle in a triangle. In this case it is more convenient to use the sine formula in the form

$$\frac{\sin\hat{A}}{a} = \frac{\sin\hat{B}}{b} = \frac{\sin\hat{C}}{c}$$

However care must be taken when two sides and the non-included angle is the only information given about a triangle.

In this triangle, for example,
using the sine rule to find $\hat{B}$ gives

$$\frac{\sin\hat{B}}{10} = \frac{\sin 64°}{14}$$

$$\Rightarrow \quad \sin\hat{B} = \frac{10 \times \sin 64°}{14} = 0.641\ldots$$

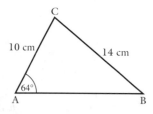

Using a calculator gives $\hat{B} = 39.9°$

But, from the work at the beginning of the chapter, we know that the sines of supplementary angles are equal, i.e. $\sin(180° - 39.9°) = 0.641\ldots$

Therefore another possible value of $\hat{B}$ is $(180° - 39.9°) = 140.1°$

In this case we can reject this possibility because the side opposite $\hat{B}$ is shorter than the side opposite $\hat{A}$, therefore $\hat{B} < \hat{A}$, so $\hat{B}$ is acute.

Now consider this triangle.
This time the side opposite $\hat{B}$ is longer
than the side opposite $\hat{A}$, so it is
possible that $\hat{B}$ may be acute or obtuse.

This diagram shows the two possible triangles that can be drawn from the information given.

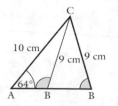 i.e. 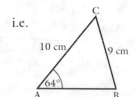 and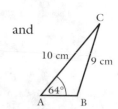

EXERCISE 11H

In questions **1** to **6** find the size of the marked angle. If there are two possible values for this angle, give both.

1

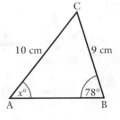

4

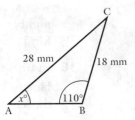

2

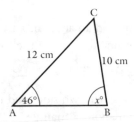

5

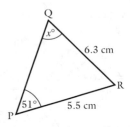

3

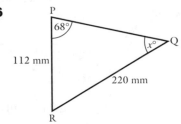

6

7 In triangle ABC, each measurement is given correct to 2 significant figures. Find the smallest possible size of Â.

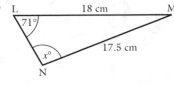

8 **a** Which is the largest angle in triangle PQR?

b Explain why angle P cannot be obtuse.

c Can you use the sine rule to find angle P?

Explain your answer.

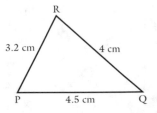

When we know the lengths of the three sides of a triangle but none of the angles, we cannot use the sine formula to find an angle because there will be two unknown angles whichever pair of fractions we choose.

For cases like this where the sine rule fails we need a different formula.

Consider a triangle ABC divided into two right-angled triangles by a line BD, perpendicular to AC. Let the length of AD be x so that $DC = b - x$.

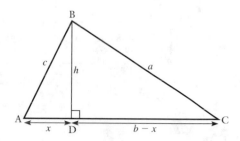

Using Pythagoras' theorem in triangles ABD and CBD gives

$$c^2 = h^2 + x^2$$

and
$$a^2 = h^2 + (b - x)^2$$
$$= h^2 + b^2 - 2bx + x^2$$
$$= b^2 + (h^2 + x^2) - 2bx$$
$$= b^2 + c^2 - 2bx$$

in $\triangle ABD$, $x = c \cos \widehat{A}$. Therefore

$$a^2 = b^2 + c^2 - 2bc \cos \widehat{A}$$

This result is called the *cosine rule*.

If we were to draw a line from A perpendicular to BC, or from C perpendicular to AB, similar equations could be obtained,

i.e.
$$b^2 = a^2 + c^2 - 2ac \cos \widehat{B}$$
$$c^2 = a^2 + b^2 - 2ab \cos \widehat{C}$$

Note that, in each version of the cosine rule, the side on the left and the angle on the right have the same letter.

When using the cosine rule it is a good idea to put brackets round the term containing the cosine

i.e.
$$a^2 = b^2 + c^2 - (2bc \cos \widehat{A})$$

EXERCISE 11I

In a triangle ABC, $AB = 6$ cm, $BC = 7$ cm and $\widehat{B} = 60°$.
Find AC.

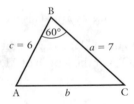

The sine rule fails here because we do not know either of the angles opposite given sides.

The unknown side is b, and $\widehat{B}$ is known, so we use the version of the cosine rule that starts with b^2.

$$b^2 = a^2 + c^2 - (2ac\cos\widehat{B})$$
$$= 7^2 + 6^2 - (2 \times 7 \times 6\cos 60°)$$
$$= 49 + 36 - (84 \times \cos 60°)$$
$$= 85 - 42 = 43$$
$$\Rightarrow \qquad b = \sqrt{43} = 6.557\ldots$$

Therefore AC is **6.56** cm correct to 3 s.f.

In this exercise the lengths of the sides of each triangle are measured in centimetres.

1 Find a.

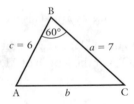

4 Find m.

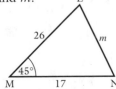

2 Find c.

5 Find q.

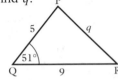

3 Find q.

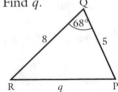

6 Find a.

If the given angle is obtuse its cosine is negative and extra care is needed in using the cosine rule; brackets are even more helpful in this case.

Triangle ABC is such that
BC = 11 cm, AC = 8 cm
and $\widehat{C} = 130°$.
Find AB.

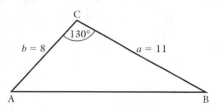

Using the cosine rule

$$c^2 = a^2 + b^2 - (2ab \cos \widehat{C})$$

$$= 11^2 + 8^2 - (2 \times 11 \times 8 \cos 130°)$$

$$= 298.13\ldots$$

$$\Rightarrow \qquad c = \sqrt{298.13\ldots} = 17.26\ldots$$

Therefore AB is 17.3 cm correct to 3 s.f.

7 Find BC.

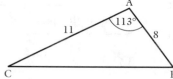

10 Find a.

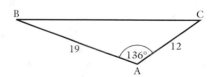

8 Find PQ.

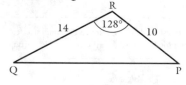

11 Find p.

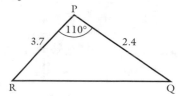

9 Find LN.

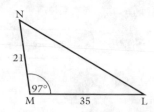

12 Find e.

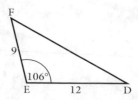

The cosine rule can be used to find an angle when three sides of a triangle are known.

In triangle ABC, AB $= 5$ cm, BC $= 6$ cm and AC $= 8$ cm. Find the smallest and the largest angle in this triangle.

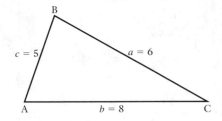

The smallest angle is opposite to the shortest side, so we are looking for $\widehat{C}$ and will use the cosine rule starting with c^2.

$$c^2 = a^2 + b^2 - (2ab \cos \widehat{C})$$
$$5^2 = 6^2 + 8^2 - (2 \times 6 \times 8 \cos \widehat{C})$$
$$25 = 36 + 64 - (96 \cos \widehat{C})$$

$96 \cos \widehat{C} + 25 = 100$ Adding $96 \cos \widehat{C}$ to each side.

$96 \cos \widehat{C} = 75$ Subtracting 25 from each side.

$$\cos \widehat{C} = \frac{75}{96} = 0.7812\ldots$$

Therefore $\widehat{C} = 38.6°$ (correct to 1 d.p.)

i.e. the smallest angle is $38.6°$ correct to 1 d.p.

The largest angle is opposite to the longest side, so we are looking for $\widehat{B}$ and will use the cosine rule starting with b^2.

$$b^2 = a^2 + c^2 - (2ac \cos \widehat{B})$$
$$8^2 = 6^2 + 5^2 - (2 \times 5 \times 6 \cos \widehat{B})$$
$$64 = 36 + 25 - (60 \cos \widehat{B})$$

$60 \cos \widehat{B} = 61 - 64 = -3$

$$\cos \widehat{B} = \frac{-3}{60} = -0.05$$ $\cos \widehat{B}$ is negative so $\widehat{B}$ is obtuse

Therefore the largest angle, $\widehat{B}$, is $92.9°$ correct to 1 d.p.

13 Find $\widehat{A}$.

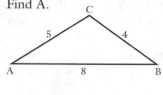

14 Find $\widehat{Q}$.

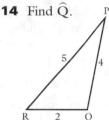

15 In △LMN, LM = 8 cm, MN = 5 cm and LN = 6 cm. Find $\widehat{N}$.

16 In △ABC, AB = 3 cm, BC = 2 cm and AC = 4 cm. Find the smallest angle in △ABC.

17 In △XYZ, XY = 7 cm, XZ = 9 cm and YZ = 5 cm. Find the largest angle in △XYZ.

18 In △DEF, DE = 2.1 cm, EF = 3.6 cm and DF = 2.7 cm. Find the middle-sized angle in △DEF.

19

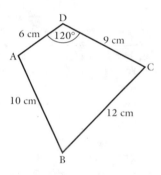

Use the information given in the diagram to find

a the length of AC   **b** A$\widehat{B}$C

20 a Use the information in the diagram to find, as a fraction, the cosine of $\widehat{A}$.

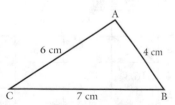

b What does your answer in part **a** tell you about the size of $\widehat{A}$?

21 In △ABC, AB = 41 mm, BC = 28 mm and AC = 36 mm. Each measurement is correct to the nearest millimetre. Find the smallest possible value of $\widehat{A}$.

If three independent facts are given about the sides and/or angles of a triangle and we are asked to find one or more of the unknown quantities, first look for a right-angled triangle or an isosceles triangle (which can be divided into two right-angled triangles). When no such triangle exists, we must then decide whether to use the sine rule or the cosine rule.

The sine rule is the easier to work out so it is chosen whenever possible and that is when the given information includes a side and the angle opposite to it (remember that, if the two angles are given, the third angle is also known). The cosine rule is chosen only when the sine rule cannot be used.

EXERCISE 11J

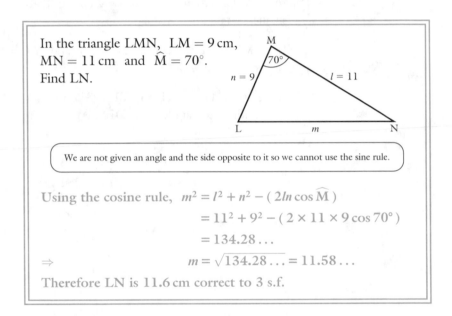

In the triangle LMN, LM $= 9$ cm, MN $= 11$ cm and $\widehat{M} = 70°$.
Find LN.

We are not given an angle and the side opposite to it so we cannot use the sine rule.

Using the cosine rule, $m^2 = l^2 + n^2 - (2ln \cos \widehat{M})$

$$= 11^2 + 9^2 - (2 \times 11 \times 9 \cos 70°)$$
$$= 134.28\ldots$$
$$\Rightarrow \qquad m = \sqrt{134.28\ldots} = 11.58\ldots$$

Therefore LN is 11.6 cm correct to 3 s.f.

Each question from **1** to **8** refers to a $\triangle ABC$. Fill in the empty spaces.

	a	b	c	$\widehat{A}$	$\widehat{B}$	$\widehat{C}$
1	11.7		✕	39°	66°	✕
2		128	86	63°		✕
3	✕		65	✕	79°	55°
4	16.3	12.7		✕	✕	106°
5		263		✕	47°	74°
6	14			53°	82°	✕
7		✕	17.8	107°		35°
8		16	16	81°	✕	✕

THE AREA OF A TRIANGLE

We already know that the area, A, of a triangle can be found by multiplying half the base, b, by the perpendicular height, h.

In some cases, however, the perpendicular height is not given, so an alternative formula is needed.

Consider a triangle ABC in which the lengths of BC and CA, and the angle C, are known.

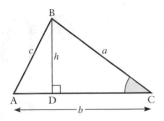

The line BD, drawn from B perpendicular to AC, is a perpendicular height of the triangle. Therefore the area of the triangle is $\frac{1}{2}bh$.

But, in triangle BDC, $\sin \widehat{C} = \dfrac{h}{a}$ i.e. $h = a\sin\widehat{C}$

Therefore the area of the triangle is $\frac{1}{2}ab\sin\widehat{C}$, i.e. $A = \frac{1}{2}ab\sin\widehat{C}$

Alternatively we could draw perpendicular heights from A or from C, giving similar expressions for the area,

i.e. $A = \frac{1}{2}bc\sin\widehat{A}$ and $A = \frac{1}{2}ac\sin\widehat{B}$

Each of these expressions involves two sides and the included angle

i.e.   Area $\triangle = \frac{1}{2} \times$ product of two sides $\times$ sine of the included angle

EXERCISE 11K

Find the area of $\triangle$PQR if
$\widehat{P} = 120°$, PQ $= 132$ cm
and   PR $= 95$ cm.

> r and q are given and $\widehat{P}$ is the included angle.

Area $= \frac{1}{2}qr\sin\widehat{P}$

$= \frac{1}{2} \times 95 \times 132 \times \sin 120° = 5429.9\ldots$

Therefore area of $\triangle$PQR $= 5430$ cm² correct to 3 s.f.

Find the area of each triangle.

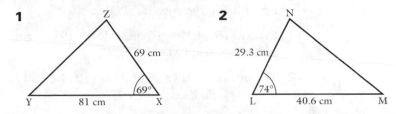

3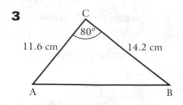

4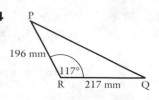

5 $\triangle ABC$; $a = 18.1\,\text{cm}$, $c = 14.2\,\text{cm}$, $\widehat{B} = 101°$

6 $\triangle PQR$; $PQ = 234\,\text{cm}$, $PR = 196\,\text{cm}$, $\widehat{P} = 84°$

7 $\triangle XYZ$; $x = 9\,\text{cm}$, $z = 10\,\text{cm}$, $\widehat{Y} = 52°$

8 $\triangle ABC$; $AC = 3.7\,\text{m}$, $AB = 4.1\,\text{m}$, $\widehat{A} = 116°$

In triangle ABC, $AB = 15\,\text{cm}$,
$\widehat{A} = 60°$ and $\widehat{B} = 81°$.
Find the area of $\triangle ABC$.

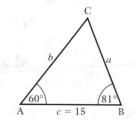

> To use the formula to find the area of $\triangle ABC$, we need two sides and the included angle. We know only one side, so we will use the sine formula to find a. First we must calculate $\widehat{C}$.

$$\widehat{C} = 180° - 60° - 81° = 39°$$

$$\boxed{\frac{a}{\sin \widehat{A}}} = \frac{b}{\sin \widehat{B}} = \boxed{\frac{c}{\sin \widehat{C}}}$$

$$\frac{a}{\sin 60°} = \frac{15}{\sin 39°}$$

$$a = \frac{15 \sin 60°}{\sin 39°} = 20.64\ldots$$

Using $\text{area} = \frac{1}{2} ac \sin \widehat{B}$ gives

$$\text{area} = \frac{1}{2} \times 20.64\ldots \times 15 \times \sin 81° = 152.9\ldots$$

Therefore area $\triangle ABC$ is $153\,\text{cm}^2$ correct to 3 s.f.

---

9 In $\triangle ABC$, $BC = 7\,\text{cm}$, $AC = 8\,\text{cm}$, $AB = 10\,\text{cm}$. Find $\widehat{C}$ and the area of the triangle.

10 $\triangle PQR$ is such that $PQ = 11.7\,\text{cm}$, $\widehat{Q} = 49°$ and $\widehat{R} = 63°$. Find PR and the area of $\triangle PQR$.

11 In $\triangle LMN$, $LM = 16\,\text{cm}$, $MN = 19\,\text{cm}$ and the area is $114.5\,\text{cm}^2$. Find $\widehat{M}$ and LN.

12 The area of $\triangle ABC$ is $27.3\,\text{cm}^2$. If $BC = 12.8\,\text{cm}$ and $\widehat{C} = 107°$ find AC.

APPLICATIONS   In many problems a description of a situation is given which can be illustrated by a diagram. Our aim is to find, in this diagram, a triangle in which three facts about sides and/or angles are known. A second diagram, showing only this triangle, can then be drawn and the appropriate rules of trigonometry applied to it.

EXERCISE 11L

From a port P a ship Q is 20 km away on a bearing of 125° and a ship R is 35 km away on a bearing of 050°.
Find the distance between the two ships.

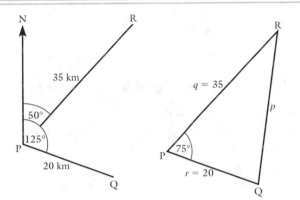

△PQR is a suitable triangle since PR and PQ are known and QP̂R can be found.

$Q\hat{P}R = 125° - 50° = 75°$

The distance between the ships is QR so we must calculate p in △PQR.

Using the cosine rule in △PQR gives

$$p^2 = q^2 + r^2 - (2qr \cos \hat{P})$$
$$= 35^2 + 20^2 - (2 \times 35 \times 20 \times \cos 75°)$$
$$= 1625 - 362.3\ldots = 1262.6\ldots$$
$$\Rightarrow \qquad p = 35.53\ldots$$

Therefore the distance between the ships is 35.5 km correct to 3 s.f.

1 Starting from a point A, an aeroplane flies for 40 km on a bearing of 169° to B, and then for 65 km on a bearing of 057° to C. Find the distance between A and C.

2 From two points A and B, on level ground, the angles of elevation of the top of a radio mast PQ are found to be 39.1° and 57.2°. If the distance between A and B is 25 m, find

a AP̂B

b the height of the radio mast.

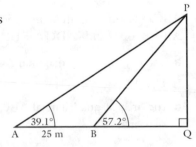

3 A children's slide has a flight of steps of length
2.7 m and the length of the straight slide is 4.2 m.
If the distance from the bottom of the steps to
the bottom of the slide is 4.9 m find, to the
nearest degree, the angle between the steps
and the slide.

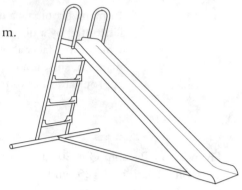

4 Using the information given in the diagram

   a find the area of △ABC

   b use the formula area △ABC $= \frac{1}{2} ac \sin \widehat{B}$
      to find $\widehat{B}$

   c find AC.

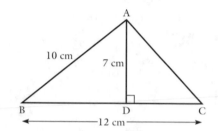

5 A helicopter leaves a heliport A and flies 2.4 km on a bearing of 154° to a checkpoint B. It
then flies due east to its base C. If the bearing of C from A is 112° find the distances AC
and BC. The helicopter flies at a constant speed throughout and takes 5 minutes to fly
from A to C. Find its speed.

6 P, Q and R are three points on level ground.
From Q, P is 60 m away on a bearing of 325°
and R is 94 m away on a bearing of 040°.

   a Find cos Q.

   b Find the distance between P and R.

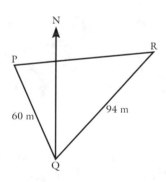

7 ABCD is a quadrilateral in which AB = 4.1 cm, BC = 3.7 cm, CD = 5.3 cm,
A$\widehat{B}$C = 66° and A$\widehat{D}$C = 51°. Find

   a the length of the diagonal AC

   b C$\widehat{A}$D

   c the area of quadrilateral ABCD, considering it as split into two triangles by the
      diagonal AC.

8 The diagram shows three survey points, A, B and C, which are on an east-west line on level ground. From point A the bearing of the foot of a tower T is 051°, while from B the bearing of the tower is 042°. Find

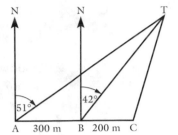

    a TÂB and AT̂B   **b** AT   **c** CT

9 The diagram shows the end wall of a bungalow. The roof has one face inclined at 30° to the horizontal and the other inclined at 55° to the horizontal. Find

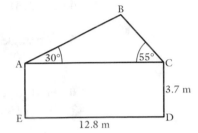

    a the length of AB   **c** the area of the end wall

    b the length of BC   **d** the height of B above ED.

10 In a quadrilateral ABCD, DC is of length 3 cm, the length of the diagonal BD is 10 cm, BÂD = 30°, BD̂A = 45° and BD̂C = 60°. Calculate

    a the length of **i** AB   **ii** BC

    b the area of the quadrilateral.

11 The points A, B and C are on the circumference of a circle with centre O and radius 10 cm. The lengths of the chords AB and BC are 8 cm and 3 cm respectively. Calculate

    a AÔB   **b** BÔC   **c** the length of the chord AC

    d the area of quadrilateral ABCO.

    (Remember that OA = OB = OC = 10 cm.)

12 The diagram represents the positions of Derby, Coventry and Wolverhampton. Coventry is 37 miles due south of Derby. Wolverhampton is 34 miles from Derby on a bearing of 226°.

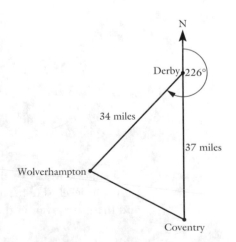

    a Calculate the distance and bearing of Wolverhampton from Coventry.

    b How far is Wolverhampton

      i north of Coventry

      ii west of Derby?

1 If $\cos \widehat{A} = \frac{5}{13}$ and $\widehat{A}$ is acute, find $\sin \widehat{A}$ and $\tan \widehat{A}$.

2 Find two angles between $0°$ and $180°$ such that the sine of each is 0.3667.

3 If $\cos \widehat{P} = 0.43$ find, without using a calculator, $\cos(180° - \widehat{P})$.

4 In $\triangle ABC$, $BC = 161\,cm$, $\widehat{B} = 109°$ and $\widehat{A} = 51°$. Find AC.

5 A triangle PQR is such that $QR = 7.6\,cm$, $PQ = 5.9\,cm$ and $\widehat{Q} = 107°$. Find PR.

6 Find the area of $\triangle ABC$ if $AB = 8.2\,cm$, $BC = 11.3\,cm$ and $\widehat{B} = 125°$.

7 A boat sails $11\,km$ from a harbour on a bearing of $220°$. It then sails $15\,km$ on a bearing of $340°$. How far is the boat from the harbour?

8 a Use the information in the diagram to find $\cos \widehat{A}$ giving your answer as a fraction.

   b Hence find
     i $\sin \widehat{A}$ in surd form.
     ii the area of $\triangle ABC$ in surd form.

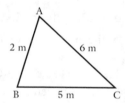

Brendan and May are asked if they can find the distance across a canyon at a particular point where their civil engineering company would like to construct a bridge.

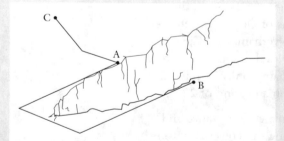

Brendan discovers that the ground from A and B to the end of the canyon is level. He makes several measurements all on the same level and these are given in the following diagram.

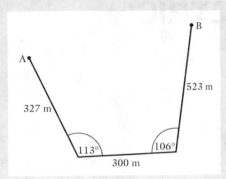

Investigate whether or not Brendan has sufficient information to find the distance AB. If he has, find it. If he has not, can you suggest another measurement which he needs? Investigate the minimum information needed to 'fix' a quadrilateral.

May's approach is quite different. She finds that a short distance back from A in the line BA the ground slopes up at a constant angle. She walks 54 metres up the slope to a point C and from this point she measures the angles of depression of A and B. Her measurements are given in the next diagram.

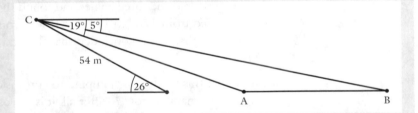

Does May have enough information to find AB? If she has, find it. If she has not, can you suggest another measurement she could make which will then make it possible?

Investigate whether there are other ways of finding the distance AB using your present knowledge.

GEOMETRIC PROOF

12

Jim has drawn about thirty different triangles of all shapes and sizes. For each one he measured the three angles and found their sum. The results he obtained varied from 178° to 181.5°. It was from results such as these in Book 7A that it was concluded that the sum of the angles of *any* triangle is 180°.

Could it be that this method is 'jumping to conclusions' and is unsatisfactory for many reasons? After all, it is impossible to draw a line, for a line has no thickness and if it did not have thickness we could not see it! Furthermore it is impossible to measure angles with absolute accuracy. The protractor Jim uses is probably capable of measuring angles at best to the nearest degree. The only conclusion that Jim can draw from his results is 'it seems likely that the angle sum of any triangle is 180°' but he must remain aware that 'proof' by examining particular cases leaves open the possibility that somewhere, as yet unfound, there lurks an exception to the rule.

Jim needs to know if the result can be *proved* to be true for every triangle. If it can, several other results follow. For example, if the angle sum of any triangle is 180°, the angle sum of the four angles in every quadrilateral must be 360° since one diagonal always divides a quadrilateral into two triangles.

This chapter shows how certain geometric properties can be proved and how other properties follow from them.

DEDUCTIVE
PROOF

Learning geometrical properties from demonstrations gives the impression that each property is isolated. However geometry can be given a logical structure where one property can be deduced from other properties. This forms the basis of deductive proof; we quote known and accepted facts and then make logical deductions from them.

For example, if we accept that

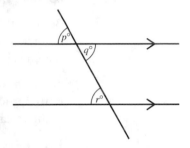

- vertically opposite angles are equal
- corresponding angles are equal,

then, using just these two facts, we can prove that alternate angles are equal.

In the diagram
$$p° = q° \qquad \text{(vertically opposite angles)}$$
$$p° = r° \qquad \text{(corresponding angles)}$$
$$\Rightarrow \quad q° = r°$$

Therefore the alternate angles are equal.

The symbol $\Rightarrow$ means 'implies that' and indicates the logical deduction made from the two stated facts.

This proof does not involve angles of a particular size; $p°$, $q°$ and $r°$ can be any size. Hence this proves that alternate angles are *always* equal whatever their size.

As a further example of deductive proof we will prove that in *any* triangle, the sum of the interior angles *is* 180°. Note that angles on a straight line by definition, add up to 180°.

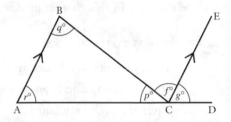

If $\triangle ABC$ is any triangle and if AC is extended to D and CE is parallel to AB then

$$p° + f° + g° = 180° \qquad \text{(angles on a straight line)} \qquad (1)$$
$$f° = q° \qquad \text{(alternate angles)} \qquad (2)$$
$$g° = r° \qquad \text{(corresponding angles)} \qquad (3)$$
$$\Rightarrow \quad p° + q° + r° = 180°$$

i.e. the sum of the interior angles of *any* triangle is 180°.

The statements on page 275 also lead to another useful fact about angles in triangles:

$$(\, 2 \,) \text{ and } (\, 3 \,) \quad \Rightarrow \quad f^\circ + g^\circ = q^\circ + r^\circ$$

i.e. an exterior angle of a triangle is equal to the sum of the two interior opposite angles.

Because this proof does not involve measuring angles in a particular triangle it applies to all possible triangles thus closing the loophole that there may exist a triangle whose angles do not add up to 180°.

Notice how this proof uses the property proved in the first example, that is, this proof follows from the previous proof. The angle sum property of triangles can now be used to prove further properties.

Euclid was the first person to give a formal structure to Geometry. He started by making certain assumptions, such as 'there is only one straight line between two points'. Using only these assumptions (called axioms), he then proved some facts and used those facts to prove further facts and so on. Thus the proof of any one fact could be traced back to the axioms.

However when *you* are asked to give a geometric proof you do not have to worry about which property depends on which; you can use *any* facts that you know. One aspect of proof is that it is an argument used to convince other people of the truth of any statement, so whatever facts you use must be clearly stated.

It is a good idea to marshal your ideas before starting to write out a proof. This is most easily done by marking right angles, equal angles and equal sides etc. on the diagram.

The exercises in this chapter give practice in writing out a proof.

For the next exercise the following facts are needed;

> vertically opposite angles are equal,
>
> corresponding angles are equal,
>
> alternate angles are equal,
>
> interior angles add up to 180°,
>
> angle sum of a triangle is 180°,
>
> an exterior angle of a triangle is equal to the sum of the interior opposite angles,
>
> an isosceles triangle has two sides of the same length and the angles at the base of those sides are equal,
>
> an equilateral triangle has three sides of the same length and each interior angle is 60°.

EXERCISE 12A

In a triangle ABC the bisectors of angles B and C intersect at I.
Prove that $\widehat{BIC} = 90° - \frac{1}{2}\widehat{A}$

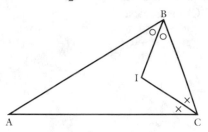

In triangle BIC

$\widehat{BIC} + \widehat{IBC} + \widehat{ICB} = 180°$ (angles in a $\triangle$)

i.e.

$\widehat{BIC} + \frac{1}{2}\widehat{B} + \frac{1}{2}\widehat{C} = 180°$ (BI bisects $\widehat{B}$ and CI bisects $\widehat{C}$) (1)

But $\widehat{A} + \widehat{B} + \widehat{C} = 180°$ (angles in a $\triangle$)

i.e. $\widehat{B} + \widehat{C} = 180° - \widehat{A}$

so $\frac{1}{2}\widehat{B} + \frac{1}{2}\widehat{C} = 90° - \frac{1}{2}\widehat{A}$

Substituting in (1)

$\widehat{BIC} + 90° - \frac{1}{2}\widehat{A} = 180°$

i.e. $\widehat{BIC} = 90° + \frac{1}{2}\widehat{A}$

1

Prove that $\widehat{ACD} = \widehat{ABC} + \widehat{DEC}$.

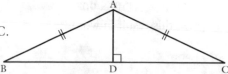

2

Prove that $\widehat{ACB} = 2\widehat{CDB}$.

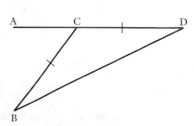

3

Prove that AD bisects $\widehat{BAC}$.

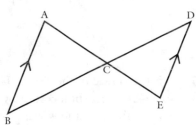

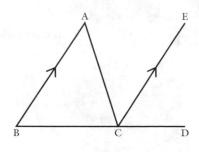

4 CE bisects $A\widehat{C}D$ and CE is parallel to BA.
Prove that $\triangle ABC$ is isosceles.

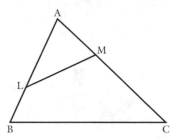

5 $A\widehat{M}L = A\widehat{B}C$.
Prove that $A\widehat{L}M = A\widehat{C}B$.

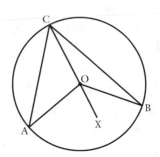

6 O is the centre of the circle.

   a Prove that $A\widehat{O}X = 2A\widehat{C}O$

   b Prove that $A\widehat{O}B = 2A\widehat{C}B$.
     Express this result in words.

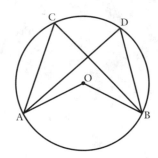

7 O is the centre of the circle. Use the second result you
obtained in question **6** to prove that $A\widehat{C}B = A\widehat{D}B$.
Express this result in words.

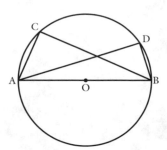

8 O is the centre of the circle and $A\widehat{O}B = 180°$.
Use the results from questions **6** and **7** to prove
that $A\widehat{C}B = A\widehat{D}B = 90°$.
Express this result in words.

We saw in the last section that drawing a few triangles and measuring the angles led us to say that 'it looks as though' the angles of any triangle add up to 180°. At that stage we had a *hypothesis*, which we then *proved* to be true for any triangle.

It is also important to be able to show that certain hypotheses are in fact false.

Suppose that students were asked to investigate the relationship between the number of lines drawn across a circle and the number of regions that the circle is divided into by those lines.

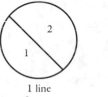 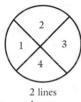 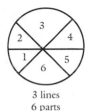

1 line   2 lines   3 lines
2 parts   4 parts   6 parts

These three drawings led John to the hypothesis that n lines drawn across a circle give $2n$ regions.

Jocelyn however, drew the lines this way, showing that 3 lines can give 7 regions, and therefore that John's hypothesis is false.

Jocelyn used a *counter example* to disprove the hypothesis.

Now consider the hypothesis 'the product of two irrational numbers is itself irrational'. This can be shown to be untrue using this counter example: $\sqrt{2}$ and $\sqrt{8}$ are both irrational, but $\sqrt{2} \times \sqrt{8} = \sqrt{16} = 4$, which is rational.

You may like to see if you can find a counter example to disprove that all prime numbers are odd.

Not every hypothesis can be either proved or shown to be false. In mathematics there are several in this category that are well known, one being Goldbach's conjecture. That is that every even number greater than or equal to 6, can be written as the sum of two odd prime numbers. At the time of writing no one has yet proved this to be true; on the other hand no one has found a counter example.

In questions **1** to **4** see if you can find a counter example to disprove each hypothesis.

1   The square root of a positive number is always smaller than the number.

2   If the side of a square is x cm long, the number of units of area of the square is always different from the number of units of length in the perimeter.

3   The diagonals of a parallelogram never cut at right angles.

4   The sum of any two angles in a triangle is always greater than the third angle.

Questions **5** and **6** give 'proofs' that are obviously invalid since they lead to contradictions. Find, in each case, the flaw in the argument.

5   It is a fact that $4 - 10 = 9 - 15$

Adding $\frac{25}{4}$ to each side gives $4 - 10 + \frac{25}{4} = 9 - 15 + \frac{25}{4}$

Factorising $(2 - \frac{5}{2})(2 - \frac{5}{2}) = (3 - \frac{5}{2})(3 - \frac{5}{2})$

i.e. $(2 - \frac{5}{2})^2 = (3 - \frac{5}{2})^2$

Take the square root of each side $2 - \frac{5}{2} = 3 - \frac{5}{2}$

Add $\frac{5}{2}$ to each side $2 = 3$ which is

plainly absurd.

6   Let $x = y$

and obviously $x^2 - xy = x^2 - xy$

Now $x = y$ so $xy = y^2$

i.e. line 2 can be rewritten $x^2 - xy = x^2 - y^2$

Factorise $x(x - y) = (x - y)(x + y)$

Divide both sides by $(x - y)$ $x = x + y$

but $x = y$, so $x = x + x$

i.e. $x = 2x$

i.e. $1 = 2$ which is obviously

absurd.

Two figures are congruent if one figure is an exact copy of the other. If the figures are drawn on squared paper it is easy to determine if they are congruent. If the shapes are drawn accurately on plain paper, we can use tracing paper to see whether they appear to be congruent but we need precise information about the lengths of sides and the sizes of angles to determine whether they really are congruent.

CONGRUENT TRIANGLES

Triangles are simple figures and not very much information is needed to determine whether one triangle is an exact copy of another triangle.

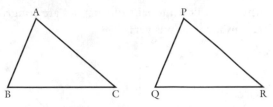

If △s $\begin{array}{c} ABC \\ PQR \end{array}$ are congruent it follows that

$$\left.\begin{array}{l} AB = PQ \\ AC = PR \\ BC = QR \end{array}\right\} \quad \text{and} \quad \left\{\begin{array}{l} \hat{A} = \hat{P} \\ \hat{B} = \hat{Q} \\ \hat{C} = \hat{R} \end{array}\right.$$

To make an exact copy of these triangles we do not need to know the lengths of all three sides and the sizes of all three angles: three measurements are usually enough and we now investigate which three measurements are suitable.

EXERCISE 12C

In each of the following questions, make a rough sketch of △ABC. Construct a triangle with the same measurements as those given for △ABC. Is your construction an exact copy of △ABC? (Try to construct a different triangle with the given measurements.)

1 △ABC, in which AB = 8 cm, BC = 5 cm, AC = 6 cm.

2 △ABC, in which $\hat{A} = 40°$, $\hat{B} = 60°$, $\hat{C} = 80°$

3 △ABC, in which AB = 7 cm, BC = 12 cm, AC = 8 cm.

4 △ABC, in which $\hat{A} = 20°$, $\hat{B} = 40°$, $\hat{C} = 120°$.

5 What extra information do you need about △ABC in questions **2** and **4** in order to make an exact copy?

THREE PAIRS OF SIDES

From the last exercise you should be convinced that an exact copy of a triangle can be made if the lengths of the three sides are known. Therefore,

> two triangles are congruent if the three sides of one triangle are equal to the three sides of the other triangle.

However if the three angles of one triangle are equal to the three angles of another triangle they may not be congruent (but they are similar).

EXERCISE 12D

Decide whether the following pairs of triangles are congruent.
Give brief reasons for your answers.

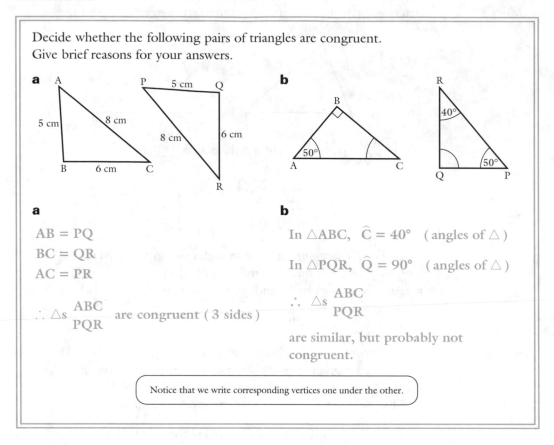

a

AB = PQ

BC = QR

AC = PR

∴ △s $\begin{array}{c}ABC\\PQR\end{array}$ are congruent (3 sides)

b

In △ABC, $\widehat{C}$ = 40° (angles of △)

In △PQR, $\widehat{Q}$ = 90° (angles of △)

∴ △s $\begin{array}{c}ABC\\PQR\end{array}$

are similar, but probably not congruent.

> Notice that we write corresponding vertices one under the other.

In questions **1** to **6** state whether or not the two triangles are congruent. Give a brief reason for your answers. All lengths are in centimetres.

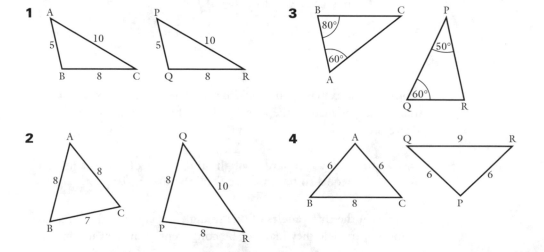

5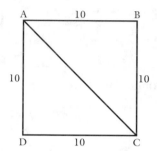

6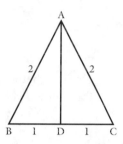

Give brief reasons for your answers to questions **7** to **10**.

7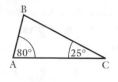

Are △ADC and △ABC congruent?

9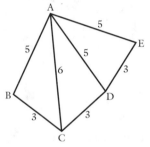

Are △ABD and △ACD congruent?

8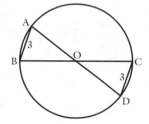

Which triangles are congruent?

10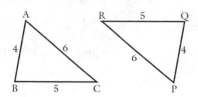

The point O is the centre of the circle and the radius is 5 cm. Are △ABO and △CDO congruent?

TWO ANGLES AND A SIDE

To make an exact copy of a triangle we need to know the length of at least one side.

EXERCISE 12E

1 Construct △ABC, in which AB = 6 cm, $\widehat{A} = 30°$, $\widehat{B} = 60°$.

2 Construct △PQR, in which PR = 6 cm, $\widehat{P} = 30°$, $\widehat{Q} = 60°$.

3 Construct △LMN, in which LM = 6 cm, $\widehat{L} = 30°$, $\widehat{M} = 60°$.

4 Construct △XYZ, in which YZ = 6 cm, $\widehat{X} = 30°$, $\widehat{Y} = 60°$.

5 How many of the triangles that you have constructed are congruent?

6 How many different triangles can you construct from the following information: one angle is 40°, another angle is 70° and the length of one side is 8 cm?

Now you can see that we are able to make an exact copy of a triangle if we know the sizes of two of its angles and the length of one side, provided that we place the side in the same position relative to the angles in both triangles, i.e.

> two triangles are congruent if two angles and one side of one triangle are equal to two angles and the *corresponding* side of the other triangle.

EXERCISE 12F

Decide whether these triangles are congruent. Give a brief reason for your answer.

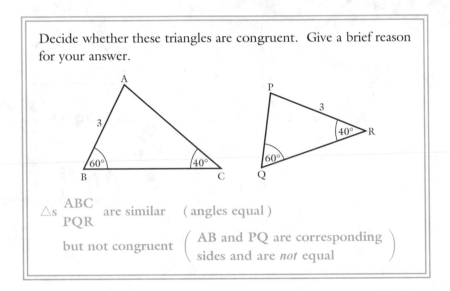

$\triangle s$ $\dfrac{ABC}{PQR}$ are similar (angles equal)

but not congruent $\left(\begin{array}{l} \text{AB and PQ are corresponding} \\ \text{sides and are } \textit{not} \text{ equal} \end{array} \right)$

In questions **1** to **8** state whether or not the two triangles are congruent. Give brief reasons for your answers. All lengths are in centimetres.

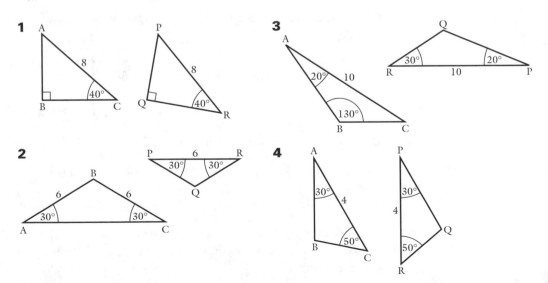

5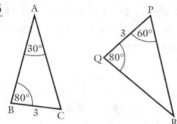

7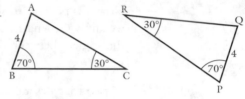

6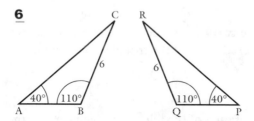

8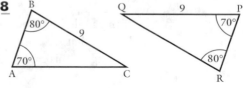

9 Are △ABC and △ADC congruent?

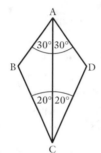

10 Are △ABC and △ADC congruent?

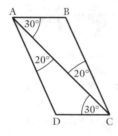

**TWO SIDES
AND AN ANGLE**

We are now left with one more possible combination of three measurements: if we know the lengths of two sides and the size of one angle in a triangle, does this fix the size and shape of the triangle?

EXERCISE 12G

Can you make an exact copy of the following triangles from the information given about them? (Try to construct each triangle.)

1 △ABC, in which AB = 8 cm, BC = 5 cm, $\widehat{B} = 30°$.

2 △XYZ, in which XY = 8 cm, XZ = 5 cm, $\widehat{Y} = 30°$.

3 △PQR, in which $\widehat{Q} = 60°$, PQ = 6 cm, QR = 8 cm.

4 △LMN, in which LM = 8 cm, $\widehat{M} = 20°$, LN = 4 cm.

5 △DEF, in which DE = 5 cm, $\widehat{E} = 90°$, EF = 6 cm.

Now it is possible to see that we can make an exact copy of a triangle if we know the lengths of two sides and the size of one angle, provided that the angle is between those two sides. Therefore

> two triangles are congruent if two sides and the *included* angle of one triangle are equal to two sides and the *included* angle of the other triangle.

If the angle is not between the two known sides, then we cannot always be sure that we can make an exact copy of the triangle. We will now investigate this case further.

EXERCISE 12H

Can you make an exact copy of each of the following triangles from the information given about them?

1 $\triangle ABC$, in which $AB = 6\,cm$, $\hat{B} = 90°$, $AC = 10\,cm$.

2 $\triangle PQR$, in which $PQ = 8\,cm$, $\hat{Q} = 40°$, $PR = 6.5\,cm$.

3 $\triangle XYZ$, in which $XY = 5\,cm$, $\hat{Y} = 90°$, $XZ = 13\,cm$.

4 $\triangle LMN$, in which $LM = 5\,cm$, $\hat{M} = 60°$, $LN = 4.5\,cm$.

5 $\triangle DEF$, in which $DE = 7\,cm$, $\hat{E} = 90°$, $DF = 10\,cm$.

6 $\triangle RST$, in which $RS = 5\,cm$, $\hat{S} = 120°$, $RT = 8\,cm$.

7 Can you calculate any further information about any of the triangles in questions **1** to **6**?

From question **7** you can see that, when the given angle is 90° the length of the remaining side of the triangle can be calculated.

Therefore, if we are told that one angle in a triangle is a right angle and we are also given the length of one side and the hypotenuse, then this information fixes the shape and size of the triangle since it is equivalent to knowing the lengths of the three sides.

> Two triangles are congruent if they both have a right angle, and the hypotenuse and a side of one triangle are equal to the hypotenuse and a side of the other triangle.

EXERCISE 12I In questions **1** to **8** state whether or not the two triangles are congruent. Give brief reasons for your answers. All lengths are in centimetres.

1
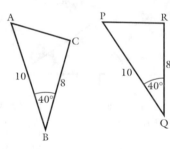

5
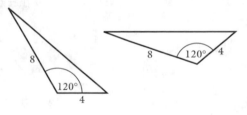

2
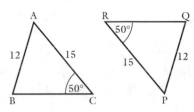

6
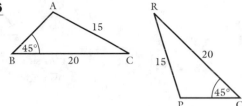

3
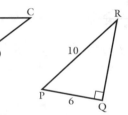

7
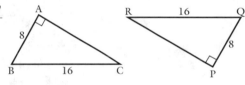

4
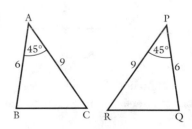

8
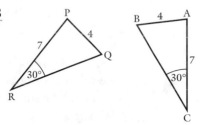

9 Are △ABD and △ACD congruent?

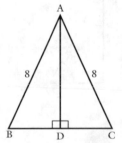

10 Are △ABD and △ACD congruent?

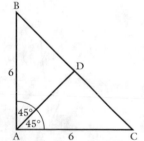

Summing up, two triangles are congruent if:

either   the three sides of one triangle are equal to the three sides of the other triangle (S S S)

or   two angles and a side of one triangle are equal to two angles and the corresponding side of the other triangle (A A S)

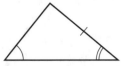 

or   two sides and the included angle of one triangle are equal to two sides and the included angle of the other triangle (S A S)

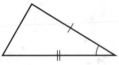 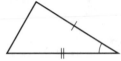

or   two triangles each have a right angle, and the hypotenuse and a side of one triangle are equal to the hypotenuse and a side of the other triangle (R H S).

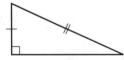 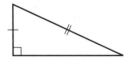

EXERCISE 12J   State whether or not each of the following pairs of triangles are congruent. Give brief reasons for your answers. All measurements are in centimetres.

1
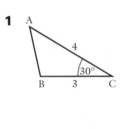 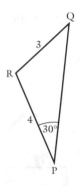

2
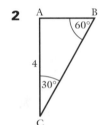 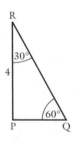

3
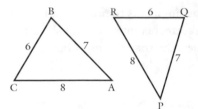

8
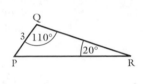

4
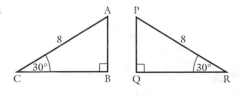

9
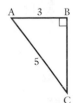

5
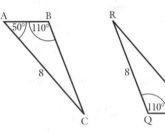

10
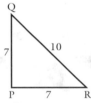

6

11
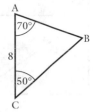

7
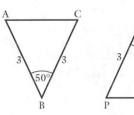

12
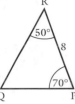
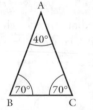
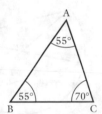
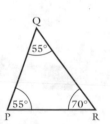
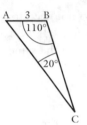

We do not need to know actual measurements to prove that triangles are congruent. If we can show that a correct combination of sides and angles are the same in both triangles, the triangles must be congruent.

In quadrilateral ABCD, AB = DC and AD = BC. The diagonal BD is drawn. Prove that △ABD and △CDB are congruent.

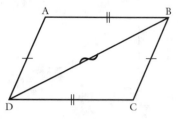

> Mark on your diagram all the information given and any further facts that you discover. The symbol ⌒ on the line BD indicates that it is common to both triangles.

In △s ABD, CDB   AB = CD   (given)
                  AD = CB   (given)
                  DB is the same for both triangles

∴ △s ABD
       CDB   are congruent (S S S).

1

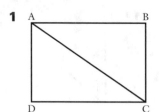

ABCD is a rectangle. Prove that △ABC and △CDA are congruent.

2

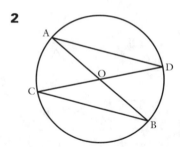

AB and CD are diameters of the circle and O is the centre. Prove that △AOD and △COB are congruent.

3

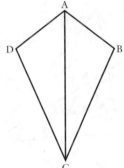

ABCD is a kite in which AD = AB and CD = BC. Prove that △ADC and △ABC are congruent.

4

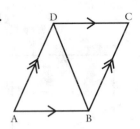

ABCD is a parallelogram. Prove that △ABD and △CDB are congruent.

5

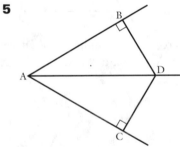

AD bisects BÂC, DB is perpendicular to AB and DC is perpendicular to AC. Prove that △ABD and △ACD are congruent.

6

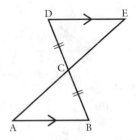

Prove that △ABC and △EDC are congruent.

7

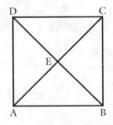

ABCD is a square. Show that △s ABE, BCE, CDE and DAE are all congruent.

8

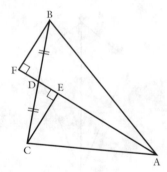

D is the midpoint of BC. CE and BF are perpendicular to AF. Find a pair of congruent triangles.

9

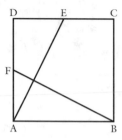

ABCD is a square. E is the midpoint of DC and F is the midpoint of AD. Show that △ADE and △BAF are congruent.

10

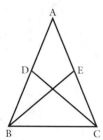

ABC is an isosceles triangle in which AB = AC. D is the midpoint of AB and E is the midpoint of AC. Prove that △BDC is congruent with △CEB.

11 ABCD is a rectangle and E is the midpoint of AB. Join DE and CE and show that △ADE and △BCE are congruent.

12 ABCD is a rectangle. E is the midpoint of AB and F is the midpoint of DC. Join DE and BF and show that △ADE and △CBF are congruent.

USING CONGRUENT TRIANGLES

Once two triangles have been shown to be congruent it follows that the other corresponding sides and angles are equal. This gives a good way of proving that certain angles are equal or that certain lines are the same length.

EXERCISE 12L

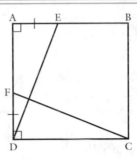

ABCD is a square and AE = DF
Show that DE = CF.

In △s DAE and CDF
$$AE = DF \quad (\text{given})$$
$$DA = CD \quad (\text{sides of a square})$$
$$D\widehat{A}E = C\widehat{D}F \quad (\text{angles of a square are } 90°)$$

$\therefore$ △s $\begin{matrix} \text{DAE} \\ \text{CDF} \end{matrix}$ are congruent (SAS).

> We have written the triangles so that corresponding vertices are lined up. We can then see the remaining corresponding sides and angles.

$\therefore$ DE = CF

1

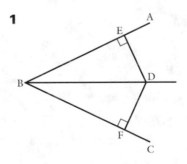

BD bisects $A\widehat{B}C$. BE and BF are equal. Show that triangles BED and BFD are congruent and hence prove that ED = FD.

2

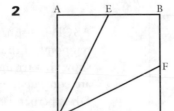

ABCD is a square and E and F are the midpoints of AB and BC. Show that △ADE and △CDF are congruent and hence prove that DE = DF.

3

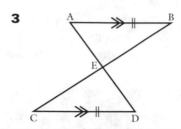

AB and CD are parallel and equal in length. Show that $\triangle$AEB and $\triangle$DEC are congruent and hence prove that E is the midpoint of both CB and AD.

ABCD is a square and P, Q and R are points on AB, BC and CD respectively such that $AP = BQ = CR$.

Show that $P\hat{Q}R = 90°$.

> If you cannot see where to start, work backwards from what you need to prove. In this case, if $P\hat{Q}R = 90°$ then $B\hat{Q}P + C\hat{Q}R = 90°$, so $B\hat{Q}P = C\hat{R}Q$, i.e. $\triangle$s $\begin{matrix} PBQ \\ QCR \end{matrix}$ are congruent.
>
> Therefore we will first prove that $\triangle$PBQ and $\triangle$QCR are congruent.

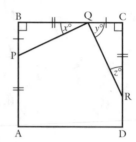

In $\triangle$PBQ and $\triangle$QCR

$$BQ = CR \qquad\qquad\qquad\qquad (\text{given})$$
$$P\hat{B}Q = Q\hat{C}R = 90° \qquad\qquad (\text{angles of a square})$$

$\left.\begin{matrix} AB = BC \quad (\text{sides of a square}) \\ AP = BQ \quad (\text{given}) \end{matrix}\right\} \Rightarrow AB - AP = BC - BQ$

i.e. $\quad PB = QC$

$\therefore \triangle$s $\begin{matrix} PBQ \\ QCR \end{matrix}$ are congruent $\qquad$ (SAS)

$\therefore \qquad\qquad\qquad x° = z°$

In $\quad \triangle$QRC $\quad y + z = 90 \qquad\qquad$ (angles of triangle)

$\therefore \qquad\qquad x + y = 90$

But $\quad x° + P\hat{Q}R + y° = 180° \qquad$ (angles on straight line)

$\therefore \qquad\qquad\qquad P\hat{Q}R = 90°$

4

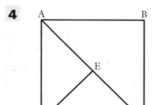

ABCD is a square and E is the midpoint of the diagonal AC. First show that triangles ADE and CDE are congruent and hence prove that DE is perpendicular to AC.

5

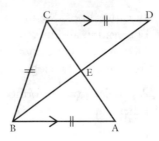

CD is parallel to BA and CD = CB = BA

Show that △CDE and △BAE are congruent and hence show that
CA bisects BD.

6 Using the same diagram and the result from question **5**, show that
△BEC and △CED are congruent. Hence prove that CA and BD cut
at right angles.

7

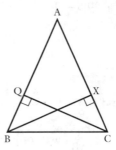

Triangle ABC is isosceles, with AB = AC.
BX is perpendicular to AC and CQ is perpendicular to AB.
Prove that BX = CQ.
(Find a pair of congruent triangles first.)

8

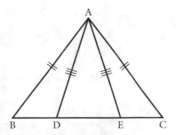

In the diagram, AB = AC and AD = AE.
Prove that BD = EC. (Consider triangles ABD and ACE.)

9 AB is a straight line. Draw a line AX perpendicular to AB. On the
other side of AB, draw a line BY perpendicular to AB so that BY is
equal to AX. Prove that $A\widehat{X}Y = B\widehat{Y}X$.

In earlier books we investigated the properties of parallelograms by observation and measurement of a few particular parallelograms. Now we can use congruent triangles to prove that these properties are true for all parallelograms.

A parallelogram is formed when two pairs of parallel lines cross each other.

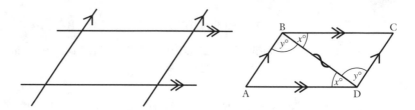

In the parallelogram ABCD, joining BD gives two triangles in which

the angles marked $x°$ are equal   They are alternate angles with respect to the parallels AD and BC.

the angles marked $y°$ are equal   They are alternate angles with respect to the parallels AB and DC.

and BD is the same for both triangles.

$\therefore \triangle s \begin{matrix} \text{BCD} \\ \text{DAB} \end{matrix}$ are congruent $(AAS) \Rightarrow BC = AD$ and $AB = DC$

i.e.   the opposite sides of a parallelogram are the same length.

Also, from the congruent triangles,

$$\widehat{A} = \widehat{C}$$

and $$\widehat{ABC} = \widehat{CDA} \quad (y° + x° = x° + y°)$$

i.e.   the opposite angles of a parallelogram are equal.

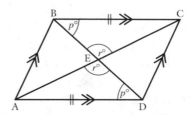

Drawing both diagonals of the parallelogram gives four triangles.

Considering the two triangles BEC, DEA

$$BC = AD \quad (\text{opposite sides of parallelogram})$$
$$E\hat{B}C = E\hat{D}A \quad (\text{alternate angles})$$
$$B\hat{E}C = A\hat{E}D \quad (\text{vertically opposite angles})$$

∴ △s $\begin{array}{c} \text{BEC} \\ \text{DEA} \end{array}$ are congruent (A A S) ⇒ BE = ED and AE = EC

i.e. the diagonals of a parallelogram bisect each other.

The diagrams below summarise these properties.

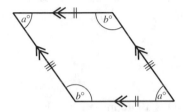 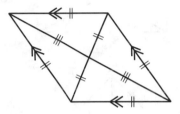

It is equally important to realise that, in general,
the diagonals are *not* the same length,
the diagonals do *not* bisect the angles of a parallelogram.

In the exercise that follows, you are asked to investigate the properties of some of the other special quadrilaterals.

EXERCISE 12M

1

ABCD is a rhombus (a parallelogram in which all four sides are equal in length). Join AC and show that △ABC and △ADC are congruent. What does AC do to the angles of the rhombus at A and C? Does the diagonal BD do the same to the angles at B and D?

2

ABCD is a rhombus. Use the results from question **1** to show that △s ABE and BCE are congruent. What can you now say about

a the angles AEB and BEC

b the lengths of AE and EC

c the lengths of BE and ED?

3

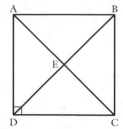

ABCD is a square (a rhombus with right-angled corners). Use the properties of the diagonals of a rhombus to show that △AED is isosceles. Hence prove that the diagonals of a square are the same length.

Are the two diagonals of *every* rhombus the same length?

4

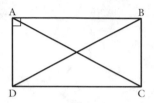

ABCD is a rectangle (a parallelogram with right-angled corners). Prove that △s ADB and DAC are congruent. What can you deduce about the lengths of AC and DB?

5

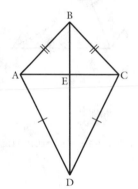

ABCD is a kite in which AB = BC and AD = DC. Does the diagonal BD bisect the angles at B and D? Does the diagonal AC bisect the angles at A and C? Is E the midpoint of either diagonal? What can you say about the angles at E?

6

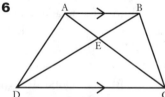

ABCD is a trapezium: it has just one pair of parallel sides. Are there any congruent triangles in this diagram?

7

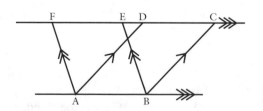

In the diagram, ABCD and ABEF are parallelograms. Show that △s ADF and BCE are congruent.

By considering the shape ABCF and then removing each of the triangles AFD and BEC in turn, what can you say about the areas of the two parallelograms?

This question proves that

> Two parallelograms with the same base, and drawn between the same pair of parallel lines, are equal in area.

**PROPERTIES OF
SPECIAL
QUADRILATERALS**

Next we summarise the results from **Exercise 12M** for special quadrilaterals. The properties of parallelograms are summarised on page 297.

A quadrilateral in which each angle is 90° is called a *rectangle*.

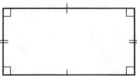

A rectangle has opposite sides that are equal and parallel and diagonals that are equal and bisect each other.

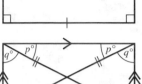

A quadrilateral with four sides of equal length and each angle 90° is called a *square*.

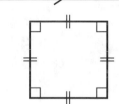

A square also has opposite sides that are parallel and equal diagonals that bisect each other at right angles.

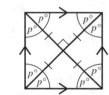

A quadrilateral with four equal sides (but not four equal angles) is called a *rhombus*.

The diagonals of a rhombus bisect each other at right angles (but are not the same length), and bisect the angles of the rhombus. The opposite sides are parallel and the opposite angles are equal.

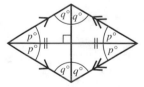

A quadrilateral with two pairs of equal adjacent sides is called a *kite*.

The diagonals cut at right angles, but only one diagonal is bisected.

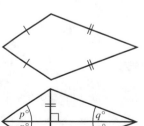

Any of these properties can be quoted and used as part of a solution.

EXERCISE 12N

1

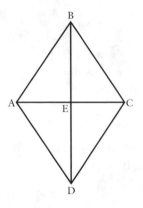

ABCD is a rectangle. The diagonals AC and DB cut at E. How far is E from BC?

2

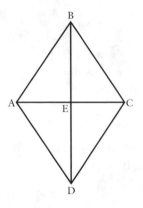

ABCD is a rhombus in which AC = 6 cm and BD = 8 cm. Find the length of AB.

3

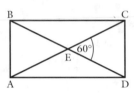

ABCD is a rectangle in which CÊD = 60°. Find EĈD.

4

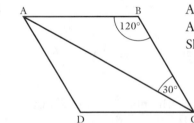

ABCD is a parallelogram in which AB̂C = 120° and BĈA = 30°. Show that ABCD is also a rhombus.

5 In a rectangle ABCD, AB = 6 cm and the diagonal BD is 10 cm. Make a rough sketch of the rectangle and then construct ABCD. Measure AD.

6 In a rhombus ABCD, the diagonal AC is 8 cm and the diagonal BD is 6 cm. Construct the rhombus and measure AB. (Remember first to make a rough sketch.)

7 ABCD is a parallelogram in which the diagonal AC is 10 cm and the diagonal BD is 12 cm. AC and BD cut at E and AÊB = 60°. Make a rough sketch of the parallelogram and then construct ABCD. Measure BC.

8 Construct a rhombus ABCD in which the sides are 5 cm long and the diagonal AC is 8 cm long. Measure the diagonal BD.

9 Construct a square ABCD whose diagonal AC is 8 cm long. Measure the side AB.

ABCD is a parallelogram. E is the midpoint of BC and F is the midpoint of AD. Prove that BF = DE.

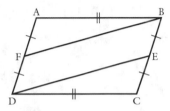

In △s ABF and CDE

$\quad$ AF = EC $\quad$ ($\frac{1}{2}$ opposite sides of parallelogram)

$\quad$ AB = DC $\quad$ (opposite sides of parallelogram)

$\quad$ F$\hat{A}$B = E$\hat{C}$D $\quad$ (opposite angles of parallelogram)

∴ △s $\begin{matrix} ABF \\ CDE \end{matrix}$ are congruent (SAS)

∴ BF = DE

10

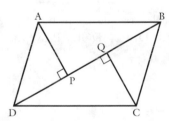

ABCD is a parallelogram. AP is perpendicular to BD and CQ is perpendicular to BD. Prove that AP = CQ.

11

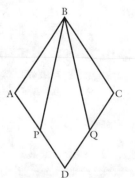

ABCD is a rhombus. P is the midpoint of AD and Q is the midpoint of CD.
Prove that BP = BQ.

12

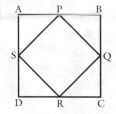

ABCD is a square and P, Q, R and S are the midpoints of AB, BC, CD and DA.
Prove that PQRS is a square.

13

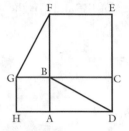

ABCD is a rectangle. ABGH and BCEF are squares.
Show that GF = BD.

PARALLELOGRAMS, POLYGONS AND CONGRUENT TRIANGLES

The next exercise uses the following facts in addition to those already used.

In a polygon

the sum of the exterior angles is 360°,
the sum of the interior angles is $(180n - 360)°$ where n is the number of sides.

If the polygon is regular, all the sides are equal and all the interior angles are equal.

EXERCISE 12P

ABC is an isosceles triangle in which AB = AC. A point D is inside the triangle and $D\hat{B}C = D\hat{C}B$. Prove that AD bisects $B\hat{A}C$.

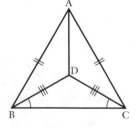

$$D\hat{B}C = D\hat{C}B \quad (\text{given})$$
$$\Rightarrow \quad \triangle BCD \text{ is isosceles}$$
$$\Rightarrow \quad BD = CD$$

In △s ADB and ADC $\qquad$ BD = CD $\quad$ (proved)
$\qquad\qquad\qquad\qquad\qquad$ AB = AC $\quad$ (given)
$\qquad\qquad\qquad\qquad\qquad$ AD is common

$\therefore \quad \triangle s \genfrac{}{}{0pt}{}{\text{ADB}}{\text{ADC}} \quad$ are congruent (SSS)

$\therefore \quad B\hat{A}D = C\hat{A}D$, i.e. AD bisects $B\hat{A}C$.

1

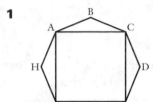

ABCDEFGH is a regular octagon.
Prove that ACEG is a square.

2

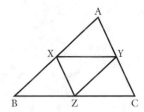

X, Y and Z are the midpoints of sides AB, AC and BC respectively. Prove that △XYZ is congruent with △YZC. Hence prove that BXYZ is a parallelogram.

3

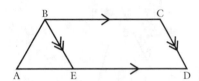

ABCD is a trapezium with BC parallel to AD and AB equal to CD. BE is parallel to CD and $\widehat{CDE} = 60°$. Prove that △ABE is equilateral.

4 ABCDEF is a hexagon in which AB is parallel and equal to ED and BC is parallel and equal to FE.

Join B to E and prove that $\widehat{ABC} = \widehat{FED}$.
Hence prove that △ABC and △FED are congruent.
Hence prove that ACDF is a parallelogram.

5

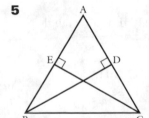

AB = AC,
BD is perpendicular to AC and CE is perpendicular to AB.
Prove that △BDC and △BEC are congruent and hence prove that △AED is isosceles.

MIXED EXERCISE

EXERCISE 12Q

1 A village primary school has four classes. Next year the total number of children on the school register is due to increase. The sizes of three of the classes are definitely going to increase. The hypothesis is that the size of the fourth class must also increase. Give some examples, using numbers, to disprove this hypothesis.

2 Decide whether or not the following pairs of triangles are congruent. Give brief reasons for your answers.

a

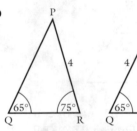

c

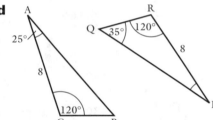

b

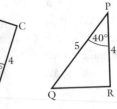

d

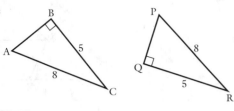

3 AD = BC.
Prove that △ADE and △BCE are congruent.

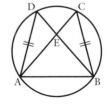

4

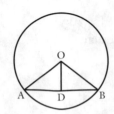

O is the centre of a circle and D is the midpoint of AB.
Prove that OD is perpendicular to AB.

5 ABCDEF is a regular hexagon. Prove that ABDE is a rectangle.

6 M is the midpoint of the side AB of △ABC.
The line through M parallel to BC meets at AC in H.
The line through M parallel to AC meets BC in K.
Show that **a** MH = BK **b** MK = AH

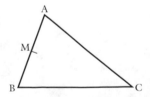

PUZZLE

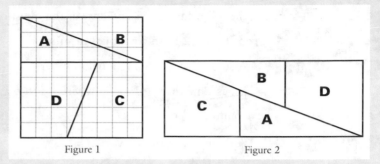

Figure 1   Figure 2

Draw a square of side 8 cm on centimetre graph paper. Divide the square into two congruent triangles and two congruent trapeziums as shown in Figure 1.

Rearrange the four shapes to form the rectangle in Figure 2. This rectangle measures 13 cm by 5 cm so has an area of $13 \times 5 \, \text{cm}^2 = 65 \, \text{cm}^2$.

However, the area of the original square is $8 \times 8 \, \text{cm}^2 = 64 \, \text{cm}^2$.

How do you explain this apparent contradiction?

PRACTICAL
WORK

a Draw a rectangle measuring 14 cm by 8 cm and cut it into four pieces as shown in the diagram.

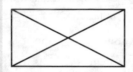

Put all four pieces together to form
  i a parallelogram
  ii a large equilateral triangle
  iii a large isosceles triangle
  iv a kite
  v two congruent triangles.

b Draw another triangle, this time measuring 12 cm by 8 cm. Can you make the same shapes as in part **a**? If your answer is 'yes', do so. If your answer is 'no', explain what is special about the first rectangle so that all the shapes can be made.

c Give the dimensions of another rectangle that will allow you to make all the shapes listed in part **a**. Are there many more?

Study the following proofs and answer the questions that follow.

1 Proof that $\sqrt{2}$ is an irrational number

1 Assume that $\sqrt{2}$ is a rational number,

   i.e. assume that $\sqrt{2} = \dfrac{a}{b}$ where a and b are integers with no common factor.

2 Squaring both sides gives $2 = \dfrac{a^2}{b^2}$

3 i.e. $2b^2 = a^2$

4 But $2b^2$ is obviously divisible by 2, so a^2 is an even number.

5 And if a^2 is even then a is even

6 So $a = 2c$ for some whole number c

7 i.e. $a^2 = 4c^2$

8 But we know that $a^2 = 2b^2$

9 so $2b^2 = 4c^2$

10 i.e. $b^2 = 2c^2$

11 This means that b^2 must be even, i.e. b is even

12 Hence $\dfrac{a}{b}$ cannot be in its simplest form since both numbers are even numbers.

13 This contradicts the original assumption which must therefore be false.

14 Since $\sqrt{2}$ cannot be expressed as $\dfrac{a}{b}$ where a and b are integers, $\sqrt{2}$ is irrational.

a This is called a proof by contradiction. Which two lines contradict each other?

b Why is line 5 true?

c Is it true that the square root of any even whole number is always even? If it is not what special condition must hold for it to be true?

d Is it true that the square root of any odd whole number is always odd or is the statement true for particular odd numbers only?

e Use a similar argument to show that $\sqrt{3}$ is an irrational number.

f Use this method to try to show that $\sqrt{4}$ is an irrational number? Where and why does the argument break down?

2 Euclid's proof that there must be an infinite number of prime numbers

1 Assume that the largest prime number is p.

2 When the number $2 \times 3 \times 5 \times 7 \times 11 \times 13 \times 17 \times \ldots \times p + 1$ is divided by any prime number it leaves a remainder of 1.

3 But every number greater than 1 is exactly divisible by at least one prime number.

4 This gives a contradiction.

5 Therefore the assumption in line 1 is wrong and there cannot be a largest prime number, so there must be an infinite number of prime numbers.

a What are the next three numbers after 17 in the second line of the proof?

b What is the answer when $2 \times 3 \times 5 \times 7 \times 11 \times 13 \times 17 + 1$ is divided by **i** 13   **ii** 5?

c What do the dots in line 2 represent?

d Why is line 2 correct?

e Why is line 3 correct?

f Prove that 30031 is a prime number.

g Find a prime number that is greater than 1 000 000 000, and state why you are sure that it is prime.

CIRCLES AND TANGENTS

The early work on angles in a circle is found in Book 9A, Chapter 20.

The main results in that chapter were

- angles standing on the same arc
  of a circle and in the same segment
  are equal

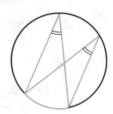

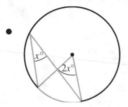

the angle which an arc of a circle subtends at
the centre is equal to twice the angle it
subtends at any point on the remaining
circumference

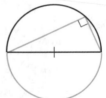

- the angle in a semicircle is a
  right angle.

You have proved these results if you did questions **6** to **8** in
Exercise 12A.

In this chapter we extend our knowledge of circles by studying cyclic
quadrilaterals, tangents to circles and harder loci questions, many of
which involve circles or arcs of circles.

CYCLIC
QUADRILATERALS

EXERCISE 13A

Copy the following diagrams making them at least twice as large. For
each diagram measure the angles denoted by $p°$ and $q°$. What do you
notice about their sum?

1

2

3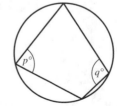

The results from **Exercise 13A** demonstrate that

the opposite angles of a cyclic quadrilateral are supplementary.

A proof of this result is given below.

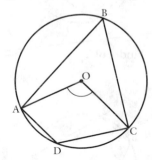

ABCD is a quadrilateral inscribed in a circle centre O.

obtuse angle AOC $= 2\,\widehat{ABC}$ (angle at centre result)

and   reflex angle AOC $= 2\,\widehat{ADC}$ (angle at centre result)

But obtuse angle $\widehat{AOC}$ + reflex angle $\widehat{AOC} = 360°$ (angles at a point)

$\therefore$ $2\,\widehat{ABC} + 2\,\widehat{ADC} = 360°$

$\Rightarrow$ $\widehat{ABC} + \widehat{ADC} = 180°$

i.e. the opposite angles of a cyclic quadrilateral are supplementary.

EXERCISE 13B

Find the marked angle.

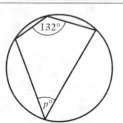

$p° + 132° = 180°$ (opp. $\angle$s cyclic quad. supplementary)

$\therefore$ $p° = 180° - 132° = 48°$

In questions **1** to **4** find the marked angles.

1
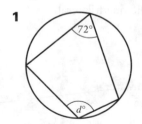

2

3
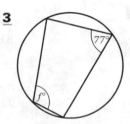

4
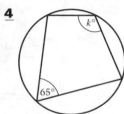

5

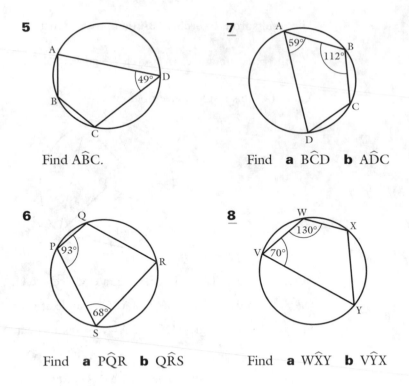

Find $\widehat{ABC}$.

7

Find **a** $\widehat{BCD}$ **b** $\widehat{ADC}$

6

Find **a** $\widehat{PQR}$ **b** $\widehat{QRS}$

8

Find **a** $\widehat{WXY}$ **b** $\widehat{VYX}$

**INTERIOR AND
EXTERIOR
ANGLES**

If the side AB of the cyclic quadrilateral ABCD is produced to E, the angle $\widehat{CBE}$ is an exterior angle of quadrilateral ABCD.

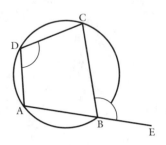

Now $\qquad \widehat{ABC} + \widehat{CBE} = 180°$ (∠s on a straight line)

and $\qquad \widehat{ABC} + \widehat{ADC} = 180°$ (opp. ∠s cyclic quadrilateral)

Hence $\qquad\qquad \widehat{CBE} = \widehat{ADC}$

i.e.

> any exterior angle of a cyclic quadrilateral
> is equal to the interior opposite angle.

EXERCISE 13C

Copy the following diagrams making them at least twice as large. For each diagram measure the angles denoted by the letters. What result do they confirm?

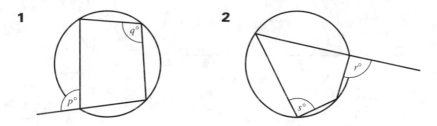

1

2

In questions **3** to **6** find the angles denoted by the letters.

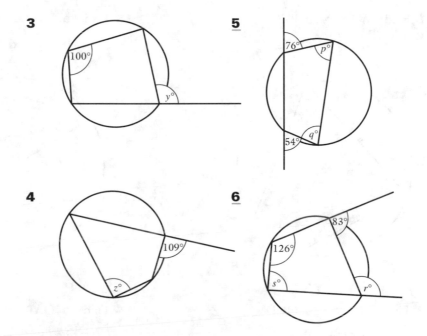

3

5

4

6

The remaining questions in this exercise bring together all the results seen so far. In some questions more than one of those results is required. In questions **7** to **10** find the marked angles.

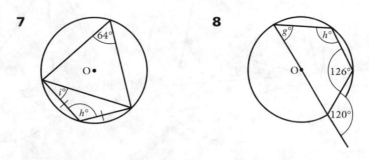

7

8

9

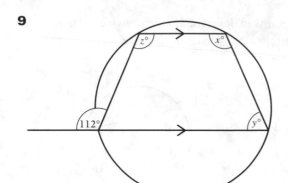

10

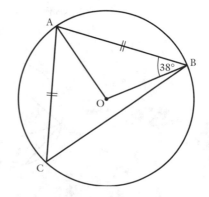

11 Find   **a** PR̂Q   **c** PŜR

         b PQ̂R   **d** RP̂S

13 Find   **a** PR̂S   **c** PR̂Q

         b SQ̂R   **d** QŜR

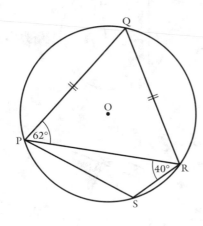

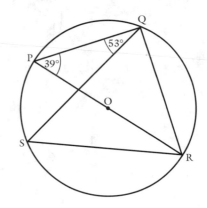

12 Find   **a** AÔD   **c** OĈD

         b AD̂E   **d** AB̂C

14 Find   **a** OÂB   **c** AĈB

         b AÔB   **d** OB̂C

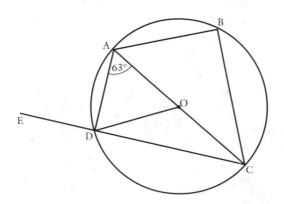

A straight line which cuts a circle in two distinct points is called a *secant*. The section of the line inside the circle is called a *chord*.

PQ is a secant and AB is a chord.

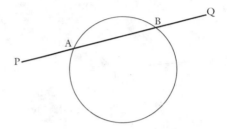

Imagine that the secant PQ is pivoted at P. As PQ rotates about P, we get successive positions of the points A and B where the secant cuts the circle. As PQ moves towards the edge of the circle, the points A and B move closer together, until eventually they coincide.

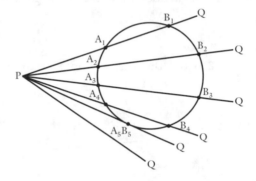

When PQ is in this position it is called a *tangent* to the circle and we say that PQ touches the circle. (When PQ is rotated beyond this position it loses contact with the circle and is no longer either a secant or a tangent.)

We therefore define a tangent to a circle as a straight line which touches the circle (in the same way as we define a tangent to a curve as a line that touches the curve).

The point at which the tangent touches the circle is called the point of contact.

PT is a tangent to the circle.
T is the point of contact.

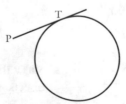

The *length of a tangent* from a point P outside the circle is the distance between that point and the point of contact. In the diagram the length of the tangent from P to the circle is the length PT.

1

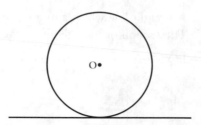

The diagram shows a disc, of radius 20 cm, rolling along horizontal ground. Describe the path along which O moves as the disc rolls.

At any one instant,

a how many points on the disc are in contact with the ground

b how far is O from the ground

c how would you describe the line joining O to the ground and what angle does it make with the ground?

2 Copy the diagram and draw any line(s) of symmetry.

3 Copy the diagram and draw any line(s) of symmetry.

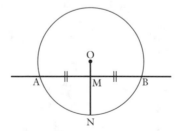

4

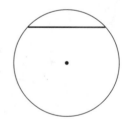

a Show that the chord AB is perpendicular to the radius ON which bisects AB. (Join OA and OB.)

b Now imagine that the chord AB slides down the radius ON. When the points A and B coincide with N, what has the line through A and B become? What angle does this line make with ON?

FIRST TANGENT PROPERTY

The investigational work in the last exercise suggests that

> a tangent to a circle is perpendicular to the radius drawn from the point of contact.

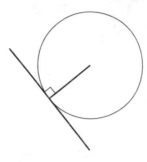

The general proof of this property is an interesting exercise in logic. We start by assuming that the property is *not* true and end up by contradicting ourselves. (This is called 'proof by contradiction'.)

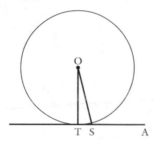

TA is a tangent to the circle and OT is the radius from the point of contact.

If we *assume* that $\widehat{OTS}$ is *not* 90° then it is possible to draw OS so that OS *is* perpendicular to the tangent, i.e. $\widehat{OST} = 90°$.

Therefore △OST has a right angle at S.

Hence   OT is the hypotenuse of △OST

i.e.   OT > OS

∴   S is inside the circle, as OT is a radius.

∴   the line through T and S must cut the circle again.

But this is impossible, as the line through T and S is a tangent.

Hence the assumption that $\widehat{OTA} \neq 90°$ is wrong, i.e. $\widehat{OTA}$ *is* 90°

EXERCISE 13E   Some of the questions in this exercise require the use of trigonometry.

The tangent from a point P to a circle of radius **4.2** cm is 7 cm long. Find the distance of P from the centre of the circle.

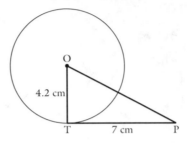

$$O\hat{T}P = 90° \qquad (\text{ tangent perpendicular to radius })$$
$$OP^2 = OT^2 + TP^2 \quad (\text{ Pythagoras' theorem })$$
$$= (4.2)^2 + 7^2$$
$$= 17.64 + 49 = 66.64$$
$$\therefore \qquad OP = 8.163\ldots$$

The distance of P from O is 8.16 cm, correct to 3 s.f.

In questions **1** to **8**, O is the centre of the circle and AB is a tangent to the circle, touching it at A.

1

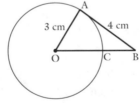

Find OB and CB.

3

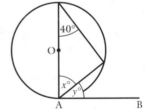

Find the marked angles.

2

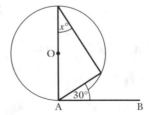

Find the marked angle.

4

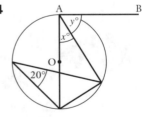

Find the marked angles.

5

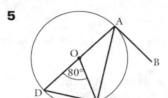

Find **a** DÂC **b** BÂC

6

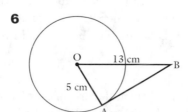

Find AB and OB̂A.

7

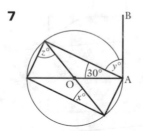

Find the marked angles.

8

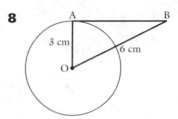

Find AB̂O.

9

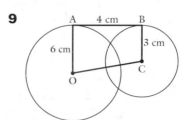

AB is a tangent to the circles
with centres O and C, touching
them at A and B respectively.
Find OC.

10

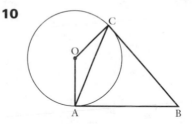

AB and BC are tangents to the
circle centre O touching it at A
and C.
Show that △ABC is isosceles.

11 AB is a chord of the larger circle
and a tangent to the smaller circle.
If O is the centre of both circles,
find the length of AB.

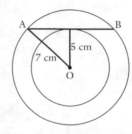

CONSTRUCTIONS

EXERCISE 13F   (Remember to draw a rough sketch before doing the construction.)

1 Draw a circle of radius 5 cm. Label the centre O and mark a point T
on the circumference. Construct the tangent to the circle at T.
(Use the fact that the radius OT is perpendicular to the tangent.)

2 Draw a circle of radius 4 cm. Label the centre of this circle C. Mark a
point P distant 10 cm from C. Draw another circle on PC as
diameter. Label the points where the two circles cut, A and B. What
is the size of CÂP? Describe the lines PA and PB in relation to the
circle with centre C.

3 Draw a circle of radius 3 cm and mark a point P distant 6 cm from the
centre of the circle. Use the method described in question **2** to
construct the two tangents from P to the circle.

4 a The diagram shows a circle, centre O, inscribed in a square
(i.e. the sides of the square are tangents to the circle).
The radius of the circle is 2 cm.
Find the length of a side of the square.

b Draw a square of side 8 cm. Construct the inscribed circle of the
square.

For questions **5** and **6**, use a ruler and compasses only to construct the
figure. Measure the marked length.

5

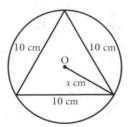

6

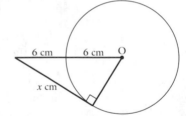

PROOFS

EXERCISE 13G

AD is the diameter of a circle and AB is a tangent to the circle at A. BD meets the circle again at E and DE = EB.
Prove that $\widehat{EAB} = 45°$.

AD is a diameter

$\therefore$ $\widehat{DEA} = 90°$ (angle in semicircle)

In $\triangle AED$ and $\triangle AEB$

   DE = EB   (given)

AE is common

   $\widehat{DEA} = \widehat{AEB}$ (both 90°)

$\therefore$ $\triangle$s $\begin{matrix} AED \\ AEB \end{matrix}$ are congruent   (S A S)

$\therefore$ $\widehat{DAE} = \widehat{EAB}$

But $\widehat{DAB} = 90°$ (angle between tangent and radius)

$\therefore$ $\widehat{DAE} = 45°$

1   AB is the diameter of a circle and D is a point on the circumference of the circle. A circle is drawn on AD as diameter. Prove that BD is a tangent to this circle.

2   P is a point outside a circle with centre O. Tangents from P to the circle touch the circle at R and S. Prove that $\triangle$ROP and $\triangle$SOP are congruent. Hence show that tangents from P to the circle are equal in length.

3   A circle centre A is drawn to cut a circle, centre B, at points C and D such that $\widehat{ACB} = 90°$. Prove that AC is a tangent to the circle centre B.

4   AOB is a diameter of a circle, centre O. AD is a tangent to the circle at A and DB meets the circle again at C. Prove that $\widehat{DAC} = \widehat{ABC}$.

5   AOB is a diameter of a circle centre O. AP is a tangent to the circle at A. A chord AC is drawn so that C and P are on the same side of AB. Prove that $\widehat{CAP} = \widehat{ABC}$.

SECOND
TANGENT
PROPERTY

The tangent property proved in question **2** of the last exercise can be quoted, i.e.

> the two tangents drawn from an external point to a circle are the same length.

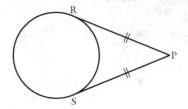

EXERCISE 13H

1

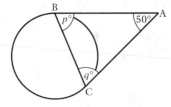

Find the marked angles.

2

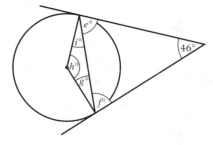

Find the marked angles.

3

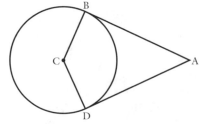

a If BĈD = 130°, find BÂD.

b What type of quadrilateral is ABCD and why?

4

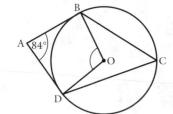

Find **a** BÔD   **b** BĈD

5

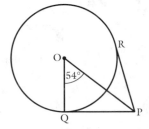

Find **a** OP̂Q   **b** OP̂R

6

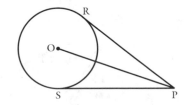

PR = 8 cm and OP = 10 cm.

Calculate

a the radius of the circle

b the angle between the tangents.

7 The diagram shows the cross-section through the centre of a ball placed in a hollow cone. The vertical angle of the cone is 60° and the diameter of the ball is 8 cm. Find the depth of the vertex of the cone below the centre of the ball.

8 A second ball, of diameter 20 cm, is now placed in the cone described in question **7**. Will it touch the first ball?

9 The circle, centre O, is inscribed in the equilateral triangle ABC (i.e. it is the circle that fits inside the triangle and touches all three sides). The sides of the triangle are each 20 cm long. Calculate the radius of the circle.

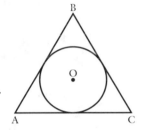

10 A circle of radius 4 cm is circumscribed by an equilateral triangle (i.e. the triangle is outside the circle and its sides touch the circle). Write down the angles between the sides of the triangle and the lines joining the centre of the circle to the vertices of the triangle. Hence calculate the lengths of the sides of the triangle.

11 A circle of radius 4 cm is circumscribed by an isosceles right-angled triangle. Find the lengths of the sides of the triangle.

12 ABCD is a quadrilateral circumscribing a circle. If AC goes through the centre of the circle, prove that ABCD is a kite.

13 Construct a circle, centre O and radius 4 cm. Mark a point A on the circumference. Construct $O\hat{A}B = 90°$ and hence draw the tangent AB. Mark any two points D and C on the circumference. Join A to D and A to C.
Measure $C\hat{A}B$ and $A\hat{D}C$. How do they compare?

14 a Construct △ABC with $\hat{A} = 90°$, AB = 24 cm and AC = 10 cm.

  b Find by construction the centre of the circle which touches all three sides of △ABC.

  c Find by construction the radius of this circle and hence draw the circle (which is called the inscribed circle of △ABC).

THIRD TANGENT
PROPERTY

Alternate segment theorem

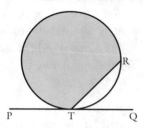

PQ is a tangent to the circle and TR is a chord. The major segment
(which is shaded) is called the alternate (or other) segment with respect
to the angle $R\widehat{T}Q$. Similarly the minor (unshaded) segment is alternate
to the angle $P\widehat{T}R$.

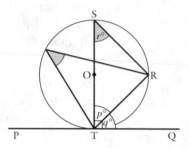

If TS is a diameter then

$$S\widehat{R}T = 90° \quad \text{(angle in semi-circle)}$$
$$S\widehat{T}Q = 90° \quad \text{(angle between tangent and radius)}$$

Now $p° + q° = 90°$
and $p° + r° = 90°$ (angles of $\triangle$)
$\Rightarrow \qquad q° = r°$

But $r°$ is equal to any angle subtended by the chord TR, i.e.

the angle between a tangent and a chord drawn from the point
of contact is equal to any angle in the alternate segment.

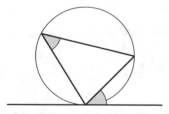

The result is known as the *alternate segment theorem* and can be quoted.

EXERCISE 13I

In questions **1** to **4**, copy the diagram and shade the alternate segment with respect to the angle marked $x°$.

1

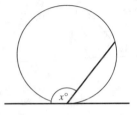

3

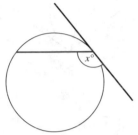

2

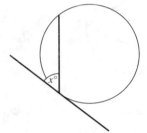

4

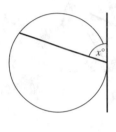

Find the size of the angles marked $x°$ and $y°$ in the diagram.

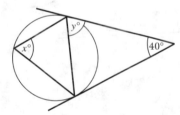

$y° = 70°$ (base angle of isosceles triangle)

$x° = y°$ (alternate segment theorem)

$\therefore \ x° = 70°$

Find the sizes of the angles marked by the letter.

5

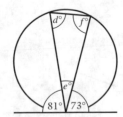

6

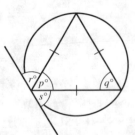

7

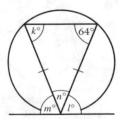

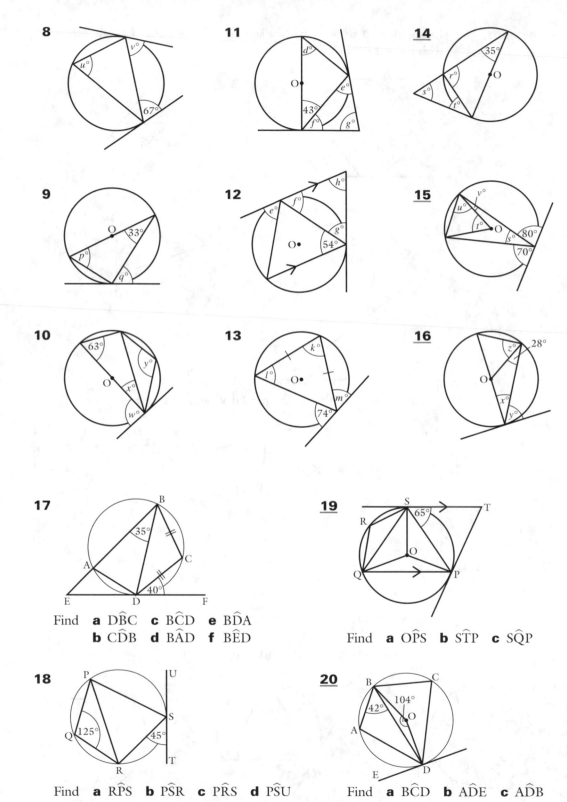

8

$v°$
$u°$
$67°$

11

$d°$
O•
$e°$
$43°$
$f°$
$g°$

14

$35°$
$r°$
•O
$s°$
$t°$

9

O•
$33°$
$p°$
$q°$

12

$h°$
$e°$
$f°$
$g°$
O•
$54°$

15

$v°$
$u°$
$t°$ •O
$s°$ $80°$
$70°$

10

$63°$
$y°$
O•
$x°$
$w°$

13

$k°$
$l°$
O•
$m°$
$74°$

16

$z°$ $28°$
O•
$x°$
$y°$

17

B
$35°$
C
A
$40°$
E   D   F

Find   **a** $\hat{DBC}$ **c** $\hat{BCD}$ **e** $\hat{BDA}$
       b $\hat{CDB}$ **d** $\hat{BAD}$ **f** $\hat{BED}$

19

S $65°$ T
R
O
Q   P

Find   **a** $\hat{OPS}$ **b** $\hat{STP}$ **c** $\hat{SQP}$

18

P   U
S
Q $125°$ $45°$
R   T

Find   **a** $\hat{RPS}$ **b** $\hat{PSR}$ **c** $\hat{PRS}$ **d** $\hat{PSU}$

20

B   C
$42°$ $104°$
•O
A
E   D

Find   **a** $\hat{BCD}$ **b** $\hat{ADE}$ **c** $\hat{ADB}$

21 AE is a tangent at E to the circle centre O.

   a Find, in terms of x **i** AÊC

                       ii AB̂D

                      iii BÂE

   b What can you deduce about

      i the lines AB and ED

      ii the line BE?

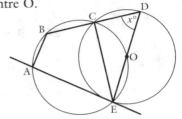

22 EDF is a tangent and BC is parallel to AD.

   a Find   **i** DB̂C

              ii BÂD

             iii BĜC

   b What kind of triangle is △BCG?

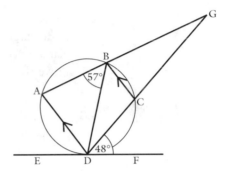

23 DE is a tangent at D to a circle centre O.

   Find **a** BD̂C   **c** BÂD

         b BĈD   **d** AD̂B

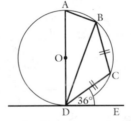

24 Find

   a ED̂B

   b ED̂F

   c BÂE

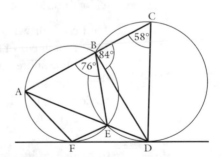

25 **a** Find the value of x.

   b Hence find the size of

      i CF̂D

      ii BÂD

      iii BD̂C

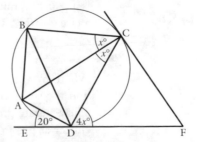

The remaining questions use the circle facts to deduce other results.

26 AB is a diameter and O is the centre of the circle. AC = BD and E, F are the midpoints of AC, BD. Prove that △AEO and △BFO are congruent. Hence prove that

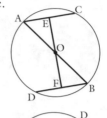

  a EOF is a straight line
  b AC and DB are parallel.

27 AB is a diameter and O is the centre of the larger circle. AO is a diameter of the smaller circle. Prove that CO is parallel to DB.

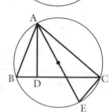

28 AE is a diameter of the circle and AD is perpendicular to BC. Prove that △AEC and △ABD are equiangular.

29

AOB is a diameter of the circle and OD bisects AÔC.
Prove that OD is parallel to BC.

LOCI

Four standard loci were considered in Book 9A, Chapter 18. To remind your self of these look at the summary on page 15 at the beginning of this book.

To these four we now add one more. This is the locus of a point P at which a fixed line subtends a given angle. If the line is AB and the angle is $x°$, the locus of P is the pair of arcs of circles with AB as a chord.

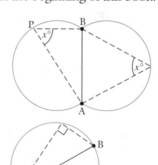

In particular, if $x° = 90°$, the locus is a pair of semicircles; these form a circle with AB as diameter.

When drawing a locus accurately, first draw a rough sketch and use it to find the shape of the locus and to calculate any necessary information. The accurate drawing should be as simple and as clear of unnecessary clutter as possible.

LINKAGES

A linkage is a mechanism for producing a locus. An example is the wheel and rod below, where the circular motion of point Q about O gives the linear motion of P along the rod. The reverse of this linkage is used in a steam engine where the linear motion of the piston produces the circular motion of the wheels.

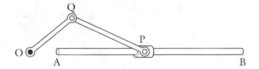

EXERCISE 13J

1 A and B are two fixed points. Describe the locus of C if $A\widehat{C}B = 90°$.

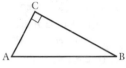

2 M is the midpoint of a chord AB. Describe the locus of M as the chord AB moves, parallel to itself, up the circle.

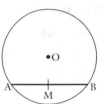

3 A and B are two fixed points. Describe the locus of C if $A\widehat{C}B = 60°$.

4 TA is of fixed length and is a tangent to the circle centre O. Describe the locus of T as A moves around the given circle.

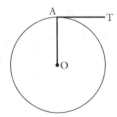

5 Draw the locus of the centre of a circle that touches both AB and BC.

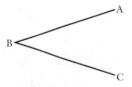

6 Two look-out points A and B lie one on each side of a sea channel of width 30 km. The sea channel runs east to west and B is due north of A. A light-buoy is to be placed so that it is equidistant from A and B but not more than 20 km from either. Show on a sketch the possible positions of the light-buoy.

7 A circle is rolled along a straight line.

a What is the locus of the centre C of the circle?

b Sketch the locus of P, a point on the edge of the circle.

c Repeat with a square in place of the circle and with the point P

i at a vertex **ii** at a midpoint of a side.

This linkage is a simplified version of a windscreen wiper mechanism. A and B are fixed points and AC rotates through 360° about A. C is linked to a point D on the wiper.

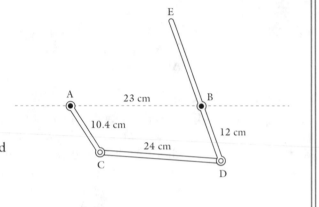

a Sketch the loci of C and D.

b Using an accurate drawing, find the extreme positions of D. Hence find the angle through which the wiper turns.

a The locus of D is part of a circle, radius 12 cm.

$C_1 D_1 = C_2 D_2 = 24$ cm

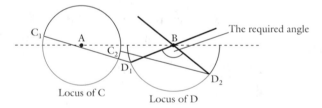

b

Draw the line AB, the circle and the semicircle. With compasses set at a radius of 24 cm, find D_1 and D_2 by trial. It should become clear that $C_1 AD_1$ and $AC_2 D_2$ are straight lines. We have used a scale of 1 cm to 6 cm to save space but this is too small for accuracy. A better scale to use is 1 cm to 2 cm.

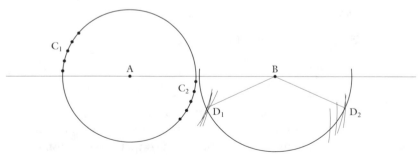

The angle turned through is 130°.

8

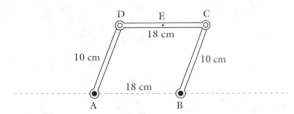

In the linkage above, A and B are fixed points. DA rotates about A. D starts on AB and AD turns through 180°. Sketch and describe the locus of

a D **b** C **c** E, the midpoint of DC

d Sketch the locus of F, the midpoint of AC and make an accurate drawing to find four possible positions of F.

9 ABCDE is a freely jointed linkage; A and D are fixed points; DCE is rigid and BE is an elastic string. F, G and H are the midpoints of DC, BC and BE respectively.

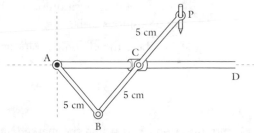

AB = DC = CE = 6 cm

and AD = BC = 8 cm.

a AB rotates about A.
Sketch and describe the locus of

i B **ii** E **iii** F

b Make an accurate drawing of these loci and draw the locus of

i G **ii** H

c Describe the loci of G and H.

10

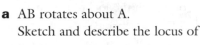

A linkage is formed of three rods AB, AD and BP, freely jointed at A and B. AD is fixed but C is free to slide along AD. A pencil P traces out a curve as C moves along AD.

Draw AD about 20 cm long. Choose a position for C, say C_1, and find the corresponding position, B_1, of B. Now mark the position of P. By plotting about ten more points find the locus of P. Make sure that you have found the extreme positions. Assume that C can actually reach a position at A.

11

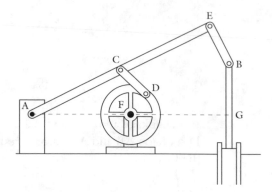

The diagram shows a 'nodding donkey', which can be used to pump oil from the ground. An engine causes the wheel, centre F, to rotate and this constrains the beam AE to move so that point E moves through an arc of a circle; this in turn makes the piston move up and down in a vertical shaft.

The linkage is freely jointed at points A, B, C, D and E.

$AC = CE = 3\,m$, $CD = 1\,m$, $EB = 1.25\,m$ and the radius of the wheel is $0.75\,m$. AFG is horizontal and $AF = FG = 3\,m$.

a Draw on a sketch the line AFG, the locus of D, the arcs of the circles on which the loci of C and E lie, and the vertical line on which the locus of B lies.

b By reference to the sketch drawn for part **a**, make an accurate scale drawing. Use 2 cm to represent 1 m. Mark a position for D at the lowest point of the wheel and construct the corresponding position of B.

c Now mark D at the highest point on the wheel and find the corresponding position of B. What is the distance between the two positions of B?

d Are these the extreme positions of B?

MIXED EXERCISE

EXERCISE 13K   In questions **1** to **4** find the marked angles.

1

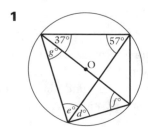

2

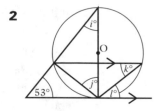

3

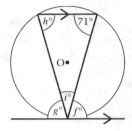

6

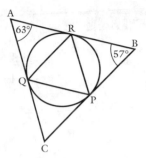

Find **a** $Q\widehat{R}P$ **b** $R\widehat{Q}P$ **c** $Q\widehat{P}R$

4

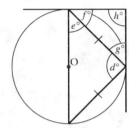

7 If $B\widehat{O}D = x°$ find,
in terms of x

    a $O\widehat{A}B$ **b** $O\widehat{B}C$ **c** $O\widehat{D}C$

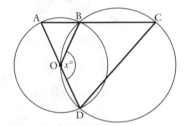

5

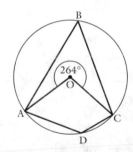

Find **a** $A\widehat{D}C$ **b** $A\widehat{B}C$

8 $AB = AD$ and ED is a tangent
to the circle at D.

    Find **a** $B\widehat{A}D$ **b** $A\widehat{E}D$

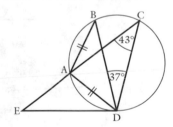

9

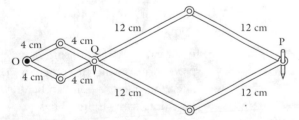

This linkage is a pantograph, which is used in drawing. O is a fixed
point. If Q is moved round a drawing of a square, the mechanism
moves the pen P so that it draws a shape. Describe the shape. How
does it compare with the original drawing?

INVESTIGATIONS

1 If 4 dots are equally spaced around the circumference of a circle and 3 or more of them are joined to form a polygon we can form 2 shapes, namely an isosceles triangle or square.

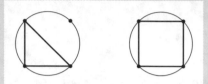

If 5 dots are equally spaced around the circumference of a circle and 3 or more are joined by straight lines to form a polygon, the different shapes we can draw are: an isosceles triangle, a different isosceles triangle, a trapezium and a regular pentagon; that is 4 different polygons.

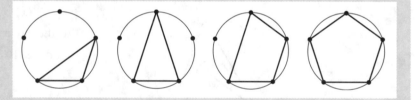

a Investigate the different polygons that can be drawn by joining, with straight lines, up to 6 points equally spaced around the circumference of a circle.

b Repeat part **a** when there are 7 dots and again when there are 8 dots.

c Investigate any relationship between the number of equally spaced dots on the circumference of a circle and the number of different polygons that can be drawn by joining 3 or more of these dots with straight lines.

d Investigate any relationship between the number of equally spaced dots on the circumference of a circle and the total number of polygons, including repeats, that can be drawn by joining the dots with straight lines.

2 A chord of a circle divides the circle into 2 regions, while two intersecting chords divide a circle into 4 regions, and 3 intersecting chords divide a circle into at most 7 regions.

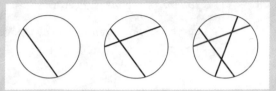

Investigate the greatest number of regions a circle can be divided into if the number of chords drawn is

a 4   **b** 5   **c** 6   **d** 7

Hence find a formula for the maximum number of regions into which a circle can be divided if n chords are drawn.

SUMMARY 4

CONES AND SPHERES

The *volume of a cone* is given by $V = \frac{1}{3}\pi r^2 h$

The *curved surface area of a cone* is given by $A = \pi r l$

The *volume of a sphere* is given by $V = \frac{4}{3}\pi r^3$

The *surface area of a sphere* is given $A = 4\pi r^2$

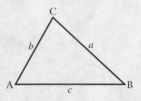

TRIGONOMETRY

The *sine and cosine of an obtuse angle* can be found using

$$\sin x° = \sin(180° - x°), \qquad \cos x° = -\cos(180° - x°)$$

In any triangle ABC, the *sine rule* is

$$\frac{a}{\sin \widehat{A}} = \frac{b}{\sin \widehat{B}} = \frac{c}{\sin \widehat{C}}$$

the *cosine rule* is $a^2 = b^2 + c^2 - 2bc \cos \widehat{A}$

the *area* is given by $\text{Area} = \frac{1}{2}bc \sin \widehat{A}$

GEOMETRY

Congruent triangles
Two triangles are congruent if

either the three sides of one triangle are equal to the three sides of the other triangle,

or two angles and a side of one triangle are equal to two angles and the corresponding side of the other triangle,

or two sides and the included angle of one triangle are equal to two sides and the included angle of the other triangle,

or two triangles each have a right angle, and the hypotenuse and a side of one triangle are equal to the hypotenuse and a side of the other triangle.

Special quadrilaterals

The properties of the special quadrilaterals are given in the diagrams below.

Rectangle

Parallelogram

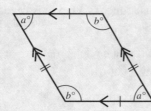 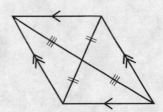

Square

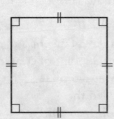 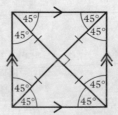

Rhombus

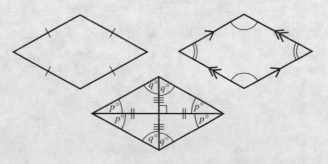

Kite

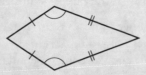 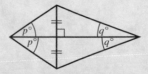

Circles and tangents

The *opposite angles of a cyclic quadrilateral* are supplementary
and an *exterior angle* is equal to the interior opposite angle.

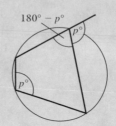

A straight line which cuts a circle in two points is called a *secant*. The section of the line inside the circle is a *chord*.
A line that touches a circle is called a *tangent*.

A *segment* of a circle is the part of a circle cut off by a chord.

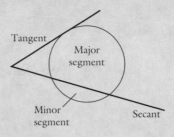

Tangent properties

A tangent to a circle is perpendicular to the radius drawn through the point of contact.

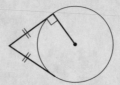

Two tangents drawn from an external point to a circle are the same length.

The angle between a tangent and a chord drawn through the point of contact is equal to the angle in the alternate segment.
This result is called the *alternate segment theorem*.

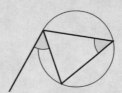

**REVISION
EXERCISE 4.1
(Chapters 10
and 11)**

1 Find **a** the length of the minor arc AB

b the area of the shaded sector.

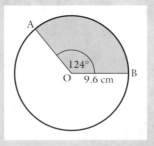

2 Which container has the greatest capacity and by how much, compared with the next one in size:

   a cylinder radius 5.6 cm, height 13 cm

or   a sphere of radius 6.5 cm

or   a right circular cone base radius 9 cm, height 15 cm?

3 a Which has the greater percentage waste: a square cut from a circle of radius 10 cm or a circle cut from a square of side 20 cm?

b A solid is formed from two equal cones whose diameters are equal to their heights. The distance between the vertices of the cones is 12 cm. Find

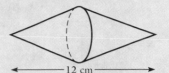

i the volume of the solid

ii its total surface area.

4 A cylinder has a radius of 5.2 cm and a height of 12.3 cm. If both values are correct to 1 decimal place, find

a the greatest possible value of the radius

b the lowest possible value of the height

c the upper and lower bounds of the volume of the cylinder.

(Give each value correct to 3 significant figures.)

5 A cylindrical piece of wood of radius 2.8 cm and height 7.8 cm has a conical hole cut in it. The cone has the same radius as the cylinder but its depth is half the height of the cylinder. Find

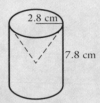

a the amount of wood removed

b the volume of wood remaining

c the density of the wood if the mass of the finished solid is 110 g.

6 a If $\sin \widehat{A} = \frac{1}{2}$ find, in surd form   **i** $\cos \widehat{A}$ **ii** $\tan \widehat{A}$

b If $\tan \widehat{A} = \frac{2}{3}$ find, in surd form, $\sin \widehat{A}$ and $\cos \widehat{A}$, and use these values to show that $\sin^2 \widehat{A} + \cos^2 \widehat{A} = 1$

7 a If $\sin 65° = 0.9063$ what is $\sin 115°$?

b Find an obtuse angle whose cosine is equal to $-\cos 54°$.

c Find two angles each with a sine of 0.8.

8

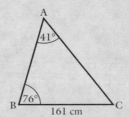

Find AC.

9 In △PQR, PR = 18 cm, QR = 16 cm and $\widehat{Q} = 46°$.
Find $\widehat{P}$ and $\widehat{R}$.

10 In △ABC, AB = 11.2 cm, AC = 8.9 cm and $\widehat{A} = 47.1°$.
Find **i** BC   **ii** the area of ABC.

11

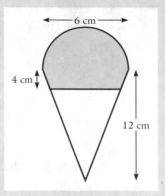

A 'corno' consists of ice cream in a biscuit cone.
The diameter of the top of the cone is measured as 6 cm and its
vertical height as 12 cm.
The shaded part of the diagram shows the ice cream in the cone.
The ice cream goes down to a depth of 4 cm in the cone and forms a
hemisphere on the top of the cone.

Based on the measurements above, calculate the volume of ice
cream in a 'corno' to an appropriate degree of accuracy.   (MEG)

12 In the triangle ABC, the length of
side AB is 42 cm to the nearest
centimetre. The length of side AC
is 35 cm to the nearest centimetre.
The angle C is 61° to the nearest
degree.

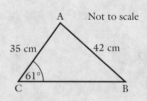

What is the largest possible size that angle B could be?   (MEG)

**REVISION
EXERCISE 4.2
(Chapters 12
and 13)**

1 Decide whether or not the two given triangles are congruent. Give
brief reasons to support your answer.

a

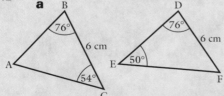

b

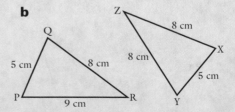

2 M is the midpoint of a chord AB in a circle centre O.
Are triangles OAM and OBM congruent?
Give brief reasons.

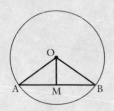

3 For each triangle say whether or not you can make an exact copy. If you cannot, give reasons to support your answer.

a △ABC in which AB = 7 cm, AC = 8 cm, $\widehat{C}$ = 50°.

b △PQR in which PQ = 5 cm, PR = 7 cm, $\widehat{P}$ = 90°.

c △XYZ in which YZ = 9 cm, $\widehat{X}$ = 40°, $\widehat{Z}$ = 65°.

d △RST in which RS = RT = 5 cm, $\widehat{S}$ = 40°.

4 Two straight lines AB and CD intersect at O. M is the foot of the perpendicular from C to AB and N is the foot of the perpendicular from D to AB.
If CM = DN prove that triangles OCM and ODN are congruent.

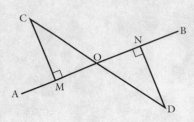

5 In the diagram AM = BN and AN = BM.
Prove that

a triangles AMN and MBN are congruent

b $M\widehat{A}N = M\widehat{B}N$

c triangles AMX and BNX are congruent

d $X\widehat{M}N = X\widehat{N}M$

e MX = NX.

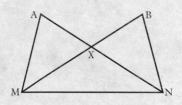

6 Find the marked angles.

a

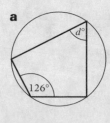

b

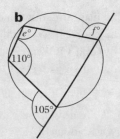

c

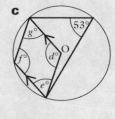

7 PT and PS are the two tangents
from P to a circle centre O.
PT = 8 cm and OP = 10 cm.
Find the length
of **a** OT   **b** RP

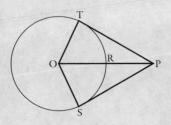

8 CAB is the tangent at A to a circle
centre O.
Find the marked angles.

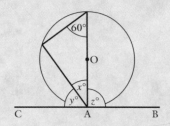

9 A bar ABC is bent so that A$\widehat{B}$C = 90°.
It is free to turn about A and BC
passes through a sleeve D which can
move freely along a wire AE.
Initially C is at D. Draw the locus of
C as AB turns until it becomes
horizontal.

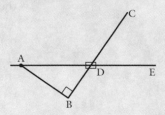

10

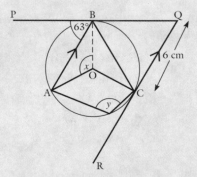

The diagram shows a circle, centre O.
The chord BA is parallel to the tangent QC.
PBQ and QCR are tangents.
Angle PBA = 63°. QC = 6 cm.

a Calculate the value of angle x and angle y.

b Write down the value of angle PQR and hence calculate the area
of triangle BQC.

(SEG)

11

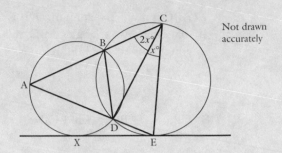

Not drawn accurately

ABC and ADE are straight lines. CE is a diameter.
Angle DCE $= x°$ and angle BCD $= 2x°$.

a Find, in terms of x, the sizes of the angles

   i ABD   **ii** DBE   **iii** BAD

b Explain why BE × AC = AE × CD.   (London)

**REVISION
EXERCISE 4.3
(Chapters 10
to 13)**

1 The length of the arc AB is 5 cm and
the arc subtends an angle of 63° at the
centre of the circle.

Find **a** the radius of the circle

       b the area of the sector.

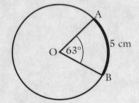

2 The diameter of a cylinder is two-thirds its height. If the volume of
the cylinder is 100 cm^3 find its diameter.

3 A child's ball, which has a diameter of 6 cm, just fits into a square box.
Find the amount of space inside the box that is not occupied by the ball.

4 Find the lengths of AB and BC in $\triangle$ABC if AC = 7.3 cm,
$\hat{A} = 49°$ and $\hat{C} = 78°$.

5 a $\cos x° = 0.123$ and $\cos y° = -0.123$. If $x°$ is acute and $y°$ is
obtuse find y in terms of x.

   b In $\triangle$ABC, $b = 4.9$, $c = 5.3$ and $\hat{A} = 57.2°$. Find a.

6 State whether or not the two triangles are congruent. Give reasons
for your answers.

a

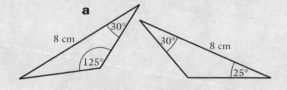

b

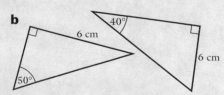

7 ABCD is a parallelogram. DB is a diagonal. Are triangles ABD and BCD congruent? Give brief reasons.

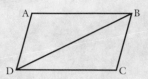

8 Find **a** $\widehat{ABC}$ **b** $\widehat{BCD}$

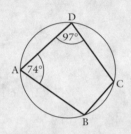

9 Find the marked angles.

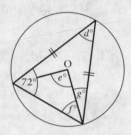

10 Draw a circle of radius 4 cm and mark a point P, 7 cm from the centre of the circle. Construct the two tangents from P to the circle. Measure and write down the length of each tangent.

REVISION EXERCISE 4.4 (Chapters 1 to 13)

Do not use a calculator for any of the questions in this exercise.

1 a Express as a fraction in its lowest terms **i** $0.0\dot{2}$ **ii** $1.\dot{7}$

b Rationalise the denominator and express your answer in terms of the simplest possible surds.

i $\dfrac{\sqrt{5}}{\sqrt{50}}$ **ii** $\dfrac{1}{\sqrt{27}}$ **iii** $\dfrac{8 - 3\sqrt{2}}{\sqrt{2}}$

2 a If $(3x + p)^2 = ax^2 + 12x + c$ for all values of x, find the values of p, a and c.

b The sum of the squares of two consecutive positive whole numbers is 365. Find them.

3 Solve the equation $x^2 - 5x - 3 = 0$ giving your answers in surd form.

4 The product of three numbers p, q and r is W.
Give a formula for

   a W in terms of p, q and r **b** p in terms of W, q and r

5 Solve the inequality $3x^2 > 8x - 4$

6

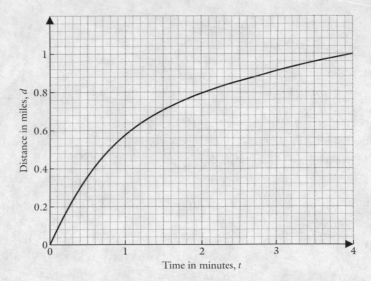

This distance–time graph shows the journey of a cyclist for the first 4 minutes of his ride.

   a How far was he from his starting point after $2\frac{1}{2}$ minutes?

   b Estimate his speed when $t = 1$ in

   i miles per minute   **ii** mph

7 The base of a pyramid is a horizontal square ABCD. The vertex of the pyramid, E, is vertically above A. $AB = 6\,cm$ and $AE = 6\,cm$.

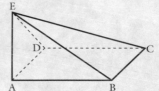

   a Find, giving answers in an exact form, the length of

   i AC   **ii** EB   **iii** EC

   b Find the volume of the pyramid.

   c Draw a sketch of a net.

8 The radius of a cylindrical drum is $20\,cm$ and the drum is $120\,cm$ high. Find as a multiple of π

   a the capacity of the drum in   **i** cm^3 **ii** litres

   b the total external surface area of the drum.

9 In △ABC AB = 5 mm, sin Â = 0.5
and sin Ĉ = 0.2
Find the length of BC.

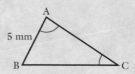

10 AB and AC are tangents
to the circle centre O.
Find the marked angles.

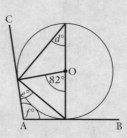

**REVISION
EXERCISE 4.5
(Chapters 1
to 13)**

1 a Simplify

i $\dfrac{\sqrt{3}-1}{\sqrt{3}}$ **ii** $(3+\sqrt{2})(3-\sqrt{2})$ **iii** $(1+2\sqrt{7})^2$

b Use your calculator, giving your answer correct to 3 significant
figures, to find   **i** $(1.4)^{\frac{2}{3}}$ **ii** $\sqrt[5]{0.2}$ **iii** $2.4^{-\frac{3}{5}}$

2 a Factorise   **i** $5x^2 - 37x + 14$ **ii** $3x^2 + 19x - 14$

b Solve the equation   **i** $11x - 3x^3 = 0$ **ii** $25x^2 + 10x = 3$

c If $(3x+k)^2 = 9x^2 + px + 49$ for all values of x find all the
possible values of k and p.

3 Solve the equation $4x^2 - 9x + 3 = 0$ giving your answers correct
to 2 decimal places. Show clearly each stage of your working.

4 a Make c the subject of the formula $A = a\left(b + \dfrac{c}{3}\right)$

b Given that $x - y = 2$ and that $x^2 + y^2 = 20$, use the first
equation to find an expression for x in terms of y. Substitute this
value for x into the second equation to give a quadratic equation
in y. Simplify this equation and factorise it. Hence find the
values of x and y that satisfy both the given equations.

5 The height of a cylinder is 7.8 cm and the cylinder has a volume of
450 cm³. Find, correct to 3 significant figures, the radius of the
cylinder.

6 In △PQR, PQ = 6 cm and PR = 8 cm. S is the foot of the
perpendicular from Q to PR and QS = 3.5 cm.

a Find   **i** the area of △PQR   **ii** angle P.

b Use the cosine rule to find the length of QR.

7 The diagonals of a rhombus ABCD intersect at E.
Which triangles are congruent to △AEB and why?

8

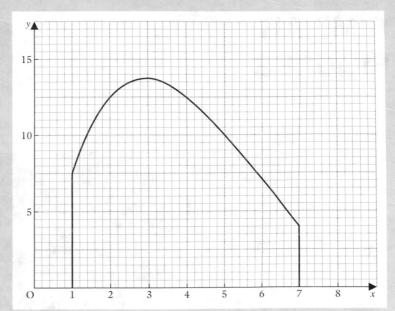

Use the trapezium rule with six equal strips to find, approximately, the area under the curve from $x = 1$ to $x = 7$.

9 R_1 is a rotation 90° anticlockwise about O.

R_2 is a rotation of 180° about O.

X is a reflection in the x-axis.

Y is a reflection in the y-axis.

Draw x- and y-axes, each for values from -6 to 6.

Draw △ABC with A(-4, 1), B(-1, 3), C(-1, 1).

Label this triangle P.

a Draw and label   **i** $R_2(P)$ **ii** $XR_2(P)$

b Describe the single transformation that maps P onto $XR_2(P)$.

10 PT is a tangent at T to a circle centre O.

Find, giving reasons   **a** $R\hat{Q}T$ **b** $Q\hat{R}T$ **c** $O\hat{Q}T$

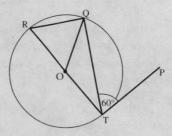

SIMILAR FIGURES

The design process for a new building involves making a model and, for a large project such as a new opera house, includes landscaping details for the site together with existing nearby features. This model is an exact scaled down version of the intended building, so the model and the intended building are mathematically similar.

The model can be used to give an impression of the space that the finished building will occupy, together with the area of features such as landscaped terraces, car parks, and so on.

- If the scale is known, we can use the model to work out, fairly precisely, the lengths, areas and volumes of any intended features. To be able to do this we need to know the relationships between the lengths, areas and volumes of similar shapes.

Remember that when two figures are mathematically similar (that is, one figure is an enlargement of the other), corresponding lengths are in the same ratio. This ratio, when expressed as a fraction, gives the scale factor.

The next exercise investigates the relationship between the ratio of corresponding lengths and the ratio of the areas of similar figures.

EXERCISE 14A

1 These four rectangles are similar.

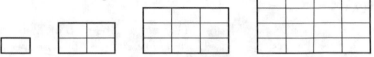

a Write down the ratio of the lengths of their bases.

b Write down the ratio of their heights.

c By counting rectangles, write down the ratio of their areas. Is there a relationship between this ratio and the ratios you got in parts **a** and **b**?

d What is the ratio of the lengths of the diagonals of the four rectangles?

2

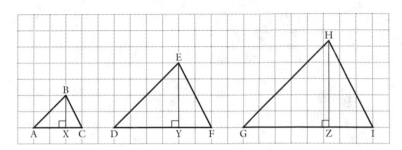

In triangle ABC the length of the base, AC, is 3 units
the perpendicular height, BX, is 2 units
the area of $\triangle ABC$ is $\frac{1}{2} \times 3 \times 2$, i.e. 3 square units.

a Write down the length of **i** DF   **ii** EY

b What is the area of $\triangle DEF$?

c Write, as a fraction in its lowest terms, the value of

  i $\dfrac{AC}{DF}$ **ii** $\dfrac{AC^2}{DF^2}$ **iii** $\dfrac{\text{area } \triangle ABC}{\text{area } \triangle DEF}$

d Triangles ABC and GHI are similar.

  Find the value of   **i** $\dfrac{AC}{GI}$ **ii** $\dfrac{AC^2}{GI^2}$ **iii** $\dfrac{\text{area } \triangle ABC}{\text{area } \triangle GHI}$

  Hence find the area of triangle GHI and use your result to find the perpendicular height, HZ, of triangle GHI.

3 The parallelograms are similar.
First calculate the length
of HG and then find
the area of each figure.
Compare DC:HG with
area ABCD:area EFGH.

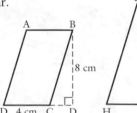

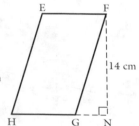

AREAS OF SIMILAR FIGURES

The results from the previous exercise lead us to the conclusion that

for similar figures, the ratio of their areas is equal to the square of the ratio of corresponding lengths.

EXERCISE 14B

Parallelograms ABCD and PQRS are similar. Find the ratio of the area of ABCD to the area of PQRS.

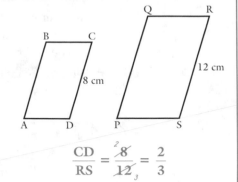

CD and RS are corresponding sides.

$$\frac{CD}{RS} = \frac{\overset{2}{\cancel{8}}}{\underset{3}{\cancel{12}}} = \frac{2}{3}$$

Therefore

$$\frac{\text{area ABCD}}{\text{area PQRS}} = \frac{2^2}{3^2} = \frac{4}{9}$$

For each question from **1** to **6** write down the ratio of the areas of the pair of similar figures.

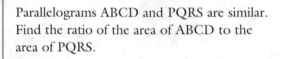

1

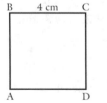

4

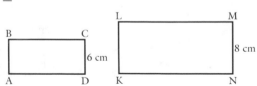

2

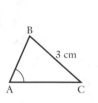

5

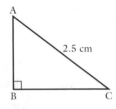

3

6

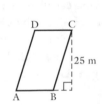

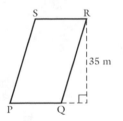

In questions **7** and **8** the pictures are from catalogues, but the dimensions given are those of the actual object.
Assume that the picture represents an object that is mathematically similar to the real article.

7 The width of the picture of the door is 20 mm. Find the ratio of the area of the picture of the door to the area of the actual door.

←— 700 mm —→

8 The width of the picture of the chest is 3 cm Find the ratio of the area of the front of the chest in the picture to the area of the front of the actual chest of drawers.

←——— 60 cm ———→

9 A photograph is enlarged by a scale factor of 1.6. The area of the original is $25.4 \, \text{cm}^2$. Find the area of the enlargement.

Triangles ABC and XYZ are similar and $\widehat{C} = \widehat{Z}$. If the area of △ABC is $3.2\,\text{cm}^2$ and the area of △XYZ is $1.8\,\text{cm}^2$, find the value of AB : XY.

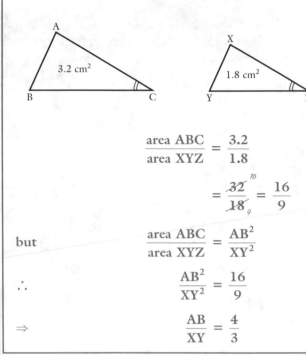

$$\frac{\text{area ABC}}{\text{area XYZ}} = \frac{3.2}{1.8}$$

$$= \frac{\overset{16}{\cancel{32}}}{\underset{9}{\cancel{18}}} = \frac{16}{9}$$

but

$$\frac{\text{area ABC}}{\text{area XYZ}} = \frac{AB^2}{XY^2}$$

$$\therefore \quad \frac{AB^2}{XY^2} = \frac{16}{9}$$

$$\Rightarrow \quad \frac{AB}{XY} = \frac{4}{3}$$

Find the value of AB : XY for each of the following pairs of similar figures.

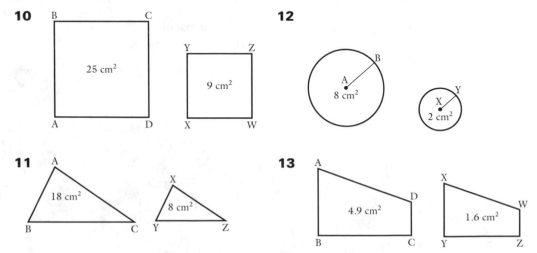

10

11

12

13

14 An enlargement increases the area of a photograph by 44%. Find the scale factor of the enlargement.

Triangles ABC and PQR are similar, with $\widehat{A} = \widehat{P}$ and $\widehat{C} = \widehat{R}$.
If $AC = 4\,cm$, $PR = 3\,cm$ and the area of $\triangle PQR = 4.5\,cm^2$, find the area of $\triangle ABC$.

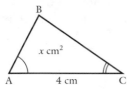

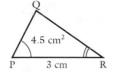

AC and PR are corresponding sides and $\dfrac{AC}{PR} = \dfrac{4}{3}$

$\therefore$

$$\dfrac{area\ \triangle ABC}{area\ \triangle PQR} = \dfrac{16}{9}$$

i.e.

$$\dfrac{x}{4.5} = \dfrac{16}{9}$$

$$4.5 \times \dfrac{x}{4.5} = \dfrac{16}{9} \times 4.5$$

$$x = 8$$

$\therefore$ area $\triangle ABC = 8\,cm^2$

15

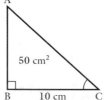

Triangles ABC and XYZ are similar.
From the information given in the
diagram, find the area of $\triangle XYZ$

17

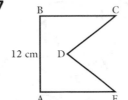

ABCDE and PQRST are similar shapes
If $AB = 12\,cm$, $PQ = 9\,cm$
and area $PQRST = 36\,cm^2$,
find the area of ABCDE.

16

ABCD and PQRS are squares and
$AB : PQ = 3 : 2$. If the area of
ABCD is $36\,cm^2$, find the area of PQRS.

18

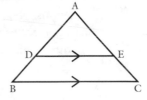

DE is parallel to BC. If $AE = 10\,cm$,
$EC = 4\,cm$ and the area of $\triangle ABC$
is $98\,cm^2$, find the area of $\triangle ADE$.

19 A document is enlarged on a photocopier in such a way that its area is quadrupled. The
original document measures $8.6\,cm$ by $10.5\,cm$. Find the dimensions of the
enlargement.

In the remaining questions, it may be necessary first to show that triangles are similar.

20 ABCD is a square of area $12\,\text{cm}^2$. P is the midpoint of AB and Q is the midpoint of AD. Find the area of $\triangle$APQ.

21 Triangles ABC and PQR are similar. If the area of $\triangle$ABC is four times that of $\triangle$PQR and AB and PQ are corresponding sides, what is the value of AB : PQ?

22 The scale of a map is $1 : 1000$. On the map, the area representing a mansion is $2\,\text{cm}^2$. What is the actual area in square metres occupied by the mansion?

23 The area of the larger circle is sixteen times that of the smaller circle. What is the ratio of the radii of the two circles?

24 ABC is a triangle with X a point on AB and Y a point on AC such that XY is parallel to BC. If $AY = 3\,\text{cm}$, $YC = 4\,\text{cm}$ and $XB = 3\,\text{cm}$, find

    a AX   **b** $\dfrac{\text{area } \triangle\text{AXY}}{\text{area } \triangle\text{ABC}}$ **c** $\dfrac{\text{area } \triangle\text{AXY}}{\text{area trapezium XYCB}}$

25 The diagram shows three regular hexagons. The sides of the smallest hexagon are each 1 unit long. Find the ratio of the areas of the three hexagons.

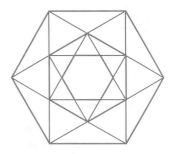

26 Triangle ABC has a right angle at A and AD is perpendicular to BC. The area of $\triangle$ABD is $4\,\text{cm}^2$ and the area of $\triangle$ADC is $5\,\text{cm}^2$. Find the ratio of the area of $\triangle$ABD to the area of $\triangle$ABC and hence the value of AB : BC.

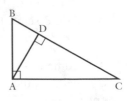

VOLUMES OF SIMILAR SHAPES

We start the next exercise by investigating, for similar figures, the relationship between the ratio of the lengths of corresponding sides and the ratio of the volumes.

EXERCISE 14C

1 The diagram shows three cubes.

a Write down the ratio of the lengths of their bases.

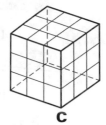

b By counting the number of cubes equal in size to cube **A**, write down the ratio of their volumes.

Is there a relationship between your answers to parts **a** and **b**?

2

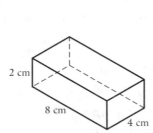

The diagram shows two similar rectangular boxes.

a Write down the ratio of their
   i longest edges   **ii** widths   **iii** heights.

b How many cubes of side 1 cm are needed to fill each box completely? Write down the ratio of their volumes.

Is there any relationship between the ratios in parts **a** and **b**?

3 The diagram shows three similar cylindrical cans.

a Write down the ratio of
   i their heights   **ii** their base radii.

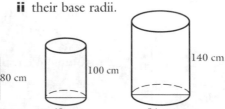

b Express the capacity of each can as a multiple of π. Hence find the ratio of their capacities.

Is there a relationship between your answers to parts **a** and **b**?

From these questions we conclude that

> the ratio of the volumes of similar figures is equal to the cube of the ratio of corresponding lengths.

In the same way, the ratio of the capacities of similar containers is equal to the cube of the ratio of corresponding linear dimensions.

A sculptor is commissioned to create a bronze statue 2 m high. He begins by making a clay model 30 cm high.

a Express, in its simplest form, the ratio of the height of the completed bronze statue to the height of the clay model.

b If the total surface area of the model is 360 cm^2, find the total surface area of the statue.

c If the volume of the model is 1000 cm^3 find the volume of the statue.

a $\dfrac{\text{height of bronze statue}}{\text{height of clay model}} = \dfrac{200}{30} = \dfrac{20}{3}$

b $\dfrac{\text{surface area of statue}}{\text{surface area of model}} = \dfrac{20^2}{3^2}$

i.e. $\dfrac{\text{surface area of statue}}{360} = \dfrac{400}{9}$

$\therefore$ surface area of statue $= \dfrac{400}{9_{\,1}} \times 360^{\,40}\,\text{cm}^2$

$\qquad\qquad\qquad\qquad = 16\,000\,\text{cm}^2$

$\qquad\qquad\qquad\qquad = 1.6\,\text{m}^2$

c $\dfrac{\text{volume of statue}}{\text{volume of model}} = \dfrac{20^3}{3^3}$

i.e. $\dfrac{\text{volume of statue}}{1000} = \dfrac{8000}{27}$

$\therefore$ volume of statue $= \dfrac{8000}{27} \times 1000\,\text{cm}^3$

$\qquad\qquad\qquad\qquad = \dfrac{8000 \times 1000}{27 \times 1\,000\,000}\,\text{m}^3$

$\qquad\qquad\qquad\qquad = \dfrac{8}{27}\,\text{m}^3 = 0.296\,\text{m}^3$ (correct to 3 s.f.)

4 This figure is made from 1 cm cubes. It is enlarged by a scale factor of 3. How many 1 cm cubes are required to make the enlarged figure?

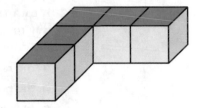

In these questions, assume that the figures are mathematically similar.

5 The sides of two cubes are in the ratio $2:1$. What is the ratio of their volumes?

6 The radii of two spheres are in the ratio $3:4$. What is the ratio of their volumes?

7 Two regular tetrahedrons have volumes in the ratio $8:27$. What is the ratio of their sides?

8 Two right cones have volumes in the ratio $64:27$. What is the ratio of
  a their heights **b** their base radii?

9 Two similar bottles are such that one is twice as high as the other. What is the ratio of
  a their surface areas **b** their capacities?

10 Each linear dimension of a model car is $\frac{1}{10}$ of the corresponding car dimension. Find the ratio of
  a the areas of their windscreens
  b the capacities of their boots
  c the widths of the cars
  d the number of wheels they have.

11 Three similar jugs have heights 8 cm, 12 cm and 16 cm. If the smallest jug holds $\frac{1}{2}$ pint, find the capacities of the other two.

12 Three similar drinking glasses have heights 7.5 cm, 9 cm and 10.5 cm. If the tallest glass holds 34.3 centilitres find the capacities of the other two.

13 The capacities of three similar jugs are 48.6 cl, 115.2 cl and 225 cl.
  a If the jug with the largest capacity is 15 cm high, find the heights of the other two.
  b If the base area of the smallest jug is 36 cm^2 find the base areas of the other two.

14 A toy manufacturer produces model cars which are similar in every way to the actual cars. If the ratio of the door area of the model to the door area of the car is $1:2500$ find

    a the ratio of their lengths

    b the ratio of the capacities of their petrol tanks

    c the width of the model, if the actual car is $150\,cm$ wide

    d the area of the rear window of the actual car if the area of the rear window of the model is $3\,cm^2$.

15 A wax model has a mass of $1\,kg$. Find the mass of a similar model which is twice as tall and made from metal eight times as heavy as wax.

16 A medicine dispenser is made from the top part of a cone as shown in the diagram. The capacity of the dispenser is $20\,ml$. Find the capacity of the complete cone.

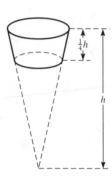

The radius of a spherical soap bubble increases by 5%. Find, correct to the nearest whole number, the percentage increase in

a its surface area   **b** its volume.

> If the original radius is $r\,cm$, the increased radius is 105% of $r\,cm$, i.e. $1.05r\,cm$

$$\frac{\text{new radius}}{\text{old radius}} = \frac{1.05r}{r} = \frac{1.05}{1}$$

a $\dfrac{\text{new surface area}}{\text{original surface area}} = \left(\dfrac{1.05}{1}\right)^2 = 1.1025$

i.e. new surface area $= 1.1025$ of the original surface area

so   new surface area $= 1.1025 \times 100\%$ of original surface area

$$= 110.25\% \text{ of the original surface area.}$$

The surface area has therefore increased by 10% (to the nearest whole number).

b $\dfrac{\text{new volume}}{\text{original volume}} = \left(\dfrac{1.05}{1}\right)^3 = 1.157\ldots$

i.e. new volume $= 1.157\ldots$ of the original volume

$$= 115.7\ldots\% \text{ of the original volume}$$

The volume has therefore increased by 16% (to the nearest whole number).

17 The radius of one sphere is 10% more than the radius of another sphere. Find, correct to the nearest whole number, the percentage difference in

a their surface areas   **b** their volumes.

18 The radius of a spherical snowball increases by 80%. Find, correct to the nearest whole number, the percentage increase in

a its surface area   **b** its volume.

19 The edge of one cube is 20% greater than the edge of another. Find, correct to the nearest whole number, the percentage difference in

a their surface areas   **b** their volumes.

20 The volume of a cone increases by 100%. Find the percentage increase in

a its height   **b** its base radius   **c** its surface area.

Give your answers correct to the nearest whole number.

21 A spherical grapefruit has a diameter of 10 cm. If its peel is 1 cm thick, find, correct to the nearest whole number, the percentage of the volume of the whole grapefruit that is thrown away as peel.

22 These two bowls are mathematically similar.

500 ml   1.5 litre

The diameter of the top of the smaller bowl is 16 cm. What is the diameter of the top of the larger bowl?

23 Solid oak balls are available in different sizes. The smallest has a diameter of 6 cm and costs £8.50. Assuming that the cost is directly proportional to the mass, find the cost of a ball of diameter 10 cm.

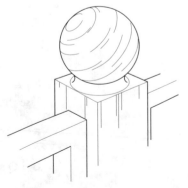

24 The pendants for a chandelier are made from glass; some are hollow and some are solid. The shapes of both types are mathematically similar and come in two sizes, 5 cm high and 2 cm high. The larger solid pendant weighs 400 g and the larger hollow pendant weighs 70 g. The mass of a hollow pendant is proportional to its surface area. A complete chandelier uses 5 large pendants and 20 smaller pendants.
Find the difference between the weights of a chandelier made with solid pendants and one made with hollow pendants.

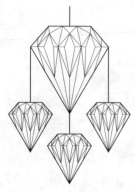

MIXED EXERCISE

EXERCISE 14D

1 Two similar rectangles have areas in the ratio 49 : 81. What is the ratio of

a their longer sides   **b** their shorter sides?

2

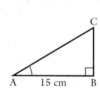
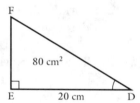

Triangles ABC and DEF are similar. From the information given in the diagrams, find

a the area of △ABC   **b** the length of FE   **c** ratio AC : FD

3

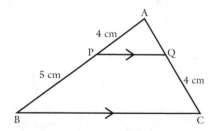

Use the information given in the diagram to find

a AQ

b PQ : BC

c $\dfrac{\text{area } \triangle APQ}{\text{area } \triangle ABC}$

d $\dfrac{\text{area } \triangle APQ}{\text{trapezium PQCB}}$

4 An inverted hollow cone is filled with water to half its depth. What fraction of the available capacity is filled?

5 These two boxes are mathematically similar.

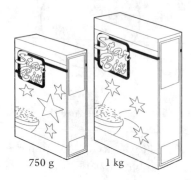

750 g   1 kg

The smaller box holds 750 g of cereal. The larger box holds 1 kg of cereal. Find the ratio of

a the heights of the boxes

b the area of cardboard used to make the boxes.

PUZZLE

Metric paper sizes, A2, A3, A4,..., are such that when any one sheet is cut in half widthwise, each half is mathematically similar to the original sheet. Find the ratio of the length to the width of a sheet of paper of any metric size.

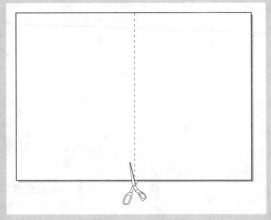

INVESTIGATIONS

1 An ellipse can be formed by stretching a circle in one direction.

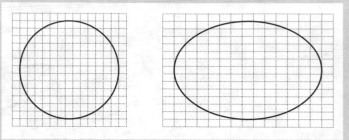

Find a formula for the area of an ellipse.

2 You will need a computer, with scalable fonts installed, and a printer. Scalable fonts can be made any size. The size is defined in 'points'.

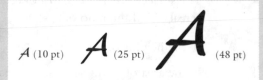

Investigate the relationship between the point size and the scaling factor.

Another way of describing the size of a font is in picas. Investigate the relationship between the size of a font in picas and its actual size.

STANDARD DEVIATION

One way in which the results of the Key Stage 2 tests for 11-year-olds are published is to take the percentage of children in a school who achieved Level 4 or higher in English, in mathematics and in science and then add these percentages together. This gives a maximum score of 300 for any one school. For a group of schools there is a possible spread of scores from 0 to 300.

A summary of these results for the schools in one education authority is

mean: 187,
range: 45–269,   interquartile range: 156–223

- From the summary we can deduce some information about how the results of individual schools are spread throughout the range; one quarter of the schools had scores ranging from 223 to 269, three quarters achieved 156 or better and a quarter of the schools had scores ranging from 45 to 156.

  We cannot however tell how the scores are spread within any one of these quarters. In the lowest quarter, for example, we do not know if just one school had a score of 45 and the others scores were much closer to 156 or if several of these schools had very low results. This means that we need another way of measuring the dispersion of individual items in a distribution.

EXERCISE 15A

1 This is a summary of the results from another education authority.

Range: 78–260   Interquartile range: 165–216   Mean: 189

Discuss whether the following statements can be justified from the information given.

a More than half the schools had scores better than 189.

b More than half the schools had scores better than 190.

c Several schools had scores below 100.

d Well over half of the schools had scores better than 150.

e In well over half of the schools, half of all the pupils achieved level 4 or better.

f Only one school had a score of 216.

2 These are distributions of the marks obtained in a test by four groups of students.

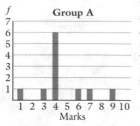

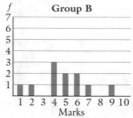

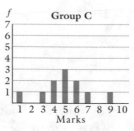

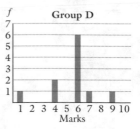

a Find the range and the interquartile range of the marks for each group.

b Discuss how the marks are distributed for each group.

c The marks for a fifth group of 23 candidates ranged from 2 to 10 with lower and upper quartiles of 5 and 8 respectively. Sketch two bar charts showing two possible distributions of those marks.

3 These two bar charts show the numbers of students taking Russian GCSE in all schools in two areas.

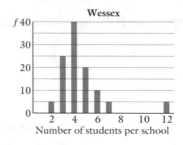

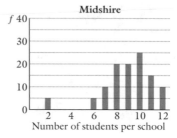

Discuss

a the usefulness or otherwise of using just the range for describing how the values are distributed in these two examples

b how the mark of 2 affects the range of numbers for Midshire

c how the mark of 12 affects range of numbers for Wessex.

STANDARD DEVIATION

The way in which values are distributed within a data set is called *dispersion*.

From the last exercise we can see that using the range to describe the dispersion of values has serious disadvantages because it uses only two values and can be strongly influenced by one extreme value. The interquartile range is not influenced by the extreme values but it still has the disadvantage of not using all the values from the distribution. For these reasons we need a measure of dispersion that uses all the values. The one used most often is based on finding the difference between each value and the mean and then averaging the squares of these. The square root of this average is called the *standard deviation* (s.d.) and gives a measure of the scatter of the values about the mean value.

Standard deviation is measured in the same unit as the values are and is defined as follows.

The standard deviation, s.d., of n values $x_1, x_2, x_3, \ldots, x_n$ is given by

$$\text{s.d.} = \sqrt{\frac{\sum(x - \overline{x})^2}{n}} \equiv \sqrt{\frac{\sum x^2}{n} - \overline{x}^2}$$

where $\overline{x}$ is the mean value.

The symbol $\equiv$ means 'is equivalent to', and the symbol $\sum$ means 'the sum of'. Either version of the formula for the standard deviation may be used but in practice $\sqrt{\dfrac{\sum x^2}{n} - \overline{x}^2}$ is easier to work with.

Since the standard deviation of a set of values measures the scatter of the values about their mean value, we would expect the set of masses of the apples on the left to have a smaller standard deviation than those on the right.

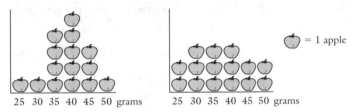

25 30 35 40 45 50 grams   25 30 35 40 45 50 grams

We can describe this difference by saying that the masses of the apples on the left are less variable than those on the right.

EXERCISE 15B

Find the standard deviation of the following masses of five apples.

$$25\,\text{g}, \ 27\,\text{g}, \ 27\,\text{g}, \ 27\,\text{g}, \ 30\,\text{g}$$

To find the s.d. using $\sqrt{\dfrac{\sum x^2}{n} - \overline{x}^2}$, we need first to work out the mean value, then square each value and add these squares.
It is easier to keep track of the calculations when they are in a table.

x	x^2
25	625
27	729
27	729
27	729
30	900
$\sum x = 136$	$\sum x^2 = 3712$

mean $\overline{x} = \dfrac{\sum x}{n} = \dfrac{136}{5} = 27.2\,\text{g}$

$\text{s.d.} = \sqrt{\dfrac{\sum x^2}{n} - \overline{x}^2}$

$= \sqrt{\dfrac{3712}{5} - 27.2^2}\,\text{g}$

$= 1.6\,\text{g}$

1 Find the mean and standard deviation for each of the following data sets.

   a The marks out of 20 that Chris scored in five tests: 3, 5, 9, 12, 14

   b The heights in centimetres of some geraniums: 56, 72, 49, 24, 85.

   c The masses of four letters: 16 g, 38 g, 27.5 g, 56.7 g

   d Sales figures at a department store, in thousands of pounds, for the four quarters of last year: 431, 448, 453, 473

2 The lengths, in centimetres, of a sample of ten leaves from my lime tree were

$$8.6, \ 7.4, \ 9.3, \ 10.2, \ 7.6, \ 11.4, \ 8.9, \ 9.2, \ 8.5, \ 10.6$$

Find the standard deviation for these lengths.

3 The data given below shows the fat content in grams per 100 g for ten different varieties of biscuit.

$$25.8, \ 24.6, \ 21.9, \ 28.1, \ 21.9, \ 25.3, \ 29.2, \ 20.1, \ 15.6, \ 21.2$$

Calculate the mean and standard deviation for the fat content of these biscuits.

4 Sarah and Kevin each kept a record of the number of hours they spent watching television for one week.

Sarah's record

Monday	– 1 hour
Tuesday	– 1½ hours
Wednesday	– 1 hour
Thursday	– 3 hours
Friday –	
Saturday	– 2 hours
Sunday	– 5 hours

Kevin's record

Monday	– ½ hour
Tuesday	– 1 hour
Wednesday	– ½ hour
Thursday	– 2 hours
Friday	– ½ hour
Saturday	– 1 hour
Sunday	– 2 hours

   a Without doing any calculation, write down estimates for the mean and standard deviation of each set of times.

   b Calculate the mean and standard deviation of each set.

5 The annual salaries of the directors of Eduwell PLC are

£60 000, £60 000, £60 000, £60 000, £75 000, £75 000,
£80 000 and £150 000.

Calculate the mean and standard deviation for the annual salaries of the Board of Directors of Eduwell PLC.
(You may find it easier to work in thousands of pounds, e.g. £60K)

6 The annual salaries of the directors of Watersons plc are

£60 000, £70 000, £75 000, £80 000, £85 000, £90 000,
£100 000 and £110 000.

a Say, giving reasons, whether you would expect the standard deviation of this set of salaries to be greater than or less than the standard deviation of the set given in question **5**.

b Calculate the standard deviation of these salaries.

**USING A
CALCULATOR**

Finding the standard deviation of a large number of values is easier when a calculator is used. Most scientific and graphics calculators have statistical functions built in.
Calculators vary but the basic steps are similar:

first make sure the calculator is in statistics mode (usually SD mode) and that the memory is empty, then enter the data,
to find the standard deviation, press $\boxed{\sigma_n}$ (usually accessed with the shift, or 2nd, button). *Do not* use the σ_{n-1} function.

It is not necessary to find the mean first; if you do want the mean, press $\boxed{\overline{x}}$

EXERCISE 15C

Use your calculator to find the standard deviation of each set of values given in **Exercise 15B**.

**STANDARD
DEVIATION OF
A FREQUENCY
DISTRIBUTION**

When the data is presented in a frequency table, each value of x^2 has to be multiplied by its frequency.

If the data is grouped, the midclass value is used for x. Since the midclass value is an estimate for the mean of the values within a group, the standard deviation calculated using the midclass value is also an estimate.

The standard deviation of a frequency distribution is given by

$$\text{s.d.} = \sqrt{\frac{\sum f(x - \overline{x})^2}{\sum f}} \equiv \sqrt{\frac{\sum fx^2}{\sum f} - \overline{x}^2}$$

where $\overline{x}$ is the mean value.
For a grouped distribution, x is the midclass value and the formula gives an estimate for the s.d.

As before, we will use the second version of the formula as it makes calculation easier. For an ungrouped frequency distribution, we need another column in the table for values of fx^2. For a grouped frequency distribution, we need yet another column for the midclass values.

EXERCISE 15D

Each pupil in Year 10 took part in a short quiz to raise money for charity. The table shows the distribution of their scores. Find the mean score and the standard deviation.

Score	0	1	2	3	4	5	6	7	8	9	10
Frequency	0	0	1	4	5	15	20	10	2	0	0

> It is easier to work with the table set vertically.

Score, x	Frequency, f	fx	x^2	fx^2
0	0	0	0	0
1	0	0	1	0
2	1	2	4	4
3	4	12	9	36
4	5	20	16	80
5	15	75	25	375
6	20	120	36	720
7	10	70	49	490
8	2	16	64	128
9	0	0	81	0
10	0	0	100	0
	$\sum f = 57$	$\sum fx = 315$		$\sum fx^2 = 1833$

Mean score $\bar{x} = \dfrac{\sum fx}{\sum f} = \dfrac{315}{57} = 5.53$ (correct to 3 significant figures)

$\text{s.d.} = \sqrt{\dfrac{\sum fx^2}{\sum f} - \bar{x}^2} = \sqrt{\dfrac{1833}{57} - \left(\dfrac{315}{57}\right)^2}$

> Notice that we do not use the corrected value found above for the mean.

$= 1.27$ (correct to 3 significant figures)

1 Find the mean and standard deviation of each of the following distributions.

a

Age, x years	Frequency
5	4
6	9
7	12
8	6

b

Number of people, x	Frequency
4	12
5	10
6	9
7	6
8	4
9	0

c

Shoe size, x	Frequency
3	2
$3\frac{1}{2}$	2
4	4
$4\frac{1}{2}$	5
5	4
$5\frac{1}{2}$	2

2 Use the statistics functions on your calculator to find the standard deviation of each distribution in question **1**.

3 These are the distributions of the masses of apples given on page 363.

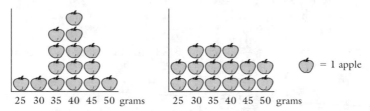

a Construct a frequency table for each distribution and use it to find the standard deviation of each set of 15 masses.

b Explain whether your answers are what you expected.

4 A single plant cell was placed on each of 20 petri dishes and incubated for 24 hours, after which the cells on each dish were counted. This experiment was repeated with a different culture medium. The diagrams show the results of the two experiments.

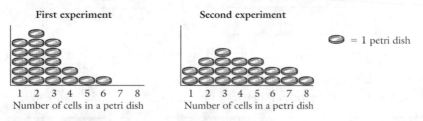

a Which of these two experiments do you expect to have the smaller standard deviation, and why?

b Explain why the standard deviation cannot be larger than half the range.

c If, in a third experiment, the standard deviation was equal to half the range, sketch a bar chart showing a possible distribution of the number of cells.

The table shows the distribution of the heights of tomato plants that were measured three weeks after the seeds were sown.

Height, h cm	$0 \leqslant h < 3$	$3 \leqslant h < 6$	$6 \leqslant h < 9$	$9 \leqslant h < 12$
Frequency	4	6	5	2

Find the mean height and the standard deviation.

Height, h cm	Frequency, f	Midclass value, x	fx	x^2	fx^2
$0 \leqslant h < 3$	4	1.5	6	2.25	9
$3 \leqslant h < 6$	6	4.5	27	20.25	121.5
$6 \leqslant h < 9$	5	7.5	37.5	56.25	281.25
$9 \leqslant h < 12$	2	10.5	21	110.25	220.5
	$\sum f = 17$		$\sum fx = 91.5$		$\sum fx^2 = 632.25$

Mean height $\bar{x} = \dfrac{\sum fx}{\sum f} = \dfrac{91.5}{17}$ cm $= 5.38$ cm (correct to 3 significant figures)

s.d. $= \sqrt{\dfrac{\sum fx^2}{\sum f} - \bar{x}^2} = \sqrt{\dfrac{632.25}{17} - \left(\dfrac{91.5}{17}\right)^2}$ cm

$$= 2.87 \text{ cm (correct to 3 significant figures)}$$

5 The table shows, in groups, the number of damaged apples in 20 boxes of apples.

Number of damaged apples	0–4	5–9	10–14	15–19
Frequency	12	4	3	1

Calculate the mean number of damaged apples per box and their standard deviation.

6 The table shows the grouped masses of potatoes.

Mass, m grams	$118 \leqslant m < 126$	$126 \leqslant m < 135$	$135 \leqslant m < 144$	$144 \leqslant m < 153$	$153 \leqslant m < 162$	$162 \leqslant m < 171$	$171 \leqslant m < 180$
Frequency	9	12	26	25	15	9	4

Calculate the mean mass and the standard deviation of the masses.

7 The bar chart shows the result of an examination of boxes of screws.

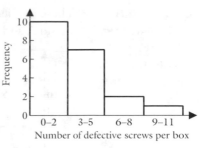

  a Use the bar chart to make a frequency table.

  b Find the mean and standard deviation of this distribution.

8 This bar chart shows the grouped scores of the Key Stage 2 tests used to introduce this chapter.
Find the mean and the standard deviation of these scores.

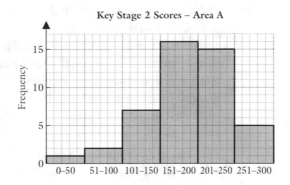

9 These are the grouped scores from a second area, a summary of which is given in **Exercise 15A**.

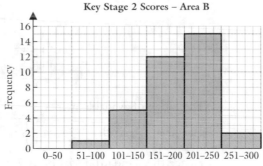

Find the mean and the standard deviation of these scores.

10 The mean score for area A and area B, given first on page 361, and calculated from the raw data are

　　　　Area A: mean 187　　　Area B: mean 189

  a Compare your mean values calculated from the grouped data with the values given and explain the differences.

  b Make at least two comparisons between the two sets of scores.

USING MEAN AND STANDARD DEVIATION TO COMPARE DISTRIBUTIONS

These frequency polygons show the results of testing a sample of Brand A and Brand B light bulbs to find out how long they last.

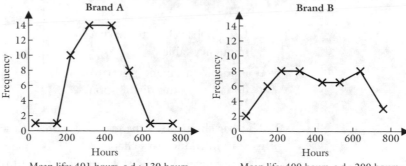

Mean life: 401 hours, s.d.: 130 hours   Mean life: 400 hours, s.d.: 200 hours

The mean is approximately in the middle of each distribution. The mean and range of both samples are very nearly the same, but the standard deviation of the Brand A sample is much smaller than that of Brand B. This means that more Brand A bulbs have a life closer to the mean than Brand B bulbs, and that fewer Brand A bulbs are likely to fail after a short time than Brand B bulbs, that is Brand A bulbs are less variable. This can be confirmed from the frequency polygons: one Brand A bulb failed before 150 hours whereas five Brand B bulbs failed in the same time interval.

The standard deviation of a distribution can be expressed as a percentage of its range. This gives a way of measuring the dispersion in terms of the total spread.

This bar chart, for example, illustrates the results of a test taken by a group of students.

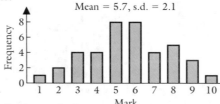

The range of available marks is

$$10 - 0 = 10, \quad \text{and} \quad \frac{\text{s.d.}}{\text{range}} = \frac{2.1}{10} = 0.21 = 21\%$$

Hence the standard deviation is 21% of the range.

This is useful when we want to compare two distributions with different ranges. The same group of students took another test, this time marked out of 20 and the standard deviation of the results is 3.2 marks.

For this test, the standard deviation is $\frac{3.2}{20}$ of the range of marks available, that is 16% of the range. Therefore we can say that the marks for this test are less variable than those for the first test.

Note that we do not know the mean mark for the second test so it is not possible to make any other comparison of the two sets of results.

**THE EFFECT OF
CHANGING ALL
VALUES BY THE
SAME AMOUNT**

Sometimes all the values in a distribution are changed by the same amount. Suppose that all the students who took the first test referred to above had their marks increased by 2 (for good spelling).

The effect of this on a frequency polygon is to shift it by 2 units to the right.

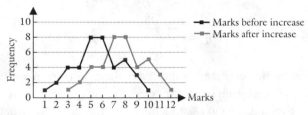

The shapes of the two distributions are the same so there has been no change in the variability of the marks, that is the standard deviation is not altered.

This means that when all the values in a distribution are increased (or decreased) by the same amount, *the standard deviation is unchanged.*

However the shift has clearly changed the mean value. As each mark has increased by 2, the mean mark has also increased by 2.

EXERCISE 15E

1 The first table shows the number of times that the various numbers of heads should theoretically be obtained when 6 coins are tossed together 64 times. The second table shows the number of heads that were obtained when six coins were tossed together 64 times.

Number of heads	0	1	2	3	4	5	6
Theoretical frequency	1	6	15	20	15	6	1

Number of heads	0	1	2	3	4	5	6
Experimental frequency	0	4	18	22	14	4	2

Draw frequency polygons to illustrate each set of data. Use a calculator to find the mean number of heads and the standard deviation for the theoretical distribution and for the experimental results. Use these, together with the shapes of the two frequency polygons, to compare the two distributions, giving reasons for any conclusions you draw.

2 Ken has only a very small plot in which to grow potatoes and wants to choose the variety that will give the best crop. He takes his wife Wendy with him to help decide on the variety of seed potato he will buy. They decide to choose between two varieties, which are:

Winchester which, according to the details given, should yield potatoes with a mean weight of 202 g and a standard deviation of 31.4 g

King Harold, which should yield a mean weight of 198 g and a standard deviation of 39.7 g.

Wendy advises him to buy Winchester seed potatoes. Does she give the best advice? Justify your answer.

3

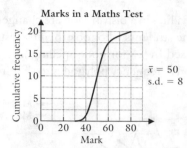

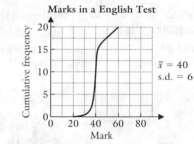

The curve in the left diagram illustrates the results from a test in mathematics and the curve in the right diagram illustrates the results from a test in English. Both tests were taken by the same group of students. Use the given information to determine whether there are any substantial differences in the two sets of results.

4 A mathematics examination was marked out of 60 and an English examination was marked out of 95. The mean mark for mathematics was 28 and for English it was 51.
Explain how these mean marks can be written in a form which allows them to be compared.

5 The mean and standard deviation masses of potatoes grown under normal conditions are 100 g and 18 g respectively.
The mean and standard deviation mass of potatoes grown under a variety of experimental conditions were

> A: 150 g, 40 g   B: 80 g, 10 g   C: 120 g, 18 g   D: 100 g, 34 g

a Compare each distribution with the potatoes grown under normal conditions.

b State, with reasons, whether you consider any of the experimental conditions offer an improvement regarding the masses of the potatoes grown.

6 These are the masses of ten letters as weighed by an automatic franchising machine.

> 26 g, 30 g, 42 g, 70 g, 36 g, 29 g, 84 g, 56 g, 71 g, 48 g

a Find the mean and the standard deviation of these masses.

b After the letters had been weighed, it was discovered that the machine was set incorrectly; each mass should be 10 g greater than the mass recorded. Write down the mean and the standard deviation of the correct masses.

7 A small company employs 10 people. The salaries of the employees are

> £10 000, £12 000, £15 000, £15 000, £18 000,
> £20 000, £20 000, £22 000, £25 000, £60 000

a Calculate the mean and the standard deviation of the salaries.

The company has a profit-sharing scheme. At the end of the financial year, the company can distribute the profit share by giving each employee either £1085 or 5% of their salary.

b What is the effect on the mean and standard deviation of giving each employee £1085?

c What is the effect on the mean and standard deviation of giving each employee 5% of their salary?

d Which of these two methods of distribution benefits the greater number of employees?

PRACTICAL
WORK

1 The table shows the theoretical results when an unbiased dice is tossed 120 times.

Score	1	2	3	4	5	6
Theoretical frequency	20	20	20	20	20	20

Throw a dice 120 times and compare your distribution of scores with the theoretical distribution.

2 These are recent Key Stage 2 results for two different education authorities. They are presented as published in one newspaper. Comment on the form in which they are presented.
Compare and contrast these results.

Area X

269%	207%	158%	141%	121%	89%	50%
267%	206%	156%	140%	113%	84%	45%
261%	200%	155%	134%	110%	82%	40%
237%	200%	153%	133%	108%	78%	33%
233%	189%	149%	129%	105%	69%	
223%	189%	147%	127%	102%	64%	
223%	186%	146%	125%	100%	63%	
	176%	145%	125%	97%	60%	
	176%	141%	124%	94%	60%	
	174%	141%	121%	91%	59%	

Area Y

234%	146%	129%	99%	77%
204%	146%	128%	99%	77%
197%	145%	127%	93%	77%
184%	143%	122%	90%	72%
180%	143%	120%	89%	68%
180%	141%	117%	89%	57%
178%	140%	117%	86%	56%
170%	139%	115%	84%	55%
160%	138%	110%	82%	52%
147%	131%	106%	78%	48%
				43%
				34%

INFORMATION FROM STRAIGHT LINE GRAPHS

16

Kevin repairs domestic equipment. He charges a call-out fee together with an hourly charge. Customers often ask for an estimate before the work is begun and as Kevin does not know how long a job will take before he starts it, he gives this graph to customers to help them get an idea of likely charges.

- Some detailed information can be read from this graph, for example a repair taking 2 hours will cost about £48.
- Some information cannot be read: the cost of a repair taking 6 hours, for example. We can estimate the cost by trying to judge where the line would be if we mentally extended both axes. This is likely to give a very rough estimate.
- A much better estimate can be obtained by using the information on the graph to work out the equation of the line and then use the equation to calculate the cost of a repair taking 6 hours.

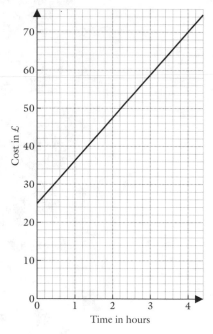

EXERCISE 16A

1 What does Kevin charge for a repair that takes $2\frac{1}{2}$ hours?

2 What is Kevin's call-out fee?

3 Discuss with a group how you can find an equation for this line.

**FINDING THE
EQUATION OF A
LINE FROM A
GRAPH**

To find the equation of any line, we start with the fact that the equation of a straight line is of the form $y = mx + c$ where m is the gradient of the line and c is the intercept on the y-axis.

374

This graph shows the relationship between quarterly domestic electricity bills from a supply company and the number of units consumed.

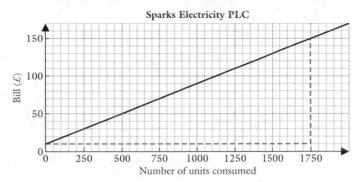

The graph has no x-axis or y-axis, but there are two variables: the number of units consumed and the size of the quarterly bill.

If we let n be the number of units consumed and £C be the quarterly bill, then, comparing with the equation $y = mx + c$ which refers to x- and y-axes, we see that n is equivalent to x and C is equivalent to y.

Hence we are looking for a relationship between n and C in the form $C = mn + c$ where m is the gradient of the line and c is the intercept on the vertical axis.

Reading from the graph, $c = 10$ and $m = \dfrac{140}{1750} = 0.08$

> Remember, we find the gradient of a line by calculating $\dfrac{\text{increase in } y\ (\text{or equivalent})}{\text{increase in } x\ (\text{or equivalent})}$
> when moving from any one point on the line to any other point on the line.

Therefore the equation of this line is $C = 0.08n + 10$

Note that $C = 0.08n + 10$ is not an exact relationship between C and n because we have read values from a graph.

EXERCISE 16B

1 **a** Use the graph above this exercise to find

   i the fixed charge payable per quarter irrespective of the number of units used.

   ii the bill for a quarter in which 900 units are used

   iii the cost of 1 unit of electricity.

b How are the answers to parts **i** and **iii** above related to the equation of the line?

c Any two points on a line can be used to calculate the gradient of that line. Discuss why we chose to take the points as far apart as practical.

d Use the equation $C = 0.08n + 10$ to find

   i the value of C when $n = 2500$ **ii** the value of n when $C = 450$

e Ari shares a house with 8 other people. He tells his housemates that the next quarter's electricity bill must be less than £500. What is the maximum number of units that can be used by the household?

2 Use the information from the graph to find the equation of the line.

a
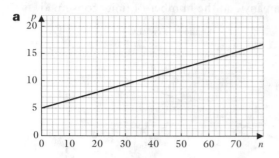

c
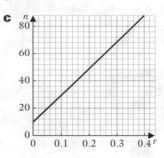

b
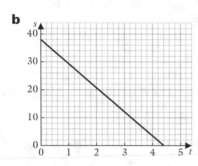

d
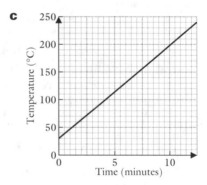

3 For each graph give the value of the gradient and what the gradient means in the context of the graph.

a
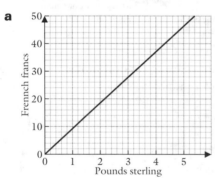

c
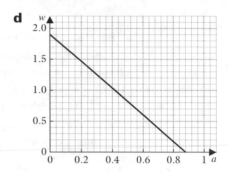

b
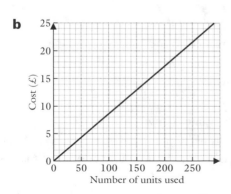

d
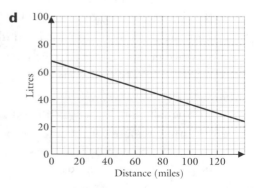

4 This graph shows how the quantity of water in a reservoir varies with time over a nine-day period in August one year.
When full the resevoir contains 2 000 000 gallons.

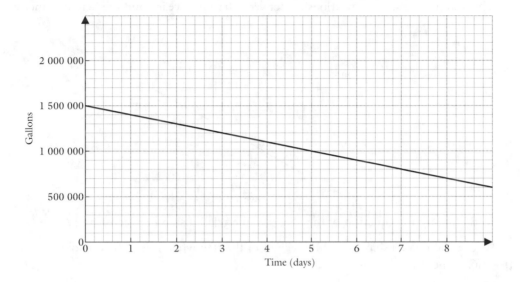

a Use the graph to find

i the volume of water in the reservoir after three days

ii after how many days the reservoir is half empty.

b What is the gradient of the line and what does it represent?

c What is the value of the intercept on the vertical axis and what does it represent?

d What do you think the weather was like during the period referred to?

e Use this graph to predict when the reservoir will be empty. Write a short paragraph commenting on the reliability of this prediction.

5 Use Kevin's graph on page 374 to find the equation of the line. Hence find

a the cost of a job that takes 6 hours

b how long Kevin had to spend on a repair to earn £100

c Kevin's hourly charge rate.

It is not always possible to see from a graph where a straight line cuts the vertical axis. The next worked example shows how to find the equation of a line in such circumstances.

The graph illustrates the relationship between the age, t years, and the height, h metres, of a tree.

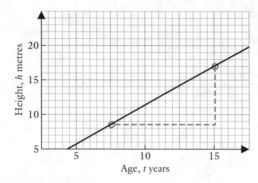

a By finding the equation of the line, give the relationship between h and t.

b Use the relationship to find the height of the tree when it is 100 years old. Comment on the answer.

a

> We can use any two points on the line to find its gradient.
> However, neither axis starts at zero, and we cannot read the value of c from the graph.

The equation is in the form $h = mt + c$

From the graph $m = \dfrac{8.5}{7.5} = 1.13\ldots$

Therefore $h = (1.13\ldots)t + c$

> We can now substitute the values of t and h at one point on the line into this equation to find c.
> We will use the higher point used to find the gradient.

When $t = 15$ and $h = 17$, $17 = (1.13\ldots) \times 15 + c$

i.e. $17 = 17 + c \quad \Rightarrow \quad c = 0$

therefore $h = 1.13t$ | Giving m correct to 3 s.f.

b When $t = 100$, $h = 1.13 \times 100$

$\qquad\qquad\qquad\quad = 113$

i.e. when the tree is 100 years old, it will be about 113 metres high. A tree is not likely to grow to over 100 metres high; the relationship found between h and t is probably not valid once the tree has reached its mature height.

6 The graph shows how, under controlled conditions, the temperature of hot metal changes after it has been removed from the furnace.

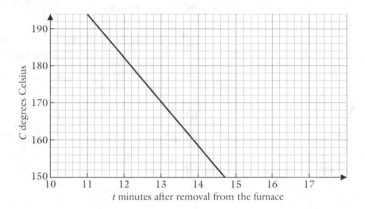

a Find the equation of the line.

Assuming that the rate of cooling remains the same,

b what was the temperature of the metal when it was removed from the furnace

c how long after the metal was removed from the furnace does it take for its temperature to fall to $50\,^{\circ}C$?

7 The graph shows the velocity, v m/s, of a stone t seconds after it is dropped from the top of a cliff.

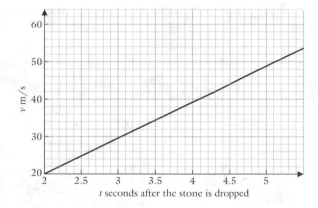

a Find the relationship between v and t.

b What does the gradient of the line mean?

c Assuming that the cliff is high enough, find the velocity of the stone 10 seconds after it is dropped.

LINE GRAPHS

The graph in the picture shows the weekly sales in a company over several months. It is constructed by marking the sales figures for each week and joining the marks with straight lines. A graph constructed in this way is called a *line graph*.

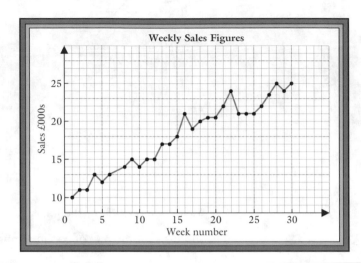

- A quick glance at the graph immediately shows that sales are increasing as time passes.

  Looking more closely, some detailed information can be read straight from the graph; for example £15 000 of sales were made in week 9, sales remained steady in week 14, they rose more rapidly in week 16, and so on.

- Some information cannot be read from this graph; for example it does not tell us the sales on individual days of a week. In fact, the lines between the dots do not tell us anything; they are there to help show the movement of sales figures over time.

- The vertical axis does not start at zero. We can start the axes where we choose. We are also free to choose the scales on the axes. This diagram shows how a different choice affects first visual impressions.

The rise in sales does not now look as impressive as it does on the first version.

EXERCISE 16C

1 When Adam went into hospital, his temperature was taken once every hour and recorded on this chart.

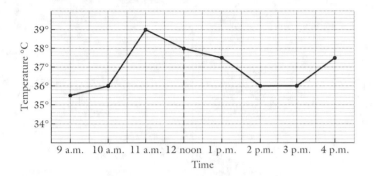

a What was Adam's temperature at 3.30 p.m.? Explain your answer.

b Discuss the visual effect on a temperature chart of scaling the vertical axis from 0° to 50° and whether this is desirable.

2 The trustees of a personal pension fund aim to increase the value of the fund at a rate faster than that of the stock exchange index.

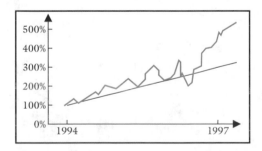

The green line on this chart shows the changes in the percentage value of funds invested by the trustees over a three-year period. The black line represents the value of all shares on the stock exchange.

a The value of all the shares on the stock exchange goes up and down from day to day. Discuss what you think the straight line is and how it is obtained. Discuss also why you think the straight line has been used instead of a line graph.

b Discuss how you would present the graph to show this information in its best possible light for the trustees.

c Discuss how you would present the graph to show this information in its worst possible light.

LINE OF BEST FIT This is the sales graph given on page 380, with the lines omitted. It is now a scatter graph.

There is a strong correlation between the sales figures and the week number. If we draw the line of best fit for these points, this averages out the weekly fluctuations in the sales figures and gives a visual picture of the trend in the sales figures.

We can use the line to get further information.

From this graph, the gradient of the line is $\dfrac{10\,500}{20} = 525$.

This tells us that, for the period shown, sales are increasing at an average rate of £525 per week..

The line cuts the vertical axis at 10 000; we cannot give a meaning to this figure because we do not know what week zero represents. (It could be the last week of the previous year or it could be the week the company started trading.) We can, however, use the intercept on the vertical axis, together with the gradient, to write down the equation of the line of best fit.

If n is the week number and $£S$ the weekly sales, then the equation of the line is $S = 525n + 10\,000$

We can now use this line to predict the weekly sales for, say, week 50; when $n = 50$, $S = 525 \times 50 + 10\,000$
$$= 36\,250$$
i.e. the predicted sales for week 50 are £36 250.

Note that this figure is an estimate and is based on the assumption that the trend stays the same. We can also see that the sales figure on the graph can be as much as £3000 above or below the line of best fit so it may be more reasonable to say that the predicted sales figures for week 50 are in the range £33 000 to £39 000; that is there is a margin of error of about $\pm£3000$.

EXERCISE 16D

1 The scatter diagram shows the level of a pollutant in a lake over the years 1990 to 1997.

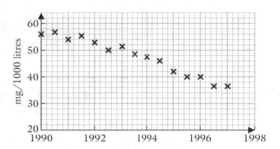

Copy the graph and draw the line of best fit.
Assuming that the trend shown in the graph continues,

a in which year is the level of pollutant expected to fall below 30 mg/1000 litres

b what is the level of pollutant expected to be in the year 2010?

2 The scatter diagram shows the prices and mileages of some second-hand cars of the same make and model.

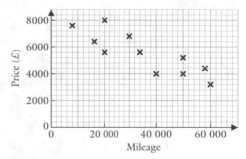

Copy the graph and draw the line of best fit.
Find the equation of your line and use it to estimate

a the price of a car with a mileage of 100 000

b the mileage of a car priced at £8000.

c Give an estimate of the margin of error in your answers to parts **a** and **b**.

3 The number of bad peaches per box after different delivery times are shown in the table.

Number of bad peaches	0	0	1	2	2	3	4	5
Hours in transit	4	2	3	6	10	7	12	14

a Plot this information on a scatter diagram using graph paper and 1 cm ≡ 2 hours and 1 cm ≡ 1 peach.

b Draw the line of best fit and use it to estimate the number of bad peaches in a box that has been in transit for 24 hours. Give an indication of the range of error in your estimate.

4 The scatter diagram shows the values of a share index at the end of each four-week period from the start of 1996 to April 1997.

Draw the line of best fit and find its equation.

Assuming that the trend continues, estimate the value of the share index at the end of the 30th four-week period.

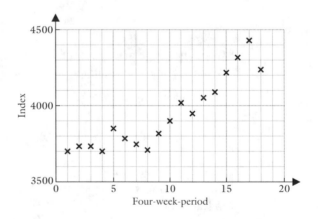

5 The table shows the population living in a town each year from 1980.

Year	1980	1982	1984	1986	1988	1990	1992	1994
Population (000s)	10	11	11.5	13	14	14	15	16.5

a Plot these figures on a scatter diagram. Scale the time axis from 1979 and use 1 cm for one year. Scale the population axis from 8000 and use 1 cm for 1000 people.

b Draw the line of best fit and use it to predict the population in the year 2020. How reliable do you think this prediction is and why?

Drawing a line of best fit by eye relies on personal judgement and the position of the line will inevitably vary from person to person. We can reduce this variability by defining a fixed point that the line must pass through – the point we take has coordinates that are the mean values of the variables.

The table gives information gathered by a researcher about the height and weight of 10 twenty-year-old men.

Height, cm	154	162	190	175	165	181	198	173	186	177	Mean 176.1
Weight, kg	60	63	74	77	65	75	82	71	74	69	Mean 71

a Plot these points on a scatter graph and draw the line of best fit.

b Use your line to estimate the weight of a twenty-year-old man of height 170 cm.

a

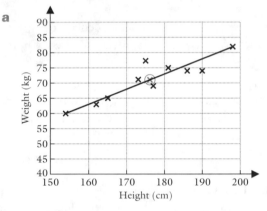

The point representing the mean height and weight is ringed. We draw the line of best fit through this point, aiming again to get the sum of the distances from the line of points above and below about equal.

b The weight of a person 170 cm tall is about 68 kg.

---

6 The height and shoe size of each of twelve women are given in the table.

Height (cm)	158	160	161	163	164	166	166	167	168	170	171	174	Mean 165.7
Shoe size (continental)	37	36	38	39	37	40	38	37	39	42	41	40	Mean 38.7

a Draw a scatter graph to illustrate the information. Scale the height axis from 154 cm using 1 cm for 2 cm of height. Scale the shoe size axis from 35 and use 1 cm for 1 unit.

b Draw the line of best fit to pass through the mean values.

c Find the equation of your line and use it to estimate the shoe size of a woman who is 180 cm tall.

d Explain why it is not sensible to use your line to estimate the shoe size of a girl who is 120 cm tall.

7 The table gives the French mark and the maths mark of each of 10 pupils in an end-of-term examination.

French	45	56	59	65	65	70	71	73	76	80
Maths	50	38	56	70	75	79	64	85	82	75

a Show this information on a graph; use a scale of 1 cm for 5 marks on each axis. Mark the horizontal axis from 40 to 85 for the French mark and the vertical axis from 35 to 90 for the maths mark.

b Calculate the mean French mark and the mean maths mark. Draw the line of best fit using these values.

c Use your line to predict the maths mark of a pupil who had a French mark of 68.

8 a Use the information given in question **3** to calculate the mean number of bad peaches per box and the mean number of hours of a box in transit.

b Use the scatter graph drawn for question **3** and redraw the line of best fit using the mean values found in part **a**. Do not calculate the equation of your new line but estimate the difference it makes to your answer for part **b** of question **3**.

LINEAR RELATIONSHIPS

Sometimes we know that two quantities that can vary are related by a particular law. For example, the resistance, R ohms, of a length of wire is related to the temperature, $t\,°C$ of the wire by the law

$$R = at + b$$

where a and b are constants that depend on the nature and length of the wire.

When we compare $R = at + b$ with the equation $y = mx + c$, we see that the relationship between values of R and t is the same as the relationship between the coordinates of points on a straight line.

Any relationship that can be compared directly with $y = mx + c$ is called a *linear relationship*.

Because $R = at + b$ can be compared directly with $y = mx + c$, we can see that if we plot corresponding values of R and t for a particular length of wire, we expect them to lie on a straight line where a is the gradient of the line and b is the intercept on the R-axis.

First we need some values of R for different values of t. These can be found from measurements in an experiment.

For example,

$t\,^{\circ}C$	20	30	40	50
R ohms	6.62	6.81	7.10	7.29

When we plot these points on a graph, we expect them to lie more or less on a straight line; they are unlikely to lie exactly on a straight line because there is probably some experimental error. We expect some values to be greater than the true values and some to be less.

The graph shows the points, together with the line of best fit which we draw to average out the variation of the points from the line.

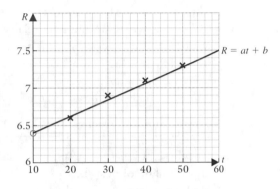

We can now find the equation of the line of best fit.

From the line, the gradient $= \dfrac{1.1}{50} = 0.022$

i.e. we estimate that $a = 0.022$,
giving $R = 0.022t + b$,

$R = 6.4$ when $t = 10$, giving $6.4 = 0.22 + b$,
so we estimate that $b = 6.18$

Therefore the estimated relationship is $R = 0.022t + 6.18$.

EXERCISE 16E

1 These questions refer to the example above this exercise.

   a Discuss why the values found for a and b are estimates.

   b Explain why we used points on the line rather than points plotted from the table to estimate the values of a and b.

   c An alternative method for finding values of a and b without using a graph is to use two pairs of values of R and t from the table and substitute these into the relationship $R = at + b$. This will give a pair of equations that can be solved to find a and b.
This method is much quicker than using a graph as described.
Explain why it is likely to give a poorer estimate for the relationship between R and t.

2 The table shows values of x and y obtained from an experiment.

x	3	5	8	12	15	18
y	2.9	4.4	7.0	10.1	12.4	15.0

These values are related by the equation $y = ax + b$.
Plot these values on a graph and draw the line of best fit.
Use the line to find approximate values for a and b.
Hence estimate the value of y when $x = 20$.

3 The load, M newtons, attached to a spring stretches the spring
to l metres where M and l are related by the law $M = kl + c$
where k and c are constants. The table shows the length of a spring
when different loads attached to it.

Load, M newtons	6	8	12	20	40
Extension, l metres	0.2	0.3	0.4	0.7	1.2

Plot these points on a graph with values of M on the vertical axis and
draw the line of best fit.
Find the equation of the line and hence find estimates for the values
of k and c for this spring.

4 When a train accelerates with constant acceleration, its speed, v km/h,
is related to the time it has been accelerating for, by the equation

$$v = u + at$$

The driver makes a note of the speed at different times as the train
accelerates.

Time, t sec	5	10	20	40	60
Speed, v km/h	12	15	16	22	25

a Compare $v = u + at$ with $y = mx + c$ and state

i whether v or t should be on the horizontal axis

ii whether it is u or a that represents the gradient of the line.

b Plot these points on a graph and state why one of the readings
made by the driver is probably wrong. Which one is it?

c Draw the line of best fit and use your line to find approximate
values of u and a.

d Estimate for how long the train has been accelerating when its
speed reaches 40 km/h.

5 When a train driver applies the brakes so that a train decelerates at a constant rate, the relationship between its speed, v km/h and the time for which it has been braking is $v = u + at$

The table shows the speed of the train at different times.

t sec after applying the brakes	30	60	75	100	180
Speed, v km/h	91	89	87	84	76

a Plot these points on a graph and draw the line of best fit.

b Assuming the deceleration is constant, estimate

  i the speed of the train when the brakes were applied,

  ii how long the train has to brake before it stops.

6 The table shows the water level in a reservoir at weekly intervals during a prolonged drought.

Number of weeks since rain, n	1	2	3	4	5	6	7	8
Water level, h metres	28	26	24	23	21	19	17	15

h and n are connected by the relationship $h = kn + c$.

a Plot these points on a graph and draw the line of best fit.

b Use your line to estimate the water level in the reservoir when it last rained.

c The water company has to stop drawing water from the reservoir when the level falls below 5 metres. Estimate when this will happen if there is no more rain.

7 The air temperature, t °C, outside an aircraft and the height, h metres, at which it is flying are related by the law $t = mh + n$ where m and n are constants.

The table shows some values of t for different values of h.

h metres	1000	2500	5000	7500	10 000
t °C	8	-1	-18	-34	-50

Plot these values of t against h on a graph.

Use your graph to estimate

a the temperature outside the aircraft when it is flying at 9000 m

b the height which the aircraft must not exceed if it is dangerous to fly when the outside temperature falls below -56 °C.

NON-LINEAR RELATIONSHIPS

When a car increases speed at a constant rate, the distance, D metres, it travels is related to its speed, V km/h, by the equation $D = kV^2 + c$. The relationship between D and V is quadratic so if we plot experimental values of D against values of V we expect them to lie more or less on a parabola. Trying to draw 'a best fit' parabola to a set of points is not easy.

However, if we compare $\qquad D = k(V^2) + c$

with $\qquad y = mx + c$

we see that values of D plotted against values of V^2 give points that lie on a straight line.

The gradient of the line gives the value of k and the intercept on the D-axis gives the value of c.

EXERCISE 16F

1 A car accelerated slowly so that the speed increased at a constant rate. The passenger took the following readings from the speedometer and mileometer which was set at zero when the acceleration started.

V mph	10	20	30	40	50
D miles	0.15	0.45	1.00	1.65	2.60

The relationship between D and V is given by $D = kV^2 + c$

a Copy and complete this table.

V mph	10	20	30	40	50
V^2	100				
D miles	0.15	0.45	1.00	1.65	2.60

b Plot values of D against values of V^2. Draw the line of best fit.

c Find estimates for the values of k and c.

d Estimate

  i the speed of the car when it started to accelerate
  ii how far the car had travelled when the speed reached 45 mph.

e Assuming that the car had continued to accelerate at the same rate, estimate how far it would have travelled when the speed reached 70 mph.

2 When doing an emergency stop, the distance, s km, travelled by a car is related to its speed, v km/h, before the brakes are applied, by the law

$$s = kv^2$$

where k is a constant.

The following information was recorded for a car doing emergency stops from different initial speeds.

v km/h	40	60	80	100	120
s km	0.04	0.10	0.17	0.24	0.38

a Copy the table and add another row for values of v^2.

b Plot corresponding values of v^2 and s on a graph and draw the line of best fit.

c Estimate the value of k.

d Estimate the distance travelled by a car doing an emergency stop from a starting speed of 200 km/h.

3 Values of X and Y are related by the equation

$$Y = A\left(\frac{1}{X}\right) + B$$

where A and B are constants.

The table gives corresponding values of X and Y obtained by experiment.

X	2.2	4.5	6.1	7.9
Y	3.0	2.3	2.2	2.1

a Compare $Y = A\left(\frac{1}{X}\right) + B$ with $y = mx + c$ to determine what values should be plotted against Y to give a straight line.

b Copy the table and add another row for the values to be plotted against Y.
Calculate these values correct to 2 significant figures.

c Plot the points on a graph and hence estimate the values of A and B.

4 In each part, the relationship between x and y is given together with a table of corresponding values of x and y. In each case state, in terms of x, the values that need to be calculated so that a straight line is obtained when these values are plotted against the corresponding values of y.

Check your answer by adding the appropriate values to the table and then use squared paper to make a rough plot of these values against the corresponding values of y.

a $y = A(1 - x)^2 + B$

x	1	2	3	4
y	5	7	13	23

b $y = A\sqrt{x} + B$

x	1	2	3	4
y	5	6.7	8.0	9.0

c $y = Ax^3 + B$

x	1	2	3	4
y	1	-2.5	-12	-30

5 Judy thinks that the time taken, t seconds, for a disc to slide from rest down a rough slope, is related to the roughness, μ, of the slope by the equation $\mu = A - \dfrac{k}{t^2}$ where k is a constant.

(μ is a Greek letter pronounced 'mew'.)

She gathers the information in the table by timing the disc as it slides down different slopes all of the same length.

t	1.5	2.6	5	7.4	8.1
μ	0.9	5.6	7.3	7.6	7.7

a Judy then plots values of $\dfrac{1}{t^2}$ against the corresponding values of μ to determine whether the relationship is correct. Explain what she should find when she does this.

b Plot values of $\dfrac{1}{t^2}$ against the corresponding values of μ on a graph and describe the result.

INVESTIGATION

Regression lines

The line of best fit drawn on a scatter diagram is called a *regression line*. It is possible to calculate the equation of a regression line. Consider this set of points.

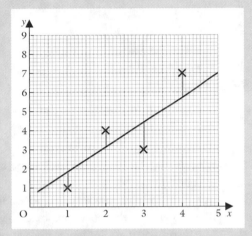

In this investigation we are aiming to find the line which assumes that the x-values are correct, so we work with the difference in the y-values of the plotted points and the corresponding y-values on the line. This is called the regression line of y on x.

Because some points are above the line and others are below the line, we use the squares of the differences in y-values.

If the line is $y = ax + b$, we need to find values of a and b so that the sum of the squares of the lengths of the blue lines on the diagram is a minimum.

Investigate how these values can be found.

Can you generalise the result?

PROBABILITY

There are 4 blue discs
and 5 black discs in this bag.

One disc is to be taken out.
The probability that this disc will be black is $\frac{5}{9}$ and the probability that it will be blue is $\frac{4}{9}$.
A second disc is now to be removed from the bag. Before we can find the probability that it will be black we need to know whether the first disc is returned to the bag before another one is removed.

- If the first disc is put back there are again 9 discs, 5 of which are black and 4 of which are blue. Therefore the colour of the first disc removed has no effect on the probabilities of the second disc being black or blue, that is, the two events are independent.
- If the first disc is not returned, then we know that there are 8 discs left in the bag. However, unless we know the colour of the first disc removed, we do not know whether there are 4 or 5 black discs left; that is, the number of black discs left is conditional upon the colour of the first disc removed. In the same way the number of blue discs left depends on the colour of the first disc removed. In this case, the events are not independent.

EXERCISE 17A

Determine whether the number of ways in which the event described can occur is independent of, or conditional on, the other event.

1 A blue and a red dice are thrown and the red dice scores 6.

2 A bag of sweets contains toffees and wine gums. Julie eats one sweet and then chooses a toffee.

3 Two cards are dealt from an ordinary pack of 52 playing cards and the second card is red.

4 A £1 coin and a 2 p coin are tossed and the £1 coin lands head up.

**CONDITIONAL
PROBABILITY**

Consider again the bag containing 4 blue discs and 5 black discs. If two discs are removed from the bag then, unless we know the colour of the first disc removed, we cannot find the probability that the second disc is black because we do not know how many black discs are left.

However, if we are told that the first disc is blue, then we know that there are 8 discs left of which 5 are black. In this case, the probability that the second disc is black is $\frac{5}{8}$. This probability is conditional upon the first disc being blue and we can write it as

$$P(\text{ 2nd disc black given 1st disc blue }) = \tfrac{5}{8}$$

EXERCISE 17B

A card is drawn from a pack of 52 playing cards.

a What is the probability of drawing a red card?

b If the first card is red and is not replaced what is the probability that a second card drawn is red?

a $P(\text{ red card }) = \frac{26}{52} = \frac{1}{2}$ There are 26 red cards out of 52.

b   There are now 25 red cards left out of 51 cards.

$$P(\text{ 2nd red card given 1st card red }) = \tfrac{25}{51}$$

1 A bag contains 5 red beads and 3 blue beads.

    a What is the probability of drawing   **i** a red bead   **ii** a blue bead?

    b If a red bead is drawn first and is not replaced, what is now the probability of drawing a blue bead?

    c If a red bead is drawn first and not replaced, what is the probability of drawing a second red bead?

2 A card is drawn from a pack of 52 cards.

    a Give the probability of drawing   **i** a nine   **ii** a heart.

    b If a heart is drawn and not replaced, what is now the probability of drawing a heart?

    c If a nine is drawn first and not replaced, what is now the probability of drawing a ten?

3 A hutch contains 4 white and 5 grey guinea pigs. When the door is opened they come out in random order.

   a Give the probability that the first out is white.

   b If the first out is white, what is the probability that the second out is

     i white   **ii** grey?

   c If the first out is grey, what is the probability that the second out is

     i white   **ii** grey?

The table shows the results of tossing two apparently identical 2 p coins one after the other several times. One coin is biased so that a head is more likely than a tail. The other coin is not biased.

	Head	Tail
Biased coin	296	124
Fair coin	199	221

Peter sees just one coin tossed.

a What is the probability that the coin lands head up?

b What is the probability that the coin is the biased one?

c Given that the coin lands head up, what is the probability that it is the biased coin?

a

> To find the probability that the coin lands head up, we need to find how many tosses there are and how many of these are heads.

There are $296 + 124 + 199 + 221$ tosses, i.e. 840 tosses.

There are $296 + 199$ heads, i.e. 495 heads.

Therefore $P(\text{a head}) = \frac{495}{840} = 0.59$ (correct to 2 d.p.)

b The biased coin is tossed $296 + 124$ times $= 420$ times out of a total of 840 tosses.

Therefore $P(\text{biased coin}) = \frac{420}{840} = 0.5$

c There are 495 heads of which 296 are on the biased coin.

Therefore $P(\text{coin is biased given it lands head up}) = \frac{296}{495}$

$$= 0.60 \text{ (correct to 2 d.p.)}$$

---

4 The table shows one day's sales of tins of baked beans and jars of instant coffee from two supermarkets.

	Baked beans	Instant coffee
Ascos	256	145
Blacks	494	127

Rashid went into both supermarkets that day and bought just one tin of baked beans. What is the probability that he bought it in Blacks?

5 The orders for food and alcohol of all the customers in a wine bar one evening are summarised in the table.

	Ordered a meal but not alcohol	Ordered alcohol but not a meal	Ordered both alcohol and a meal
Male	16	58	48
Female	49	30	25

One customer is chosen at random. What is the probability that the customer

a is male

b orders a meal

c orders alcohol given that the customer is male

d is female given that the customer does not order a meal?

6 The diagram shows two bags of boiled sweets.

Brown bag   White bag

One bag is chosen at random and then one sweet is chosen at random from that bag. What is the probability that

a the brown bag is chosen

b given that a black sweet is chosen, it came out of the brown bag?

7 This table shows the number of cars and off-street parking places owned by the households in a street.

	0 car	1 car	2 cars
0 off-street parking place	6	15	4
1 off-street parking place	2	27	12
2 off-street parking places	0	8	10

a How many households are there in the street?

b If one household is selected at random, what is the probability that it has no off-street parking places?

c One household owns two cars. What is the probability that it also owns two off-street parking places?

8 There are three cages of mice in the Dan Pet Shop. Ben buys a mouse.

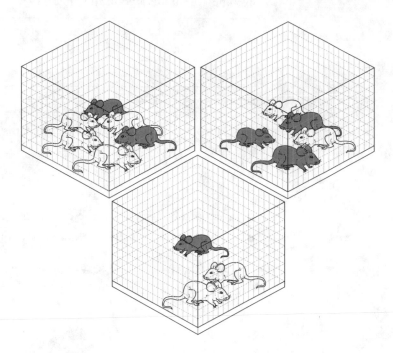

a What is the probability that he buys a white mouse?

b Given that Ben buys a white mouse, what is the probability that it came from the cage with just one black mouse in it?

9 The table shows the results of a canvass into voting intentions at the next general election.

	Conservative	Labour	Liberal Democrat	Don't know or will not vote
Male over 30	20	25	4	5
Female over 30	15	12	2	12
Male under 30	10	20	6	15
Female under 30	12	25	1	18

a How many males were canvassed?

b What percentage of the people canvassed said they would vote Labour?

c Given that one of the people canvassed, chosen at random, intends to vote Conservative, what is the probability that the person is under 30?

TREE DIAGRAMS FOR DEPENDENT EVENTS

Returning again to the bag containing 4 blue and 5 black discs, we know that, when two discs are removed, the number of ways in which a second disc can be black depends on whether the first disc removed was black or blue. To find the probability that the second disc is black, we have to consider both of these possibilities and this can be done by using a tree diagram. The next worked example shows how this is done.

EXERCISE 17C

Two discs are taken out of this bag.
Draw a tree diagram to show the possible combinations of colours of the discs and use it to find the probability that the second disc is black.

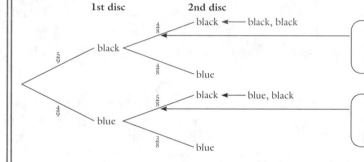

1st disc   2nd disc

black $\frac{5}{9}$ — $\frac{4}{8}$ black ← black, black

This branch comes from the first disc being black so 4 of the 8 remaining discs are black.

$\frac{4}{8}$ blue

blue $\frac{4}{9}$ — $\frac{5}{8}$ black ← blue, black

This branch comes from the first disc being blue so 5 of the 8 remaining discs are black.

$\frac{3}{8}$ blue

Now we can see that the second disc is black at the ends of two paths.
Remember that we *multiply* the probabilities when we follow a path along the branches and *add* the results of following several paths.

$$\text{P(2nd disc is black)} = \frac{5}{9} \times \frac{4}{8} + \frac{4}{9} \times \frac{5}{8}$$

$$= \frac{5}{18} + \frac{5}{18} = \frac{5}{9}$$

1 A box contains ten counters; six are black and four are white.
One counter is to be taken from the bag and then another.

  a Copy and complete the tree diagram.

  b Use your tree diagram to find the probability that   **i** both counters are white
        ii both counters are black
        iii the second counter is black.

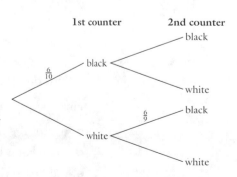

1st counter   2nd counter

black $\frac{6}{10}$ — black / white

white — $\frac{6}{9}$ black / white

2 A bag contains four green beads and five yellow beads. Two beads are withdrawn at random.

   a Find the probability that the first bead is green.

   b If the first bead is yellow find the probability that the second bead is green.

   Draw a tree diagram to show the probabilities when two beads are withdrawn and find the probability that

   c both beads are green.

   d the first bead is yellow and the second is green.

3 A hand of ten cards contains four hearts and six clubs. Two cards are drawn at random from the hand.

   a What is the probability that the first card is a heart?

   b If the first card is a heart what is the probability that the second card is a heart?

   c Draw a tree diagram and find the probability that both cards are clubs.

4 Seven cards are numbered 1 to 7 and two cards are drawn at random. Draw a probability tree to show the probabilities of drawing odd or even cards. Find the probability that

   a the first card is even

   b both cards are even

   c both cards are odd

   d the first card is even and the second is odd

   e the first card is odd and the second is even

   f one card is odd and one even in any order.

5 A birdcage contains six blue and three green budgerigars. The door is small and allows only one bird at a time to fly out and when it is opened the birds fly out in random order.

   a What is the probability that the first bird out is blue?

   b If the first bird out is blue, what is the probability that the second bird out is blue?

   Find the probability that

   c one of the first two birds is blue and one green

   d the second bird is green

   e the first three birds out are all blue.

6 Simon has six grey socks and four white ones in a drawer. He takes out two socks in the dark. What is the probability that

a the second sock taken out is grey

b the socks are of different colours?

7 Two of these cards are dealt face up.

a The first card dealt is 1. What is the probability that the second card dealt is a multiple of 3?

b What is the probability that the sum of the numbers on the cards is 9?

c In a betting game, two of these cards are dealt. The punter pays £1 before the deal and, if the sum of the numbers on the two cards dealt is 7, £1.50 is given back to the punter. What are the chances of winning money on this game?

8 Rachel works for a market research company. The table shows the numbers of each category of person she interviews for one survey.

Male aged 50 or over	Female aged 50 or over	Male over 25 but under 50	Female over 25 but under 50	Male aged 25 or less	Female aged 25 or less
5	4	9	10	8	12

Rachel's supervisor checks her work by randomly selecting two of the people interviewed and then asking them questions.
What is the probability that the supervisor selects

a two people aged 25 or less   **b** one male and one female

9 A green dice has faces marked
1, 2, 3, 6, 6, 6.
A grey dice has faces marked
1, 2, 3, 4, 5, 6.
One dice is chosen at random
and then rolled.
Copy and complete the tree diagram.

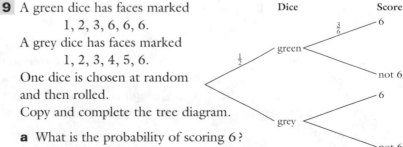

a What is the probability of scoring 6?

b Given that a six is scored, what is the probability that it was with the green dice?

Sometimes not all the branches on a tree diagram reach the right-hand edge.

Ann wants to attend a one-year Art course at Swarbridge College where competition for places on the course is high. She is told that, for a person applying now, the chance of being selected this year is 60%. However, if she fails to get in this year, her chance of being accepted for the following year is increased to 75% and should she fail to get in then her chance of being selected for the third year rises to 90%.

a Draw a tree diagram showing this information.

b Calculate the probability that Ann will be offered a place

   i next year   **ii** the year after next.

c 400 people have applied for the course this year. How many of these applicants will be likely to be accepted for this year?

d What is the chance that an applicant this year will get on the course either this year, next year or the year after?

a

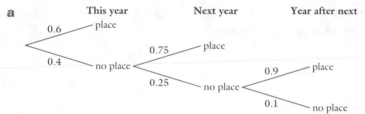

b **i** P(place next year) $= 0.4 \times 0.75 = 0.3$

   ii P(place year after next) $= 0.4 \times 0.25 \times 0.9 = 0.09$

c Probability that an applicant gets a place the year they apply is 0.6, therefore 400×0.6 of this year's applicants are likely to get a place, i.e. 240 are likely to get a place.

d P(place either this year, next year or the year after)

      $= 1 - \text{P(no place after 3 years)} = 1 - 0.4 \times 0.25 \times 0.1 = 1 - 0.01 = 0.99$

> Alternatively, we can add the probabilities of a place either this year or next year or the year after next,
> i.e. $0.6 + 0.4 \times 0.75 + 0.4 \times 0.25 \times 0.9 = 0.6 + 0.3 + 0.09 = 0.99$

10 Andy is not a very good navigator. When he enters a small town the probability that he gets lost and cannot find the correct road to continue his journey is 0.2. When he enters a large town, the probability that he does not find the correct exit road is 0.25. He starts on a journey that passes through two small towns followed by one large town. Draw a tree diagram to represent this information and use it to find the probability that

    a he reaches the second small town and leaves it on the correct road

    b he reaches the large town but fails to find the correct exit road.

11 A student at the Moneywise School of Accountancy has a 70% chance of passing an accountancy examination at the first attempt. Each time a student retakes an examination, the student's chance of passing is reduced by 10%, i.e. there is a 60% chance of passing after one failure and so on.

a Copy the tree diagram given below and fill in the missing probabilities.

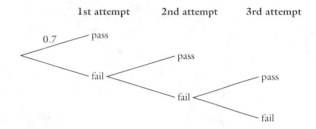

b Calculate the probability that a Moneywise student chosen at random will pass

   i at the second attempt
   ii at the third attempt.

c Out of 100 Moneywise students chosen at random how many should pass

   i at the first attempt
   ii at the second attempt
   iii at the third attempt?

d What is the chance that a student chosen at random will pass at either the first or the second or the third attempt?

12 Amjun and Sabina play a game with a dice. The game is won by rolling a 6.

a What is the probability that a 6 is scored when the dice is rolled?

b Amjun goes first. Draw a tree diagram to show the probabilities after each player has had up to two turns.

c What is the probability that

   i Sabina wins on her first turn
   ii Amjun wins either on his first turn or on his second turn?

d They play the game 500 times, taking it in turns to go first. Should they win approximately the same number of games each? About how many games should Sabina win on her first turn?

13 Hannah and Ted play a game by tossing two coins together. Hannah plays first and the first to get two heads wins.

  a For one turn in any game, what is the chance

  i of getting two heads   **ii** of not getting two heads?

  b Copy the tree diagram and fill in the missing probabilities.

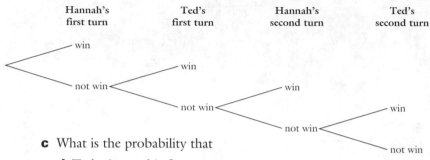

Hannah's first turn Ted's first turn Hannah's second turn Ted's second turn

win — not win — win — not win — win — not win — win — not win

  c What is the probability that

  i Ted wins on his first turn
  ii Hannah wins on her second turn?

  d They play the game 256 times. How many of these is Ted likely to have won on his second turn?

14 An analysis of the pass rates at a driving school shows that 70% of their pupils pass the driving test at their first attempt, 65% of those who retake pass at their second attempt and 60% of those who retake again pass at their third attempt. Find the probability that

  a a pupil passes the test at the second attempt

  b a pupil fails to pass after three attempts.

15 A bag contains 8 red discs, 5 white discs and 3 blue discs. All the discs are identical apart from their colour. The bag and its contents are to be used in a game for two players. Players take a disc from the bag in turn and do not replace it; the object of the game is to select two discs of the same colour. The first person to do this wins. Alison goes first and selects a red disc. Betty goes next and selects a white disc.

  a What is the probability that Alison will win on her next turn?

  b What is the probability that Betty will win on her next turn? (Remember that this infers that Alison did not select a red disc for her second turn.)

  c Explain why this is not a fair game.

  d They decide to change the rules to make it fairer. Betty will make her second selection before Alison. Repeat parts **a** and **b**. Is the game any fairer now? Explain your answer.

MIXED EXERCISE

This exercise contains a variety of probability problems. Some problems involve one event, others involve more than one event which may or may not be independent. Read each question carefully.

EXERCISE 17D

1 A multiple choice test has five questions. Each question has five possible answers, only one of which is correct.

a Robin knows that he has got one question wrong. What is the probability that he gets full marks?

b Hanna knows the correct answers to three questions but has to guess the other two. What is the probability that she gets full marks?

c Tom guesses all the answers. What is the probability that he gets full marks?

2 A card is drawn from a well-shuffled pack of 52 playing cards. Find the probability that the card is

a an ace   **b** a spade   **c** either an ace or a spade.

3 Two cards are dealt face up on the table from a well-shuffled pack. Find the probability that

a the first card is an ace

b if the first card is an ace, the second card is also an ace

c one of the cards is an ace.

4 A game consists of dealing two cards from a well-shuffled pack of 52 playing cards. If both cards are the same suit, the player can select a prize from a selection on a table. What are the chances of winning a prize?

5 A coin is biased so that when it is tossed, the probability that it lands head up is 0.8.
This coin is tossed three times. What is the probability that more tails than heads appear?

6 Three coins are tossed. Two of the coins are fair and one is biased so that the probability that it lands head up is 0.8. What is the probability that more tails appear than heads?

7 Three coins are such that two are fair and one is biased so that the probability that it lands head up is 0.8. One of these coins is selected at random and then tossed. Given that it lands head up, what is the probability that it is the biased coin?

8 The diagram shows part of a snakes and ladders board.

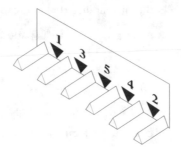

Helen's counter is on square 13. On her next turn, what is the probability that

a she goes down the snake

b she goes up the ladder

c she misses both the snake and the ladder?

9 In a sideshow, a player has to roll two balls towards five channels marked with the scores 1 to 5. The ball must go into one of the channels.

The probabilities of getting the ball into the different channels are
$P(1) = \frac{1}{10}$, $P(2) = \frac{1}{10}$, $P(3) = \frac{1}{5}$, $P(4) = \frac{1}{5}$, $P(5) = \frac{2}{5}$
A player wins £5 if the total score from both balls is 4 or less.

a Find the probability that a player wins £5.

b It costs £1 to play this game. The organisers expect 500 people to play the game on the day of the fête. How much money do they expect to make?

10 Two sprinters, Linford and Harold, are due to run in the 100 m and 200 m in the county sports.
The probability that Linford will win the 100 m is $\frac{1}{5}$ and that he will win the 200 m is $\frac{3}{10}$ while, irrespective of Linford's performance, the probability that Harold will win the 100 m is $\frac{1}{4}$ and the probability that he will win the 200 m is $\frac{1}{7}$. Find the probability that

a Linford will win both races

b Harold wins the 100 m and Linford wins the 200 m

c neither wins either race

d the two win one race between them.

11 This table summarises a survey of children under the age of 16. Each child was asked if he/she had smoked or consumed alcohol in the previous seven days.

	Smoked only	Drunk alcohol only	Both	Neither
Boys	6	35	8	20
Girls	10	27	14	30

  a One of these children is selected at random. What is the probability that the child is a girl?

  b How many of the boys questioned smoked?

  c Two of these children are selected at random. The first child is a girl. What is the probability that the second child is also a girl?

  d Copy and complete the tree diagram.

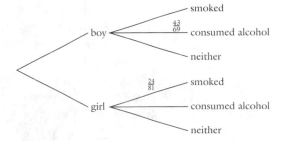

  e Use the tree diagram to find the probability that one of these children selected at random neither smoked nor drank alcohol.

  f Explain why the tree diagram cannot be used to find the probability that a randomly selected child did not smoke.

PUZZLE

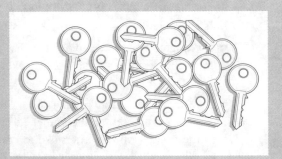

One student decided to play a trick on the other 20 students in his group. He borrowed the keys to their lockers and removed all identification from the keys. As the keys look the same, there is no way of telling which key fits which lock. The other students get their revenge by making him sort the keys out by trying the keys in the locks until he finds the ones that fit. What is the *maximum* number of times that he may have to try keys in locks until all are sorted?

INVESTIGATION

This is a game for two players.

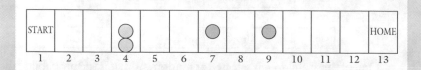

Each player has two counters, and they take turns to throw two dice.
At the start of the game, both counters are off the board.
The player who throws can either move one counter by the total
number shown on the dice or move one counter by the number on
one dice and the other counter by the number on the second dice.
If a counter lands on a square occupied by the other player's counter,
that other player's counter has to start again.
The object of the game is to get both counters to the home square
before the other player. If a counter is, say, on square 11, any score
greater than 1 can be used to get the counter to the home square.

For example, in the diagram the two blue counters belong to Amy
and the two grey counters belong to Tim. It is Amy's turn and she
throws a 3 and a 6. She has the choice of moving one counter nine
places to get one counter home or she can move one counter three
places, so making Tim start again with one of his counters, and her
other counter six places, which then makes both counters vulnerable
to being landed on when Tim has his next turn.

a Which of the two options would you advise Amy to take and why?

b Is this a game of pure chance? Justify your answer.

c Investigate whether Amy or Tim has the better chance of winning
from the position shown if Amy takes the option of moving both
counters.

d Investigate this game further; find a partner to play with a few
times to get a feel for the game.
Some points you may then like to consider are
What is the least number of turns needed to win?
Is the best policy always to move just one counter as far as
possible
Does the player who starts have an advantage?

SUMMARY 5

**SIMILAR
FIGURES**

The *ratio of the areas of similar figures* is equal to the square of the ratio of their sides.

The *ratio of the volume of similar figures* is equal to the cube of the ratio of their sides.

**STANDARD
DEVIATION**

The standard deviation of n values, $x_1, x_2, x_3, \ldots, x_n$, is given by

$$\text{s.d.} = \sqrt{\frac{\sum(x - \bar{x})^2}{n}} \equiv \sqrt{\frac{\sum x^2}{n} - \bar{x}^2}$$

where $\bar{x}$ is the mean value.

The standard deviation of a frequency distribution is given by

$$\text{s.d.} = \sqrt{\frac{\sum f(x - \bar{x})^2}{\sum f}} \equiv \sqrt{\frac{\sum fx^2}{\sum f} - \bar{x}^2}$$

where $\bar{x}$ is the mean value.

For a grouped distribution, x is the midclass value and the formula gives an estimate for the standard deviation.

PROBABILITY

When the number of ways in which an event can happen depends on what has already happened, the probability that the second event occurs is conditional on what happened first.

For example, if two discs are removed from a bag containing 2 red and 2 yellow discs then the probability that the second disc to be removed is red depends on the colour of the first disc removed. If the first disc is red, $P(\text{2nd red}) = \frac{1}{3}$, but if the first disc is yellow, $P(\text{2nd red}) = \frac{2}{3}$.

**REVISION
EXERCISE 5.1
(Chapters 14
and 15)**

1

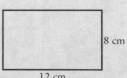

5 cm

8 cm

12 cm

These two rectangles are similar. Find

a the length of the smaller rectangle   **b** the ratio of their areas.

2

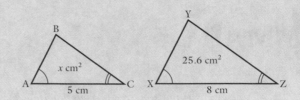

Triangles ABC and XYZ are similar, with $\widehat{A} = \widehat{X}$ and $\widehat{C} = \widehat{Z}$. If $AC = 5\,cm$, $XZ = 8\,cm$ and the area $\triangle XYZ = 25.6\,cm^2$ find the area of $\triangle ABC$.

3 The radii of two spheres are in the ratio $5:4$. What is the ratio of their volumes?

4 In $\triangle ABC$, $AX = 3\,cm$, $AB = 7\,cm$ and XY is parallel to BC. Find

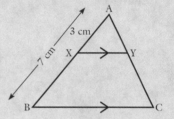

a $\dfrac{AY}{YC}$ **b** $\dfrac{XY}{BC}$ **c** $\dfrac{\text{area } \triangle AXY}{\text{area } \triangle ABC}$

5 The ratio of the areas of two similar labels on two similar cylindrical cans is $25:36$. Find the ratio of

a the heights of the two cans   **b** their capacities.

6 The masses of 5 letters which are to be sent by first class post are:

$$52\,g \quad 34\,g \quad 62\,g \quad 35\,g \quad 27\,g$$

Find the standard deviation of these masses.

7 Ian and Jean each kept a record for one week of the time in hours they spent doing homework. The details are given in the table.

	Mon	Tues	Wed	Thurs	Fri	Sat	Sun
Ian	$1\frac{1}{2}$	1	$\frac{1}{2}$	2	–	–	2
Jean	1	2	$1\frac{1}{2}$	$\frac{1}{2}$	1	2	4

a Without doing any calculations, write down estimates for the mean and standard deviation of each set of times.

b Calculate the mean and standard deviation of each set.

c Compare the two sets of times.

8 The table shows the number of sweet pea plants per pot that have germinated after two weeks.

Number of plants	3	4	5	6	7
Frequency	2	5	6	4	1

Calculate the mean number of sweet pea plants per pot and find the standard deviation.

9 **a** This bar chart shows the council tax levied in the different local authorities of a region of the United Kingdom for properties in Band C.
Find the mean and standard deviation of these values.

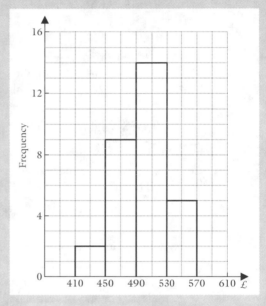

b This bar chart shows similar information for a second region of the country.
Find the mean and standard deviation for this data.

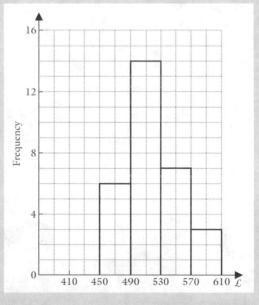

c Make at least two comparisons between the council tax levied for Band C properties in these two regions of the UK.

10 Sabina weighed 10 tomatoes separately using her kitchen scales. She recorded their masses as 85 g, 104 g, 100 g, 93 g, 143 g, 84 g, 88 g, 93 g, 109 g and 105 g.

a Find the mean and standard deviation of these masses.

b When she has finished she noticed that the scales was set at 25 g instead of 0. Write down the correct mean and standard deviation for these 10 tomatoes.

11 The diagram represents a metal cone of height 90 cm made in two parts, labelled T and S. The top part, T, has a height of 45 cm.

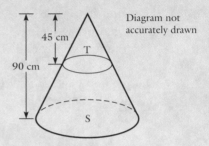

Given that the volume of S and T together is $10\,500\,\pi\,cm^3$

a calculate the volume of S.

A second cone is also made up of two parts A and B. The radius of the top part is 20 cm and the radius of the base of B is 30 cm. The height of bottom part B is 120 cm.

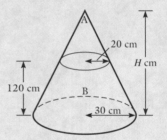

b Calculate the height, H cm, of the cone. (London)

12 This set of marks was obtained by 10 pupils in an English GCSE examination.

   73, 70, 62, 67, 69, 76, 55, 65, 61, 82

The mean of this set of marks is 68.

a Calculate the standard deviation of these marks. All the ten pupils had their marks increased by 3 for good spelling.

b Write down for the *new* set of marks

   i the mean
   ii the standard deviation. (London)

1 Use the information on the graph to find the equation of the line.

a   **b**

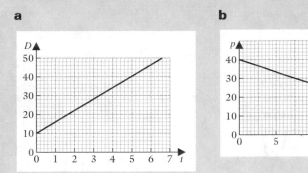

2 Find the gradient of each line. Give a meaning to the gradient in the context of the graph.

a   **b**

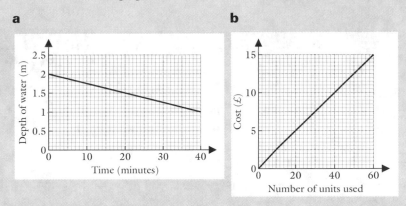

3 The advertising costs and profits of eight small companies over a period of one year are given in the table.

Advertising costs £000s, A	20	50	10	25	35	15	40	30
Profit in millions of £s, P	1.4	1.75	1.25	1.4	1.65	1.2	1.66	1.55

a Plot these points on a graph and comment on the relationship between A and P. Draw the line of best fit.

b From your graph estimate

  i the profit when the amount spent on advertising is £44 000.
  ii the cost of advertising that should give a profit of £1.5m.

c The relationship between A and P is given by the equation $P = mA + c$ where m and c are constants.
Use your graph to estimate the value of **i** m **ii** c.
Hence write down the equation connecting P and A.

4

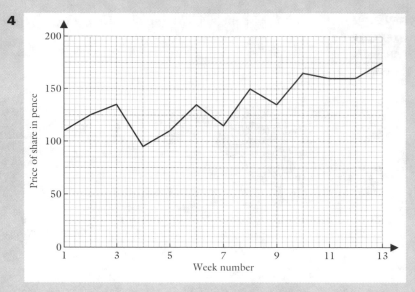

Week number

This graph shows the price of Supermark Plc ordinary shares at the close of business each week for a 13-week period.

a What was the price of the share at the close of business on week 11 ?

b Which week produced the greatest gain ? How much was this gain ?

c Which week produced the greatest loss ? How much was this loss ?

d How would you describe the general trend in the share price ?

e If this trend continues, what do you predict the price will be at the end of week 19 ?

5 The flow of water, x litres per minute, through a circular hole in the bottom of a tank is believed to obey the relationship $x = k\sqrt{H}$, where H metres is the depth of water in the tank. For the hole in one particular tank the following results were obtained.

Depth of water, H m	2	3	4.5	6
Rate of flow, x litres per minute	113	139	170	196

a Copy the table and add another row for the values of $\sqrt{H}$.

b Plot the corresponding values of $\sqrt{H}$ and x on a graph and draw the line of best fit.

c Estimate

   i the value of k

   ii the flow of water through the hole when the depth of water is 4 metres.

6 A card is drawn at random from an ordinary pack of 52 cards.

   a What is the probability of drawing **i** an ace   **ii** a spade?

   b If a spade is drawn and not replaced, what is the probability that a second card drawn will be a spade?

   c If an ace is drawn first and not replaced what is the probability that a king is the next card drawn?

7 A bag contains 8 counters; 5 are red and the remainder are blue. Two counters are taken from the bag.

   a What is the probability that the first counter is red?

   b If the first counter is blue what is the probability that the second counter is red?

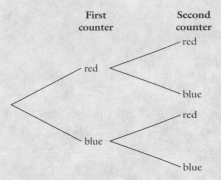

Copy and complete the tree diagram.

   c Use your tree diagram to find the probability that

     i both counters are red
    ii both counters are blue
   iii the second counter is blue.

8 A box contains 18 cartons of yoghurt; 6 are banana-flavoured, 4 are peach-flavoured and the remainder are strawberry-flavoured. Two cartons are taken at random from the box. What is the probability that the yoghurts are

   a both banana-flavoured

   b both of the same flavour

   c of different flavours?

9 A coin is biased so that when it is tossed the probability that it lands 'head up' is 0.4. This coin is tossed 3 times. What is the probability that more tails than heads appear?

10 One question in a holiday questionnaire was 'Where did you take your main holiday last year – in the UK or abroad?'. The results, which are divided into three categories, are given in the table.

	Abroad	UK	Did not take a holiday
Self-employed	16	8	33
Employee	39	21	12
Retired or not working	24	16	8

a How many people were interviewed?

b If one person is selected at random, what is the probability that that person took their main holiday abroad?

c Given that one of the people interviewed had their last holiday in the United Kingdom, what is the probability that the person is an employee?

11 Alex needs to pass a driving test. The probability that he will pass the test on his first attempt is 0.4.

If he fails his first test, then the probability that he will pass the test on any subsequent attempt is 0.7.

a Calculate the probability that Alex needs two attempts, and passes the test on his second attempt.

b Calculate the probability that Alex passes the test on either his third or fourth attempt.

(SEG)

12

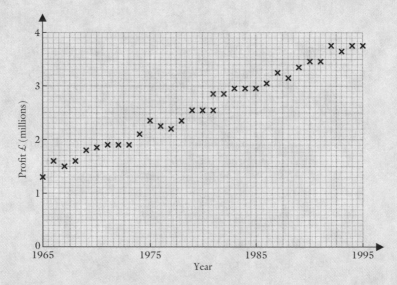

The scatter diagram represents the profits made by a company over the years 1965 to 1995.

Use the diagram to calculate an estimate of the profit the company could expect to get in the year 2000 if this trend continues.

(NEAB)

**REVISION
EXERCISE 5.3
(Chapters 14
to 17)**

1

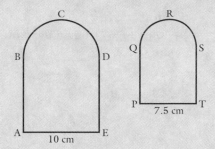

ABCDE and PQRST are similar shapes. If AE = 10 cm,
PT = 7.5 cm and the area of ABCDE is 96 cm², find the area of
PQRST.

2 The areas of the squares ABCD and WXYZ are respectively 98 cm²
and 50 cm².

Find the value of AB : WX.

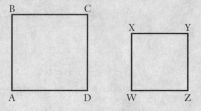

3 a Write down expressions for the surface area A cm² and volume
V cm³ of a sphere of radius r cm.

b The radius of a sphere is increased by 50%. What is the new
radius in terms of r? Hence write down an expression for the
new value of A in terms of r and π.

c By how much, in terms of r and π has the surface area increased?
Express this increase, correct to the nearest whole number, as a
percentage of the original surface area.

d Find, correct to the nearest whole number, the percentage
increase in the volume of the sphere if its radius increases by
50%.

4 The masses of 10 tablets are:

242 g, 253 g, 249 g, 248 g, 242 g, 254 g, 251 g, 240 g, 252 g and 248 g

Find the mean and standard deviation of these masses.

5 The bar chart shows the number of points per match scored by the home rugby team in the Northern League on the first Saturday of the season.

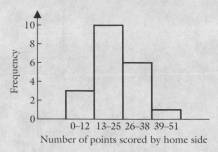

Number of points scored by home side

a Use the bar chart to make a frequency table.

b Find the mean and standard deviation of this distribution.

6 Different masses were attached to a spring and the resulting length of the spring was measured. The results are given in the table.

Length of spring, L cm	16.3	18.5	20.6	23.4	24.3	26.5
Mass, M g	50	100	150	200	250	300

These values are related by the equation $L = aM + b$
Plot these values on a graph and draw the line of best fit.

a Hence estimate   **i** the value of L when $M = 240$
                 ii the value of M when $L = 25$

b The equation of this line can be used to predict the length of the spring when a mass of 30 kg is attached to it. Explain why this prediction is very unlikely to be correct.

7 A trolley accelerates down a slope. Its speed v m/s was measured for different times, t seconds, and the results recorded in the following table.

Time, t seconds	10	20	30	40	50	60
Speed, v m/s	2.2	4.4	6.7	9	11.8	13.4

The values for v and t are connected by the relationship
$v = u + at$ where u and a are constants.

a Plot these values on a graph. (Plot t on the horizontal axis.)

b Draw a line of best fit and use it to estimate the values of u and a.

c Which reading for v is probably wrong? Estimate a better value.

d Explain what meaning you can give to u.

8

	Score	
	6	Not 6
Biased dice	50	153
Unbiased dice	16	84

The table shows the results of rolling two apparently identical dice. One dice is biased so that it is more likely to give a 6. The other dice is unbiased. Paul sees just one dice rolled.

a What is the probability that the dice shows a 6?

b Before he sees the score what is the probability that the dice is the unbiased one?

c Given that the dice shows a 6, what is the probability that it is the unbiased one?

9 A bag contains 40 counters labelled 1 to 40. A prize is awarded if a multiple of 10 is drawn. Nia draws two counters at random.

a What is the probability that the number on the first counter ends in 0?

b If the number on Nia's first counter ends in 0 what is the probability that the number on the second counter also ends in 0?

c

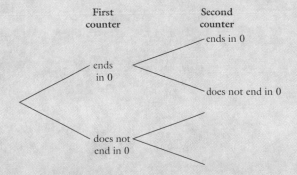

Copy the tree diagram and fill in the missing probabilities. Use it to find the probability that

i Nia wins one prize with two draws

ii Nia wins a prize with both draws.

10 Doug is a photographer and uses a particular type of high speed film. From experience he knows that there is a 75% chance that he can get film when he visits Shorts, a 65% chance when he visits Wetstones and a 50% when he goes to Fetters. Naturally he always visits the shops in the order that gives him the best chance of getting his film.

a Copy the tree diagram given below and fill in the missing probabilities.

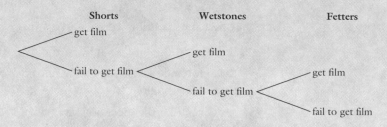

Shorts   Wetstones   Fetters

get film / fail to get film / get film / fail to get film / get film / fail to get film

b Calculate the probability that when Doug next wants film he will get it **i** at Wetstones **ii** at Fetters.

c Doug anticipates that over the next 2 years he will go to buy film on about 50 occasions. On how many of these should he

  i get a film at Wetstones

  ii fail to get film at any one of the three shops?

REVISION EXERCISE 5.4

(Chapters 1 to 17)

Do not use a calculator for any question this exercise.

1 a Express in terms of the simplest possible surd

  i $\sqrt{3} \times \sqrt{8}$ **ii** $\sqrt{50} - \sqrt{18}$

  b Find **i** $(36)^{\frac{1}{2}}$ **ii** $(0.09)^{-\frac{1}{2}}$ **iii** $\left(\frac{1}{27}\right)^{\frac{2}{3}}$

2 a Factorise

  i $2x^2 + 13x + 18$ **iii** $15 + t - 2t^2$

  ii $35x^2 + 4x - 4$ **iv** $3x^2 - 12x - 63$

  b Find the value of $0.6544^2 - 0.3456^2$

  c Solve the equation

  i $(3x - 2)(x - 9) = 0$ **ii** $15x^2 - 28x - 32 = 0$

3 Rewrite $\dfrac{5}{x - 1} + \dfrac{3}{x + 2} = 4$ in the form $ax^2 + bx + c = 0$

Hence solve the equation $\dfrac{5}{x - 1} + \dfrac{3}{x + 2} = 4$.

4 Sketch on the same axes the graphs of $y = x^2$ and $y = 4 - x$ for values of x in the range -5 to 5. Estimate the values of x at the points of intersection of the two graphs.
What equation has these values of x as roots?

5 The graph illustrates the velocity of a train over a six-second interval in a journey.

   a Find the time at which the acceleration is zero.

   b Is the train accelerating or decelerating from $t = 0$ to $t = 4$?

   c Use the trapezium rule with 3 strips to estimate the distance covered by the train in the 6 seconds.

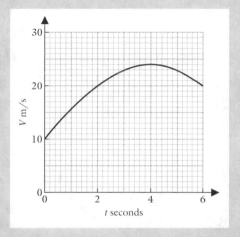

6 Copy the diagram and draw the image of the given shape when it is rotated $90°$ anticlockwise about the point $(2, 2)$ followed by a translation defined by the vector $\begin{pmatrix} 2 \\ -4 \end{pmatrix}$. Mark the final image P.
Describe the transformation that maps the given shape directly onto P.

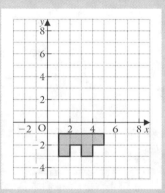

7 a Is it possible to draw a triangle in which AB = 6.3 cm,
AC = 12.6 cm and $\widehat{A} = 60°$?
Give a reason for your answer.

b In △DEF, EF = 12 cm, DF = 9 cm and $\cos \widehat{F} = 0.5$.
Find DE.

8 PA and PB are the tangents from
P to a circle centre O.

Find   **a** A$\widehat{C}$B   **b** A$\widehat{P}$B

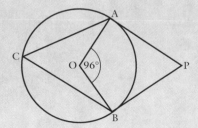

9 The table shows the estimated cost of printing different numbers of
copies of a poster.

Number of copies, n	25	50	100	150
Cost, £C	25	28.50	31.50	35

Plot these points on a graph and draw the line of best fit. Scale both
axes from zero. Use your graph to estimate

a the cost of 80 copies of the poster

b how many posters I could expect to get for £30.

Give a meaning to the value of C at the point where the line of best
fit crosses the C-axis.

10 Two cards are dealt face up on the table from a well-shuffled pack.
Find the probability that

a the first card is a court card. (The court cards of a suit are the
Jack, Queen and King.)

b if the first card is a court card the second car is also a court card

c one of the cards is a court card.

**REVISION
EXERCISE 5.5
(Chapters 1
  to 17)**

1 Solve the equation

a $x^2 - 7x + 5 = 0$ giving your answer correct to 2 decimal places.

b $3x^2 + 13x + 7 = 0$ giving your answers in surd form.

2 a Express as a single fraction

  i $\dfrac{5}{x^2 - 9} + \dfrac{2}{x - 3}$ **ii** $\dfrac{1}{x + 3} - \dfrac{6}{x^2 - 9}$

  b Make g the subject of the formula $T = 2\pi\sqrt{\dfrac{L}{g}}$

3 A curve goes through the points given in the table.

x	0	1	2	3	4	5	6
y	19	32.5	39.5	40	38.5	30	19

Draw a rough sketch of the curve. Use five strips to find the area under the curve from $x = 1$ to $x = 6$. Is your answer greater than or less than the actual area? Justify your answer.

4

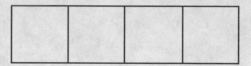

Four identical squares, of side 4.5 cm correct to 1 decimal place, are laid side by side in a line to form a rectangle.

a Find **i** the upper bound of the length of the rectangle
      ii the lower bound of the area of the rectangle.

b The four squares are placed together to form a square. Is the upper bound of the area of the square larger, smaller or the same as the upper bound for the area of the rectangle? Justify your answer.

5 This funnel, for putting oil into an engine, is in the shape of a cone combined with a cylinder of equal radius. The depth of the conical part is equal to its radius and the depth of the cylindrical part is twice the depth of the cone. The funnel is plugged at its base and holds 1.5 litres of oil when full. Find, correct to 3 significant figures

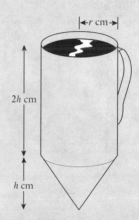

a the depth of the cylindrical part

b the dimensions of the funnel.

6 In △LMN, MN = 14.2 cm, LN = 17.3 cm and LM = 11.8 cm.

Find **a** the smallest angle in the triangle

b the largest angle in the triangle.

7 P is any point on the line that bisects
AB̂C. M is the foot of the
perpendicular from P to AB and N is
the foot of the perpendicular from P to
BC. Show that triangles PMB and
PNB are congruent. What can you
conclude about the lengths of PM and
PN?

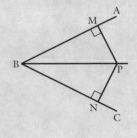

8 A and B are two fixed points.
C is a point which moves so
that AĈB is always 90°.
Describe the locus of C.

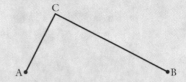

9 Triangles ABC and XYZ are similar. If the area of △ABC is $2\frac{1}{4}$
times that of △XYZ and AB and XY are corresponding sides, what is
the value of AB : XY?

10 The number of tangerines in several packs on a supermarket shelf
were counted and the results recorded in the following table.

Number of tangerines in a pack	6	7	8	9	10
Frequency	3	7	8	6	3

Find the mean and standard deviation for this set of data.

ANSWERS

Answers are supplied to questions asking for estimates but there is no 'correct' estimate; we have given a likely value.

Allow a reasonable margin of error for answers read from graphs. Possible answers are given to questions asking for opinions or reasons or interpretation; any reasonable alternative is also valid.

Diagrams given are intended only to give an indication of shape; no scales are given and axes are not labelled.

Numerical answers are given corrected to three significant figures unless specified otherwise.

The Examination Boards accept no responsibility whatsoever for the accuracy, method or working in the answers given to past examination questions. These answers are the sole responsibility of the authors.

Summary 1

Revision Exercise 1.1 (p. 21)

1. a 9810 **e** 21 024 **i** 8
  b 28 184 **f** 13 776 **j** 17
  c 11 017 **g** 43 **k** 11
  d 35 084 **h** 46 **l** 21

2. a -10 **g** -18 **l** -1.5 **r** 14
  b $-1\frac{1}{3}$ **h** -3 **m** -2 **s** -1
  c 16 **i** -15 **n** $-2\frac{2}{3}$ **t** -13
  d -2 **j** -4 **p** -16 **u** 4
  e 12 **k** 6 **q** 5 **v** -2
  f 42

3. a i 230 **iv** 0.000 12
  ii 860 000 **v** 38.3
  iii 0.0057 **vi** 0.000 045 8
  b i 4.7×10^{-2} **iv** 8.2×10^{7}
  ii 8×10^{-5} **v** 9.2×10^{-5}
  iii 5.07×10^{3} **vi** 9.08×10^{2}

4. a $1\frac{3}{20}$ **f** $4\frac{1}{6}$ **k** $\frac{5}{8}$ **q** $1\frac{3}{8}$
  b $\frac{1}{8}$ **g** $7\frac{4}{9}$ **l** $2\frac{2}{3}$ **r** $3\frac{1}{2}$
  c $1\frac{11}{12}$ **h** $2\frac{7}{20}$ **m** $\frac{2}{5}$ **s** 0
  d $1\frac{1}{2}$ **i** $1\frac{7}{8}$ **n** $3\frac{1}{12}$
  e $19\frac{1}{3}$ **j** $1\frac{1}{2}$ **p** $\frac{2}{3}$

5. a 10.2 **g** 2.8 **m** 0.0004
  b 19.18 **h** 0.268 **n** 0.0009
  c 1.28 **i** 1.28 **p** 0.0004
  d 0.481 **j** 0.02 **q** 0.000 004
  e 1.96 **k** 0.056 **r** 10.2
  f 0.0382 **l** 0.841 68 **s** 0.001

6. a 2.7 **d** 2.5 **g** 0.036
  b 6.2 **e** 8.22 **h** 0.935
  c 0.029 **f** 7.5

7. a i $\frac{1}{8}$ **ii** $\frac{1}{9}$ **iii** $\frac{1}{5}$
  b i 3^{-1} **ii** $4^{-1} (= 2^{-2})$ **iii** 3^{-3}

8. a 2^{7} **e** 4^{-1} **i** 3^{0} **m** 3^{9}
  b 5^{8} **f** 10^{5} **j** b^{3} **n** 5^{1}
  c 3^{7} **g** 7^{-3} **k** p^{1} **p** 4^{1}
  d a^{6} **h** a^{4} **l** 2^{8}

9. a i 6 ●———————○ 10
  ii -3 ○———————● 3
  iii 0 ●———————○ 0.2
  iv 0.04 ○———————○ 0.15
  b i 2.45 ●———————○ 2.55
  ii 0.445 ●———————○ 0.455
  iii 0.055 ●———————○ 0.065
  iv 7.15 ●———————○ 7.25
  c 41 500 to 42 499

Revision Exercise 1.2 (p. 23)

1. a i 0.84 **ii** 0.35 **iii** 0.34 **iv** 0.125
  b i $\frac{3}{4}$ **ii** $\frac{23}{25}$ **iii** $\frac{21}{50}$ **iv** $\frac{3}{8}$
  c i 24% **ii** 36% **iii** 246% **iv** 82.5%
  d i $\frac{9}{20}$ **ii** 0.45 **e i** 3.75 **ii** 375%

2. a i $<$ **ii** $>$ **iii** $>$ **iv** $<$
  b i $\frac{32}{9}$ **ii** $\frac{11}{7}$ **iii** $\frac{27}{5}$ **iv** $\frac{19}{4}$
  c i $4\frac{1}{5}$ **ii** $3\frac{1}{4}$ **iii** $5\frac{7}{8}$ **iv** $3\frac{1}{9}$

3. a i 33 kg **iii** 54.4 g **v** 13.5 m
  ii 374 cm **iv** 168 mm **vi** £342
  b i £243 **v** 1298 m^2
  ii £612 **vi** 30.8 cm^3
  iii £114.31 **vii** 173.25 m
  iv 3.864 m **viii** £163.40
  c i 10.3 m **iv** 7.18 cm^3
  ii 244 cm^2 **v** 5.78 cm^3
  iii 20.9 cm^2 **vi** 100 m

4. a $\frac{18}{25}$ **c** 0.9 **e** 9.5%
  b 40% **d** $\frac{1}{12}$ **f** 0.56

5. a £56.86 **b** £60.84 **c** £7680

6. a i 3:5 **iii** 2:3 **v** 5:4:6
  ii 1:2:5 **iv** 9:7 **vi** 18:8:9
  b i 2:5 **iii** 17:60 **v** 2:125
  ii 2:3 **iv** 7:20 **vi** 15:1
  c i $1\frac{7}{8}$ **iii** $\frac{3}{4}$ **v** $\frac{25}{3}$
  ii $\frac{16}{9}$ **iv** $\frac{21}{8}$ **vi** 14
  d i 1:2.5 **iii** 1:1.38 **v** 1:1.13
  ii 1:1.71 **iv** 1:1.43 **vi** 1:0.385

7. a i 40 cm, 48 cm **iii** 0.5 kg, 1.5 kg, 2 kg
  ii £63, £72 **iv** 4, 16, 32 litres
  b i $\frac{2}{5}$ **ii** $\frac{7}{12}$ **iii** $\frac{4}{9}$

8. a i 71.68 g **ii** 5.376 g **f** $2\frac{1}{2}$ hours
  b £87.15 **d** 2 sweets
  c 16 boxes **e** 3 hours

9. a £60 **d** £1500 **g** £14
  b £90 **e** £80 **h** £7.50
  c £220 **f** £64

10. £30

Revision Exercise 1.3 (p. 25)

1. a i 3.972 m   **iii** 139 inches
    ii 1176.46 g   **iv** 38 oz
   b i 5.4 m   **viii** $0.7 \, \text{m}^2$
    ii 6.3 cm   **ix** 288 sq inches
    iii 3 feet   **x** $80 \, \text{cm}^3$
    iv 24 feet   **xi** $5000 \, \text{cm}^3$
    v $1000 \, \text{mm}^2$ **xii** $3 \, \text{m}^3$
    vi $4000 \, \text{cm}^2$ **xiii** $2500 \, \text{cm}^3$
    vii 72 sq ft   **xiv** 2000 litres

2. a 35 pints   **d** 11 lb   **g** 80 inches
   b 45 litres   **e** 64 km   **h** 6.25 miles
   c 62.5 acres   **f** 55 m

3. a i length   **iii** area
    ii volume   **iv** length
   b i volume   **ii** length   **iii** area
   c i length   **iii** length
    ii volume   **iv** area

4. a i 62 cm   **ii** $168 \, \text{cm}^2$
   b i 48.7 cm   **ii** $166 \, \text{cm}^2$
   c i 88 cm   **ii** $432 \, \text{cm}^2$
   d i 15 cm   **ii** $9.375 \, \text{cm}^2$

5. a i 35.2 cm   **iii** 18.5 cm
    ii 7.33 cm   **iv** $20.5 \, \text{cm}^2$
   b 5.64 cm

6. a $37.5 \, \text{cm}^2$ **b** $2625 \, \text{cm}^3$ **c** 2231.25 g

7. a $126 \, \text{cm}^3$ **c** $72 \, \text{cm}^3$
   b $308 \, \text{cm}^3$ (3 s.f.)   **d** $403.2 \, \text{cm}^3$

8. a i 1 h 20 min   **ii** 4 h 20 min
   b i 45 km   **ii** 13.5 km
   c i 60 km/h   **ii** 60 km/h   **iii** 12 km/h
   d i 15 min   **iii** 3.5 km, 30 min
    ii 2.5 km   **iv** 7 km/h

Revision Exercise 1.4 (p. 28)

1. a $3x + 6$ **f** $8ac + 2ad + 4bc + bd$
   b $4a - 12$ **g** $5xz - yz + 15x - 3y$
   c $7xy + 14xz$ **h** $12x - 3xy + 8 - 2y$
   d $5ab - 10ac$ **i** $4ac - 12a - bc + 3b$
   e $ac + bc - ad - bd$

2. a $x^2 + 9x + 20$ **j** $12ab - 16a - 3b + 4$
   b $a^2 + 10a + 21$ **k** $6c^2 + 13c - 15$
   c $a^2 + 3a - 10$ **l** $a^2 + 8a + 16$
   d $x^2 - 13x + 36$ **m** $x^2 - 6x + 9$
   e $x^2 - 6x + 8$ **n** $3 - x - 2x^2$
   f $2x^2 + 5x + 3$ **p** $12 - x - x^2$
   g $3x^2 + 26x + 35$ **q** $6 + 5x - 4x^2$
   h $10x^2 + 19x + 6$ **r** $12 + x - 6x^2$
   i $6a^2 - 7a - 20$ **s** $25x^2 + 30x + 9$

3. a $\dfrac{x}{3}$ **e** $\dfrac{1}{5x}$ **i** $\dfrac{2}{a}$
   b $\dfrac{b}{2}$ **f** $\dfrac{2a}{5b}$ **j** $\dfrac{5}{(p - 2q)}$
   c $\dfrac{3}{q}$ **g** $\dfrac{1}{(3 - a)}$ **k** $\dfrac{3}{(a + b)}$
   d $\dfrac{2}{3y}$ **h** $\dfrac{1}{4}$ **l** $\dfrac{2}{p}$

4. a $\dfrac{a}{c}$ **d** $\dfrac{1}{2p}$ **g** ab
   b $\dfrac{a}{2b}$ **e** $\dfrac{x}{4y}$ **h** $\dfrac{a^2}{32}$
   c $\dfrac{a^2 b^2}{c}$ **f** $\dfrac{2a}{b}$ **i** $\dfrac{3p}{2}$

5. a $\dfrac{2b + 3a}{ab}$ **d** $\dfrac{5b - 9a}{15ab}$ **g** $\dfrac{7}{4x}$
   b $\dfrac{1}{2x}$ **e** $\dfrac{9x^2 + 4y^2}{12xy}$ **h** $\dfrac{21}{10a}$
   c $\dfrac{19}{8x}$ **f** $\dfrac{14b - 15a}{18ab}$

6. a $\dfrac{9x + 11}{20}$ **d** $\dfrac{9x + 22}{30}$ **g** $\dfrac{9x - 10}{x^2 - 2x}$
   b $\dfrac{4x + 22}{21}$ **e** $\dfrac{-23}{6}$ **h** $\dfrac{7x - 12}{10x^2 + 15x}$
   c $\dfrac{7x + 2}{15}$ **f** $\dfrac{110x - 99}{20}$ **i** $\dfrac{19x - 35}{3x^2 - 15x}$

7. a $x(x + 6)$ **m** $(x + 14)(x - 3)$
   b $3x(x - 3)$ **n** $(x - 3)^2$
   c $(x + 12)(x + 1)$ **p** $(a + 2b)(a - 2b)$
   d $(x + 15)(x + 2)$ **q** $(8 - x)(3 + x)$
   e $(x - 9)(x - 3)$ **r** $(14 + x)(2 - x)$
   f $(x - 12)(x - 4)$ **s** $2(x - 5)(x + 3)$
   g $(x + 4)(x - 3)$ **t** $(x + y)(x - y)$
   h $(x + 5)(x - 3)$ **u** $2(x - 4)(x + 3)$
   i $(x + 8)(x - 8)$ **v** $2(x - 3)(x - 5)$
   j $3(x + 5)(x + 1)$ **w** $2pq(p - 5q)$
   k $(x - 16)(x - 2)$ **x** $2a^2 b(2b + 3a)(2b - 3a)$
   l $(x + 4)(x - 5)$ **y** $3xy^2(3x^2 + 4y^2)$

Revision Exercise 1.5 (p. 29)

1. a 10   **b** 21   **c** -5 **d** 5
2. a 1   **b** $\frac{11}{15}$ **c** 10   **d** 20
3. a -4 **b** 36   **c** 1.4   **d** 0.2
4. a 3, 8, 15, 24, 120   **b** $n^2 + 1$

5. a $a = 2b + \dfrac{c}{2}$ **b** 9   **c** $c = 2(a - 2b)$

6. a $b = a - 2c$ **f** $t = \dfrac{(u - v)}{10}$

   b $v = u + 6$ **g** $s = \dfrac{1}{3}(4q - P)$

   c $q = 2p$ **h** $b = 4(a - c)$

   d $y = \dfrac{x}{5}$ **i** $y = 5(x - z)$

   e $r = \dfrac{C}{2\pi}$ **j** $r = \dfrac{1}{3}(P - q)$

7. a $x = 3$ **e** $x = 50$ **i** $x = \frac{7}{2}$
   b $x = 2$ **f** $x = 50$ **j** $x = 3$
   c $x = 3$ **g** $x = 37.5$ **k** $x = \frac{7}{2}$
   d $x = 0.3$ **h** $x = \frac{4}{13}$ **l** $x = 4$

8. a $x = 3, y = 2$ **e** $p = 2, q = -1$
   b $x = 4, y = 3$ **f** $x = 3, y = -2$
   c $x = 2, y = 3$ **g** $x = 1, y = 2$
   d $x = 4, y = -2$ **h** $x = 4, y = 3$

i $x = 3, y = -1$ **k** $x = -3, y = 4$
j $x = 2, y = -3$ **l** $x = 5, y = 2$
9. a $x = 3, y = 4$ **d** $x = 3, y = 2$
  b $x = 4, y = 10$ **e** $x = 1.5, y = 2$
  c $x = 4, y = -2$ **f** $x = 2, y = 5$
10. a $x = 0$ or -4 **j** $x = -\frac{1}{2}$
  b $x = -3$ or 7 **k** $x = 6$
  c $x = -2$ or 3.5 **l** $x = 2$ or 4
  d $x = 2$ or 3 **m** $x = 3$ or 4
  e $x = -2$ or -6 **n** $x = -2$ or 4
  f $x = 3$ or -2 **p** $x = -3$ or 2
  g $x = -8$ or 3 **q** $x = 8$ or -3
  h $x = 0$ or $-\frac{5}{8}$ **r** $x = -7$ or 3
  i $x = 0$ or $\frac{3}{7}$ **s** $x = -4$ or 2
11. a $x > -1$ **d** $x < -2$ **g** $x \geqslant 0$
  b $x > -3$ **e** $x \leqslant 1$ **h** $x \geqslant 1\frac{1}{3}$
  c $x < 13$ **f** $x \leqslant 2$ **i** $x < 16$
12. a i $x \leqslant -1$ **ii** $\frac{1}{2} < x \leqslant 5$
  b i $2 < x < 5$ **iv** $0 < x < 2$
     ii $x < -1$ **v** $x < -4$
     iii $-3 \leqslant x \leqslant 2$ **vi** $1 < x < 3$

Revision Exercise 1.6 (p. 31)

1. a i -6 **ii** 8 **iii** -3
  b i -8 **ii** 10 **iii** $-1\frac{1}{2}$
  c i $(2, 4), (-2, 4), (-1, 4)$
     ii $(-2, -4)$ **iii** $(4, -1)$
  d i 3 **ii** $-\frac{1}{2}$
2. a $y = 2x + 2$ **c** $y = -\frac{5}{3}x + 5$
  b $y = -3x - 2$ **d** $y = \frac{1}{2}x + 4$
3. B   **4. D**
5. a $x \leqslant 4, y \leqslant x, y \geqslant 2 - x$
  b

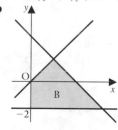

6. a **B**   **b** **D**   **c** **A**   **d** **C**
7. a $y = 4$ **b** $y = x - 4$ **c** $y = -\frac{5}{2}x + 5$
8. a cubic
  b 3 values: $x = -3, x = 1$ and $x = 4$

Revision Exercise 1.7 (p. 33)

1. a $a = 56°$ $b = 118°$ $c = 31°$
  b $d = 64°$ $e = 52°$ $f = 64°$
  c $h = 98°$ $g = 82°$ $i = 98°$ $j = 90°$
  d $x = 127$
2. a $135°$ **c i** 12 **ii** 18
  b i 8 **ii** 10   **d i** 9 **ii** no **iii** 6
3. a not similar   **b** similar   **c** similar
4. a $6\frac{2}{3}$ cm   **b** 12.5 cm

5. a not similar   **b** similar, $\widehat{A} = \widehat{F}$
6. a $x = 5\frac{1}{3}$ cm   **c** $x = 3$ cm, $y = 2$ cm, $2\frac{2}{3}$ cm
  b $y = 7.5$ cm   **d** $x = 3.5$ cm
7. a $a = 63°$ $b = 117°$
  b $c = 63°$ $d = 54°$ $e = 27°$
  c $f = 141°$
  d $g = 35°$ $h = 51°$
  e $i = 52°$ $j = 142°$ $k = 90°$ $l = 19°$
  f $m = 119°$ $n = 20°$ $p = 70°$ $q = 41°$

Revision Exercise 1.8 (p. 35)

1. a 6.20 cm   **b** 51.8 mm
2. a BC = 8.39 cm   **b** angle Z = 90°
3. 3.80 cm
4. a i 38.0°   **ii** 56.8°   **iii** 36.9°
  b i 25.2°   **ii** 46.2°   **iii** 41.8°
  c i 22.6°   **ii** 77.1°   **iii** 33.6°
5. a 43.1°   **b** 52.0°   **c** 38.8°
6. a 9.04 cm   **b** 16.4 cm   **c** 12.4 cm
7. a 26°   **b** 17°
8. a BQ = 7.58 m   **b** 9.31 m
9. b C = 90°   H = 57°   P = 33°
  c i 770 m   **ii** 918 m

Revision Exercise 1.9 (p. 37)

1. mean = 14   mode = 19   median = 13
2. a athletics team: mean = 15.55 range = 3
     band: mean = 14.7   range = 8
  b The second group has a lower mean age
     ($\simeq 1$ year less) but a much larger age range
     than the first group.
3. a Only range is given; we do not know where
     the scores are in that range.
  b i 90   **ii** 116
  d i 37   **ii** 49 and 27 **iii** 30
4. a 149 cm
  b The midclass value has been used as an
     estimate of the mean height in that group.
5. a i $\frac{1}{6}$ **ii** $\frac{1}{3}$ **iii** $\frac{1}{2}$ **iv** 0   **v** 1
  b i $\frac{5}{6}$ **ii** $\frac{1}{2}$
6. a i 0.25   **ii** 0.75
  b i 50   **ii** unlikely due to randomness
     iii surprised, 1 or both coins may be biased
     but could be due to randomness
7. a $\frac{2}{13}$ **b** $\frac{2}{13}$ **c** $\frac{1}{169}$

Chapter 1

Exercise 1B (p. 40)

1. $\frac{4}{5}$, $0.01\dot{4}\dot{2}$, $\sqrt{36}$, $(\sqrt{2})^2$
2. a BC = 2   BD = 1
     $\widehat{B} = 60°$ AC = $\sqrt{3}$
  b $\sin B = \dfrac{(\sqrt{3})}{2}$, irrational

     $\cos B = \frac{1}{2}$, rational
     $\tan B = \sqrt{3}$, irrational

Exercise 1C (p. 41)

1. $\frac{2}{9}$

2. $\frac{2}{3}$

3. $\frac{8}{9}$

4. $1,\ 1 - 0.\dot{9} = 0.\dot{0}$

5. $\frac{1}{6}$ **8.** $\frac{11}{75}$ **11.** $\frac{5}{33}$ **14.** $\frac{7}{110}$

6. $\frac{11}{45}$ **9.** $\frac{367}{900}$ **12.** $\frac{19}{165}$ **15.** $\frac{5}{11}$

7. $\frac{1}{15}$ **10.** $\frac{1}{11}$ **13.** $\frac{175}{333}$ **16.** $\frac{752}{4995}$

Exercise 1D (p. 42)

1. $2\sqrt{2}$ **15.** $5\sqrt{2}$ **29.** $8\sqrt{2} - 12$

2. $2\sqrt{3}$ **16.** 4 **30.** 0

3. $4\sqrt{2}$ **17.** 7 **31.** $\dfrac{3\sqrt{2}}{2}$

4. $3\sqrt{3}$ **18.** 6 **32.** $\dfrac{\sqrt{5}}{5}$

5. $5\sqrt{2}$ **19.** 5 **33.** $\dfrac{\sqrt{2}}{4}$

6. $3\sqrt{5}$ **20.** $3\sqrt{6}$ **34.** $\dfrac{\sqrt{10}}{5}$

7. $10\sqrt{2}$ **21.** 1 **35.** $\dfrac{\sqrt{6}}{2}$

8. $4\sqrt{3}$ **22.** $2\sqrt{2} - 2$ **36.** $\dfrac{\sqrt{2}}{2}$

9. $6\sqrt{2}$ **23.** $3\sqrt{5} + 5$ **37.** $\dfrac{2\sqrt{6}}{3}$

10. $10\sqrt{5}$ **24.** $4 - \sqrt{2}$ **38.** $\dfrac{\sqrt{15}}{5}$

11. $5\sqrt{10}$ **25.** $7 - \sqrt{14}$ **39.** $\sqrt{15}$

12. $3\sqrt{2}$ **26.** $5\sqrt{3} + 9$ **40.** $\sqrt{3}$

13. $\sqrt{6}$ **27.** $\sqrt{30} - 5$ **41.** $\sqrt{2}$

14. $3\sqrt{2}$ **28.** $6\sqrt{3} - 12$ **42.** $\dfrac{5\sqrt{2}}{3}$

43. a $3\sqrt{3}$ c $3\sqrt{2} + 3\sqrt{3}$
      b $2\sqrt{5}$ d $\sqrt{3}$

44. $\dfrac{2\sqrt{3} - 3}{3}$ **47.** $\dfrac{\sqrt{2} - 6}{4}$

45. $1 + \dfrac{\sqrt{5}}{5}$ **48.** $\dfrac{5\sqrt{14} + 7\sqrt{2}}{28}$

46. $2\sqrt{2} - \sqrt{6}$ **49.** $\dfrac{3 + \sqrt{2}}{3}$

50. a $\dfrac{3\sqrt{2}}{2}$ f $7 + 4\sqrt{3}$

   b $\dfrac{5\sqrt{3}}{3}$ g 1

   c $18 - 8\sqrt{2}$ h -4

   d $\dfrac{2\sqrt{3}}{3} + 2\sqrt{2}$ i $\sqrt{7} + 8$

   e $\dfrac{11\sqrt{5}}{10}$

51. a $24\sqrt{3}$ c $40\sqrt{5}$ e $100\sqrt{10}$
       b $9\sqrt{3}$ d $54\sqrt{2}$ f $24\sqrt{3}$

52. a irrational   d irrational   g irrational
       b rational   e rational   h rational
       c rational   f rational   i rational

53. rational; $AB^2 = 25 + (\sqrt{11})^2 = 36 \Rightarrow AB = 6$

54. e.g. **a** $\sqrt{2} \times \sqrt{8} = \sqrt{16} = 4$
       b $(1 + \sqrt{2}) + (1 - \sqrt{2}) = 2$

55. $\sin A = \dfrac{2}{\sqrt{13}}$ $\cos A = \dfrac{3}{\sqrt{13}}$

58. Suppose that $\sqrt{-4} = a$, then squaring gives $-4 = a^2$. But the square of a rational or of an irrational number is positive so a, i.e. $\sqrt{-4}$ is neither.

Exercise 1E (p. 45)

1. a 3 b -3 c 4 d -5 e 10

2. a 3 b 2 c 5 d 10 e 2

3. a 4 b -8 c 1000

4. a rational   b rational   c rational

5. a $\frac{2}{1}$ b $\frac{3}{2}$ c $\frac{1}{2}$

Exercise 1F (p. 46)

1. 3 **5.** 5 **9.** $\frac{1}{2}$ **13.** $\frac{1}{3}$

2. 4 **6.** 4 **10.** $\frac{2}{3}$ **14.** 7

3. 6 **7.** $\frac{1}{2}$ **11.** 0.5 **15.** 0.1

4. 2 **8.** 0.2 **12.** $\frac{2}{3}$ **16.** $\frac{3}{2}$

Exercise 1G (p. 47)

1. 9 **9.** 4 **17.** $\frac{1}{4}$ **25.** $x^{\frac{1}{2}}$

2. $\frac{1}{4}$ **10.** 100 **18.** $\frac{1}{8}$ **26.** x^2

3. 8 **11.** 0.001 **19.** $\frac{1}{2}$ **27.** y^2

4. 25 **12.** 100 **20.** 1000 **28.** a^2

5. 0.04 **13.** 3 **21.** 0.01 **29.** x^6

6. 1728 **14.** $3\frac{1}{2}$ **22.** 27 **30.** x^4

7. 0.216 **15.** 5 **23.** $11\frac{1}{9}$ **31.** xy^3

8. 27 **16.** $\frac{3}{2}$ **24.** $\frac{2}{5}$ **32.** $p^{-3}q$

33. a $x^{\frac{1}{3}}$ b $x^{-\frac{1}{3}}$ c $x^{\frac{2}{3}}$ d $x^{-\frac{3}{2}}$

34. a $2\frac{1}{2}$ b 0.064 c 0.0256 d 1

35. $x = \frac{5}{2}$ **38.** $x = -1$ **41.** -2

36. $x = 6$ **39.** $x = -1$ **42.** $\frac{3}{4}$

37. $x = \frac{3}{2}$ **40.** $-\frac{1}{2}$ **43.** 0

44. a 5^2 b 5^3 c 5^{-1} d $5^{\frac{1}{2}}$

45. a 4^2 b $4^{\frac{1}{2}}$ c $4^{\frac{5}{2}}$ d $4^{\frac{3}{2}}$

46.

Number	Powers of			
	3	9	27	81
1	3^0	9^0	27^0	81^0
3	3^1	$9^{\frac{1}{2}}$	$27^{\frac{1}{3}}$	$81^{\frac{1}{4}}$
9	3^2	9^1	$27^{\frac{2}{3}}$	$81^{\frac{1}{2}}$
27	3^3	$9^{\frac{3}{2}}$	27^1	$81^{\frac{3}{4}}$
81	3^4	9^2	$27^{\frac{4}{3}}$	81^1

47. a irrational   c irrational
       b rational   d rational

48. a $\dfrac{a^5}{2}$ b $8x^6y^{15}$ c $\dfrac{1}{3x^2y^2}$

Exercise 1H (p. 49)

1. 2.88   **6.** 1.48   **11.** 0.681
2. 4.90   **7.** 7.95   **12.** 2.22
3. 3.16   **8.** 2.45   **13.** 2.621 cm
4. 2.93   **9.** 0.381   **14.** 0.949
5. 0.215   **10.** 1.08

Exercise 1I (p. 50)

1. a $10\sqrt{2}$ **b** $\dfrac{5\sqrt{3}}{3}$ **c** 2

2. a $\frac{121}{999}$ **b** $\frac{3}{110}$ **c** $\frac{43}{90}$ **d** $\frac{101}{999}$
3. a $\frac{1}{16}$ **d** 9 **f** 4 **h** $\frac{1}{2}$
   b 1 **e** y^8 **g** 27 **i** $3\frac{3}{8}$
   c $\frac{5}{2}$
4. a $x^{\frac{3}{2}}$ **b** p^2
5. a 2^6 **b** 4^3 **c** $16^{\frac{3}{2}}$
6. a 2^5 **b** $4^{\frac{5}{2}}$ **c** $\frac{1}{2}^{-5}$
7. a $x = 7$ **b** $x = \frac{5}{4}$
8. a 0.027 **c** 411.5 to 4 s.f.
   b 0.09
9. b, c, e, f and **g**
10. b $-\frac{1}{1}$ **e** $\frac{1}{2}$ **g** $\frac{5}{3}$
   c $\frac{2}{1}$ **f** $\frac{611}{4950}$

Chapter 2

Exercise 2B (p. 53)

1. $(x + 3)(x + 5)$ **11.** $(x + 4)(x - 4)$
2. $(x + 11)(x + 2)$ **12.** $(x - 7)(x + 3)$
3. $(x + 9)(x + 7)$ **13.** $(x + 6)(x - 5)$
4. $(x + 8)(x + 5)$ **14.** $(x + 12)(x - 1)$
5. $2(x + 3)(x - 4)$ **15.** $(x + 11)(x - 3)$
6. $(x - 4)(x - 6)$ **16.** $(x + 8)(x - 9)$
7. $(x - 7)(x - 8)$ **17.** $(x - 8)(x - 9)$
8. $(x - 10)(x - 11)$ **18.** $(6 + x)(7 - x)$
9. $(x - 9)(x - 5)$ **19.** $2(2 + x)(2 - x)$
10. $2(x - 1)(x - 9)$ **20.** $(4 + x)(3 - x)$

Exercise 2C (p. 55)

1. $(2x + 1)(x + 1)$ **11.** $(2x + 1)(x - 2)$
2. $(3x - 2)(x - 1)$ **12.** $(3x + 4)(x - 1)$
3. $(4x + 3)(x + 1)$ **13.** $(5x + 2)(x - 3)$
4. $(2x - 1)(x - 3)$ **14.** $(4x - 3)(x + 2)$
5. $(3x + 1)(x + 4)$ **15.** $(3x - 2)(x + 4)$
6. $(3x - 2)(x - 2)$ **16.** $(7x + 2)(x - 3)$
7, $(2x + 1)(x + 4)$ **17.** $(6x + 5)(x - 2)$
8. $(5x - 2)(x - 3)$ **18.** $(5x - 4)(x - 3)$
9. $(2x + 3)(x + 4)$ **19.** $(3x + 4)(x - 5)$
10. $(7x - 1)(x - 4)$ **20.** $(4x - 3)(x + 5)$

Exercise 2D (p. 56)

1. $(3x + 2)(2x + 1)$ **3.** $(5x + 2)(3x + 1)$
2. $(3x + 5)(2x + 3)$ **4.** $(6x + 5)(2x + 3)$

5. $(7x + 2)(5x + 2)$ **13.** $(7x - 4)(3x + 2)$
6. $(3x - 1)(2x - 3)$ **14.** $(10x + 3)(8x - 3)$
7. $(3x - 2)(3x - 4)$ **15.** $(8x - 5)(3x + 4)$
8. $(8x - 1)(2x - 1)$ **16.** $(3a - 5)(2a + 3)$
9. $(5x - 3)(3x - 7)$ **17.** $(3t - 2)(2t + 1)$
10. $(5x - 2)(4x - 3)$ **18.** $(3b - 2)^2$
11. $(4x + 1)(2x - 3)$ **19.** $(5x + 3y)(x - 2y)$
12. $(5x - 2)(3x + 1)$ **20.** $(4x - 3)(x - 2)$

Exercise 2E (p. 56)

1. $(2x + 5)(2x - 5)$ **5.** $(3x + 5)(3x - 5)$
2. $(3x + 2)(3x - 2)$ **6.** $(2a + 1)(2a - 1)$
3. $(6a + 1)(6a - 1)$ **7.** $(4a - 3b)(4a + 3b)$
4. $(4a + b)(4a - b)$ **8.** $(5s + 3t)(5s - 3t)$
9. $(10x + 7y)(10x - 7y)$
10. $(3y + 4z)(3y - 4z)$
11. $(2x - 7y)(2x + 7y)$
12. $(9x + 10y)(9x - 10y)$
13. $(3a + 2b)(3a - 2b)$
14. $(8p + 9q)(8p - 9q)$
15. $(3M - 2N)(3M + 2N)$
16. $3(a + 3b)(a - 3b)$ **24.** $6(2a + 3b)(2a - 3b)$
17. $2(3t + 5s)(3t - 5s)$ **25.** $\frac{1}{2}(a + 2b)(a - 2b)$
18. $3(3x + y)(3x - y)$ **26.** $\left(\dfrac{a}{2} + \dfrac{b}{3}\right)\left(\dfrac{a}{2} - \dfrac{b}{3}\right)$
19. $5(3x + 2)(3x - 2)$ **27.** $3\left(3x + \dfrac{y}{3}\right)\left(3x - \dfrac{y}{3}\right)$
20. $5(a + 2)(a - 2)$ **28.** $\left(\dfrac{x}{4} + \dfrac{y}{5}\right)\left(\dfrac{x}{4} - \dfrac{y}{5}\right)$
21. $5(3 + b)(3 - b)$ **29.** $\frac{1}{18}(3 + x)(3 - x)$
22. $2(p + 2q)(p - 2q)$ **30.** $\frac{1}{8}(x + 2y)(x - 2y)$
23. $3(2 + x)(2 - x)$

Exercise 2F (p. 57)

1. $5(3x + 2)(x + 1)$ **14.** $5(5x - 2)(4x - 3)$
2. $2(2x + 1)(x - 2)$ **15.** $4(3x - 2)(2x + 1)$
3. $3(2x + 1)(x + 1)$ **16.** $7(3x - 2)(x + 4)$
4. $3(6x + 5)(x - 2)$ **17.** $(4 + 3x)(1 - 2x)$
5. $2(4x - 3)(x + 5)$ **18.** $(4 - 3x)(4x + 3)$
6. $2(x + 1)(4x + 3)$ **19.** $(7 - x)(4x + 3)$
7. $5(5x + 2)(x - 3)$ **20.** $2(x - 2)(x - 6)$
8. $3(3x + 4)(x - 1)$ **21.** $2(2 - 3x)(x + 4)$
9. $2(3x + 1)(x + 4)$ **22.** $(9 - x)(x + 1)$
10. $5(3x - 2)(x + 4)$ **23.** $(1 - x)(x + 12)$
11. $2(3x - 2)(3x - 4)$ **24.** $2(3x + 2)^2$
12. $3(8x - 1)(2x - 1)$ **25.** $5(x - 3)^2$
13. $2(3x + 2)(2x + 1)$ **26.** $5(3x + 2)(x + 2)$

Exercise 2G (p. 58)

1. $(3x + 1)(2x + 1)$ **7.** $(x + 10)(x - 9)$
2. $(5x - 2)(x + 1)$ **8.** $(4x + 1)(2x - 1)$
3. $(4x - 1)(3x - 1)$ **9.** $(5p - 4)(3p - 2)$
4. $(x - 3)(x - 7)$ **10.** $2(5x - 2)(3x + 1)$
5. $(3t + 2)(2t - 3)$ **11.** $(7 - x)(x + 4)$
6. $(2x - 3)(x + 5)$ **12.** $5(3x + 2)(2x + 1)$

13. $(a+3)(a-6)$ **28.** $(11x-2)(x-3)$
14. $2(2a-1)(2a-3)$ **29.** not possible
15. $(3x+1)(2x-7)$ **30.** $3(2a+7)(a+3)$
16. $(3x+4)(2x-1)$ **31.** $(a+b+c)(a+b-c)$
17. $4(x+2y)(x-2y)$ **32.** $(29x+1)(4x-1)$
18. $(2-x)(x+14)$ **33.** $(x+16)(x+7)$
19. $(t+8)(t+10)$ **34.** not possible
20. $(4x-3)(3x-2)$ **35.** $(4x^2+1)(2x+1)$
21. $(5b+2)(b-4)$ **36.** $(3a-7)(a-8)$
22. $(7c-1)(c+2)$ **37.** $2(x+7)(x-11)$
23. $(2-a)(a-5)$ **38.** $(2x-y+z)(2x+y-z)$
24. $(5-t)(t+4)$ **39.** $(ab+18)(ab-19)$
25. $2(3x+4)(x-2)$ **40.** $(x^3+2)(2x-1)$
26. $(1-t)(t+3)$ **41.** 199
27. $(4x-3)(3x-4)$ **42.** $11\,997$

43. $24\,690\,246\,911$
44. $1\,975\,308\,643\,975\,308\,641$
45. $0.135\,78$ **46.** $19\,752.086\,424\,6$
47. $0.975\,308\,642$ **48.** $0.555\,533\,331\,11$

Exercise 2H (p. 60)

1. $x=1$ or $\frac{5}{2}$ **11.** $x=2$ or $\frac{7}{3}$
2. $x=4$ or $\frac{2}{3}$ **12.** $x=\frac{1}{2}$ or $\frac{5}{3}$
3. $x=\frac{3}{4}$ or $\frac{4}{5}$ **13.** $x=0$ or $\frac{1}{3}$
4. $x=0$ or $\frac{5}{4}$ **14.** $x=0$ or $\frac{3}{7}$
5. $x=0$ or $\frac{3}{10}$ **15.** $x=3$ or $-\frac{3}{2}$
6. $x=7$ or $-\frac{2}{5}$ **16.** $x=\frac{5}{2}$ or $-\frac{3}{4}$
7. $x=\frac{2}{3}$ or $-\frac{5}{6}$ **17.** $x=\frac{4}{5}$ or $-\frac{9}{10}$
8. $x=\frac{3}{8}$ or $-\frac{5}{2}$ **18.** $x=\frac{2}{3}$ or $-\frac{9}{4}$
9. $x=\frac{8}{7}$ or $-\frac{15}{4}$ **19.** $x=\frac{12}{5}$ or $-\frac{7}{2}$
10. $x=-\frac{3}{4}$ or $-\frac{3}{2}$ **20.** $x=-\frac{3}{4}$ or $-\frac{8}{5}$

Exercise 2I (p. 61)

1. $x=2$ or $\frac{1}{2}$ **16.** $x=\frac{3}{2}$ or $\frac{3}{4}$
2. $x=4$ or $\frac{3}{2}$ **17.** $x=\frac{5}{2}$ or $-\frac{5}{6}$
3. $x=4$ or $\frac{5}{2}$ **18.** $x=-\frac{1}{2}$ or $-\frac{3}{2}$
4. $x=-\frac{2}{3}$ or -1 **19.** $x=-\frac{2}{3}$ or $-\frac{3}{4}$
5. $x=\frac{5}{2}$ or -7 **20.** $x=\frac{7}{2}$ or $-\frac{3}{5}$
6. $x=3$ or $\frac{2}{3}$ **21.** $x=\frac{1}{4}$ or $-\frac{7}{3}$
7. $x=2$ or $\frac{1}{3}$ **22.** $x=\pm\frac{5}{4}$
8. $x=\frac{3}{2}$ or -4 **23.** $x=\pm\frac{9}{10}$
9. $x=-\frac{2}{3}$ or -3 **24.** $x=\pm\frac{5}{2}$
10. $x=-\frac{2}{5}$ or -5 **25.** $x=\pm\frac{4}{3}$
11. $x=\frac{2}{3}$ or $-\frac{1}{2}$ **26.** $x=\pm\frac{12}{5}$
12. $x=\frac{2}{5}$ or $-\frac{4}{3}$ **27.** $x=\pm\frac{2}{3}$
13. $x=\frac{1}{3}$ or $\frac{1}{4}$ **28.** $x=\pm\frac{5}{9}$
14. $x=\frac{5}{2}$ or $-\frac{1}{3}$ **29.** $x=\pm\frac{2}{5}$
15. $x=-\frac{1}{5}$ or $-\frac{3}{4}$ **30.** $x=\pm\frac{5}{6}$

Exercise 2J (p. 62)

1. $x=4$ or $-\frac{1}{3}$ **3.** $x=\frac{4}{3}$ or $-\frac{3}{4}$
2. $x=\frac{3}{2}$ or $-\frac{1}{3}$ **4.** $x=\frac{2}{13}$ or $-\frac{3}{2}$

5. $x=\frac{3}{2}$ or $-\frac{1}{5}$ **17.** $x=3$ or $-\frac{3}{7}$
6. $x=2$ or $\frac{5}{3}$ **18.** $x=\frac{3}{4}$ or $\frac{2}{5}$
7. $x=\frac{1}{5}$ or $-\frac{1}{2}$ **19.** $x=0$ or 1 or 2
8. $x=\frac{1}{5}$ or $\frac{1}{7}$ **20.** $x=0$ or 3 or -4
9. $x=3$ or $\frac{2}{5}$ **21.** $x=0$ or 2 or $\frac{5}{2}$
10. $x=3$ or $\frac{1}{2}$ **22.** $x=0$ or 1
11. $x=7$ or $-\frac{1}{2}$ **23.** $x=0$ or $-\frac{1}{2}$ or -4
12. $x=2$ or $\frac{1}{3}$ **24.** $x=0$ or 6 or 7
13. $x=\frac{5}{3}$ or $\frac{3}{5}$ **25.** $x=0$ or 5 or -2
14. $x=\frac{5}{3}$ or $-\frac{3}{2}$ **26.** $x=0$ or 5 or $-\frac{7}{3}$
15. $x=\frac{2}{3}$ or $-\frac{5}{3}$ **27.** $x=0$ or $\pm\frac{3}{2}$
16. $x=\frac{3}{2}$ or $-\frac{1}{5}$ **28.** $x=0$ or 2 or 4

Exercise 2K (p. 63)

1. $x=\pm\frac{1}{3}$ **13.** $x=0$ or $\frac{5}{2}$
2. $x=2$ or $-\frac{7}{2}$ **14.** $x=2$ or $-\frac{1}{3}$
3. $x=-3$ **15.** $x=\pm\frac{1}{2}$
4. $x=\pm\frac{2}{5}$ **16.** $x=9$ or $\frac{7}{2}$
5. $x=-\frac{1}{2}$ or $-\frac{4}{3}$ **17.** $x=\frac{5}{3}$ or -2
6. $x=\frac{1}{3}$ or $\frac{1}{4}$ **18.** $x=\frac{3}{4}$ or $\frac{2}{3}$
7. $x=\pm\frac{1}{4}$ **19.** $x=\frac{3}{4}$ or $\frac{5}{8}$
8. $x=\frac{1}{2}$ or $-\frac{2}{3}$ **20.** $x=-\frac{2}{9}$ or $-\frac{2}{3}$
9. $x=2$ or $-\frac{1}{3}$ **21.** $x=\frac{9}{2}$ or -2
10. $x=\frac{1}{3}$ or $-\frac{5}{2}$ **22.** $x=\pm2$
11. $x=-\frac{1}{2}$ or $-\frac{3}{2}$ **23.** $x=\frac{4}{5}$ or $\frac{3}{4}$
12. $x=\frac{4}{5}$ or $-\frac{5}{3}$ **24.** $x=\frac{1}{13}$ or $-\frac{1}{11}$
25. a $x=50$ or $\frac{2}{3}$ **b** $x=28$ or $-9\frac{1}{2}$

Exercise 2L (p. 64)

1. $9x^2+24x+16$ **6.** $a=81, b=36, c=4$
2. $49x^2-28x+4$ **7.** $k=\pm5, p=\pm20$
3. $25x^2-20x+4$ **8.** $k=\pm4, p=\mp24$
4. $a=64, b=48, c=9$ **9.** $a=4, c=25, p=5$
5. $p=6, q=9$ **10.** $a=4, k=2$
11. $p=4$ and $q=7$ or $p=-4$ and $q=-7$
12. $p=1, q=6, r=0$ or $p=-1, q=-6, r=0$

Exercise 2M (p. 65)

1. 9 and 5 **4.** 5 cm and 9 cm
2. 4 and 2 **5.** 8 cm and 5 cm
3. 5 and 6
6. $2x^2+6x-80=0, x=8$ and 5
7. 5 cm, 12 cm and 13 cm
8. 2 cm and 8 cm
9. 10 cm, 8 cm and 6 cm
10. 6 cm and 8 cm **12.** 8 and 11
11. 12 and 7 **13.** 4 cm and 9 cm
14. a 12 cm **b** 7 cm
15. parallel sides 5 cm and 7 cm; $2\frac{1}{2}$ cm apart
16. 24
17. 12

18. $t = 4$ or 2 seconds. One time is on the way up, the other on the way down.
19. 15 cm and 20 cm
20. 60p   **21.** 9, 10 and 11

Chapter 3

Exercise 3A (p. 69)

1. $x = -0.55$ or -5.45 **13.** $x = 0.59$ or 3.41
2. $x = -6.37$ or -0.63 **14.** $x = 6.54$ or 0.46
3. $x = -3.62$ or -1.38 **15.** $x = 1.27$ or 4.73
4. $x = -7.27$ or 0.27 **16.** $x = 5.85$ or -0.85
5. $x = -4.65$ or 0.65 **17.** $x = 4.56$ or 0.44
6. $x = -7.37$ or -1.63 **18.** $x = 2.62$ or 0.38
7. $x = -5.73$ or -2.27 **19.** $x = 9.22$ or -0.22
8. $x = -11.32$ or 1.32 **20.** $x = -1.61$ or 5.61
9. $x = -6.87$ or 0.87 **21.** $x = -7.27$ or 0.27
10. $x = -9.11$ or 0.11 **22.** $x = 0.56$ or -3.56
11. $x = -4.19$ or 1.19 **23.** $x = 2 - \sqrt{7}, 2 + \sqrt{7}$
12. $x = -5.32$ or 1.32
24. $x = \frac{1}{2}(7 + \sqrt{61})$ or $\frac{1}{2}(7 - \sqrt{61})$
25. $x = -(4 + \sqrt{11})$ or $\sqrt{11} - 4$
26. $x = 1 - \sqrt{5}$ or $1 + \sqrt{5}$
27. $x = -3.19$ or -0.31 **37.** $a = 0.69$ or -0.29
28. $x = -2.78$ or -0.72 **38.** $b = -1.99$ or -0.26
29. $x = -1.54$ or -0.26 **39.** $S = 2.22$ or -0.22
30. $x = 2.78$ or 0.72 **40.** $x = 1.79$ or -1.12
31. $x = 1.64$ or 0.15 **41.** $R = -0.30$ or -1.41
32. $x = -1.77$ or -0.57 **42.** $n = -5.06$ or 0.06
33. $x = -1.59$ or -0.16 **43.** $p = -0.30$ or 0.15
34. $x = 1.54$ or 0.26 **44.** $x = -0.95$ or -0.18
35. $x = -2.14$ or 0.47 **45.** $A = -0.56$ or -4.44
36. $x = 0.22$ or -2.51 **46.** $n = 0.04$ or -6.04

Exercise 3B (p. 72)

1. $x = 5.08$ or -1.08 **11.** $x = 3.27$ or -0.77
2. $x = 2.32$ or -0.32 **12.** $x = -1.55$ or 0.22
3. $x = -2.14$ or 0.47 **13.** $x = 1.21$ or -0.21
4. $x = 0.88$ or -0.68 **14.** $x = -2.59$ or 0.26
5. $x = 1.39$ or 0.36 **15.** $x = 0.72$ or 0.28
6. $x = 4.16$ or -0.16 **16.** $x = 0.42$ or -0.30
7. $x = 1.78$ or -0.28 **17.** $x = 1.89$ or -0.20
8. $x = -1.55$ or 0.80 **18.** $x = 0.58$ or -0.14
9. $x = 2.76$ or 0.24 **19.** $x = 0.16$ or -4.03
10. $x = 1.86$ or -0.36 **20.** $x = 2.06$ or 0.79

Exercise 3C (p. 73)

1. $x = 0.5$ or -2 **7.** $x = 2.19$ or -0.69
2. $x = -1.58$ or -0.42 **8.** $x = 0.25$ or -1.5
3. $x = -0.5$ or $-\frac{2}{3}$ **9.** $x = -1.40$ or 0.24
4. $x = -2.19$ or 0.69 **10.** $x = 1.18$ or -0.43
5. $x = 2.39$ or 0.28 **11.** $x = \dfrac{-4 \pm \sqrt{30}}{7}$
6. $x = 3$ or -0.33 **12.** $x = \dfrac{3 \pm \sqrt{29}}{10}$

13. $x = 2$ or $\frac{1}{3}$ **17.** $x = \dfrac{-4 \pm \sqrt{6}}{5}$
14. $x = \dfrac{-6 \pm \sqrt{3}}{11}$ **18.** $x = \dfrac{7 \pm \sqrt{73}}{4}$
15. $x = \frac{1}{5}$ or $-\frac{3}{4}$ **19.** $x = \frac{1}{2}$ or -5
16. $x = 3$ or $\frac{5}{3}$ **20.** $x = \dfrac{5 \pm \sqrt{73}}{12}$

Exercise 3D (p. 74)

1. $x + \dfrac{30}{x} + 11$ **10.** $x = 5$ or $\frac{8}{9}$

2. $1 - 3x + \dfrac{30}{x}$ **11.** $x = 2.8$ or -5

3. $5x - \dfrac{12}{x} - 17$ **12.** $x = 10$ or 3

4. $3x - 26 + \dfrac{35}{x}$ **13.** $x = 8$ or -20

5. $32 - 5x - \dfrac{48}{x}$ **14.** $x = \frac{12}{5}$ or -7

6. $\dfrac{5}{x} - 4x + 8$ **15.** $x = -3\frac{1}{2}$ or $-2\frac{2}{9}$

7. $\dfrac{4}{x} - 15x + 17$ **16.** $x = -0.8$ or -12

8. $10x - \dfrac{18}{x} + 3$ **17.** $x = -\frac{9}{7}$ or -4

9. $3x - 11 + \dfrac{6}{x}$

18. a $x^2 - x - 12 = 0$ **b** $x = 4$ or -3
19. a $x^2 - 11x + 2 = 0$ **b** $x = 10.82$ or 0.18
20. a $x^2 - 3x - 5 = 0$ **b** $x = 4.19$ or -1.19
21. a $x^2 - 7x + 2 = 0$ **b** $x = 6.70$ or 0.30
22. a $4x^2 + x - 2 = 0$ **b** $x = -0.84$ or 0.59
23. a $2x^2 + 5x - 5 = 0$ **b** $x = -3.27$ or 0.77
24. $x = 2$ or $-1\frac{4}{7}$ **30.** $x = 4$ or $\frac{1}{3}$
25. $x = -1$ or 8 **31.** $x = -3.42$ or 2.92
26. $x = 6$ or -3 **32.** $x = -4.30$ or -0.70
27. $x = 1.5$ or -2 **33.** $x = -4.55$ or 2.80
28. $x = 6$ or $2\frac{2}{3}$ **34.** $x = -4.27$ or 3.27
29. $x = 5$ or -1 **35.** $x = 0.55$ or 5.45

Exercise 3E (p. 77)

1. 1.13 and 8.87   **6.** 4 cm, 6 cm and 10 cm
2. $\frac{47}{6}$ and $\frac{7}{6}$ **7.** 3 cm, 5 cm and 10 cm
3. 0.05 and 19.95   **8.** 42 years
4. 6.22 and 3.22 cm   **9.** 21 m and 28 m
5. 8.46 cm   **10.** 6 cm by 13 cm
11. BNC = 24 cm, AN = 5 cm
12. a $\dfrac{420}{x}$ pence   **d** 14 grapefruit at 30p each

   b $\left(\dfrac{420}{x} + 5\right)$ pence

13. a £$\dfrac{240}{x}$ **e** 20 books at £12 each

   b £$\left(\dfrac{240}{x} - 2\right)$

14. 4 cm

15. 60 mph

16. 30p

17. £6 or £9

18. 3 cm × 3 cm and 6 cm × 9 cm or $\frac{51}{7}$ cm × $\frac{51}{7}$ cm and $\frac{27}{7}$ cm × $\frac{18}{7}$ cm

19. 42

20. 20p

21. Len: 3 mph, 5 hours   Mandy: 4 mph, $4\frac{1}{2}$ hours

22. George: 6 km/h   Liam: 4 km/h

Puzzle (p. 82)   6.071 m

Chapter 4

Exercise 4B (p. 85)

1. a 8.4×10^5 **d** 1.15×10^{-5}
   b 1.08×10^{10} **e** 3.2×10^2
   c 1.54×10^{-4} **f** 7.8×10^{-2}

2. a 2×10^3 **d** 1.4×10^{-5}
   b 7×10^4 **e** 3×10^0
   c 3×10^{-2} **f** 1.25×10^8

3. a 3.2×10^3 **d** 4.13×10^{-3}
   b 3.2×10^{-2} **e** 2.59×10^{-2}
   c 3.31×10^5 **f** 2.8×10^6

4. a 6×10^3 **c** 1.2005×10^5
   b 2.4×10^6 **d** $2.399\,999 \times 10^6$

5. a 8.64×10^{-12} **c** 1.128×10^{-5}
   b 6×10^{-2} **d** 1.06

6. a 1.3×10^3 **c** 2.6005×10^3
   b 5.2×10^7 **d** 2.5995×10^4

7. 1.49×10^{-10}

8. 2.23×10^{-3}

9. a 15 minutes
   b 2.12×10^8 km
   c b gives one distance between the orbits; this is the distance between the planets only when they are in line with their sun and on the same side of it.

10. a 9.1×10^{10} km   **c** 6×10^5 s
   b $1:0.49$

11. 4.77×10^{-3} to 3 d.p.

12. a 1.3×10^{-6} m² to 3 d.p.
   b 2.5×10^{-2} m² to 3 d.p.

13. £2.90×10^8

Exercise 4C (p. 88)

1. a $T = a + b + c$ **b** $a = T - b - c$

2. $C = 6p + 8q$

3. $y = 20(N + 1)$

4. a $x - 6$ **b** $P = 6(x - 6)$

5. $T = N(S - C)$

6. $A = xy$

7. a 25   **b** $x = 3n + 1$

8. a $AB = 30 - 2x$, $BC = 40 - 2x$
   b $V = 4x(20 - x)(15 - x)$

9. a area $= x(300 - x)$ **b** 120 m and 180 m

10. a area $= x^2 - 5$ **c** $x = 5$ cm
   b volume $= x^3 - 5x$

11. a height $= \dfrac{144}{x^2}$ cm   **b** 5.66 cm and 11.3 cm

12. 10 sides

13. a $12x°$ **c** 5.45° to 3 s.f.
   b hour hand: $(60 + x)°$,   minute hand: $(12x)°$

15. gasket: x cm by y cm by z cm thick, square; side a cm, volume of cork, $V = z(xy - a^2)$

16. dose rate $= x$ mg/kg bodyweight
   bodyweight $= y$ kg
   dose, $D = xy$

Exercise 4D (p. 91)

1. $\dfrac{3x - 1}{(x + 1)(x - 1)}$ **21.** $\dfrac{1}{2x + 1}$

2. $\dfrac{3x - 1}{(x + 2)(x - 2)}$ **22.** $\dfrac{-1}{x + 3}$

3. $\dfrac{-4x - 13}{(x + 4)(x - 4)}$ **23.** $\dfrac{1}{(x + 2)(x + 1)}$

4. $\dfrac{4x + 11}{(x + 3)(x - 3)}$ **24.** $\dfrac{2}{(x + 1)(x - 3)}$

5. $\dfrac{x}{(x + 2)(x - 2)}$ **25.** $\dfrac{-3}{x + 2}$

6. $\dfrac{9 + 2x}{(x + 1)(x - 1)}$ **26.** $\dfrac{-4}{2x + 1}$

7. $\dfrac{3x - 17}{(x + 5)(x - 5)}$ **27.** $\dfrac{2}{x + 4}$

8. $\dfrac{-9x - 58}{(x + 7)(x - 7)}$ **28.** $\dfrac{3}{(x + 5)(x + 2)}$

9. $\dfrac{4x - 13}{(x + 4)(x - 4)}$ **29.** $\dfrac{15x + 11}{12}$

10. $\dfrac{3x - 8}{2x(x - 2)}$ **30.** $\dfrac{5x - 2}{20}$

11. $\dfrac{5x - 9}{3x(x + 3)}$ **31.** $\dfrac{1}{ab}$

12. $\dfrac{5x - 12}{(x + 3)(x - 3)}$ **32.** $\dfrac{b}{a}$

13. $\dfrac{1}{x - 1}$ **33.** $\dfrac{1}{6d}$

14. $\dfrac{1}{2 - x}$ **34.** $\dfrac{3}{4}$

15. $\dfrac{1}{x - 4}$ **35.** $\dfrac{2(3s + 4)}{(s + 2)(s - 2)}$

16. $\dfrac{1}{x - 3}$ **36.** $\dfrac{-(2x + 13)}{(x + 2)(x - 1)(x - 4)}$

17. $\dfrac{1}{x - 4}$ **37.** $\dfrac{2}{x - 2}$

18. $\dfrac{1}{x - 2}$ **38.** $\dfrac{8p}{rq}$

19. $\dfrac{1}{x + 1}$ **39.** $3(T - 1)$

20. $\dfrac{2}{x - 1}$ **40.** $\dfrac{2}{(x - 2)(x - 4)}$

41. $\dfrac{p}{2}$

42. $\dfrac{1}{(3m+1)(2m-1)}$

43. $\dfrac{2(n+1)}{n(n+2)}$

Exercise 4E (p. 94)

1. $x = 1\frac{1}{2}$

2. $x = \dfrac{c}{a} - b$

3. $x = 2\frac{3}{4}$

4. $x = \dfrac{y - ma}{2a}$

5. $x = \dfrac{8 - b}{2}$

6. $x = \dfrac{4 - p}{5p}$

7. $q = \dfrac{1 - pr}{p}$

8. $P = \dfrac{2 + 3Q}{3}$

9. $c = \dfrac{10Y + X}{5Y}$

10. $A = \dfrac{L + BD}{D}$

11. $T = \dfrac{v - 2 + S}{2S}$

12. $y = \dfrac{2 + xz}{x}$

13. $p = \dfrac{m(1 - r)}{r}$

14. $a = \dfrac{2A - bh}{h}$

15. $R = \dfrac{C}{2\pi} - r$

16. $h = \dfrac{2(A - b)}{b}$

17. a $\dfrac{h}{3} - 30$ **b** only applies to adults

18. a $a = -2$ **b** $a = \dfrac{A}{3n} - l$

19. a $t = \dfrac{u - v}{g}$
b $t = 25.0\,\text{s}$
c substitute all 4 values into original formula

20. a $n = 8$ **b** $n = \dfrac{3 \pm \sqrt{9 + 8N}}{2}$

Exercise 4F (p. 96)

1. $x = \pm 2$

2. $x = \pm\frac{5}{3}$

3. $x = \pm\sqrt{\frac{5}{3}}$

4. $x = \pm\sqrt{p}$

5. $x = \pm\sqrt{\frac{q}{p}}$

6. $x = \pm q\sqrt{\dfrac{1}{p}}$

7. $x = \pm\sqrt{p + q}$

8. $x = \pm\sqrt{\dfrac{bc}{a}}$

9. 4 ± 3

10. $a \pm \sqrt{b}$

11. $3 \pm \frac{2}{3}$

12. $5 \pm \sqrt{\dfrac{s}{t}}$

13. $2 \pm \sqrt{\dfrac{2A}{t}}$

14. $\frac{1}{2}a \pm \frac{1}{4}\sqrt{\frac{p}{3}}$

15. $a \pm \sqrt{\dfrac{R}{2}}$

16. $x = 16$

17. $x = \frac{4}{9}$

18. $x = 27$

19. $x = a^2$

20. $x = \dfrac{q^2}{p^2}$

21. $x = \dfrac{r^2}{p}$

22. $x = p^2 q$

23. $x = 16 - a$

24. $x = 49$

25. $x = (a - b)^2$

26. $x = 10$

27. $x = (s - t)^2 + t$

28. $p = \dfrac{\pm\sqrt{q}}{2}$

29. $p = \dfrac{a^2}{4}$

30. $a = b^2 - x$

31. $a = \pm\sqrt{c - b}$

32. $A = C^2 - B$

33. $h = \dfrac{2D^2}{3}$

34. $a = z - b$

40. a ± 3 **b** $x = \pm\sqrt{\dfrac{z - 2y^2}{2}}$

41. a 20 **b** $Q = P^2 - R$

35. $x = \pm\sqrt{b^2 - a^2}$

36. $m = Q \pm \sqrt{\dfrac{R}{s}}$

37. $x = (p - a)^2$

38. $b = a - (c - 2a)^2$

39. $r = \dfrac{\pm p\sqrt{l}}{1 \pm \sqrt{l}}$

Exercise 4G (p. 98)

1. $x = 24$

2. $x = \frac{15}{2}$

3. $x = \frac{8}{5}$

4. $x = \frac{12}{5}$

5. $x = pq$

6. $x = \dfrac{pq}{q - p}$

7. $x = \dfrac{pr}{a}$

8. $x = r(p + q)$

9. $x = a(c - b)$

10. $x = \dfrac{a^2 + b^2}{b - a}$

11. $x = a$

12. $x = \dfrac{bc}{a + b}$

13. $R = \dfrac{100I}{PT}$

14. $n = \dfrac{2A}{a + 1}$

15. $Q = 4P - R$

16. $b = \dfrac{4a + 3c}{6}$

17. $x = \dfrac{ab}{b + a}$

18. $x = p + q + r$

19. $x = \dfrac{s - r}{t}$

20. $q = \dfrac{4p}{a^2}$

21. $l = \dfrac{gT^2}{4\pi^2}$

22. $H = \dfrac{ht}{2h - t}$

23. $X = \dfrac{-(b^2 + c)}{a^2 b}$

24. $B = \dfrac{2aM}{L} + b$

25. $t = \dfrac{v - u}{a}$

26. $h = \dfrac{2A}{b}$

27. $c = \pm\sqrt{a^2 - b^2}$

28. $v = \dfrac{2s}{t} - u$

29. $t = \dfrac{2s}{u + v}$

30. $h = \dfrac{2A}{a + b}$

31. $f = \dfrac{uv}{u + v}$

32. $a = \dfrac{2A}{h} - b$

33. $u = \dfrac{fv}{v - f}$

34. $a = \dfrac{v^2 - u^2}{2s}$

35. $h = \dfrac{A - \pi r^2}{\pi r}$

36. $u = \pm\sqrt{v^2 - 2as}$

37. $a = \pm\sqrt{\dfrac{v^2}{\omega^2} + x^2}$

38. $h = \pm\sqrt{\dfrac{A}{\pi^2 r^2} - r^2}$

39. $u = \dfrac{2s - at^2}{2t}$

40. $a = \dfrac{2s - 2ut}{t^2}$

41. $p = \dfrac{2A}{q \sin R}$ **43.** $g = \dfrac{4\pi^2 l}{T^2}$

42. $u = \pm \sqrt{\dfrac{mv^2 - 2E}{m}}$ **44.** $R = \dfrac{100(A - P)}{PT}$

45. a $p = \dfrac{100(S - C)}{C}$ **b** $C = \dfrac{100S}{p + 100}$

Exercise 4H (p101)

1. $q = a(1 + a - p)$ **4.** $V = \dfrac{Ar}{2}$

2. $U = \dfrac{s}{2}(3s - T)$ **5.** $s = \dfrac{v^2 - u^2}{2a}$

3. $F = \dfrac{12}{6 - n}$

6. a $A = \pi r^2$ **b** $A = 4\pi t$, $754 \, \text{cm}^2$

7. $T = \dfrac{25t - 475}{14}$

8. a $2x^2 - 6x + 9 = 17$
   b $x = 4, y = 1$ or $x = -1, y = 4$

9. a   neither x nor y will be eliminated
   b $x = 2, y = 1$ or $x = 1, y = 2$

10. a $x = 2, y = 2$ or $x = 1\frac{1}{2}, y = 2\frac{1}{2}$
    b $x = 4, y = -2$ or $x = -\frac{8}{3}, y = \frac{14}{3}$
    c $x = 3, y = 4$ or $x = 4, y = 3$

11. a $V = x^3 - 16x$ **c** $59.3 \, \text{cm}^3$
    b $A = 6x^2 - 32$

12. a $l = \sqrt{r^2 + h^2}$ **c** $V = \dfrac{r}{3}\sqrt{A^2 - \pi^2 r^4}$

    b $A = \pi r^2 \sqrt{r^2 + h^2}$

13. a $p_n = \dfrac{1}{n}, q_n = n^2 + 1$ **b** $q_n = \dfrac{1}{p_n^2} + 1$

Exercise 4I (p. 103)

1. a 1.8×10^{-9} **b**   8

2. a $6.738 \times 10^9 \, \text{km}$ **b** $5.162 \times 10^9 \, \text{km}$

3. a $\dfrac{2(3x + 4)}{(x + 2)(x - 2)}$ **c** $\dfrac{M(2M - 1)}{(M + 2)(M - 2)(M - 3)}$

    b $\dfrac{3(x + 2)}{2}$ **d** $\dfrac{3x + 1}{2x - 1}$

4. a   4.92 s to 3 s.f.   **b** $l = \dfrac{gT^2}{4\pi^2}$

5. a   330 cm   **c** $c = \sqrt{d^2 - a^2 - b^2}$
    b   20.42 cm to 4 s.f.

Chapter 5

Exercise 5B (p. 108)

1. a 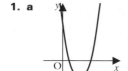   **b**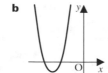

c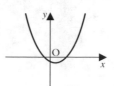

d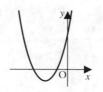

e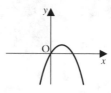

f

g

h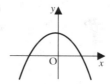

i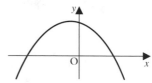

j

2. a   A$(0, 6)$, B $(2, 0)$, C $(3, 0)$ **b** $y = 6 - 2x$
3. a $p = -1, q = -20$ **b** $(0, -20)$

4. a A $(-3,0)$, B $(0,9)$

b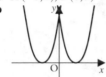

5.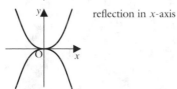
$-y = x^2 + 2$
$-y = x^2$
$-y = x^2 - 1$

6. reflection in x-axis

7. 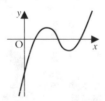 reflection in x-axis

8. a A $(-3,0)$, B $(0,9)$, C $(3,0)$

b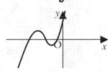

9. a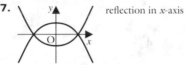

b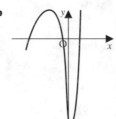

c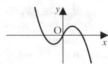

d

e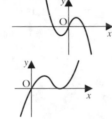

f

10. A $(-3,0)$, B $(4,0)$ **11.** $a = 0, b = -16$

12. $y = x(x-2)^2$ **13.**

14. 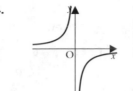   **16.** C
17. C
18. B
19. D

15.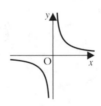

Exercise 5C (p. 112)

1. a $-2 \leqslant x \leqslant 2$ **c** $1 < x < 2$
   b $-5 \leqslant x \leqslant 5$
2. a $x < -6$ and $x > 6$ **d** $2 \leqslant x \leqslant 4$
   b $0 < x < 7$ **e** $x \leqslant -4$ or $x \geqslant 4$
   c $-1 < x < 5$ **f** $x < -3$ or $x > 1$
3. a $\dfrac{-1 \pm \sqrt{13}}{2}$ **b** $\dfrac{-1 - \sqrt{13}}{2} < x < \dfrac{-1 + \sqrt{13}}{2}$
4. a i $x = 3.2$ or -1.2 **ii** $x = 2.4$ or -0.4
   b i $-1.2 < x < 3.2$
     ii $x \leqslant -0.4$ or $x \geqslant 2.4$
   c The least value of y on the curve is -1.
5. a i $x = -2, 0$ or 2
     ii $x = -1.6, -0.4$ or 2.2
   b i $-2 < x < 0$ and $x > 2$
     ii $x < -1.6$ and $-0.4 < x < 2.2$
6. a $x^2 + (x+2)^2 = (x+5)^2$, $x = 8.5$
   b $x^2 + (x+2)^2 > (x+5)^2$, $x > 8.5$
7. $1.5 < x < 4$, $1.5\,\text{m} < \text{width} < 4\,\text{m}$
8. a n^2 **b** $n^2 > 10\,000$, 101st term
9. b $x < 0$ and $2 < x < 3$
   c 2 inches $< \text{width} < 3$ inches
10. a $4n^2 + 4$ **b** 15

11. a $1 < t < 8$ **b** 7 seconds
12. $n < 10$; 10, 5, $3\frac{1}{3}$, $2\frac{1}{2}$, 2, $1\frac{2}{3}$, $1\frac{3}{7}$, 1.25, $1\frac{1}{9}$
13. a i $\dfrac{110}{x}$ hours   **ii** $(x + 10)$ mph

iii $\left(\dfrac{180}{x + 10}\right)$ hours

b Speed is always positive.
c 66.6 mph to 70 mph

Exercise 5D (p. 116)

1. $0 < x < 6$
2. $-5 < x < 0$
3. $-7 < x < 7$
4. $x < 1$ and $x > 4$
5. $x < 1.5$ and $x > 3$
6. $-1 < x < 7$
7. $x < -9$ and $x > 0$
8. $0 < x < 1.5$
9. $x < -1$ and $x > \frac{1}{3}$
10. $x < -5, 0 < x < 2$
11. $x^2 + 1 = 0$ has no solution

Exercise 5E (p. 117)

1. a $x^2 - x - 7 = 0$ **d** $x^2 + 3x - 5 = 0$
  b $x^2 - 2x - 5 = 0$ **e** $x^2 + 3x + 2 = 0$
  c $x^2 - 6x + 4 = 0$ **f** $2x^2 - x - 6 = 0$
2. a $y = 2x + 1$ **c** $y = -6x - 4$
  b $y = 7x - 2$ **d** $y = -\frac{3}{2}x - 1$
3. estimate: $x = -1.6$ and 2.6, $x^2 - x - 4 = 0$
4. estimate: $x = -3$ and 8, $x^2 - 5x - 20 = 0$
5. estimate: $x = 0$ and 1, $x^2 - x = 0$
6. estimate: $x = \frac{1}{2}$ and -2, $x^2 + 2x - 1 = 0$
7. b $x = \pm 3.5$ **e** $y = 2 - x$; 3.7, -2.7
  d $x^2 + 2x - 5 = 0$; -3.5, 1.5
8. a $y = 2x$
  b $x = \pm 1.414$ or 0
  c

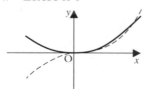

9. a

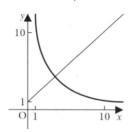

b There is a negative solution outside the range
  of the sketch.
10. $y = \frac{1}{2}x + 6$, $x = 2.7$ or -2.2
11. $y = 2 - 5x$, $x = -5.4$ or 0.4
12. $y = 6 - x$, $-3 < x < 2$
13. a $x = 10.5$ or 1.5   **c** $1.5 < x < 10.5$
  b $12x - x^2 - 16 = 0$
14. c $x = 1.7$ or 0.3   **d** $2x^2 - 4x + 1 = 0$

15. a £10 250, 3500   **c** $1438 \leqslant x \leqslant 5561$
  b 298
16. c $x = 1.94$ or 0.32
17. a 13.2 m   **c** $1568\,\text{m}^2$
  b area = $2450\,\text{m}^2$, $x = 35$ **d** $2352\,\text{m}^2$
18. b $C = 16$ and 21.16   **e** $2.74 < x < 3$
  d 3.16 feet
19. a $y = -6x - 10$ **b** lines do not cross

Summary 2

Revision Exercise 2.1 (p. 127)

1. a $\sqrt{3}$ and π
  b i $\frac{4}{9}$ **ii** $\frac{1}{300}$ **iii** $\frac{7}{90}$ **iv** $\frac{23}{99}$
2. a 10   **b** $6\sqrt{7}$ **c** $\sqrt{15}$ **d** $6\sqrt{6}$
3. a $27 + 2\sqrt{3}$ **b** $5\sqrt{3}$ **c** $\sqrt{3}$
4. a $2\sqrt{2}$ **b** $\dfrac{2\sqrt{3} + 3}{3}$ **c** $\dfrac{2\sqrt{5} + 3\sqrt{10}}{10}$
5. a i 2   **ii** -4 **iii** 0.1   **iv** 729
  b i 5   **ii** -2
6. a $(3x + 1)(x - 4)$ **c** $(5x - 2)(4x - 3)$
  b $(3x + 2)(3x - 2)$ **d** $(4x - 7)(x - 2)$
7. a $x = 2$ or $\frac{5}{3}$ **d** $x = \frac{5}{2}$ or $\frac{2}{3}$
  b $x = 0$ or $\frac{1}{5}$ **e** $x = \frac{1}{3}$ or $-\frac{4}{3}$
  c $x = -\frac{7}{3}$ or $-\frac{5}{2}$ **f** $x = \frac{7}{2}$ or $\frac{2}{5}$
8. a $a = 4, b = -28, c = 49$ **b** 29 800
9. 24 cm, 26 cm and 10 cm
10. a $x = 18$ or 3   **b** 18 cm by 3 cm
11. a $6\sqrt{3}$, irrational   **c** $\frac{5}{9}$, rational
  b $11 - 6\sqrt{2}$, irrational
12. a iii is rational   **c** $\frac{2}{55}$
  b e.g. $\sqrt{2} \times \sqrt{8} = 4$
13. a $6p(1 - 2p)$ **b** $(4t - 3)(3t - 2)$
14. a 3×10^{-1} **b** $\dfrac{a}{b^2}$

Revision Exercise 2.2 (p. 129)

1. a $x = -6.19$ or -0.81 **b** $x = -5 \pm 2\sqrt{7}$
2. a $2x - 8 - \dfrac{24}{x}$ **b** $x = 8$ or $-\frac{3}{2}$
3. a $x + 2$ **b** $x(x + 2) = 48$, 6 cm and 8 cm
4. a $\dfrac{180}{x}$ **b** $\dfrac{180}{x + 5}$ **c** 15p
5. a 2.56×10^7 **b** 4×10^1 **c** 1.12×10^5
6. a $\dfrac{10 - 3x}{(x + 2)(x - 2)}$ **c** $\dfrac{7}{(x + 3)(x + 4)}$
  b $\dfrac{2(x - 5)}{(x - 2)(x - 4)}$ **d** $\dfrac{a - 1}{(a + 3)(a - 3)}$
7. a $P = \frac{3}{4} - Q$ **c** $a = \sqrt{c^2 + b^2}$
  b $h = \dfrac{A - 2\pi r^2}{2\pi r}$ **d** $r = p^2 - 4pq + 4q^2$

8. a

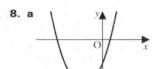

b

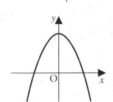

9. b $(-\sqrt{2},0), (\sqrt{2},0)$
  c i and **ii** reflection in x-axis
10. a

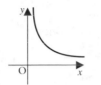

b i

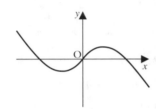

  ii

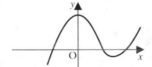

11. a $b = 75$ **b** $M = b + \sqrt{\dfrac{p}{a}}$

12. a

x	-2	-1	0	1	2	3
y	-1	2	-1	-4	-1	14

  c $-1.86, -0.25, 2.11$
13. $x = 1.63$ or 0.37

Revision Exercise 2.3 (p. 131)

1. a i $\frac{2}{9}$ **ii** $\frac{3}{11}$ **iii** $\frac{4}{45}$
  b i $16\sqrt{2}$ **ii** 27 **iii** $25\sqrt{5}$ **iv** $\frac{1}{100}$
2. a $\dfrac{\sqrt{2}+8}{4}$
  b i $16 + 7\sqrt{5}$ **ii** $14 - 6\sqrt{5}$
  c i 1.25 **ii** 0.64 **iii** 0.512
3. a i not possible   **iii** $3(3a-b)(3a+b)$
  ii $(3x+1)(x+3)$
  b i $-7, \frac{1}{4}$ **ii** $0, 6$ **iii** $-2, \frac{1}{5}$
4. a $p = -18, q = 81$ **b** $6\,cm$ by $9\,cm$

5. a $x = \dfrac{\sqrt{137}+5}{8}$ or $\dfrac{-\sqrt{137}+5}{8}$
  b $x = \dfrac{3 \pm \sqrt{11}}{2}$
6. $x = 10$ or $-\frac{1}{3}$
7. a i 1.2×10^1 **iii** 8.15×10^3
  ii 5.33×10^6 to 2 d.p.
  b i $\dfrac{4b}{3a}$ **ii** $\dfrac{14-3x}{(x+4)(x-4)}$
8. a $\dfrac{a^2+b^2}{a-b}$
  b i $a = \sqrt{A-bc}$ **ii** $a = x - 16$
9. $3 < x < 4$
10. a $y = 3x - 1$ **b** $y = \frac{3}{2} - 4x$

Revision Exercise 2.4 (p. 132)

1. a $\dfrac{\sqrt{24}}{\sqrt{2}}, \sqrt{\dfrac{12}{5}}$
  b i $10\sqrt{3}$ **ii** $2\sqrt{14}$ **iii** $6\sqrt{5}$
2. a i 4.16 **ii** 1.73 **iii** 2.78
  b i 4 **ii** a^2 **iii** -3
3. a $(3x+1)(2x+3)$ **c** $3(x+2y)(x-2y)$
  b $2(2x+1)(x+5)$ **d** $(3-x)(x+1)$
4. a $x = \frac{3}{4}$ or $-\frac{3}{2}$ **c** $x = \frac{5}{4}$ or -2
  b $x = 7$ or $\frac{3}{2}$ **d** $x = 0, 4$ or -2
5. a $x = 1.24$ or -1.07 **b** $x = 3.21$ or -0.21
6. $x = 2.59$ or 1.16
7. a $a = \dfrac{2A}{h} - b$ **c** $f = \dfrac{uv}{u+v}$
  b $c = a^2 - 2ab + b^2$ **d** $a = b \pm \sqrt{5}$
8. a $d = 2a(2a-c)$
  b i $A = 3x^2$ **ii** $x = \sqrt{\dfrac{A}{3}}$
9. a $b = -3, c = -10$ **c** $(0, -10)$
  b B: $(1\frac{1}{2}, -12\frac{1}{4})$
10. a C   **b** $y = x$

Chapter 6

Exercise 6A (p. 135)

1. a i $4.9\,cm$
  ii $0.107\,cm/s$; this is the gradient of CD
  b i $3.3\,cm$ **ii** $0.136\,cm/s$
  c i $0.95\,cm$ **ii** $0.19\,cm/s$
  d i $0.2\,cm$ **ii** $0.2\,cm/s$
  e estimate 0.2 as gradient at C
  f move the point closer to C
2. a y increases to 3.1, then decreases to -3
  b gradient $= -3$

Exercise 6B (p. 137)

1. a $\frac{1}{2}$ **c** $\frac{5}{6}$ **e** 0
  b $\frac{3}{7}$ **d** $-\frac{11}{3}$

2.

x	0	1	2	3	4	5	6	7	8
y	0	0.1	0.4	0.9	1.6	2.5	3.6	4.9	6.4

  a 0.6   **c** 0.2, 0.8, 1.2

3.

x	1	1.5	2	3	4	5	6	7	8
y	10	6.7	5	3.3	2.5	2	1.7	1.4	1.3

  a −2.5   **c** −1.1 to 2 d.p.
  b A: −10 B: −0.6
4. a 3   **b** 27
5. a i 29   **ii** 33   **b** 34
  c 5.25; number of ripe strawberries increasing
     by $5\frac{1}{4}$ a day on average from Monday to Friday
  d −6; number of ripe strawberries decreasing by
     6 a day on average from Monday to Friday
6. a −7.2; the population decreased by an average
     of 7.2 people per year
  b −11; in 1910 the population was decreasing at
     the rate of 11 people per year
7. a 800; in month 2 sales were increasing at a rate
     of 800 jars per month
  b 1800; in month 4 sales were increasing at a
     rate of 1800 jars per month

Exercise 6C (p. 140)

2. a accurately   **b** 6; accurate
3. b 18.5   **c** underestimate

Exercise 6D (p. 143)

1. a 26   **b** 27
2. 14 square units
3. 26; less
4. 11.5 square units
5. a 28.5   **b** 27.375
6. b $183.75\,\text{m}^2$ **d** 165 573 000 litres
  c 45 940 litres

Chapter 7

Exercise 7A (p. 146)

1. a The second graph shows acceleration/
     deceleration
  b 1.7 m/s. Either graph gives this information.
     (Total distance/total time)
2. a No. The dip shows where the driver slows
     down and then speeds up so he goes round
     the roundabout.
  b B attempts to show the direction of travel as
     well as the speed – the velocity. Negative
     speed shows travel in the opposite direction;
     but the car does not travel only in two
     directions in a line.

Exercise 7B (p. 148)

1. a 12.5 m   **b** 6 m/s   **c** 10 m/s
2. a 450 m   **b** 80 m/s   **c** 185 m/s
3. a 31 m   **e** 62 m, 5 seconds
  b 12.4 m/s   **f** 12.4 m/s
  c 12.4 m/s   **g** gradient is zero
  h **f** gives the average speed, **g** gives the average
     velocity
  i The object did not change direction.

Exercise 7C (p. 150)

1. a speed   **c** velocity   **e** speed
  b velocity   **d** speed   **f** velocity
2. a A ———●→——— B
            2 m/s
  b A ———●→——— B
            4 m/s
  c A ———←●——— B
           10 m/s
  d A ————————●—— B   no movement
3. a 10 m/s   **c** 7.5 m/s   **e** 6 m/s
  b +10 m/s **d** −7.5 m/s
4. +0.8 m/s, then −0.4 m/s, (i.e. speed 4 m/s in
    the opposite direction), then stationary
5. a false   **c** false   **e** true
  b true   **d** true

Exercise 7D (p. 154)

1. a 140 m/s   **c i** 60 m/s   **ii** 94 m/s
  b 95 m/s
2. a after 6 seconds
  b 15 m/s
  c 17.5 m/s
  d i 20 m/s   **ii** −10 m/s   **iii** −20 m/s
3. a 15 m/s   **c** 5 m/s   **e** −15 m/s
  b 20 m/s   **d** 31 m
4.

t	0	1	2	3	4
d	0	6	8	6	0

  c $t = 2, 0\,\text{m/s}$ $t = 3, -4\,\text{m/s}$ **d** 8 m

Exercise 7E (p. 155)

1. 30 m/s, 60 seconds
2. a 0.4 m/s   **b** 15 m/s   **c** 12 m/s
3. 15 seconds
4. $2\,\text{m/s}^2$
5. a 90 km/h   **b** 300 km/h   **c** 22.5 km/h
6. $14\,\text{km/h/s}$ (= $3.89\,\text{m/s}^2$)
7. $2.78\,\text{m/s}^2$

Exercise 7F (p. 157)

1. a $2.5\,\text{m/s}^2$ **d** 2 seconds
  b less acceleration   **e** $7.5\,\text{m/s}^2$
  c 2 seconds   **f** 12 seconds

2. a 10 km/minute²   **c** 27.5 km/minute
   b 15 km/minute   **d** 2.5 km/minute
3. a 300 km/h²   **d** zero
   b 15 km/hour   **e** −300 km/h²
   c 3 minutes

Exercise 7G (p 160)

1. a i 3 m/s²   **ii** 1.5 m/s²   **c** 75 m
   b 5 seconds   **d** 337.5 m
2. a 115 m   **c** 167 m to nearest whole metre
   b 35 m
3. a 600 m/s²   **c** 1300 m/s²   **e** 4000 m/s²
   b 3.0625 m   **d** 4.125 m   **f** 0.3125 m
4. a 0.185 m/s²   **b** 1000 m
5. a 0.017 m/s²   **c** 0.025 m/s²   **e** 420 m
   b 5 m/s   **d** 300 m
6. a 0.67 m/s² to 2 d.p.   **d** 50 m
   b 1 m/s²   **e** 475 m
   c 75 m

Exercise 7H (p. 164)

1. a 5 m/s   **b** decelerating   **c** 38.5 m
2. a 98 m
   b i T   **ii** F   **iii** F   **iv** T
3. a 12 km/minute²   **d** 20 km
   b 15.5 km/minute²   **e** 44 km
   c 2.7 minutes
4. a 9 m/s² 3 seconds after release   **d** zero
   b 7 m/s   **e** 35 m
   c 4 m/s²
5. a 250 mph/min   **c** 3 minutes
   b 200 mph/min   **d** 6 miles

Exercise 7I (p. 166)

1. B   **5. D**   **8. A**
2. B   **6. C**   **9. A**
3. D   **7. D**   **10. A**
4. B

Chapter 8

Exercise 8A (p. 172)

1. 5 cm   **2.** 6.2 cm   **3.** 7 cm   **4.** 10 cm

Exercise 8B (p. 172)

1. b AB and CD are parallel – ∠ABC and ∠BCD
    add up to 180°. CD is 6 cm – △DCB is a
    3,4,5 triangle.
    ∠BAD and ∠BDA are equal – △ABD is an
    isosceles triangle.
2. b A rhombus – diagonals bisect each other at
    right angles.
3. a 30°, 30°, 120°   **b** Isosceles
4. b 1 : 100   **c i** 6.9 m   **ii** 16 m

5. a i PQ as 9.2 cm, QR as 7.6 cm
    ii PQ as 11.5 cm, QR as 9.5 cm
   b 68 m
   c 57.6 m
   d 1 cm to 10 cm is easier than 1 cm to 8 m as
    multiplication and division by 10 is easier than
    by 8. 1 cm to 5 m is easier than 1 cm to 8 m as
    multiplication and division by 5 is easier than by 8.
6. c 217 m
   d Calculated answers will be as accurate as the
    original measurements allow. Measurements from
    scale drawings will depend on accuracy and scale.
   e 108 m

Exercise 8C (p. 174)

1. angle of rotation 92°   **3.** angle of rotation 137°
2. angle of rotation 93°   **4.** angle of rotation 55°
5. Enlargement by −3, centre (−1, 6)
6. Rotation 90° clockwise about (3, 4)
7. Translation by $\begin{pmatrix} -3 \\ -7 \end{pmatrix}$
8. Reflection in the line $y = 3$
9. d Rotation 180° about O
   e Rotation 90° anticlockwise about (0.5, −1.5)
10. LMN itself
11. a i Rotation 90° clockwise about O.
    ii Reflection in the line $x = -1$
    iii Translation by $\begin{pmatrix} -8 \\ 6 \end{pmatrix}$
   b (−7, −1)
12. a (5, 4)   **b** (−1, 1)   **c** (2, 0)
13. a (2, 5)   **b** (0, 1)
14. a E, 90° clockwise   **c** Midpoint of EB, 180°
   b EB
15. a i AB = BC = PB = BQ   **ii** AC = PQ
   b 60°, 60°   **d** 105°
   c 60°, 60°   **e** 6 cm

Exercise 8D (p. 178)

1.

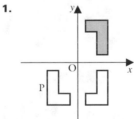

2.

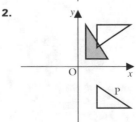

3.

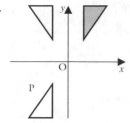

4.

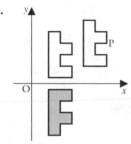

5.

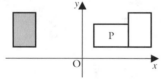

6.

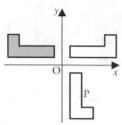

Exercise 8E (p. 180)

1.

4.

2.

5.

3.

6.

7. Rotation anticlockwise.

8. Reflect about the vertical.
9. Rotation clockwise.
10. Reflect about the horizontal.
11. e.g. Rotate clockwise, rotate clockwise.
12. e.g. Reflect about vertical, reflect about horizontal.
13. Reflect about vertical, rotate clockwise.
14. Reflect about vertical, rotate clockwise.
15. Tile B1   Rotate clockwise, reflect horizontally.
    Tile B2   Rotate, rotate.

Exercise 8F (p. 182)

1.

4.

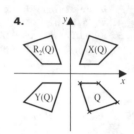

2.

5.

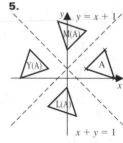

3.

6.

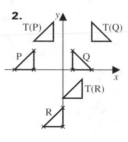

Exercise 8G (p. 184)

1. b reflection in $y = -x$
2. b i R_3 **ii** R_2
3. b Yes
   c Yes
   d Rotation $180°$ about O

4. b i Translation by $\begin{pmatrix} 4 \\ -3 \end{pmatrix}$

   ii Translation by $\begin{pmatrix} 0 \\ 6 \end{pmatrix}$

Exercise 8H (p. 185)

1. a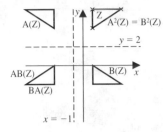

b AB and BA are both equal to a rotation of 180° about $(-1, 2)$; yes

2. b Yes   **c** Yes

3. a i $R_1{}^2 = R_2$ **ii** $R_2 R_1 = R_3$

    b i $R_3{}^2 = R_2$ **iii** $R_3 R_2 = R_1$

       ii $R_2 R_3 = R_1$

Exercise 8I (p. 186)

1. a I

    b i $R_2{}^2 = I$ **iii** $R_1 R_2 = R_3$

       ii $R_2 R_3 = R_1$

2. b i $B^2 = I$ **ii** $AB = R_2$

3. b i $DC = R_2$ **iv** $BC = R_1$

       ii $C^2 = I$ **v** $IC = C$

      iii $AC = R_3$

4. b i $A^2 = I$ **iii** $R_1 A = C$

       ii $AR_1 = D$

    c False

5. b A, B, A and B

6. a

		2nd transformation			
		A	B	C	D
1st transformation	A	I	R_2	R_1	R_3
	B	R_2	I	R_3	R_1
	C	R_3	R_1	I	R_2
	D	R_1	R_3	R_2	I

		2nd transformation			
		I	R_1	R_2	R_3
1st transformation	I	I	R_1	R_2	R_3
	R_1	R_1	R_2	R_3	I
	R_2	R_2	R_3	I	R_1
	R_3	R_3	I	R_1	R_2

b

Transformation	I	A	B	C	D	R_1	R_2	R_3
Inverse	I	A	B	C	D	R_3	R_2	R_1

A reflection in any line or a rotation of 180° will always return the object to its original position.

Exercise 8J (p. 188)

1. 2.9 cm

2.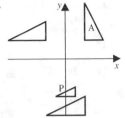

3. reflection in $x = 2$

4. a e.g. Reflect in the vertical line then rotate 90° clockwise

    b e.g. Rotate 90° anticlockwise twice.

5. b i B   **ii** A   **c i** R_3 **ii** I

Chapter 9

Exercise 9A (p. 192)

1. a 371.25 cm^2 **b** 333.25 cm^2

2. a The width of the unit may be up to 1 cm more than the width of the gap.

    b 1685.25 cm^2 **c** 86 cm^2

3. 5.9%

4. a 130.0175 cm^2 **c** 2555 litres

    b 41.6025 cm^2 **d** 109

5. 3250.2 g, 184.1 g

6. a 20.7 cm   **b** 327.7 g

7. a 25.05 cm   **c** 29.8 litres

    b 1165.25 m^2

8. C   **9. C**   **10. D**

11. 5.55 cm or 4.54 cm to 2 d.p.

12. 11.6 cm or 11.7 cm to 1 d.p.

13. 37.9° or 36.5°

14. 0.28 m

15. 11.8 cm or 11.7 cm

16. a i 15 cm   **ii** 14.8 cm

     b i 2.7 cm   **ii** 9.5 cm

17. a 85.5 cl, 84.5 cl   **d** 7

     b 11.5 cl, 12.5 cl   **e** 6 cl

     c 6

Exercise 9B (p. 200)

1. 118 cm^3 **3.** 640 cm^3

2. 72 cm^3 **4.** 107 cm^3

5. a 7.2 cm   **b** 7.08 cm

6. a 200 cm^3 **b** 7.41 cm

7. a i 6.25 cm and 6.15 cm

      ii 20.94 cm^2 and 19.99 cm^2

     iii 40.83 cm^3 and 38.31 cm^3

    b 7%

8. a 110.2 cm^2 **c** 37

    b 268.4 cm^3

Exercise 9C (p. 204)

1. **a** 10 m   **c** 36.9°   **e** 528 m²
   b 21.5 m   **d** 15.6°
2. **a** 10 cm   **c** 14.4 cm
   b 13.4 cm   **d** 22.6°
3. **a** 13.0 cm   **c** 49.1°   **e** 471 cm²
   b 45°   **d** 19.8 cm
4. **a** 21.2 cm   **c** 22.6 cm
   b 62.1°   **d** 70.7°
5. **a** 3.20 cm   **c** 38.7°
   b 51.3°   **d** 32.8°
6. **a** BD = 11.3 cm   **b** 40 cm²
   area = 56.6 cm²
7. **a** **i** 7.50 cm   **ii** 165 cm³
   b 152 cm²
8. **a** **i** 5.05 cm   **ii** 11.7 cm
   b **i** 4.95 cm   **ii** 11.6 cm
   c 23.5°
9. **a** FG = 9 cm, EG = 15 cm   **c** 720 cm³
   b HF = 5 cm, EH = 13 cm   **d** 564 cm²
10. **a** **i** $8\sqrt{2}$ cm   **ii** $4\sqrt{2}$ cm   **iii** $4\sqrt{7}$ cm
    b 167 g to 3 s.f.
11. **a** 5 cm   **c** 37.5 cm²   **e** 312 cm³
    b 5.77 cm   **d** 86.6 cm²
12. **a** 10.8 inches, 56.3°   **b** 33.7°

Exercise 9D (p. 209)

4. **a** 14.1 m   **c** 54.7°   **f** 63.4°
   b 12.2 m   **d** 11.2 m   **g** 63.4°
5. **a** AF = 5 cm, FC = 23.9 cm   **d** 22.6°
   c 12.1°   **e** 4740 g
6. **a** **i** 3 m   **ii** 2.60 m
   d 54.7°, 70.5°, 2.45 m   **e** 11.7 m²
7. **a** 26.2°   **c** 49.4°   **e** 29.5°
   b 47.3°   **d** 59.0°
8. **a** PN = 107.5 m, AN = 152.0 m
   b **i** 249 m   **ii** 272 m
   c **i** e.g. P   **ii** e.g. A
9. **a** DA = 5 m, DB = 9.43 m
   b DA: 36.9° to 1 d.p., DB: 18.5°

Exercise 9E (p. 213)

1. **a** 2.7 cm   **b** 44.3 cm   **c** 96.0 cm²
2. **a** 19.2 m   **b** 960 m³   **c** 730 m²
3. **a** 44.5 cm² and 43.5 cm²
   b 86.8 cm³ and 83.4 cm³
4. **a** 72 cm³   **b** 8 cm
5. **a** 29.5°   **b** 19.7°   **c** 55.1°   **d** 53.9°
6. 54.7°

Puzzle (p. 215)

e.g.

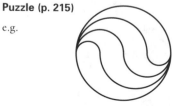

Summary 3

Revision Exercise 3.1 (p. 217)

1. 67.5 square units
2.

x	0	4	5
y	0	8	15.6

   a gradient = 4.87
   c **i** gradient = 0.375   **iii** gradient = 6
       ii gradient = 3.375
3.

x	2	2.5	3	4
y	12	11.25	9	0

   a 0   **b** −3   **c** −6
4. B   5. A and B
6. **a** after the end   **b** 18 m   **c** no
7. **a** D – shows 2 sections of journey taking place at
   the same time
   b A   **c** combination of methods
8. **a** gradient = 15, an average increase of 15 pairs
   a year from 1990 to 1993
   b gradient = 21, increasing at a rate of 21 pairs/
   year in 1993
9. **a** 0.5 m/s²   **b** 2.4 km

Revision Exercise 3.2 (p. 220)

1. 7.4 cm   2. 7.8 cm
3. **b** 1 : 200
   c **i** 17.3 m   **ii** 18.4 m   **iii** 35.8 m
4. Reflection in $y = -x$
5. **d** rotation about O of 180°
   e rotation about O of 90° clockwise
6. **a** 89.25 m²   **b** 71.25 m²
7. **a**

   b

   c

8. **a** **i** 17 cm   **ii** $\sqrt{145}$ cm   **iii** $\sqrt{306}$ cm
   b 24.6° to 3 s.f.
9. **a** **i** 8 cm   **ii** 12.5 cm   **iii** 11.0 cm
   b **i** 38.7°   **ii** 36.9°
   c 28.7°   **d** 140.4 g

10. 6.7%

11. a

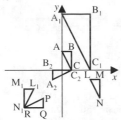

b $\begin{pmatrix} 3 \\ -4 \end{pmatrix}$ **c** reflection in $y = x$

Revision Exercise 3.3 (p. 224)

1. 35 square units

2.

x	1	2	4	6	8	10	12
y	12	6	3	2	1.5	1.2	1

    a gradient $= -0.75$ **b** -0.75

3. a 8.25 km   **b** 7.2 km/hour

4. a 1 m/s   **c** 0.6 m/s

   b 1 m/s   **d** -0.6 m/s

5. B   **6. C**, $180°$ about $(-1, 2)$

7. a $(5, -2)$ **b** $(1, 0)$

8. a 83.9 cm^2 **c** 102 litres

   b 94.6 cm^2 **d** yes

9. a 120 cm^3 **c** 37.4 cm^2 to 3 s.f.

   b 9.85 cm

10. a $45°$ **b** $35.3°$ **c** $45°$

Revision Exercise 3.4 (p. 227)

1. a i irrational **ii** rational   **iii** irrational

   b i $x = \frac{2}{3}$ **ii** $x = \frac{2}{3}$ **iii** $x = \frac{3}{2}$

2. a i $(5x - 3)(x + 6)$ **iii** $(5a + 4)(3a - 1)$

   ii $(7x - 5)(3x - 2)$

   b i $x = -\frac{4}{3}$ or $\frac{2}{7}$ **iii** $x = 0$ or 3 or -5

   ii $x = \frac{4}{5}$ or $-\frac{4}{5}$

3. a $p = 2$ and $q = 5$ **b** 8, 9 and 10

4. 8 cm

5. a i $\dfrac{a + b - 1}{(a + b)(a - b)}$ **ii** $\dfrac{x + 4}{(x + 2)(x - 2)}$

   b i $b = 2s - a - c$

     ii $\cos A = \dfrac{a^2 - b^2 - c^2}{2bc}$

6.

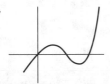

7. a 30, rate of increase in production is 30 units/
     day/month after 2 weeks

   b 115, rate of increase in production is 115
     units/day/month after 5 weeks

8. a speed   **c** speed

   b velocity   **d** velocity

9. b i C   **ii** B   **c i** R_1 **ii** R_2

10. a 120 cm^3 **b** 15 cm^2

Revision Exercise 3.5 (p. 228)

1. a i $3\sqrt{3}$ **ii** $10\sqrt{5}$

   b i $3\sqrt{3}$ **ii** $4\sqrt{2} - 3$

2. a i $(5x + 2)(3x - 7)$

    ii $(5 - x)(2x + 3)$

    iii $(4x + 9y)(4x - 9y)$

   b i $x = 2$ or $x = \frac{4}{3}$ **iii** $x = 0$ or $\frac{5}{3}$ or $-\frac{5}{3}$

    ii $x = 4$ or $-\frac{3}{2}$

3. $x = -3.69$ or 0.36

4. a 1.28×10^{-9} **c** 1.68×10^{-4}

   b 2×10^{1} **d** 9.6×10^{-3}

5. a 20   **b** 51   **7.** 119.5 square units

6. $(-5, 0), (2, 0)$ **8. A** and **C**

9. Enlargement by factor -2, centre $(-2, -1)$

10. a 69.7 cm^2 **b** 220.2 cm^3 **c** 23

Chapter 10

Exercise 10A (p. 232)

1. a 13.2 cm   **b** 79.2 cm^2

2. a 12.4 cm   **b** 46.6 cm^2

3. a 20.7 cm   **b** 58.0 cm^2

4. a 2.17 cm   **b** 4.99 cm^2

5. $66.8°$ **7.** $15.3°$ **9.** 8.91 cm

6. $43.0°$ **8.** 8.59 cm   **10.** 3.44 cm

11. a $36°$ **b** $\frac{5}{2}\pi \text{ cm}^2$

12. a $113.2°$ **b** 8.89 cm

13. a 11.7 cm   **b** 40.5 cm

14. a $79.3°$ **b** 59.2 cm

15. a 12.6 cm   **d** 37.7 cm^2

   c $120°$ **e** 50.3 cm^2

16. a 8 cm^2 **b** 4.57 cm^2

17. a 495 cm^2 **b** 106 cm^2

18. a 24.5 cm **b** 44.9 cm **c** 528 cm^2

19. 145 cm^2 **20. a** £36.20   **b** £6.20

Exercise 10B (p. 236)

1. 2.38 cm   **4.** 2.11 m   **7.** 3.37 cm

2. 2.69 cm   **5.** 16.8 cm

3. 1.73 m   **6.** 1.22 cm

Exercise 10C (p. 237)

1. 151 cm^2 **4.** 10.3 m^2 **7.** $13\,700 \text{ cm}^2$

2. 377 cm^2 **5.** 1210 cm^2 **8.** 25.9 m^2

3. 226 cm^2 **6.** 255 cm^2

9. a 377 cm^2 **b** 113 cm^2 **c** 603 cm^2

10. a 96.5 cm^2 **b** 161 cm^2

11. 209 cm^2 **13.** 4.40 m^2 **15.** $33\,900 \text{ cm}^2$

12. 928 cm^2 **14.** $16\,400 \text{ cm}^2$ **16.** 127 cm

17. a $1\,\text{m}^3$ **b** $1.03\,\text{m}$
18. $2.57\,\text{cm}$ **19.** $54\,\text{cm}$ **20.** $42\,400\,\text{cm}^3$

Exercise 10D (p. 239)

1. $1700\,\text{cm}^3$ **4.** $0.528\,\text{cm}^3$ **7.** $1150\,\text{cm}^3$
2. $29.4\,\text{cm}^3$ **5.** $27.2\,\text{cm}^3$ **8.** $330\,\text{cm}^3$
3. $19\,600\,\text{cm}^3$ **6.** $0.107\,\text{m}^3$
9. a $228\,\text{cm}^3$ **b** $5.50\,\text{g/cm}^3$

Exercise 10E (p. 241)

1. $126\,\text{cm}^2$ **4.** $15\,200\,\text{mm}^2$
2. $4.15\,\text{m}^2$ **5.** $163\,\text{cm}^2$
3. $434\,\text{cm}^2$
6. a $302\,\text{cm}^2$ **b** $10\,\text{cm}$ **c** $188\,\text{cm}^2$
7. a $\dfrac{\pi xl}{180}$ **d** sector area $= \dfrac{x\pi l^2}{360}$
   b $2\pi r$

Exercise 10F (p. 241)

1. $113\,\text{cm}^3$ **5.** $230\,000\,\text{cm}^3$
2. $1560\,\text{cm}^3$ **6.** $9200\,\text{mm}^3$
3. $24.4\,\text{m}^3$ **7.** $262\,\text{cm}^3$
4. $0.998\,\text{cm}^3$
8. a $145\,\text{cm}^3$ **b** $4.52\,\text{cm}$
9. $\dfrac{9\pi}{2}\,\text{cm}^3$ **10.** $23\,000$

Exercise 10G (p. 242)

1. $10.20\,\text{cm}^2$ **3.** $2120\,\text{cm}^2$ **5.** $3320\,\text{cm}^2$
2. $254\,\text{m}^2$ **4.** $10.2\,\text{m}^2$ **6.** 6
7. a $2.82\,\text{cm}$ **b** $94.0\,\text{cm}^3$

Exercise 10H (p. 242)

1. 596 **3.** sphere $- 25.7\,\text{cm}^3$ bigger
2. $572\,\text{cm}^3$ **4.** $239\,000\,\text{cm}^3$
5. a $15\,\text{cm}$ **b** $3020\,\text{cm}^3$
6. a $\frac{64}{3}\pi\,\text{cm}^3$ **b** $64\pi\,\text{cm}^3$ **c** $\frac{128}{3}\pi\,\text{cm}^3$
7. a $\dfrac{32\pi}{3}$ **b** $\dfrac{2048\pi}{3}$ **c** 64
8. sphere by $16.5\,\text{cm}^2$ **9.** $462\,\text{cm}^2$
10. a $15\,\text{cm}$ **b** $933\,\text{cm}^2$
11. enough paint to cover $2.4\,\text{m}^2$ still needed
12. a $2\pi\sqrt{13}$ square units   **b** 4π cubic units
13. a $1.40\,\text{cm}$ **b** $1.70\,\text{cm}^3/\text{min}$
14. $511\,\text{cm}^2$

Mixed Exercise 10I (p. 245)

1. a $18.4\,\text{cm}$ **b** $81.5\,\text{cm}$
2. a no   **b** yes   **c** no
3. a $43.2\,\text{cm}^3$ **b** $834\,\text{g}$ **4.** $20\,\text{cm}$
5. a $37.7\,\text{cm}^3$ **b** $59.0\,\text{cm}^2$ **c** $0.67\,\text{g/cm}^2$
6. C   **9. D**   **12. B**   **15. B**
7. B   **10. D**   **13. D**   **16. C**
8. A   **11. A**   **14. C**   **17. C**

Chapter 11

Exercise 11A (p. 249)

1. c $x = 90$
   d i $53°$ and $127°$
      ii $37°$ and $143°$
      iii $24°$ and $156°$
      The two angles add up to $180°$.
2. a $\sin 30° = 0.5$, $\sin 150° = 0.5$,
      $150° = 180° - 30°$
   b $\sin 40° = 0.64$, $\sin 140° = 0.64$,
      $140° = 180° - 40°$
   c $\sin 72° = 0.95$, $\sin 108° = 0.95$,
      $108° = 180° - 72°$

Exercise 11B (p. 250)

1. $\sin x° = \frac{5}{13}$ **5.** $\sin x° = \frac{7}{25}$ **9.** $x° = 28°$
2. $\sin x° = \frac{1}{2}$ **6.** $\sin x° = \frac{40}{41}$ **10.** $x° = 80°$
3. $\sin x° = \frac{2}{5}$ **7.** $x° = 15°$ **11.** $x° = 5°$
4. $\sin x° = \frac{3}{10}$ **8.** $x° = 40°$ **12.** $x° = 89°$

Exercise 11C (p. 251)

1. c $x = 90$ **d** It is negative.
   e i $37°$ **ii** $143°$
      They add up to $180°$
2. a $\cos 30° = 0.87$, $\cos 150° = -0.87$,
      $150° = 180° - 30°$
   b $\cos 50° = 0.64$, $\cos 130° = -0.64$,
      $130° = 180° - 50°$
   c $\cos 84° = 0.10$, $\cos 96° = -0.10$,
      $96° = 180° - 84°$

Exercise 11D (p. 252)

1. $\cos x° = -\frac{3}{5}$ **3.** $\cos x° = -\frac{2}{5}$
2. $\cos x° = -\frac{2}{3}$ **4.** $\cos x° = -\frac{7}{8}$
5. a $160°$ **b** $130°$

Exercise 11E (p. 253)

1. $\cos A = \frac{24}{25}$ $\tan A = \frac{7}{24}$
2. $\sin A = \frac{12}{13}$ $\tan A = \frac{12}{5}$
3. $\sin P = \frac{3}{5}$ $\cos A = \frac{4}{5}$
4. $\tan D = \frac{4}{3}$ $\sin D = \frac{4}{5}$
5. $\cos X = \frac{40}{41}$ $\tan X = \frac{9}{40}$
6. $\sin A = \frac{1}{\sqrt{2}}$ $\cos A = \frac{1}{\sqrt{2}}$
7. b i $\sin 60° = \frac{\sqrt{3}}{2}$ **iii** $\tan 60° = \sqrt{3}$
      ii $\cos 60° = \frac{1}{2}$
   c i $\sin 30° = \frac{1}{2}$ **iii** $\tan 30° = \frac{1}{\sqrt{3}}$
      ii $\cos 30° = \frac{\sqrt{3}}{2}$
8. b i $\sin 45° = \frac{1}{\sqrt{2}}$ **iii** $\tan 45° = 1$
      iii $\tan 45° = \frac{1}{\sqrt{2}}$

Exercise 11F (p. 254)

1. $\cos A = \frac{\sqrt{3}}{2}$ **a** $\frac{\sqrt{3}}{2}$ **b** $\frac{1}{2}$
2. a i 1 **ii** $\frac{1}{2}$ **b** 90° **c** 30°
3. a $-\frac{24}{25}$ **b** $\frac{7}{25}$
4. 30° and 150° **5.** −0.515 **6.** 108°
7. a $\frac{4}{5}$ **b** $\frac{3}{5}$ **c** $-\frac{3}{5}$

Exercise 11G (p. 256)

1. 4.92 cm **7.** 5.60 cm **13.** 224 cm
2. 13.0 cm **8.** 413 cm **14.** 18.4 cm
3. 9.74 cm **9.** 64.1 cm **15.** $\frac{20}{\sqrt{3}\sqrt{2}}$ cm
4. 3.68 cm **10.** 19.7 cm **16.** $\frac{20}{3}$
5. 14.6 cm **11.** 18.4 cm
6. 66.0 cm **12.** 77.0 cm

Exercise 11H (p. 260)

1. 61.7° **5.** 76.5° or 103.5°
2. 59.7° or 120.3° **6.** 28.2°
3. 42.7° **7.** 47.9°
4. 37.2°
8. a angle R
b $\hat{R} > \hat{P}$ so if $\hat{P}$ is obtuse so is $\hat{R}$ but a triangle cannot have 2 obtuse angles.
c no, no angles given

Exercise 11I (p. 262)

1. 5.73 cm **10.** 28.9 cm
2. 7.95 cm **11.** 5.05 cm
3. 7.68 cm **12.** 16.9 cm
4. 18.4 cm **13.** 24.1°
5. 7.03 cm **14.** 108.2°
6. 14.2 cm **15.** 92.9°
7. 15.9 cm **16.** 29.0° (angle A)
8. 21.6 cm **17.** 95.7° (angle Y)
9. 43.0 cm **18.** 48.2° (angle E)
19. a 13.1 cm **b** 72.3°
20. a $\frac{1}{16}$ **b** it is acute
21. 40.7°

Exercise 11J (p. 266)

	a	b	c	$\hat{A}$	$\hat{B}$	$\hat{C}$
1.		17.0				
2.	117				76.3°	
3.		77.9				
4.			23.3			
5.	308		346			
6.		17.4	12.4			
7.	29.7				38°	
8.	20.8					

Exercise 11K (p. 267)

1. 2610 cm^2 **5.** 126 square units
2. 572 cm^2 **6.** 22 800 cm^2
3. 81.1 cm^2 **7.** 35.5 square units
4. 18 900 mm^2 **8.** 6.82 m^2
9. C = 83.3°, area = 27.8 cm^2
10. PR = 9.91 cm, area = 53.8 cm^2
11. $\hat{M}$ = 48.9°, LN = 14.7 cm^2
12. AC = 4.46 cm

Exercise 11L (p. 269)

1. 62.3 km **3.** 88°
2. a 18.1° **b** 42.7 m
4. a 42 cm^2 **b** 44.4° **c** 8.52 m
5. AC = 5.76 km
BC = 4.29 km
69.1 km/hour
6. a 0.2588 **b** 97.6 m
7. a AC = 4.26 cm **c** 16.0 cm^2
b 75.1°
8. a TAB = 39°, ATB = 9°
b AT = 1430 m **c** CT = 1080 m
9. a AB = 10.5 m **c** 81.0 m
b BC = 6.42 m **d** 8.96 m
10. a i AB = 14.1 cm **ii** BC = 8.89 cm
b 81.3 cm^2
11. a AOB = 47.2° **c** AC = 10.7 cm
b BOC = 17.3° **d** area = 51.6 cm^2
12. a 27.9 miles on a bearing of 299°
b i 13.4 miles **ii** 24.5 miles

Mixed Exercise 11M (p. 272)

1. $\sin A = \frac{12}{13}$, $\tan A = \frac{12}{5}$
2. 21.5° or 158.5° **5.** 10.9 cm
3. −0.43 **6.** 38.0 cm^2
4. 196 cm to 3 s.f. **7.** 13.5 km
8. a $\frac{5}{8}$
b i $\frac{\sqrt{39}}{8}$ **ii** $\frac{3\sqrt{39}}{4}$

Chapter 12

Exercise 12B (p. 280)

1. The square root of any number between 0 and 1.
2. Not when $x = 4$.
3. Diagonals of a rhombus cut at right angles and a rhombus is a parallelogram.
4. e.g. 120°, 40° and 40°
5. square root step; i.e. $2 - \frac{5}{2} = \pm(3 - \frac{5}{2})$
6. cannot divide by $x - y$ since $x - y = 0$

Exercise 12C (p. 281)

1. yes **2.** no **3.** yes **4.** no
5. Need length of a side.

Exercise 12D (p. 282)

1. yes, sides are equal (SSS)
2. no   **4.** no   **6.** yes, SSS
3. no   **5.** no   **7.** yes, SSS
8. △ABC and △ACD   **10.** Yes, SSS
9. yes, SSS

Exercise 12E (p. 283)

5. triangles 1 and 3 are congruent
6. two triangles

Exercise 12F (p. 284)

1. yes, 2 angles and corresponding side are equal (AAS)
2. no   **5.** no   **8.** no
3. yes, AAS   **6.** yes, AAS   **9.** yes, AAS
4. yes, AAS   **7.** yes, AAS   **10.** yes, AAS

Exercise 12G (p. 285)

1. yes   **2.** no   **3.** yes   **4.** no   **5.** yes

Exercise 12H (p. 286)

1. yes   **4.** no, 2 possible
2. no, 2 possible   **5.** yes
3. yes   **6.** yes
7. can find the length of the third side in right-angled triangles

Exercise 12I (p. 287)

1. yes, SAS   **6.** not certainly
2. not certainly   **7.** yes, RHS
3. yes, RHS   **8.** not certainly
4. yes, SAS   **9.** yes, RHS
5. yes, SAS   **10.** yes, SAS

Exercise 12J (p. 288)

1. no   **5.** no   **9.** yes, RHS
2. yes, AAS   **6.** yes, SAS   **10.** yes, SSS
3. yes, SSS   **7.** no, similar   **11.** yes, AAS
4. yes, AAS   **8.** yes, AAS   **12.** no

Exercise 12M (p. 297)

1. AC and BD bisect the angles of the rhombus.
2. a $\hat{AEB} = \hat{BEC} = 90°$ **c** $BE = ED$
   b $AE = EC$
3. no   **4.** $AC = DB$
5. Yes, no, midpoint of AC, angles at E are all 90°
6. no   **7.** equal

Exercise 12N (p. 300)

1. 5 cm   **5.** 8 cm   **8.** 6 cm
2. 5 cm   **6.** 5 cm   **9.** 5.7 cm
3. 60°   **7.** 9.5 cm

Mixed Exercise 12Q (p. 304)

2. a yes, SAS   **c** yes, RHS
   b no   **d** yes, AAS

Chapter 13

Exercise 13A (p. 308)

1. 180°   **2.** 180°   **3.** 180°

Exercise 13B (p. 309)

1. $d = 108$ **3.** $f = 103$ **5.** 131°
2. $e = 84$ **4.** $k = 115$
6. a 112°   **b** 87°   **8. a** 110°   **b** 50°
7. a 121°   **b** 68°

Exercise 13C (p. 311)

1. $p = q$ **5.** $p = 54, q = 76$
2. $r = s$ **6.** $r = 126, s = 83$
3. $y = 100$ **7.** $h = 116, i = 32$
4. $z = 109$ **8.** $g = 54, h = 120$
9. $x = 112, y = 68, z = 112$
10. $l = 126, m = 63, n = 117$
11. a 62°   **b** 56°   **c** 124°   **d** 16°
12. a 54°   **b** 90°   **c** 27°   **d** 90°
13. a 53°   **b** 37°   **c** 51°   **d** 39°
14. a 38°   **b** 104°   **c** 52°   **d** 14°

Exercise 13D (p. 314)

1. O moves in a horizontal line 20 cm above the ground.
   a 1 point   **b** 20 cm   **c** radius, 90°
2.   **4. b** tangent, 90°

3.

Exercise 13E (p. 316)

1. OB = 5 cm, CB = 2 cm
2. $x = 30$
3. $x = 50, y = 40$
4. $x = 20, y = 70$
5. a 40°   **b** 50°
6. AB = 12 cm, $\hat{OBA} = 22.6°$
7. $x = 30°, y = 60°, z = 60°$
8. 30°   **9.** 5 cm
11. 9.80 cm

Exercise 13F (p. 318)

2. 90°, tangents   **5.** 5.8 cm
4. a 4 cm   **6.** 10.4 cm

Exercise 13H (p. 320)

1. $p = q = 65$
2. $e = f = 67, g = i = 23, h = 134$
3. **a** $50°$
   b kite (2 pairs of adjacent sides equal) and cyclic quadrilateral (opposite angles supplementary)
4. **a** $96°$ **b** $48°$ **5. a** $36°$ **b** $36°$
6. **a** 6 cm **b** $73.7°$ to 3 s.f.
7. 8 cm **9.** 5.77 cm to 3 s.f.
8. yes **10.** $30°$, 13.9 cm to 3 s.f.
11. 19.3 cm, 13.7 cm, 13.7 cm **14.** 4 cm
13. They are equal.

Exercise 13I (p. 323)

5. $d = 73, e = 26, f = 81$
6. $p = q = 60, r = s = 60$
7. $k = 64, l = 64, m = 64, n = 52$
8. $u = 67, v = 67$
9. $p = 57, q = 57$
10. $w = 90, x = 27, y = 117$
11. $d = 47, e = 47, f = 47, g = 86$
12. $e = 54, f = 54, g = 54, h = 72$
13. $k = 74, l = 53, m = 53$
14. $r = 90, s = 55, t = 35$
15. $s = 30, t = 60, u = 60, v = 10$
16. $x = 28, y = 62, z = 62$
17. **a** $40°$ **c** $100°$ **e** $65°$
    b $40°$ **d** $80°$ **f** $45°$
18. **a** $45°$ **b** $55°$ **c** $80°$ **d** $80°$
19. **a** $25°$ **b** $50°$ **c** $65°$
20. **a** $52°$ **b** $42°$ **c** $10°$
21. **a i** $x°$ **ii** $(180 - x)°$ **iii** $90°$
    b i parallel **ii** diameter of circle
22. **a i** $48°$ **ii** $75°$ **iii** $30°$
    b isosceles
23. **a** $36°$ **b** $108°$ **c** $72°$ **d** $18°$
24. **a** $38°$ **b** $20°$ **c** $46°$
25. **a** $x = 20$
    b i $20°$ **ii** $140°$ **iii** $60°$

Exercise 13J (p. 327)

1. Locus of C is a circle of diameter AB.
2. Locus of M is a straight line through O, perpendicular to AB.
3. Major arcs of circles on chord AB
4. A circle with centre O and radius OT
5.
6.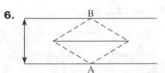

7. **a** straight line parallel to given line
   b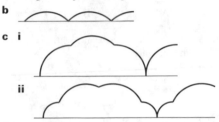
   c i
   ii

8. **a** semicircle, radius 10 cm, centre A
   b semicircle, radius 10 cm, centre B
   c semicircle, radius 10 cm, centre midpoint of AB
   d semicircle, radius 5 cm, centre midpoint of AB
9. **a** circle radius
     i 6 cm, centre A **iii** 3 cm, centre D
     ii 12 cm, centre D
   c circles, centre midpoint of AD, of radius 6 cm and 9 cm
10.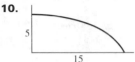
11. **c** 3.2 m **d** no

Exercise 13K (p. 330)

1. $d = 37, e = 53, f = 57, g = 33$
2. $i = 37, j = 53, k = 37, l = 37$
3. $f = 71, g = 71, h = 71, i = 38$
4. $d = 90, e = 45, f = 45, g = 45, h = 90$
5. **a** $132°$ **b** $48°$
6. **a** $60°$ **b** $61.5°$ **c** $58.5°$
7. **a** $\frac{x}{2}°$ **b** $180° - \left(\frac{x}{2}\right)°$ **c** $\frac{x}{2}°$
8. **a** $94°$ **b** $14°$
9. P draws a square three times bigger than original.

Summary 4

Revision Exercise 4.1 (p. 336)

1. **a** 20.8 cm **b** 99.7 cm^2
2. cylinder, 8.42 cm^3 bigger than cone
3. **a** square cut from circle
   b i 113 cm^3 **ii** 126 cm^2
4. **a** 5.25 cm **c** 1070 m^3 and 1020 m^2
   b 12.25 cm
5. **a** 32.0 cm^3 **b** 160 cm^3 **c** 0.687 g/cm^3
6. **a i** $\frac{\sqrt{3}}{2}$ **ii** $\frac{1}{\sqrt{3}}$
   b $\sin A = \frac{2}{\sqrt{13}}, \cos A = \frac{3}{\sqrt{3}}$
7. **a** 0.9063 **c** $53.1°$ and $126.9°$ to 3 s.f.
   b $126°$
8. 238 cm **9.** $P = 39.7°$, $Q = 94.3°$
10. **i** 8.30 cm **ii** 36.5 cm^2
11. 136 cm^3 (or 140 cm^3) **12.** $48.7°$

Revision Exercise 4.2 (p. 338)

1. a yes, ASA   **b** no
2. yes, SSS
3. a no, may be two triangles with these
    measurements
  b yes   **c** yes   **d** yes
6. a $d = 54$
  b $e = 105$, $f = 110$
  c $d = 106$, $e = 74$, $f = 127$, $g = 53$
7. a 6 cm   **b** 4 cm
8. $x = 30$, $y = 60$, $z = 90$
9. arc of circle centre A, radius AC
10. a $x = 126$, $y = 121.5$
  b $63°$, $16.0\,\text{cm}^2$
11. a i $90° - x°$ **ii** $x°$ **iii** $90° - 2x°$

Revision Exercise 4.3 (p. 341)

1. a 4.55 cm   **b** $11.4\,\text{cm}^2$
2. 4.39 cm   **3.** $103\,\text{cm}^3$ to 3 s.f.
4. AB $= 8.94\,\text{cm}$, BC $= 6.90\,\text{cm}$
5. a $y = 180 - x$ **b** 4.90 cm
6. a yes, ASA   **b** no
7. yes, SSS
8. a $83°$ **b** $106°$
9. $d = 36$, $e = 72$, $f = 54$, $g = 18$
10. both 5.7 cm

Revision Exercise 4.4 (p. 342)

1. a i $\frac{1}{45}$ **ii** $1\frac{7}{9}$
  b i $\frac{\sqrt{10}}{10}$ **ii** $\frac{\sqrt{3}}{9}$ **iii** $4\sqrt{2} - 3$
2. a $p = 2$, $a = 9$, $c = 4$ **b** 13, 14
3. $x = \dfrac{5 \pm \sqrt{37}}{2}$
4. a $W = pqr$ **b** $p = \dfrac{W}{qr}$
5. $x < \frac{2}{3}$ and $x > 2$
6. a 0.86 miles
  b i 0.4 miles per minute **iii** 24 mph
7. a i $6\sqrt{2}$ **ii** $6\sqrt{2}$ **iii** $6\sqrt{3}$
  b $72\,\text{cm}^3$
8. a i $48\,000\pi\,\text{cm}^3$ **iii** 48π litres
  b $5600\pi\,\text{cm}^2$
9. 12.5 mm
10. $d = 41$, $e = 41$, $f = 98$

Revision Exercise 4.5 (p. 344)

1. a i $\dfrac{3 - \sqrt{3}}{3}$ **ii** 7   **iii** $29 + 4\sqrt{7}$
  b i 1.25   **ii** 0.725   **iii** 0.591
2. a i $(5x - 2)(x - 7)$ **ii** $(3x - 2)(x + 7)$
  b i $x = 0$ or ± 1.91 **ii** $x = \frac{1}{5}$ or $-\frac{3}{5}$
  c $k = 7$, $p = 42$ or $k = -7$, $p = -42$
3. $x = 1.84$ or 0.41

4. a $c = \dfrac{3A}{a} - 3b$
  b $x = 2 + y$, $x = 4$ and $y = 2$, $x = -2$ and
    $y = -4$
5. 4.29 cm
6. a i $14\,\text{cm}^2$ **ii** $35.7°$ to 3 s.f.
  b 4.69 cm to 3 s.f.
7. $\triangle$s AED, BEC and CED, SSS
8. 61.5 square units
9. a

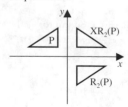

  b Y
10. a $90°$ **b** $60°$ **c** $30°$

Chapter 14

Exercise 14A (p. 347)

1. a $1 : 2 : 3 : 4$
  b $1 : 2 : 3 : 4$
  c $1 : 4 : 9 : 16$, square of the ratios
  d $1 : 2 : 3 : 4$
2. a i 6 units   **ii** 4 units
  b 12 square units
  c i $\frac{1}{2}$ **ii** $\frac{1}{4}$ **iii** $\frac{1}{4}$
  d i $\frac{3}{8}$ **ii** $\frac{9}{64}$ **iii** $\frac{9}{64}$
  area GHI $= 21\frac{1}{3}$ square units
  HZ $= 5\frac{1}{3}$
3. HG $= 7\,\text{cm}$, area ABCD $= 32\,\text{cm}^2$,
  area EFGH $= 98\,\text{cm}^2$

Exercise 14B (p. 348)

1. $\dfrac{\text{area ABCD}}{\text{area WXYZ}} = \dfrac{4}{1}$ **5.** $\dfrac{\text{area ABC}}{\text{area XYZ}} = \dfrac{25}{9}$

2. $\dfrac{\text{area ABC}}{\text{area PQR}} = \dfrac{9}{25}$ **6.** $\dfrac{\text{area ABCD}}{\text{area PQRS}} = \dfrac{25}{49}$

3. $\dfrac{\text{area AB}}{\text{area CD}} = \dfrac{4}{9}$ **7.** $1 : 1225$

4. $\dfrac{\text{area ABCD}}{\text{area KLMN}} = \dfrac{9}{16}$ **8.** $1 : 400$

9. $65.0\,\text{cm}^2$ **13.** $7 : 4$ **17.** $64\,\text{cm}^2$
10. $5 : 3$ **14.** 1.2   **18.** $50\,\text{cm}^2$
11. $3 : 2$ **15.** $8\,\text{cm}^2$
12. $2 : 1$ **16.** $16\,\text{cm}^2$
19. 17.2 cm by 21 cm   **22.** $200\,\text{m}^2$
20. $1.5\,\text{cm}^2$ **23.** $4 : 1$
21. $2 : 1$
24. a 2.25 cm   **b** $\frac{9}{49}$ cm   **c** $\frac{9}{40}$
25. $1 : 3 : 9$ **26.** $4 : 9$, AB $:$ BC $= 2 : 3$

Exercise 14C (p. 353)

1. a $1:2:3$ **b** $1:8:27$
2. a i $2:3$ **ii** $2:3$ **iii** $2:3$
b $8:27$
3. a i $4:5:7$ **ii** $4:5:7$
b $64:125:343$
4. 135 **5.** $8:1$ **6.** $27:64$ **7.** $2:3$
8. a $4:3$ **b** $4:3$ **9. a** $4:1$ **b** $8:1$
10. a $1:100$ **c** $1:10$
b $1:1000$ **d** $1:1$
11. $1\frac{11}{16}$ pints and 4 pints
12. 12.5 and 21.6 centilitres
13. a 9 cm and 12 cm **b** $64\,\text{cm}^2$ and $100\,\text{cm}^2$
14. a $1:50$ **c** 3 cm
b $1:125\,000$ **d** $7500\,\text{cm}^2$
15. 64 kg **16.** 34.6 ml
17. a 21% **b** 33% **19. a** 44% **b** 73%
18. a 224% **b** 483%
20. a 26% **b** 26% **c** 59%
21. 49% **23.** £39.35
22. 23.1 cm to 3 s.f. **24.** 1938 g difference

Exercise 14D (p. 358)

1. a $7:9$ **b** $7:9$
2. a $45\,\text{cm}^2$ **b** 8 cm **c** $3:4$
3. a 3.2 cm **b** $4:9$ **c** $\frac{16}{81}$ **d** $\frac{16}{65}$
4. $\frac{1}{8}$ **5. a** $1:1.10$ **b** $1:1.21$

Chapter 15

Exercise 15B (p. 363)

1. a mean = 8.6, s.d. = 4.13
b mean = 57.2, s.d. = 20.8
c mean = 34.55, s.d. = 15.0
d mean = 451, s.d. = 15.0
2. 1.21 **3.** mean = 23.4, s.d. = 3.84
4. b Sarah: mean = 1.93, s.d. = 1.52
Kevin: mean = 1.07, s.d. = 0.623
5. mean = £77 500, s.d. = £28 500
6. b £15 200

Exercise 15D (p. 366)

1. a mean = 6.65 yrs, s.d. = 0.935 yrs
b mean = 5.51, s.d. = 1.31
c mean = 4.34, s.d. = 0.726
3. a mean = 38.7, s.d. = 6.18
mean = 37, s.d. = 7.92
4. a first, less variation
c 10 with 1 cell, 10 with 8 cells
5. mean = 5.25, s.d. = 4.55
6. mean = 146, s.d. = 13.6
7. b mean = 3.1, s.d. = 2.53
8. mean = 187, s.d. = 55.4
9. mean = 193, s.d. = 44.6

10. estimated mean for area B is slightly high because the halfway values are not necessarily the mean values for the groups.

Exercise 15E (p. 371)

1. theoretical: mean = 3, s.d. = 1.22 to 3 s.f.
actual: mean = 3.03, s.d. = 1.13
2. e.g. Winchester because higher mean weight and less variable in weight
3. Maths test mean is 10 marks higher than English test mean (the difference in the standard deviations is not substantial).
4. As a percentage of the total for each test
5. a mean up 50 g but standard deviation double – some improvement
b mean down 20 g and s.d. less – not an improvement
c mean up 20 g and s.d. unchanged – definite improvement
d mean unchanged but s.d. nearly double – definitely not an improvement
6. a mean = 49.2, s.d. = 19.3
b mean = 59.2, s.d. = 19.3
7. a mean = £21 700, s.d. = £13 500
b mean = £22 785, s.d. = £13 500
c mean = £22 785, s.d. = £14 200
d more benefit from the first method (the variation is unchanged)

Chapter 16

Exercise 16A (p. 374)

1. £53 **2.** £25

Exercise 16B (p. 375)

1. a i £10 **ii** £82 **iii** 8 pence
b i intercept of y-axis, c **iii** gradient, m
d i 210 **ii** 5500 **e** 6124 units
2. a $p = 0.15q + 5$ **c** $n = 195r + 10$
b $s = 38 - 8.6t$ **d** $w = -2.16a + 1.9$
3. a 9.30, French francs per £1
b 0.086, cost per unit in £
c 17, increase in temperature per minute
d −0.3 litres used per mile
4. a i 1 200 000 gallons **ii** 5 days
b −100 000; water loss per day
c 1 500 000; initial amount of water in reservoir
d dry **e** 15 days from day zero
5. $c = 11.25h + 25$, $c = $ cost in £,
$h = $ number of hours
a £92.50 **c** £11.25
b 6 hours 40 minutes
6. a $C = -12t + 326$
b 326°C **c** 23 minutes
7. a $v = 9.8t + 0.4$ **c** 98.4 m/s to 3 s.f.
b acceleration

Exercise 16C (p. 381)

1. a Do not know; no reading at this time.

Exercise 16D (p. 383)

1. a 1998–1999
   b cannot tell; depends on too many unknown factors such as pollutants entering the lake
2. a £1000   **c** 15 000 miles and £1000
   b 10 500 miles
3. b 9 peaches ± 2 peaches but probably worse as this is beyond the range of the given information
4. $I = 50f + 3550$ where f is the period number, 5050
6. c 43
   d the information is about adults, children have different proportions
7. b mean French = 66, mean maths = 67.4
   c 71
8. a mean number bad peaches per box = 2.125
   mean number hours in transit per box = 7.25
   b 8 or 9 peaches

Exercise 16E (p. 387)

2. $y = 16.5$ **3.** $M = 34l - 0.8$
4. a i t on horizontal axis   **ii** a is gradient
   b 10, second reading appears to be too high
   c $u = 11.2, a = 0.24$ **d** 120 seconds
5. b i 94 km/h   **ii** 920 seconds
6. b 30 m   **c** 14th week after last rainfall
7. a $-44°C$ **b** 10 900 m

Exercise 16F (p. 390)

1. c $k = 0.001, c = 0$ **e** 5.03 miles
   d i 0   **ii** 2.1 miles
2. c $k = 0.000\,026$ **d** 1.04 km
3. a Plot $\frac{1}{X}$ against Y **c** $A = 2.8, B = 1.7$
5. a straight line graph with negative gradient
   b straight line with gradient -16 and intercept 8 on vertical axis

Chapter 17

Exercise 17A (p. 394)

1. independent   **3.** conditional
2. conditional   **4.** independent

Exercise 17B (p. 395)

1. a i $\frac{5}{8}$ **ii** $\frac{3}{8}$ **b** $\frac{3}{7}$ **c** $\frac{4}{7}$
2. a i $\frac{1}{13}$ **ii** $\frac{1}{4}$ **b** $\frac{4}{17}$ **c** $\frac{4}{51}$
3. a $\frac{4}{9}$ **b i** $\frac{3}{8}$ **ii** $\frac{5}{8}$ **c i** $\frac{1}{2}$ **ii** $\frac{1}{2}$
4. 0.66

5. a 0.54   **b** 0.61   **c** 0.87   **d** 0.34
6. a $\frac{1}{2}$ **b** $\frac{2}{3}$
7. a 84   **b** $\frac{25}{84}$ **c** $\frac{5}{13}$
8. a $\frac{4}{7}$ **b** $\frac{1}{4}$
9. a 105   **b** 41%   **c** $\frac{22}{57}$

Exercise 17C (p. 399)

1. a i $\frac{2}{15}$ **ii** $\frac{1}{3}$ **iii** $\frac{3}{5}$
2. a $\frac{4}{9}$ **b** $\frac{1}{2}$ **c** $\frac{1}{6}$ **d** $\frac{5}{18}$
3. a $\frac{2}{5}$ **b** $\frac{1}{3}$ **c** $\frac{1}{3}$
4. a $\frac{3}{7}$ **c** $\frac{2}{7}$ **e** $\frac{2}{7}$
   b $\frac{1}{7}$ **d** $\frac{2}{7}$ **f** $\frac{4}{7}$
5. a $\frac{2}{3}$ **c** $\frac{1}{2}$ **e** $\frac{5}{21}$
   b $\frac{5}{8}$ **d** $\frac{1}{3}$
6. a $\frac{3}{5}$ **b** $\frac{8}{15}$
7. a $\frac{2}{3}$ **b** $\frac{1}{3}$ **c** $\frac{1}{6}$
8. a 0.168   **b** 0.507
9. a $\frac{1}{3}$ **b** $\frac{3}{4}$
10. a 0.64   **b** 0.16
11. b i 0.18   **ii** 0.06
   c i 70   **ii** 18   **iii** 6
   d 0.94
12. a $\frac{1}{6}$ **d** Yes, 76 games
   c i $\frac{5}{36}$ **ii** $\frac{61}{216}$
13. a i $\frac{1}{4}$ **ii** $\frac{3}{4}$ **d** 27
   c i $\frac{3}{16}$ **ii** $\frac{9}{64}$
14. a 19.5%   **b** 4.2%
15. a $\frac{1}{2}$ **b** $\frac{12}{91}$
   c Alison has a higher chance of winning because if she does not win on her second selection she still has a chance of winning so the game is unfair.
   d Betty wins $-\frac{2}{7}$, Alison wins $-\frac{9}{26}$
   The game is fairer but Alison is still more likely to win after they have each selected two discs.

Mixed Exercise 17D (p. 405)

1. a 0   **b** $\frac{1}{25}$ **c** 0.000 32
2. a $\frac{1}{13}$ **b** $\frac{1}{4}$ **c** $\frac{4}{13}$
3. a $\frac{1}{13}$ **b** $\frac{1}{17}$ **c** 0.145
4. $\frac{12}{51}$ **5.** 0.104   **6.** 0.35   **7.** $\frac{4}{9}$
8. a $\frac{1}{6}$ **b** $\frac{1}{6}$ **c** $\frac{2}{3}$
9. 0.08   **b** £300
10. a $\frac{3}{50}$ **b** $\frac{3}{40}$ **c** 0.36   **d** 0.42
11. a $\frac{27}{50}$ **b** $\frac{80}{149}$ **c** 14   **e** $\frac{1}{3}$
   f Some are counted twice, e.g. those who did not smoke but did drink.

Puzzle (p. 407)   210

Summary 5

Revision Exercise 5.1 (p. 409)

1. a 7.5 cm   **b** 25:64
2. 10 cm^2 **3.** 125:64
4. a 3:4   **b** 3:7   **c** 9:49
5. a 5:6   **b** 125:216   **6.** 12.9 g
7. b Ian   mean = 1, s.d. = 0.802
Jean   mean = 1.71, s.d. = 1.06
   c Ian spent less time on average than Jean and the variation in his times was also less.
8. mean = 4.83, s.d. = 1.07 to 3 s.f.
9. a mean = £499, s.d. = £32.60
   b mean = £519, s.d. = £35.30
   c e.g. mean charge is £20 higher in area 2 and more variable.
10. a mean = 100.4, s.d. = 16.4 to 3 s.f.
   b mean = 75.4, s.d. = 16.4 to 3 s.f.
11. a 9187.5π cm^2 **c** 360 cm
12. a 7.44 to 3 s.f.   **b i** 71   **ii** 7.44

Revision Exercise 5.2 (p. 413)

1. a $D = 6t + 10$ **b** $p = 40 - 1.3q$
2. a -0.025, decrease in depth/minute
   b 0.25, cost per unit
3. a profit increases with increase in advertising costs
   b i £1.71 million   **ii** £29 000
   c i $m = 0.0145$ **ii** $c = 1.07$
   $P = 0.0145A + 1.07$
4. a 160 p   **d** upwards
   b week 7 – 35 p gain   **e** 210 p
   c week 3 – 40 p loss
5. c i $k = 80$ **ii** 160 litres per minute
6. a i $\frac{1}{13}$ **ii** $\frac{1}{4}$ **b** $\frac{4}{17}$ **c** $\frac{4}{51}$
7. a $\frac{5}{8}$ **b** $\frac{5}{7}$ **c i** $\frac{5}{14}$ **ii** $\frac{3}{28}$ **iii** $\frac{3}{8}$
8. a $\frac{5}{51}$ **b** 0.32   **c** 0.68   **9.** 0.648
10. a 177   **b** $\frac{79}{177}$ **c** $\frac{7}{15}$
11. a 0.42   **b** 0.1638   **12.** £4.2 million

Revision Exercise 5.3 (p. 417)

1. 54 cm^2 **2.** 7:5
3. a $A = 4\pi r^2$, $V = \frac{4}{3}\pi r^3$
   b $\frac{3}{2}r$, $A = 9\pi r^2$
   c Increased by $5\pi r^2$, 125% increase
   d 238% increase
4. mean = 248, s.d. = 4.72

5. b mean = 22.25, s.d. = 9.96
6. a 24.2 cm   **b** 259 g
   c Unlikely, the spring is not likely to behave in the same way for such a load.
7. b $u = 0$, $a = 0.223$ **d** starting speed
   c 11.8, 11.1
8. a $\frac{22}{101}$ **b** $\frac{100}{303}$ **c** $\frac{8}{33}$
9. a $\frac{1}{10}$ **b** $\frac{1}{13}$ **c i** $\frac{12}{65}$ **ii** $\frac{1}{130}$
10. b i 0.1625   **ii** 0.04375
   c i 8   **ii** 2

Revision Exercise 5.4 (p. 420)

1. a $2\sqrt{6}$ **ii** $2\sqrt{2}$
   b i 6   **ii** $3\frac{1}{3}$ **iii** $\frac{1}{9}$
2. a i $(2x + 9)(x + 2)$ **iii** $(3 - t)(2t + 5)$
   ii $(7x - 2)(5x + 2)$ **iv** $3(x + 3)(x - 7)$
   b 0.3088
   c i $x = 9$ or $\frac{2}{3}$ **ii** $x = \frac{8}{3}$ or $-\frac{4}{5}$
3. $x = \frac{5}{2}$ or $-\frac{3}{2}$
4. -2.6 and 1.6, $x^2 + x - 4 = 0$
5. a 4 seconds   **c** 118 m
   b accelerating
6. rotation 90° anticlockwise about (5, 1)
7. a yes, SAS   **b** $3\sqrt{13}$ cm
8. a 48°   **b** 84°
9. a £29.90   **b** 81
   Start up cost for producing posters
10. a $\frac{3}{13}$ **b** $\frac{11}{51}$ **c** $\frac{80}{221}$

Revision Exercise 5.5 (p. 422)

1. a $x = 6.19$ or 0.81
   b $x = -\dfrac{-13 + \sqrt{85}}{6}$ or $\dfrac{-13 - \sqrt{85}}{6}$
2. a i $\dfrac{2x + 11}{(x + 3)(x - 3)}$ **ii** $\dfrac{x - 9}{(x - 3)(x + 3)}$
   b $g = 4\pi^2 \dfrac{L}{T^2}$
3. 173.75 square units
   Area is less than actual as curve is above tops of trapeziums
4. a i 18.2 cm   **ii** 79.21 cm^2 **b** same
5. a 11.8 cm
   b total height = 17.7 cm, radius = 5.89 cm
6. a N = 42.6° to 3 s.f.   **b** M = 82.9° to 3 s.f.
7. PM = PN   **9.** 1.5:1
8. a circle with AB as diameter
10. mean = 7.96, s.d. = 1.17 to 3 s.f.

INDEX

Acceleration   155, 156, 163, 216
Addition, of fractions   2
  of probabilities   20
Algebraic fractions, adding   7, 91
  dividing by   8
  multiplying   8
  simplifying   7
  subtracting   7, 91
Alternate angles   12
Alternate segment theorem   322, 336
Angle, at the centre of a circle   15
  between a line and a plane   208, 217
  between two planes   208, 217
  in a semicircle   15
  of rotation   17
Angles, in circles   15
  in same segment   15
  of depression   12
  of elevation   12
Area   6
  bounded by a curve   140, 141
  of a circle   6
  of a parallelogram   6
  of a rectangle   6
  of a sector   6, 232
  of a square   6
  of a trapezium   6
  of a triangle   6, 267, 334
  under a velocity-time graph   159, 163
Areas of similar figures   348, 409
Average speed   7
Average velocity   152, 216

Bearings   13

Centre of rotation   17, 174
Chord   216, 313, 336
Circumference   6
Coefficient   7
Common factor   8, 57
Compound percentage change   4
Compound transformation   18, 178, 183
Conditional probability   395, 409
Congruence   14, 280
Congruent triangles   281, 288, 293, 334

Constructions   170, 172
Continued fractions   51
Continuous values   18
Correcting numbers   3
Correlation   19
Corresponding angles   12
Cosine, of an angle   16
  of an obtuse angle   251
  rule   261, 334
Counter example   279
Cross-section   203
Cube root   45
Cubic curves   12
Cumulative frequency   19
  curve   19
  polygon   19
Curved surface area, of a cone   240, 334
  of a cylinder   237
Cyclic quadrilaterals   308

Deceleration   216
Decimal expressed as a percentage   3
Deductive proof   275
Density   7
Difference between two squares   8
Direct proportion   4
Directed number   1
Discrete values   18
Distance   159, 163, 216
Distance–time graphs   147, 152, 216
Division, by a decimal   2
  by a fraction   2
  in a given ratio   4

Enlargement   18
Equation of a straight line   11, 374
Equilateral triangles   13
Euclid's proof (prime numbers)   307
Expansion of brackets   8, 74
Exterior angle of a cyclic quadrilateral
  310, 336
Exterior angles of a polygon   14

Factor   1
Factorising   8, 53, 54, 55

Formula   9, 83, 88, 94, 96, 98, 101
Formula for solving quadratic equations
   68, 127
Fraction, changing to a decimal   2
   expressed as a percentage   2
   of a quantity   2
Fractional indices   46, 126

Goldbach's conjecture   279
Gradient   11, 216
   of a curve   136, 216

Heronian algorithm   51
Hyperbola   12
Hypothesis   18, 279

Identities   64
Identity transformation   186
Imperial units   5
Independent events   20
Index   5
Indices   5, 47, 126
Inequalities   10, 11, 112, 115
Interest   4
Interior angles   12
   of a polygon   14
Interquartile range   19
Intersecting graphs   116
Inverse proportion   5
Inverse transformation   186
Irrational number   39, 40, 126
Isosceles triangle   13

Laws of indices   47, 126
Length of an arc   6, 232
Line graphs   380
Line of best fit   19, 382
Linear relationships   386
Linkages   327
Loci   15, 326
Lower bound   3, 191
Lower quartile   19

Map ratio   4
Mean   18, 19, 371
Median   18, 19
Metric units   5

Mirror line   17
Mixed operations   2
Modal group   19
Mode   18
Multiple   1
Multiplication, by a fraction   2
   of decimals   2
   of probabilities   20
Mutually exclusive   20

Nth root   45, 126
Nth term   9
Non-linear relationships   390
Notation for transformations   182, 183

Opposite angles of a cyclic quadrilateral
   309, 336

Parabolas   11
Parallel lines   12
Parallelogram   13
Parallelograms, properties of   296
Percentage, expressed as a decimal   3
   expressed as a fraction   3
Percentage change   3
Percentage of a quantity   3
Polygon   14
Polynomial equations   10
Power   5
Prime number   1
Prism   7, 203
Probability   20, 394, 409
Pyramid   198
Pythagoras' theorem   14

Quadratic equations   10, 60, 68, 127
Quadratic inequalities   112, 115, 127
Quadrilateral   13

Range   18, 19
Ratio   4
Rational number   40, 126
Rationalising the denominator   42
Real number   40
Reciprocal   1
Reciprocal curves   12
Rectangle   13
Rectangular number   1

Recurring decimals   3, 41, 126
Reflection   17
Regression lines   393
Regular polygon   14
Relative frequency   20
Representative fraction   4
Rhombus   13
Right circular cone   239
Right pyramid   198, 217
Rotation   17, 174
Rounding numbers   3
Ruler and compasses constructions   170
Rules of indices   5

Scalar   16
Scale   172
    drawing   172
    factor   18
Scatter graph   19
Secant   313, 336
Significant figures   3
Similar figures   14, 348, 354, 409
Similar triangles   14
Simultaneous equations   9
Sine, of an angle   16
    of an obtuse angle   250
    rule   259, 334
Sketching curves   107, 127
Slant height of a cone   240
Special quadrilaterals, properties of
    296, 299, 335
Speed   150
Square   13
    number   1
    root   1
Standard deviation   362, 365, 409
Standard form   1, 84
Straight line graphs   11, 374
Subject of a formula   9, 94, 96, 98, 127
Substitution, elimination by   101

Surds   42, 126
Surface area, of a pyramid   199, 334
    of a sphere   241, 334

Tangent, of an angle   16
    to a circle   313, 315, 320, 322, 336
    to a curve   136, 153
Tetrahedron   198
Three-figure bearings   13
Triangular number   1
Transformations   17, 174, 178
Translation   17
Trapezium   13
    rule   141, 216
Tree diagrams   20, 402
Trial and improvement   10
Triangle notation   255
Triangles   13

Units, of area   6
    of capacity   5
    of length   5
    of mass   5
    of volume   6
Upper bound   3, 191
Upper quartile   19

Vector   16
Velocity   150, 153, 216
Velocity–time graph   156, 159, 162,
    163, 216
Vertex   239
Volume   6
    of a cone   239, 334
    of a cuboid   7
    of a cylinder   7, 236
    of a prism   7
    of a pyramid   198, 217
    of a sphere   241, 334
Volumes of similar figures   354, 409